International Cases in the Business of Sport

International Cases in the Business of Sport

Edited by

Simon Chadwick and Dave Arthur

ELSEVIER

AMSTERDAM • BOSTON • HEIDELBERG • LONDON • NEW YORK • OXFORD
PARIS • SAN DIEGO • SAN FRANCISCO • SINGAPORE • SYDNEY • TOKYO
Butterworth-Heinemann is an imprint of Elsevier

Butterworth-Heinemann is an imprint of Elsevier
Linacre House, Jordan Hill, Oxford OX2 8DP, UK
30 Corporate Drive, Suite 400, Burlington, MA 01803, USA

First edition 2008

British Library Cataloguing in Publication Data
A catalogue record for this book is available from the British Library

Library of Congress Cataloging-in-Publication Data
A catalog record for this book is available from the Library of Congress

ISBN: 978-0-7506-8543-6

For information on all Butterworth-Heinemann publications
visit our web site at http://books.elsevier.com

Typeset by Charon Tec Ltd (A Macmillan Company), Chennai, India www.charontec.com

Printed and bound in Great Britain

08 09 10   10 9 8 7 6 5 4 3 2 1

Contents

Acknowledgements

Simon would like to thank Barbara and Tom for their patience and good humour as he prepared this book. He would also like to thank Dave for his wit and wisdom, both of which made the job of getting the book together so much easier. Dave would like to thank four very special people, Selena, Angus, Daisy and Charlotte, for just being there and his Mum and Dad for letting him go in the first place! Simon has been an inspiration to him throughout – without his drive and humour the book would have been impossible. Finally, Simon and Dave send massive thanks to Fran who is always supportive, enthusiastic and helpful and of course all the contributors for their tireless efforts.

Biographies

John Amis

John is an Associate Professor in the Department of Management at the University of Memphis. His work has been published in journals such as *Academy of Management Journal*, *European Marketing Journal*, *Organizational Research Methods*, *Journal of Applied Behavioral Science*, *Journal of Sport Management*, *European Sport Management Quarterly* and *Leisure Studies*. He recently co-edited (with Bettina Cornwell) Global Sport Sponsorship (Berg, 2005).

Harry Arne Solberg

Harry Arne Solberg is a Professor of Sports Economics/Sports Management at Trondheim Business School as Sør-Trøndelag University College. He has published several articles on the economics of sport and sporting activities – with special attention on impacts related to sport broadcasting and sporting events. Together with Professor, Chris Gratton, he has just come out with the book: *The Economics of Sport Broadcasting*. Harry Arne is a member of the editorial board for the International Journal of Sport Finance and European Sport Management Quarterly.

Dave Arthur (co-editor)

Dave is a Senior Lecturer in the Department of Exercise Science and Sport Management at Southern Cross University where he co-ordinates the acclaimed Master of International Sport Management degree. Although this is his first co-edited book he has published many book chapters, a range of articles in leading sport journals and is a member of the editorial board of Sport Management Review. In addition to academia he has consulted to leading sporting organizations including the National Rugby League, South Sydney Rugby League Club and the Australian Sports Commission. His abiding sporting passion however is rugby union. As a practicing journalist he was accredited for the 2003 Rugby World Cup and in 2006 he was privileged to be the Pacific Islanders' Media Manager for their three Test series versus Wales, Scotland and Ireland.

John Beech

John is the Head of Sport and Tourism Applied Research at Coventry University Business School, where he was previously Head of the Strategy and Applied Management Department and of the Leisure, Sport and Tourism Subject Group. He is a co-editor, with Simon Chadwick, of

The Business of Sport Management, *The Business of Tourism Management* and *The Marketing of Sport* (all published by Pearson Education).

Thomas Bezold

Thomas is a Professor of Sport Management and Business Administration at the Reinhold Wuerth University, Kuenzelsau, a branch of Heilbronn University Germany. He started his academic career at the University of Bayreuth and holds a master degree in Sport Economics and in European Sport Management and a PhD in Sport Science, Marketing and Business Administration. His research focus lies in sport marketing, brand management and sports & media.

Ann Bourke

Ann is Vice Principal for Teaching and Learning in the College of Business and Law at UCD and Senior Lecturer in Management at UCD Business School. She has published in many leading education and business journals and presented at international conferences and workshops. Her research interests include adult learning and curriculum design, international trade in higher education, career progression among aspiring elite athletes, sports scholarship programmes and governance of sports bodies. She is currently a Board Member of EASM (European Association of Sport Management).

Anne Braedley

Anne is a Student–Researcher in the School of Fashion at Ryerson University, working with both fashion and marketing instructors on various projects. Following the completion of her undergraduate degree in Engineering Mathematics at Queen's University in Kingston, Canada, she moved to Ryerson to study Fashion Design specializing in the design of both high-performance athletic gear and tailored garments. Anne is also an accomplished long-distance runner.

Cheri Bradish

Cheri, an Associate Professor, is entering her 11th year in the Department of Sport Management at Brock University. She has served as the Chair of the Department of Sport Management, and has worked with a number of professional sport organizations, including Nike Canada and the NBA Vancouver Grizzlies.

Simon Chadwick (co-editor)

Simon is a Professor of Sport Business Strategy and Marketing, and Leader of the Ambushing, Sponsorship and Sport Marketing Group, at Coventry University (UK). He is also a Director of the Birkbeck Sport Business Centre at the University of London. He is a co-editor, with John Beech of *The Business of Sport Management*, *The Business of Tourism Management and The Marketing of Sport* (all published by Pearson Education), and is also an editor of the *International Journal of Sports Marketing and Sponsorship*, Elsevier's Sport

Marketing book series and the Henry Stewart Sports Marketing Talk Series. He has worked with numerous organizations from across sport including FC Barcelona, Atletico Madrid, Chivas US, the four Grand Slam tennis tournaments, the Football Association (FA), Sport England, the International Tennis Federation, Sport Business, Red Mandarin and International Marketing Reports.

Graham Cuskelly

Graham is a Professor and Dean (Research) in the Griffith University Business School. He holds a Master of Science in Recreation Administration from the University of North Carolina at Chapel Hill and a PhD from Griffith University where he studied organizational commitment amongst sport volunteers. Professor Cuskelly has been awarded Australian Research Council funding for two separate projects examining volunteer and referee retention with the Australian Rugby Union and is an Associate Editor of the Sport Management Review.

Simon Darcy

Simon is an Associate Professor and Research Director in the School of Leisure, Sport and Tourism at the University of Technology, Sydney. Simon's research and teaching expertise is in sport, tourism and diversity management. He currently holds research grants investigating organizational responses to accessible tourism, sports management practices and protected area visitor management systems. All Simon's research is industry linked with the private sector, third sector or government organizations.

Michel Desbordes

Michel is a Professor at the University of Paris South, France. He is also an Associate Professor at the ISC School of Management (Paris, France). He is a specialist in sport marketing; his research focuses on the management of sport events, sports sponsorship and marketing applied to football. He is also a consultant in sport marketing and Associate Director of the company MX Sports (www.mxsports.fr).

Geoff Dickson

Geoff works at AUT University in New Zealand where he is Head of Research for the Division of Sport and Recreation as well as being an Associate Director of the New Zealand Tourism Research Institute. He is an editorial board member of the International Journal of Sports Marketing and Sponsorship, International Journal of Sport Management and Marketing, Annals of Leisure Research and the Sport Management Education Journal.

Allan Edwards

Allan is a Lecturer at Griffith University, Gold Coast campus. His research interest focuses on post-modern methodology and reflective practice. He is researching in the area of culture and surfing with Surfing Australia and the International Surfing Association. Dr Edwards has strong links with the Australian sports industry in particular the Australian Rugby League, Queensland Rubgy Union, Professional Golfers Association (PGA) and the Australian Paralympic Committee.

Alain Ferrand

Alain is Professor of marketing and Director of the business and management research centre (CEREGE) at the University of Poitiers. He is Associated Professor at University of Turin and Scuola Dello Sport in Rome (Italian National Olympic Committee). He is in charge of the Executive Masters in Sport Organisation Management (MEMOS) conducted in French. He has a large experience with the marketing issues of National Olympic Committees, National Federations and sport clubs around the world. He has written five books on sport organizations marketing.

Sean Hamil

Sean is a Lecturer at Birkbeck College, University of London. A graduate of Trinity College Dublin and the London School of Economics, he has published in the areas of corporate social responsibility and the governance & regulation of sport. He has co-edited three books on regulation and governance in the football industry; The Changing Face of the Football Business: Supporters Direct (2001); Football in the Digital Age: Whose Game is it Anyway? (2000); A Game of Two Halves? The Business of Football (1999). He is a co-founder and member of Birkbeck College's Sports Business Centre, is an elected director of Supporters Direct, and was responsible for establishing Supporters Direct's activities in Scotland. Supporters Direct is funded by the UK government with the aim of promoting and supporting the concept of democratic supporter ownership and representation at football clubs through mutual, not-for-profit structures.

Knut Helland

Knut is a Professor at Department of Information Sciences and Media Studies, University of Bergen, Norway. His two main areas of research are relations between sport and the media on the one hand, and news production and journalism on the other. In his recent research he has, in particular, been concerned with how TV sports rights challenges long established journalistic ideals in journalism.

Jaemin Hong

Jaemin works as London correspondent of South Korean daily newspaper *The Sports Seoul 21*. He studied MSc Sport Management and the Business of Football at Birkbeck, the University of London and regularly reports on the English Premiership for his newspaper.

Maria Hopwood

Maria is an Associate Professor in Public Relations at Bond University in Queensland, Australia. Her research interests are in sports public relations and marketing communications in which areas she has published a number of book chapters and journal articles. A keen follower of cricket, particularly Durham County Cricket Club, she is especially interested in the continuing developments in that sport, but her work also demands her enthusiastic involvement in both codes of rugby and Australian football with a round ball.

Russell Hoye

Dr Russell Hoye is with the School of Sport, Tourism and Hospitality Management at La Trobe University Australia. Russell is the editor of the Sport Management Series produced by Elsevier: Butterworth-Heinemann, a member of the editorial board for Sport Management Review and a board member of the Sport Management Association of Australia and New Zealand (SMAANZ).

Catharine Idle

Catharine is a Research Assistant in the Department of Sports Studies at the University of Stirling. She completed an MSc in Sports Studies at Stirling in 2006 and is now working on a number of projects related to cycling and other outdoor pursuits. Prior to post-graduate study, Catharine worked as Contracts Manager for a European leisure tour operator.

Kimio Kase

Kimio's interests lie in the area of corporate-level strategy. His recent research focuses on the transformational leadership from the viewpoint of leaders' mental scheme. Questions addressed relate to the interpretative process of business situations; 2005 saw the publication in the UK of a book he co-authored with two other academics on transformational CEOs. Dr Kase and his co-author are working on a book on the same topic due to be published in December 2007, by Palgrave UK. Dr Kimio Kase holds a BA from Tokyo University of Foreign Studies, Licenciatura en Ciencias Empresariales from ICADE, MBA from IESE and a doctor's degree in Business Administration from Manchester University.

Paul Kitchin

Paul works at London Metropolitan Business School where he is a programme leader for the MA in Sport Management. His research interests include marketing communications through sport and the marketing of new media. He is editor of the forthcoming London Journal of Tourism Sport and Creative Industries and has been on the editorial board of the International Journal of Sport Management and Marketing since 2006.

Chanil Lee

Chanil works at the Lotte, based in South Korea. He studied MBA Football Industries at the University of Liverpool and is in charge of developing, coordinating and promoting the sport business and sponsorship at the Lotte Group's headquarters.

Carlos Martí Sanchis

Carlos is an Associate Researcher at the Centre for Sport Business Management, IESE Business School, and also an Associate Professor at the Law Faculty, University of Navarra. Carlos is a PhD candidate on Strategies in Communication Enterprises at Universidad Complutense, Madrid, and has consultancy experience as partner of Key International Sport.

Jason Means

Jason completed his Masters degree in sport management at Georgia Southern University in 2006. Since then he has worked with the Chick-Fil-A Bowl, an event of the Atlanta Sports Council in Atlanta, Georgia. Currently he is an Event Manager at JW Marriott Buckhead, Buckhead, Georgia, USA.

Rudi Meir

Rudi is a Senior Lecturer at Southern Cross University. He has published numerous articles on a wide range of topics related to the management and marketing of team sport. He has a particular interest in developing strategies that facilitate and encourage 'tribal' support of fans in professional team sport.

Stephen Morrow

Stephen is Head of the Department of Sports Studies at the University of Stirling. His research concentrates on financial and governance aspects in sport and he is the author of *The People's Game? Football, Finance and Society* (Palgrave, 2003) and *The New Business of Football* (Macmillan, 1999). Stephen is a member of the editorial board of the International Journal of Sport Finance.

Paul Muller

Paul is a graduate of Southern Cross University's Master of International Sport Management. He has since left the racing industry and now resides in Tasmania. Paul currently works closely with Cricket, Australian Football and the Tasmanian Rugby Union and is continuing research in the field of sport.

Paul M. Pedersen

Paul is an Associate Professor of Sport Communication at Indiana University. His primary scholarly interests are sport communication and sport management, areas in which he has published over 40 scholarly articles. Pedersen, a former sportswriter and sports business columnist, is the author of Strategic Sport Communication (2007) and the editor of the International Journal of Sport Communication.

John Nauright

John is a Professor of Sport Management and Director of Graduate Programs in the School of Recreation, Health and Tourism at George Mason University in Virginia, USA. He is the author or editor of 9 academic books and 50 refereed journal articles including Sport, Cultures and Identities in South Africa; Rugby and the South African Nation (with David Black); and The Political Economy of Sport (with Kim Schimmel). His primary teaching areas are in international sport management and in sport policy and development. He has taught at universities in Australia, Canada, Denmark, New Zealand, Scotland and the USA.

Norm O'Reilly

Norm is Director and Associate Professor at the School of Sports Administration at Laurentian University in Sudbury, Canada, where he is also Director of the Institute of Sport Marketing. He has published in numerous refereed journals and conference proceedings in sport marketing, social marketing, sport finance, management education, ambush marketing, sport tourism and sponsorship.

Sean Phelps

Sean is a Senior Lecturer in Sport and Recreation Management at AUT University where he teaches at both the undergraduate and graduate level. He has extensive practitioner experience in sport having worked for USA Triathlon, Montana and Florida State Games, Special Olympics and the Winter Olympics.

Frank Pons

Frank Pons is an Associate Professor at Université Laval (Canada). He has published in the *Journal of Business Research, Psychology and Marketing*, the *Journal of Services Research or Sport Marketing Quarterly*. He is on the editorial board of the International Journal of Sports Marketing and Sponsorship and was guest editor of several special issues in sport marketing journals.

K.K. Ramachandran

K.K. Ramachandran is a Director of GRD School of Commerce and International Business, Coimbatore, India. He holds an MBA, MFT, MCom, MPhil and a PhD. He is an educator and an administrator. He is an adviser for a couple of brand building companies. He is an inspiring thought leader in the field of Sport marketing, Brand management and strategy. He frequently writes for top journals across the globe. He is a Brand, Marketing and Strategy specialist.

Santiago Ramallo

Santiago is the first ever sports marketing manager in Argentine Rugby with the famous San Isidro Club. He worked previously for a sports event marketing company and his research focuses on the sports sponsorship and management applied to football. He is also an Associate Professor at ESEADE for the Executive Program of Sports Business Management and a visiting lecturer and researcher in sport marketing for the University of Greenwich. He was a contributor to Marketing & Football: An International Perspective by Desbordes.

André Richelieu

André is an Associate Professor at Université Laval, specialized in Brand Management and Sport Marketing. Andre's research interests relate to: (i) how professional sports teams can leverage their brand equity by capitalizing on the emotional connection they share with their fans; (ii) how professional sports teams can internationalize their brand; (iii) how sports teams can improve fans' experience at the sport venue and increase fans' attachment to both the game and the team and (iv) how sports teams and equipment makers can capitalize on the Hip Hop/Urban movement.

German Robles

Germán, Director Centro de Estudios e Investigación of Atlético de Madrid, SAD is in charge of marketing and institutional relations. Germán has a degree in economics from Madrid's Autonomous University and works closely with IESE Business School's Centre for Sports Business Management and authored several research papers with it.

James Santomier

James is currently a Professor in the John F. Welch College of Business and Director of the Sport Management Program at Sacred Heart University, Fairfield, Connecticut, USA. He is also a Visiting Professor at the University of Bayreuth, Germany, and the University of Florence, Italy. He received a BA and MA in Physical Education from Montclair State University, and a PhD in Physical Education from the University of Utah. Areas of study included sport management and the psychosocial aspects of physical activity and sport. Dr Santomier has published extensively in the areas of sport management, sociology of sport and psychosocial aspects of sport. He has presented at international and national conferences and has appeared on numerous radio and television programmes.

Leigh Sparks

Leigh is a Professor of Retail Studies at the Institute for Retail Studies at the University of Stirling. For the last seven years he has been involved in developing and running undergraduate and postgraduate modules in Sports Marketing, including on the MSc programmes in Marketing and Sports Management. His research interests are mainly in the area of retailing and he has been adviser and consultant to many governments and private retail companies. Leigh is currently seeking to combine his interests in retailing and sport through a study of the development of sports goods retailing and experiential sports retailing. He is an avid Welsh rugby supporter, which is of course a blessing and a curse.

Dave Stotlar

Dave teaches on the University of Northern Colorado faculty in the areas of sport marketing, sponsorship and currently serves as the Director of the School of Sport & Exercise Science. He has had over 60 articles published in professional journals, has written several textbooks in sport marketing and serves as a consultant in sport marketing to multinational corporations and international sport managers.

Tracy Taylor

Tracy is a Professor of Sport Management at the University of Technology, Sydney. Her research focuses on managing people in sport, and particularly in the areas of diversity and gender.

Paul Turner

Paul is a Senior Lecturer and Discipline Coordinator of Sport Management with the Bowater School of Management and Marketing at Deakin University in Melbourne, Australia. His scholarly interests are in the areas of sport media (particularly sport broadcasting) and event management.

Ignacio Urrutia

Ignacio is an Assistant Professor in the Accounting and Control Department at IESE, Madrid. His qualifications include a PhD in Financial Economics and Accounting, Universidad Complutense de Madrid, Degree in Economic and Business Science, Universidad Complutense de Madrid. He is an academic Director of the Center for Sport Business Management where his areas of specialization include strategic and control management in sport organizations; value creation in sport organizations; sport and corporate social responsibility and business models of sport organizations.

Geoff Walters

Geoff Walters is a Research Associate of the Football Governance Research Centre at Birkbeck, University of London. He is currently working on a PhD funded by the Economic and Social Research Council looking at corporate governance in the football industry, with a specific focus on the stakeholder model of governance.

Nick Wilde

Nick Wilde lectures in Sports Marketing at the University of Liverpool and Birkbeck University on their highly acclaimed MBA's in Football Management, He is a Senior Lecturer in Marketing at the University of Greenwich and visiting lecturer at the University of Buenos Aires and ESEADE University in Argentina. He is currently writing up his PhD at the University of Liverpool, His research looks at the impact of merchandising at football clubs in England, Spain and Argentina. A frequent visitor to Argentina he works closely with Boca Juniors, Racing Football Club and Estudiantes de la Plata as well as with SIC, Argentina's leading rugby club. He is co-author of Marketing and PR with Phil Holden. Published by A&C Black the book offers practical advice for small businesses and in the process of writing a follow up book for small businesses. He is a life-long Sheffield United supporter and a 'new fan' of Argentinian football.

Brita Ytre-Arne

Brita holds a master degree in media studies from the University of Bergen. She wrote her thesis on the Norwegian football deal of 2005 and its consequences for Norwegian broadcasting. Together with Knut Helland she has written a report for the Norwegian Union of Journalists on sports rights and journalism. She is currently working as a Lecturer and Researcher at Volda University College in Norway.

Introduction

For many people, sport is a leisure time activity, a hobby, a route to good health and wellbeing, possibly even a way of life – long may this continue! Yet it is increasingly accepted that sport is also an industry in its own right and, in some cases, is even perceived as being a commercial activity. The evidence is compelling: the United Nations believe that sport may account for almost 3 per cent of global economic activity; in the European Union, the figure is thought to be around 1 per cent of Gross Domestic Product (GDP) and in the UK sport is thought to generate around 2.5 per cent of GDP. Estimates for the USA indicate that sport is worth almost $300 billion per annum to the US economy. Contributing to these figures, some sports and sporting organizations are of such a size and scale that they warrant comparison with large, global organizations. For instance, Manchester United is reputed to have 100 million fans worldwide, while Real Madrid turns over almost $300 million worth of business each year. At the same, there are numerous organizations across the world that are smaller in scale, more localized, often culturally specific, but no less important in terms of the impact they have on the commercial, economic or socio-cultural development of the countries in which they are located.

Whether large or small, national or international, rich or poor, each sport or sports organization will inevitably face its own, sometimes very distinct, challenges. This could be an industrial challenge such as the need to restructure and reorganize; it could be a marketing problem such as falling attendances; it could be an issue of technological or regulatory change such as in broadcasting; it could be a human resource matter such as motivating workers. These challenges are increasingly set against a backdrop of sporting megachange, that is events beyond the control of any one individual sport. Such events include: technological change; internationalization and globalization; social change; a growth in the power of television and the media; the proliferation of commercial sports rights markets; changes in service expectations and the rise of professionalism, managerialism and commercialism in sport.

It would be difficult, if not impossible for any book, case study or otherwise, to address all the challenges facing a large number of sports. What this book therefore sets out to achieve is an examination of the major issues facing a representative sample of sports and sporting organizations across the world. In doing so, the book aims broadly to do the following things:

- Provide case material and learning resources.
- Be an informative source about sport, especially for those seeking lecture, seminar and project materials.
- Stimulate interest in the area of international sport business management.

- Enhance readers understanding of international sport business management.
- Illustrate and highlight key concepts in international sport business management.
- Provide an insight into the practical challenges facing international sport business managers.

Reader Benefits

The book is intended to be a comprehensive resource consisting of high profile international sport business cases, analysed by leading sport experts. As such, the editors believe that readers should derive numerous benefits by reading it that include the following:

- Cutting edge analysis of major international sport business cases.
- Clear and structured presentation and examination of key issues in international sport businesses.
- Comprehensive diagnoses of leading international sport business cases.
- A strong balance of academic and practical analysis and comment.
- An informative and comprehensive resource for those seeking a better understanding of developments in international sport.

Case Study Structure

Each of the case studies appearing in this book is structured in the following way:

1 Case title.
2 Author names.
3 Case focus – a brief description of the fundamental nature of the case.
4 Keywords – up to six words characterizing the case.
5 Case summary – a paragraph summarizing the case.
6 Case elements – the main part of the case focusing on a sport, an organization or some other entity directly related to sport under examination.
7 Case diagnosis – a statement explaining the key issues relating to the case.
8 Case questions – up to six questions that can be used by students, academics and practitioners seeking to explore the case in more detail.
9 Case resources – additional readings and/or websites that are relevant to the case.
10 Further information – any other information that you feel should be included but does not fit into any of the headings above.

Learning Matrix

Rather than being written around specific themes or concepts, contributors to this book were asked to provide case studies that (a) have been written around a variety of different sports; (b) are of a geographically diverse nature and (c) are multi-disciplinary in nature. As such, to assist readers in deciding the relevance of each case to their needs, a learning matrix that provides details of the focus and content of all the cases is presented prior to the case studies.

Final Note

The editors acknowledge that there will inevitably be a natural ageing process meaning that the content of some cases becomes outdated or obsolete. In this case, readers are invited to email either the editors or the publisher with details of relevant, up to date or more specific information.

Learning Matrix

Introduction

International Cases in the Business of Sport on the face of it presents an eclectic mix of interesting sport business case studies from around the world. The range of sports from which the cases are drawn, including for example football, rugby union, cycling, cricket, ice hockey and golf is vast. Similarly the geographic location from where the cases emanate (Canada, India, Europe, South America and the Pacific Islands to name but a few) is extensive. However each contributor was invited to participate based on their expertise and knowledge in a specific area and the book was loosely designed around this.

With this in mind it is pertinent to provide readers with a general guide as to which cases apply to which area of sport business and how they interact. In short the following section provides a simple 'learning matrix' that can be used to determine which case is best suited to a given situation. The cases are therefore divided into a number of general themes – it should be noted however that some cases necessarily overlap and are therefore referred to on more than a single occasion. For example a number of cases deal with strategy as a primary concept but many also allude to strategy as a key, albeit secondary consideration.

Theme: Marketing

Primary

(8) Kitchin; (12) Ramachandran; (16) Ferrand; (22) Bezold; (23) Stotlar and Bradish; and (27) Hong and Lee.

Kitchin (8) uses the relatively recent cricket innovation of Twenty-20 to illustrate how a sport can reposition itself. Ramachandran (12) looks at the opportunities for sport marketing in India whilst Ferrand (16) utilizes the pinnacle of sport marketing as an example and suggests that brand equity is the most important factor in the marketing of the Olympic Games. Bezold (22) explores naming rights in the context of both being a marketing tool but also a financial tool in raising revenue. Stotlar and Bradish (23) examine the launch and marketing of the Starbury One basketball shoe that baulked at many of the traditions associated with releasing a new brand. Hong and Lee (27), using Korea's Lotte Giants as an example, consider aspects of marketing in a challenging, global environment.

Secondary

(1) Chadwick and Arthur; (5) Sparks; (9) Hamil; (10) Muller and Arthur; (14) Meir; (18) Hopwood and Edwards; (19) O'Reilly and Braedley; (24) Beech and (29) Ramallo and Wilde.

Theme: Strategy

Primary

(1) Chadwick and Arthur; (6) Bourke; (14) Meir; (15) Urrutia, Robles Kase and Martí; and (29) Ramallo and Wilde.

Chadwick and Arthur (1) look at the commercial development of FC Barcelona and the marketing strategy that underpinned this. Similarly Bourke (6), in examining UC Dublin football club provides an interesting perspective as to the strategy employed by the organization in a unique and challenging environment. Meir (14) in his case on tribalism offers the strategic viewpoint for the development of this important attribute in sports fans. Urrutia, Robles Kase and Martí (15) using Club Atlético de Madrid as an example show this organization's strategy in attempting to achieve internationalization. Finally Ramallo and Wilde (29), also using football, but this time Argentina's Boca Juniors, looks at the strategy used to develop the club.

Secondary

(3) Santomeir; (5) Sparks; (9) Hamil; (11) Amis; (16) Ferrand; (22) Bezold; (23) Stotlar and Bradish; and (26) Means and Nauright.

Theme: Branding

Primary

(2) Richelieu and Pons; (5) Sparks; (11) Amis; (19) O'Reilly and Braedley; and (30) Chadwick and Walters

Richelieu and Pons (2) look at the manner in which three different ice hockey franchises have branded their team and the relative success of each. Sparks (5) presents the unique challenges afforded in branding sweatyBetty, a small, women only, active wear boutique chain. Guinness is a well-known brand that Amis (11) explores to illustrate how it has been positioned in sport to provide global coherence and O'Reilly and Braedley (19) use the context of golf to show how the individual athlete can become a brand. Finally Chadwick and Walters (30) examine legal aspects of branding through the use of manufacturer's identifiers and logos.

Secondary

(1) Chadwick and Arthur; (7) Dickson and Phelps; (15) Urrutia, Robles Kase and Martí; (16) Ferrand; (19) O'Reilly and Braedley; (20) Arthur and Chadwick; (22) Bezold; (23) Stotlar and Bradish; and (30) Chadwick and Walters.

Theme: Media

Primary

(17) Pedersen and (20) Arthur and Chadwick.

Pedersen (17) looks at the 'contested terrain' between the media and the players in the professional locker room whilst the use of the media to promote Pacific Islander rugby is examined by Arthur and Chadwick (20).

Secondary

(4) Morrow and Idle; (18) Hopwood and Edwards; (19) O'Reilly and Braedley; and (21) Solberg, Helland and Ytre-Arne.

Theme: Governance

Primary

(4) Morrow and Idle; (7) Dickson and Phelps; and (25) Desbordes.

The challenge of modernizing and restructuring professional cycling is examined by Morrow and Idle (4). Using New Zealand's Coast to Coast Multisport event as a backdrop, Dickson and Phelps (7) examine governance and issues in a non-traditional sport. Desbordes (25) utilizes one of the world's premier sporting events, the Tour de France to examine the regulation of professional cycling competitions.

Secondary

(15) Urrutia, Robles Kase and Martí; and (28) Darcy, Taylor, Cuskelly and Hoye.

Theme: Technology and Broadcasting

Primary

(3) Santomier; (13) Turner and (21) Solberg, Helland and Ytre-Arne.

Santomier (3) looks at the Asian broadcasting conglomerate ESPN Star Sports as it sought to broadcast a variety of sports. Turner (13) looks at the web delivery of sport both in terms of both broadcast and technical enhancement. Using football media rights in Norway as an example, Solberg, Helland and Ytre-Arne (21) examine sports broadcasting.

Secondary

(8) Kitchin and (18) Hopwood and Edwards.

Theme: Sport Development

Primary

(18) Hopwood and Edwards; (26) Means and Nauright; and (28) Darcy, Taylor, Cuskelly and Hoye.

Hopwood and Edwards (18) explore the issues associated with cricket's evolution and development. Means and Nauright (26) address some of the issues associated with the growth of the NBA's Basketball without Barriers program in South Africa. Finally, Darcy, Taylor, Cuskelly and Hoye (28) investigate the scope of volunteer involvement in the Australian Rugby Union.

Secondary

(1) Chadwick and Arthur; (6) Bourke; (7) Dickson and Phelps; (8) Kitchin; (12) Ramachandran and (25) Desbordes.

Theme: Spectatorship

Primary

(9) Hamil; (10) Muller and Arthur; (14) Meir and (24) Beech.

Hamil (9) examines the commercial development that underpins Manchester United's phenomenal support base. Muller and Arthur (10) explore the concept of free tickets for spectators as a means of increasing attendance and other revenue streams in greyhound racing. Meir (14) through his case on tribalism considers aspects of fan segmentation. Beech (24) investigates spectatorship with particular reference to the 2007 Cricket World Cup.

Secondary

(2) Richelieu and Pons; (3) Santomier; (8) Kitchin; (12) Ramachandran; (13) Turner; (20) Arthur and Chadwick; and (27) Hong and Lee.

1

Més que un club (more than a club): the commercial development of FC Barcelona

Simon Chadwick and Dave Arthur

Case Focus

The case examines the history and commercial development of FC Barcelona in Spain, addressing some of the factors that simultaneously strengthen and constrain the football club.

Keywords

- Multisports club
- Operating environment
- Commercial strategy
- Marketing strategy
- Brand management
- Sponsorship

Case Summary

FC Barcelona is an icon of world football, successful on the field of play and popular off it. This popularity is in part based on the club's symbolism as a rallying point for Catalonia. Given its huge socio-political significance, the club is often referred to as 'més que un club' (more than a club). This has simultaneously served both to promote and to constrain the club, the latter meaning that 'Barca' has in recent years begun to lag behind rival football clubs from elsewhere in Spain and from abroad. Following the election of a new club president in 2003, new strategies were implemented to address the problem; this case study therefore examines how the club has sought to generate revenue whilst remaining true to the principles upon which FC Barcelona is built.

Case Elements

When FC Barcelona captain Carlos Puyol lifted the Champions League trophy in May 2006, following victory in the Final over Arsenal, it marked the re-emergence of a club that last won the trophy in 1992. The win also complemented Barca's back-to-back La Liga titles in Spain, achieved in the 2004/2005 and 2005/2006 seasons. For people from the semi-autonomous region of Catalonia the club's playing success is always very important, not least for the message it sends out about them, their club and the region. But playing success is just as significant because of the lucrative commercial opportunities that inevitably follow it, something that has become increasingly important to the club since the election of Joan Laporta as club president in 2003. The question is, although a team containing Ronaldinho, Eto'o and Messi may be one of the best in the world, does the club really have what it takes to succeed in business and commerce?

Barcelona was founded in 1899 by a group of Swiss, British, Spanish and Catalonian footballers. Although initially set up as a football club, it was subsequently developed as a polideportivo, that is a multiple sports club, to play professional basketball, handball, roller hockey and futsal, as well as numerous other amateur sports including rugby union and wheelchair basketball. Since 1957, Barca have played at their now iconic home – the Nou Camp stadium. With a capacity of almost 99,000, it is Europe's biggest football stadium and home games are often complete sell-outs. Whereas clubs in countries such as England and Italy have been owned by local business people or industrial families FC Barcelona was founded as a membership club. This is still the case, with the club achieving a total worldwide membership of 145,000 in 2006. These members are referred to as socios or culés and many of them are members of penés or supporter's clubs, of which there are almost 1800 worldwide. Each of these socios pays an annual membership fee that allows them, amongst other things, to vote in the club's presidential elections. Historically, Barca has held something of a stranglehold on Spanish football, along with their closest and bitterest rivals Real Madrid. This rivalry became one of the most passionate in world football following the Spanish Civil War, during which Franco's Madrid based government fought a vicious and bloody campaign against Catalan separatists. FC Barcelona became a symbol of Catalan identity and defiance and, in the minds of many football fans and Catalans alike, has helped to cement the club as 'més que un club' – it is part of their identity, an integral element of Catalan culture.

Despite being the focus for proud Catalans the world over and one of the world's most renowned football teams, the 10 years up to 2003 were not the most notable for Barca. The team failed to sustain any success in its on-field performances and the club began to encounter financial problems off the field. Moreover, whilst clubs such as Manchester United began to see revenues and profits grow dramatically, Barcelona were falling behind their rivals due to a combination of internal politics, poor management and the constraints of history. In 2003, a progressive, young reformer, Joan Laporta, successfully stood for election as club president, bringing with him a directorial board consisting of equally young, commercially minded and entrepreneurially spirited people. This marked a watershed for Barca as Laporta not only promised playing success but also a new focus on building the club's off-field commercial activities. The signing of Ronaldinho was an initial sign of Laporta's ambition for the team, with his desire for culture change and a new strategic direction being a measure of his ambition for the club.

Football has experienced dramatic changes over the last 10 years, with some estimates indicating that the global game is now worth $12 billion per annum while commentators suggest the industry grew in size by up to 25 per cent during the same period. There are many reasons for such unprecedented growth: the proliferation and growth of the television market; technology and associated revenues; the development of revenue streams such as sponsorship and naming rights; a growing recognition that many football club brands have significant latent financial value; intense competition in the sport market leading to the emergence of powerful, internationally successful sports; and the globalization of sport.

The rapid changes in football, allied to Joan Laporta and his team's vision for FC Barcelona, have therefore led to a new era at the club. At its centre is a strategy designed to re-model Barca as a global entertainment brand, something akin to Walt Disney, rather than just a regional sports club. This clearly acknowledges that the club brand has both a huge, albeit latent, financial value and the potential to compete effectively with existing successful global sports brands such as the National Basketball Association (NBA) and Manchester United. The strategy has been built upon a number of important factors including the club's strong history and heritage, an established reputation for playing exciting, entertaining football, and an arguably unrivalled popularity that is most potently symbolized by the fact that the Nou Camp is the most popular tourist attraction in Barcelona.

Barca's marketing strategy is only one part of a broader corporate strategy, elements of which include cost control, value chain management and playing a strategic role in the development of organizations such as the G14 group of leading European clubs. The marketing strategy itself essentially consists of three major elements: effective product management, revenue generating brand management and international development. The essence of product management is what happens at the football product's core, that is, the way the team plays. It would be easy to say that Barca has in recent years signed the biggest football stars in the world. Yet Ronaldinho was unexpectedly signed from Paris Saint Germain with a reputation for being something of a maverick, Samuel Eto'o was a free scoring centre forward but one who had nevertheless been previously offloaded by Real Madrid and Lionel Messi was signed at 13 years old when he had nothing but potential. In other words, Barcelona's product management has actually been based on the Catalan virtue of shrewd financial management – not for Barca the free spending of Chelsea or Real Madrid. The team, rather than a group of galacticos, is important, another characteristic of Catalan culture.

Revenue generating brand management has been centred on the proposition that Barca is more than a club. In terms of positioning, the club is not intended either to have the glamorous image of its Madrid rivals or to have the rampantly commercial reputation that characterizes some English clubs. Rather, Barca aims to have an inclusive approach that embraces the development of new products and a global network of football schools and camps. In an attempt to appeal to young people, the club even has its own product range aimed at children which is based on cartoon figures of the club's first team players. Another important element of the brand's management is the FC Barcelona membership scheme. This is a major source of revenue for the club that Laporta quickly identified as offering scope for substantial revenue growth (on average, members pay an annual membership fee of around €120). The club therefore developed a campaign called 'The Big Challenge' that invited existing and potential socios to imagine 'their' club achieving an ultimate target of a million members. Thus far, the campaign has been a success, the total membership figure increasing by almost 40,000 in the period following Laporta's 2003 election. A significant proportion of these members can be found outside Catalonia and Spain, and this signifies the importance of the international marketplace for the club. Research indicates that Barca is the most popular overseas football club in Japan, there is already a natural affinity between the club and fans in Central and South America, and some say that throughout Europe FC Barcelona is often many people's second favourite club. The potential for international growth is therefore clearly evident and Barca has built on this by pursuing a growth strategy in countries such as China and in the USA, particularly in areas of the country where there is a large community of Hispanic origin.

The signing of Lilian Thuram and Gianluca Zambrotta from Juventus, and Eidur Gundjonsson from Chelsea prior to the 2006/2007 season has confirmed Barcelona's economic approach to signing players who nevertheless have a good reputation. At the same time, continuity and stability at the club will be ensured following the unopposed re-election, in September 2006, of Joan Laporta as club president. This is especially important because it should enable Barca to continue pursuing its goal of becoming a leading global entertainment brand. This raises a series of important issues for Laporta and his board of directors, many of which simultaneously present tremendous opportunities whilst posing a major developmental threat. The most fundamental of these is the goal of becoming a global entertainment brand. The club brand is currently one that has clear and intense political associations. For Catalans, Barca is symbolic of their fight for independence from centralized control in Madrid; many of them remain committed to breaking away from Spanish rule and fans believe the club plays an important part in this process. At the same time, FC Barcelona enjoys huge support in countries to which many Catalans fled during the Spanish Civil War, such as Mexico. Add to this the close ties between the Catalan people and those in other regions such as the Basque country and Wales, and one clearly gets the sense that this is not a 'Walt Disney' type brand, just as, in the same way, Medicine Sans Frontieres or the Worldwide Fund for Nature are not entertainment brands. This consequently poses a serious challenge for the club: either its goal is inconsistent with people's perceived image of it or, strategically, the brand will have to be very carefully managed in the future.

We are already seeing evidence that club officials, acutely aware of the apparent misalignment of image and strategy, are carefully trying to manage the Barca brand's development. By the end of the 2005/2006 season, Barcelona was the only leading football club in the world that did not have a sponsor's logo on its shirts. In financial terms, this would appear to be naïve, if not misguided. When Manchester United recently signed a four-year shirt sponsorship deal with the American International Group, it was worth almost €70 million to the club. In another recent case, Arsenal signed a combined shirt sponsorship and naming rights deal with Emirates Airlines, bringing the club around €145 million over 10 years. Sponsorship is therefore a major revenue stream for any club but it would appear that Barcelona is constrained by its past and by its brand image. By not carrying a corporate logo on its shirt, the club is once more making a strong socio-political statement, something that will reinforce the club's image in the minds of many people. This clearly has a value, no matter how intangible, and helps to reinforce the view that Barca is special – the club is about community, solidarity and care. But, in an era of big name player signings and generous salaries, it also denies the club a very important source of revenue. Barcelona's solution to this problem has been to capitulate; from 2006 onwards, a logo appeared on its shirts, although this is not what it seems. In conjunction with the Barcelona charitable foundation, UNICEF's logo appeared on team shirts, highlighting the quest of both parties to address the problems of children in vulnerable situations. The theme of the agreement being 'Barca, more than a club, it is a new global hope for vulnerable children'.

So what lies behind this decision? Integrity and principles certainly, but obviously not a direct or clearly established stream of revenue. Nevertheless, the move is clever brand management because it marks out Barca as being different to other clubs in not having a commercial shirt sponsorship deal; it also reinforces the club's existing brand image as being 'més que un club'. What the deal has done therefore, is to help build equity in the Barca brand, something which has huge potential value, particularly in terms of creating an affiliation between fans, the public and the club. It is likely to prove difficult for anyone to accurately measure the direct impact of the deal on the Barca brand, but the socially responsible nature of the arrangement is a shrewd long-term move that does not undermine club philosophy but does promote a 'global feel good factor' towards it.

The sanctity of Barca's shirts therefore means the club has to think about other sources of revenue, something which it is already doing. To compensate for the revenue lost because of the absence of a shirt deal, 'The Big Challenge' was introduced and management has also put in place a series of secondary sponsorship deals with companies including Telefonica, La Caixa, TV3, Estrella Damm, Nike and Coca Cola. In revenue terms, ensuring these deals are the most lucrative available to the club requires the careful acquisition and retention of strategic partners. It is likely that we will see additions to this portfolio of commercial partners as FC Barcelona develops its commercial activities. A further additional source of revenue would be for the club to sell naming rights to the Nou Camp stadium. Arsenal have done it, in conjunction with a move away from Highbury to their new stadium; so too have many of the German Bundesliga's leading clubs. However, for the foreseeable future at least, we are unlikely to see Barca sell these rights. Just as club shirts are not for sale, the same is true of the stadium, although this is not just an issue for the Catalans. Clubs across Europe have rejected the move towards commercial naming of sports stadia, these facilities often having a strong history and being deeply embedded in the psyche of sports fans.

In stark commercial terms, one actually has less need to question Barca's objection to naming rights than may be the case elsewhere. The Nou Camp remains the most popular tourist destination in Barcelona, the club drawing thousands of people each year to its museum and to admire the spectacle of Europe's biggest football stadium. Without doubt, it is a major asset for the club, although concerns remain about the facility. FC Barca finds itself in something of a dilemma: unlike England for example, Spain has a culture of low ticket pricing and any attempts to significantly increase prices are likely to incur the wrath of, in Barca's case, their socios. This would lead ultimately to probable election defeat for the president responsible for introducing such a measure. Yet the club effectively operates at 100 per cent capacity utilization, indicating that there is excess demand for match tickets. Logically, this alternatively suggests that the club should consider increasing the size of the stadium. Yet this would also be difficult because the design and location of the Nou Camp makes further development a problematic proposition. Another option would be to relocate, just as many of Europe's other leading clubs have done, including Arsenal, Bayern Munich and Juventus. But such is the iconography, the symbolism and the overall significance of the stadium that this option has been discussed and rejected by the club. The stadium's design also prohibits the construction or development of corporate boxes, again a constraint on revenue generation. As clubs like Manchester United develop their stadia, building new capacity and developing additional facilities, Barca finds itself constrained by the very resources that make it such an important club in the first place. In order to address this concern, Barca launched a major architectural competition in 2006 aimed at identifying an innovative design for re-vamping the Nou Camp.

The election of Laporta, alongside his team of young, well qualified, enterprising board of directors, was exactly what FC Barcelona needed. Local business people, they remain acutely aware of the meaning that Barca has for Catalans and non-Catalans alike. Moreover, they recognize the need to uphold a set of values that has long been associated with the club. At the same time, it is recognized that a growing financial imperative exists for football clubs to at least break-even. Added to this, numerous league tables measuring commercial performance in football are starting to appear; as for any other club, Barca's position in these leagues is an important indicator of commercial health. One thing that does however distinguish Barca from other football clubs is their innovative approach to managing the club's strategic development. Although this may seem to some as the only way forward, it nevertheless typifies the cultural change that has taken place at the Nou Camp and shows that the board of directors see as opportunities what some may previously have perceived as developmental constraints.

Between 1999 and 2005, FC Barcelona failed to win the Spanish La Liga title or the Copa del Rey (Kings Cup). During the same period, there were no Champions League or other European titles, and the club fell behind its major competitors off the field as well. There is some evidence that progress is nevertheless being made: revenues are increasing and Barca is one of the few leading European clubs to make a profit in recent years. The question is, given that some clubs like Real Madrid and Manchester United already hold a first-mover commercial advantage over Barcelona, how long will it take the Catalan club to compete on an equal commercial footing with them? Continued success on the field is one important ingredient, astute strategic management of the brand another, but only time will tell when, if ever, it will be achieved.

Case Diagnosis

To understand FC Barcelona, one has to truly appreciate the socio-political origins of the club. That the club was formed by someone from Switzerland who ultimately changed his name to a Catalan derivative of it is telling. Catalans like to think of themselves as being open and receptive but Catalonia has a powerful impact on many people. A strong sense of self-identity and self-worth is also evident amongst Catalans, traits that were heightened during the Spanish Civil War when the Madrid government forcefully attempted to quell unrest in Barcelona. This is an especially pertinent issue today because, in an age of globalization in sport, Catalan émigrés (and Barca fans) from this period are now spread across the Spanish-speaking world and beyond. The principles of equality and fairness borne out of the unrest, also ensure that the club has always adopted a socially responsible approach to business when many other organizations have only recently been awoken to the need for responsibility in their operations. Add to this, the iconic stadium, the era when the club was dominated by Johan Cruyff, the Dutch international footballer, the string of domestic and international trophies and current players such as Ronaldinho, and one sees a football club that is as distinctive as it is complex.

In the most general of terms, the FC Barcelona case study is an excellent example of an organization that needed to change. Developments in the club's operating environment (for instance, advances in technology, new media opportunities and the commercialization of sport) have had an impact, to varying degrees, on all football clubs, although Barca was especially slow to respond to them. The election in 2003 of Joan Laporta was a watershed for the club, representing an advance in management competence that has subsequently led to a cultural change at the club. Philosophically, the club remains the same but the way in which FC Barcelona now operates has changed considerably. This raises some interesting issues that users of the case may wish to consider. In particular, how internal culture change sits within the broader context of the club's history and the more general Catalan culture is interesting, as is the impact that the club's changed culture has had on commercial strategy.

Commercially, the club faces an interesting future, particularly as it seeks to make up lost (commercial) ground on clubs such as Manchester United and Real Madrid. The extent to which this can be achieved, allied to pace of commercial change at the club, would make for an interesting debate. One argument is that Barca is actually in a better position to take advantage of new opportunities than, say, Real Madrid, which is, it could be argued, shackled by associations with the 'galacticos' team of Ronaldo, Beckham, Figo, Zidane et al. There are, however, constraints on the club, most notably the principles noted above. Some commentators argue that whilst it is noble and highly commendable to have a strong sense of corporate responsibility, it is a major constraint on the commercial development of FC Barcelona. This is a highly pertinent argument in an era when player transfer costs and associated salaries are rapidly inflating, meaning that clubs need to maximize off-field revenue generation in order to sustain on-field success. Put another way, if a club earns more, it can buy the best players and pay them more.

Such a contention is premised on an established business model that seems to prevail across world football. That is, a club needs to be like Manchester United in order to prosper: extending their brand, creating new merchandising opportunities, exploiting new media and so on. What is so interesting, and indeed refreshing, is that Barca appears to have adopted a different model. The goal is for the club to secure the same ends as clubs such as United, but the means of doing this are considerably different. Certainly the approach is socially, ethically and morally more principled. As a model of corporate social responsibility it is exemplary, certainly in football, similarly so in sport, possibly even in the business world as a whole.

Despite the strengths and merits of being a responsible business, there are a number of problems that FC Barcelona must manage if it is to realize its commercial potential. The first is centred around a very distinctive organization culture that, according to Ball (2003), has been characterized by some as arrogant and self-aggrandising. This has led to accusations that the club can be rather too presumptuous in the way it operates, divorced from the reality of its operating environment. Arguably, internal culture is likely to be partly an outcome of member ownership of the club. In many ways, Barca is a model for the way in which a football club should be owned and run. Unlike the oligarchs and 'money men' running football clubs elsewhere in the world, Barca truly reflects the wishes and desires of its fans. Yet the Catalan agenda poses a major challenge for managers of what is, in effect, a highly politicized club and brand. Similarly, the socio-culture means the club is often severely restricted in what it can do, most notably in relation to ticket prices. Once more, this in itself is not a bad thing, but for a directorial board intent on competing with the best clubs in the world, both on the field of play and off it, imposes a particular need to operate in a thoughtful, creative and innovative way. To compound matters further, the Nou Camp stadium, iconic though it may be, remains a concern. In an era when consumers have high expectations, it can be a cold, dark, intimidating, uninviting venue. Moreover, the stadium's construction and location provide little scope for further development. If club officials remain committed to revenue generation, the creativity evident in their UNICEF shirt sponsorship deal will also need to be evident in their thinking about where the club plays its football.

At the heart of Barcelona's marketing strategy is the vision that the Barca brand can become one that is akin to the Walt Disney brand. At one level, concerns about globalization and the imposition of 'Western' culture (some critics of globalization talk of corporate imperialism) are highly pertinent for Barca, especially as the club is symbolic of the struggle against an outside foe. As an aspirational brand for the club, Disney is also a worry for other reasons: firstly, it implies oppressiveness and cultural homogenization, both of which are unlikely to sit well with the socios or with Catalans in general; secondly, football is not seen by many as entertainment, it is pain, suffering, passion, identity. In the latter respect, the cultural transition from a club that constitutes a way of life for many Catalans to a global entertainment commodity is going to be an interesting challenge for club officials to manage.

With a couple of exceptions, FC Barcelona has been one of the last major clubs in the world to play without a sponsor's logo on its shirts. The recent UNICEF deal is an admirable one and a very clever one too. One question though is: Is the UNICEF arrangement simply a prelude to a major corporate deal in the future? If so, this raises some major issues for the club: credibility, identity, image, reputation and so on. If not, some commentators will remain concerned that the club is denying itself a major source of revenue by providing its shirt space to UNICEF on a not-for-profit basis. The club is already attempting to offset the revenue loss by putting in place a series of secondary sponsorship deals that may be enough to compensate the club. However, other clubs are doing the same; for instance, Barca may have a relationship with Estrella Damm, but Manchester United has a relationship with Budweiser. Putting together a package of secondary sponsors may not, therefore, be as innovative as some people at Barca might think. A final point to consider is the way in which the club leverages the UNICEF deal; is it simply a fine example of socio-political symbolism or are club officials truly convinced that it has some direct financial worth? In the case of the former, the club lays itself open to accusations of commercial naivety. In the case of the latter, the club alternatively lays itself open to accusations of cynicism and exploitation. FC Barcelona has chosen a unique and complex approach to sponsorship. In fact, this nicely sums up the club: it is unique and complex.

Case Questions

1 What do you think are the advantages and disadvantages for a sports organization of adopting a multisports club approach similar to that employed by FC Barcelona?
2 To what extent do you agree with the statement that FC Barcelona's history simultaneously constrains and strengthens the football club?
3 Evaluate whether or not you think FC Barcelona's commercial strategy is likely to be the most effective one for the club.
4 Compare and contrast the marketing challenges that FC Barcelona, Manchester United, AC Milan and Bayern Munich face.
5 How does the FC Barcelona brand differ from that of, for example, Real Madrid, and what do you think are the implications of these differences for the respective club's marketers?
6 What are the arguments for and against carrying a sponsor's logo on a team shirt? In FC Barcelona's case, what do you think will have been some of the challenges for the club in managing the introduction of a logo?

Case Resources

Reading

Ball, P. (2003). *Morbo: The Story of Spanish Football*. WSC Books, London.

Beech, J. and Chadwick, S. (2004). *The Business of Sport Management*. FT Prentice Hall, Harlow.

Beech, J. and Chadwick, S. (2006). *The Marketing of Sport*. FT Prentice Hall, Harlow.

Burns, J. (2000). *Barca: A People's Passion*. Bloomsbury, London.

Conn, D. (2006). Barcelona's model of integrity shows right is might. *The Guardian*. 17 May, http://football.guardian.co.uk/champions-league200506/story/0,,1776487,00.html.

Foer, F. (2005). *How Soccer Explains the World*. Harper Perennial, New York.

Gil-LaFuente, J. (2006). Marketing a socially complex club: FC Barcelona, in Desbordes, M. (Ed.), *Marketing and Football: An International Perspective*. Elsevier, Oxford.

Hoehn, T., Szymanski, S., Matutes, C. and Seabright, P. (1999). The americanization of european football. *Economic Policy*, Vol. 14, No. 28, pp. 203–240.

Martin, P. (2005). The europeanization of elite football – scope, meanings, significance. *European Societies*, Vol. 7, No. 1, pp. 349–368.

Richelieu, A. and Pons, F. (2006). Toronto Maple Leafs vs. Football Club Barcelona: How two legendary sports teams built their brand equity. *International Journal of Sports Marketing and Sponsorship*, Vol. 7, No. 3, pp. 231–259.

Winner, D., van Dam, L., Barend, F. and van Dorp, H. (1999). *Ajax, Barcelona, Cruyff*. Bloomsbury, London.

Websites

FC Barcelona – http://www.fcbarcelona.com/eng/home-page/home/home.shtml

Manchester United Supporters Trust – http://www.joinmust.org/forum/showthread.php?t=23742

Soccerpulse – http://www.soccerpulse.com/forum/index.php?showtopic=97837

Further Information

Users of the case may want to take a look at the Wikipedia entries for the following:

Barcelona – http://en.wikipedia.org/wiki/Barcelona
Catalunya – http://en.wikipedia.org/wiki/Catalunya
FC Barcelona – http://en.wikipedia.org/wiki/Fc_barcelona
Spain – http://en.wikipedia.org/wiki/Spain

2

Branding sport teams in a competitive context: a look at team branding strategies in the National Hockey League

André Richelieu and Frank Pons

Case Focus

This case examines branding strategies used by three teams in the National Hockey League. Despite the acknowledged importance of the strategic issue of branding, these teams present critical discrepancies in their approach that may explain why some of them struggle in their market.

Keywords

- Hockey teams
- Brand strategy
- Brand equity
- Merchandising strategy
- Communication policy
- Community involvement

Case Summary

The Montréal Canadiens, the Ottawa Senators and the Atlanta Thrashers implement different strategies to leverage their brand.

The Canadiens aim at positioning their brand as young and dynamic, while capitalizing on the winning tradition, which unfortunately seems a distant memory today. The lack of a formal brand strategy leads to major contradictions, especially in merchandising endeavours.

The Senators share the same misconception of what defines a marketing strategy. However, despite a fragmented market, their legitimate status as a Stanley Cup contender gives credibility to their ambition of becoming a regional brand that is strongly committed toward the Ottawa community.

Finally, even though they operate in a non-traditional hockey market, the Thrashers appear more proactive in leveraging their brand. Truly, their merchandising and communication strategies contribute to increase their visibility, which ensures coherence with their goal to become a reference team in the league, on and off the ice.

Case Elements

I cannot emphasize enough the importance of branding in this economy. In an era where consumers do not distinguish between broadcast and cable networks and there is so much competition among so many companies and mediums for consumer attention, it is critical that your brand serves as a beacon in a sea of choice.

George Bodenheimer, ESPN/ABC Sports President
(2004 Sports Media and Technology Conference)

In marketing consumer goods and services, branding issues have always been of primary concern for companies. Key players such as P&G or BMW have positioned branding issues as central strategic preoccupations within their respective organizations as suggested by the increasing importance and responsibilities given to brand managers. However, other than a handful of key players in each major professional sport such as the New York

Yankees, the Real Madrid or the Dallas Cowboys, sport marketers have been more reluctant to work on long-term strategic issues such as branding, focusing instead on ticket sales and other short-term issues. Structural and historical variables may explain this late interest but, in light of an over-competitive market in which fans and advertisers face many options, sport marketers are becoming increasingly immersed in finding the adequate positioning for their teams, moving toward an effective branding strategy. In fact, consumers often do not perceive the sport offering as having con-crete attributes beside the win–loss aspect. Therefore, the brand must act as a differentiator that will allow a franchise to stand, in the eye of the con-sumer, for something different than any other team. In addition, a strong brand has the potential of transcending the sports arena (event) by build-ing a 'brand community' and a reputation for the sports product. A strong brand will stir fans in every part of their lives. From an economic and finan-cial standpoint, strong brand equity attracts spectators and sponsors. It also increases revenue through television rights and merchandising.

This has become a critical issue in the sport marketing area and the National Hockey League (NHL) in particular. Coming out of a life-threatening year-long lock-out, the fourth major sport league in North America and its teams faced a double challenge of reviving fans' interest and building a business model that could grow for the years to come. For years, the league had neglected branding issues but it recently started a major repositioning, with a long-term objective in mind, and immersed itself in a branding overhaul with changes in rules, financial, broadcast and promotional content. Even though the league is now on the branding path, it will always remain as good as its weakest link. Therefore, this case attempts to present how branding issues and strategies are, or were, viewed and implemented in three different NHL teams. Using secondary data analyses (website analyses, newspaper and mag-azine contents) as well as primary data stemming from interviews with the VP marketing for three NHL teams (Montréal Canadiens, Ottawa Senators and Atlanta Thrashers), branding strategies and tactics are presented hereaf-ter, offering an insider and critic look at teams' strategic orientations. But first, a brief biography on each Vice president interviewed.

The Vice president of Marketing and Sales of the Canadiens joined the team in September 2001. In his role, he oversees the Canadiens' ticket sales, luxury suite sales, consumer products, events and all marketing pro-grams. In 1991, he became Director of Football Operations for the Montréal Machine of the World League of American Football. In 1993, he joined the National Basketball Association to launch NBA Europe. He is one of the six members of the NHL's Business Advisory Board, which focuses on generat-ing future revenue ideas for the NHL (Canadiens' website).

The Vice president, Marketing of the Ottawa Senators and Scotiabank Place was promoted to his position in August 2002. Prior to this appointment, he was Vice president, ticketing, a position he held since 1993. As Vice president, Marketing of the Ottawa Senators and Scotiabank Place, he is tasked with providing overall marketing direction for the team and building, including advertising, promotions, merchandise sales, game presentation and fan and community development programs. He has been a member of the NHL ticketing advisory committee for the past six years (Senators' Vice president office).

The Vice president Marketing, Advertising and Branding for the Thrashers started his career with the Madison Square Garden (NY). He spent nine years working for the Knicks (NBA) and the Rangers (NHL). When he left, he was the marketing director for the Rangers and he longed to pursue things outside of New York. As the NHL announced its expansion, he was hired to be the Thrashers' marketing director. After five years, Lion Spirit purchased the Thrashers and the Hawks, and he was promoted to be in charge of the marketing and branding for both teams.

The Montréal Canadiens

The Montréal Canadiens (Habs) were established in 1908 and have won the Stanley Cup (championship trophy) an NHL record 24 times. The Montréal Canadiens are one of the six original teams which were part of the NHL when the league started its operations. More than just a hockey team, it is an institution in Montréal and in Canada. The club has long been seen as the team of French Canadiens, which explains its nickname, the 'Habs' (for 'Habitants', the original French Canadian settlers). After its share of problems and a restructuring process, the team seems to be headed in the right direction now.

As far as branding is concerned, the Montréal Canadiens would like to leverage their brand based on four key attributes: (i) history and tradition, (ii) authenticity, (iii) professionalism and (iv) dynamism. First, history and tradition are linked to the longevity of the franchise (100 years in 2008), and the impressive record of the team (24 Stanley Cups). Second, the team has long been seen as authentically French Canadian. With recent changes in players draft and trade policies as well as free agency, the team currently wants to position itself more as a Canadian brand, as opposed to most American teams, and capitalize on this identity across Canada. Third, after a five-year rebuilding process under a new and competent general manager (Bob Gainey), the team shows the first signs of a revival, which boosts the professionalism of the franchise. Fourth, dynamism is an attribute the new management team wants to bring as the latest change to the conservative image of the club. This may represent the main challenge of the marketing team. In this regard, there seems to be a dramatic shift in the target market of the team, with a stronger focus on young customers: 'We want to reach the younger fans who did not live the glory days of the past. We need to get closer to these fans and make our product attractive to them' (Montréal Canadiens Vice president, Marketing). However, this shift could be made to the detriment of the traditional fan base that is more attached to the love of the game and is not interested so much in the off-ice entertainment experience.

Like other Canadian hockey teams, the Montréal Canadiens can rely on specific factors to leverage their brand efficiently. The importance given to the entertainment experience is seen as a powerful catalyst tool: 'We want the fans to have the best entertainment experience of their life' (Montréal Canadiens Vice president, Marketing). This is in total accordance with their willingness to nurture the sense of belonging and commitment of their fans, but also their goal to attract a younger audience at the arena. Getting their fans involved and thrilled is a challenge, considering the high number of regular home games (41), spread over seven months, which might alter the original exaltation.

Merchandising appears as another way to make each event special. However, merchandising must be understood as a component of an integrated marketing strategy. Otherwise, it can lead to serious incoherence and therefore, thwart the brand's equity. Unfortunately, the Montréal Canadiens embody this misconception of merchandising. While the team's colours have always been blue, white and red, selling bright orange and yellow caps with a black logo in the team's boutique is at least surprising, if not disconcerting for the fans that can hardly identify themselves with those whimsical products. Above all, the team managers have been making every effort not to alter the Canadiens' logo and colours since its creation: 'The Montréal Canadiens is a strong recognized brand, which embeds history and tradition. Hockey greats have worn the Canadiens jersey with this logo on their chest; changing it would be a sacrilege!' (Montréal Canadiens Vice president, Marketing).

Moreover, there is one more contradiction in attempting to attract a younger target: truly, no new jersey has ever been launched to introduce some kind of novelty for the fans, with the exception of the vintage jerseys, which are replicas of former Montréal Canadiens uniforms and a way to play on the nostalgia of the good old days of the team.

In fact, the marketing actions of the Montréal Canadiens seem to unveil a lack of clarity in their identity and decisiveness in their positioning: Do they want to be seen as a young and dynamic franchise targeting a younger audience or do they want to capitalize on their glorious heritage to promote the team and the beauty of the game to true Montréal Canadiens hockey fans?

The Ottawa Senators

Ottawa first had a hockey team between 1901 and 1934, before the franchise was moved to St. Louis and disappeared. The Senators (Sens) have been back in Ottawa since 1992. This situation represents a challenge for building the Senators brand. Since 2000, the team is a legitimate Stanley Cup contender.

In relation with branding, the Ottawa Senators have three key values they want to build on: (i) being part of the community, (ii) having a good product on the ice and (iii) offering good entertainment. First, community involvement aims at increasing the sympathy fans have for the players and their sense of belonging to the team. This should help the team become a brand with a social conscience and therefore build brand awareness, enhance brand image and brand personality. Examples are the team practices on the Rideau Canal, where kids are invited; a full colour poster of each Ottawa Senators player in the Ottawa Citizen, with information on his community involvement at the bottom of the poster. This showed that the players were more than just high paid sportsmen, but also that they do care for their community. It is a way to connect with the fans through players' involvement in the community, and thus trigger a sense of belonging to the team.

Second, on the ice, Ottawa has reached the elite status in the league. Competitive during the regular season, they now win division titles; the next step would be to win the Stanley Cup. And finally, the Senators aim at not only offering an entertainment experience to the fans that come to the arena (Scotiabank Place) through the game itself, but also through the animations that surround the game: music, mascot (Spartacat), contests, ambience in the stands, etc. However, the main challenge the team faces is in building their fan base in a small market. They only had the equivalent of 8,500 full season ticket holders and they still had problems filling in the 18,000 seats arena: 'We would like to reach 13,000 season ticket holders to secure revenues at the beginning of the season'. (Ottawa Senators Vice president, Marketing). A winning record and a focus on young customers to move them along the emotional continuum could help establish the Ottawa Senators brand and build a solid fan base over time. This being said, intergenerational influence, which is the transmission of information, beliefs and resources from one generation to the other within the family, could slow down the process of attracting new fans.

This is probably the reason why the Ottawa Senators try to define the Senators as a brand, not only with sympathy, but also with a social conscience. This leads the Senators to obey the laws of the cognitive retention process. In fact, their approach consists of the three following stages: building brand awareness, enhancing the brand image and thus conveying a personality to the emerging brand; a personality the fans could refer to and that will last overtime.

Although the Ottawa Senators, like the Montréal Canadiens, tend to think that marketing actions define the brand strategy, whereas it should be the other way around, this team is likely to go beyond its original constraint, which is its market's fragmentation. In spite of the well-known difficulty to allocate resources to branding in a small market, because there are many chances that local marketing actions turn out to be non-profitable in the end, the Senators seem to be on the right track. First, their winning record strengthens their visibility, hence their ability to anchor the brand locally, regionally and eventually nationally. Second, their merchandising actions, conducted up until now, are compatible with their target and their ambition to position themselves as a national brand in the long term: the introduction of a third jersey with a Canadian symbol on their shoulders does reflect it.

Not only is this coherent with the need to strengthen the Senators brand on a local scale, but also it does open the door to the recruitment of new fans elsewhere in Canada.

The Atlanta Thrashers

After the departure of the Atlanta Flames for Calgary in 1980, Atlanta remained without a major hockey league franchise for 17 years. Finally, in 1997, the city was awarded an NHL franchise in an expansion move adopted by the league. The majority owner of this new franchise was headed by Ted Warner and the media giant Time Warner. The nickname 'Thrashers', chosen after Georgia's state bird, the brown thrasher, was selected from a fan poll in early 1998. The Thrashers played their first game on 2 October 1999 (a loss to future Stanley Cup Champions, the New Jersey Devils) at the Philips Arena. This new building offered them a brand new named arena to replace the former and aging Omni, which had been home to the Flames. On 21 September 2003, the team was sold by Time Warner, along with the NBA's Atlanta Hawks, to a group of executives who formed the current ownership group, the Atlanta Spirit LLC. At the end of the 2005–2006 season, the Thrashers had never made the playoffs in their short history; they took part to one playoff round in April 2007.

Even though the Thrashers evolve in a non-traditional hockey market, their ultimate branding goals are not that different from several other teams. As the VP marketing describes it: 'We want to provide first-class entertainment for our fans … we want to put on an incredible show to complement what is going on the ice, to the degree that the results shouldn't matter but that families can still come out and have a good time … we want to make it affordable and keep our overall philosophy that the Thrashers is a classy team that puts on a fun and entertaining product'. This classy and professional positioning is well reflected in the following statement made by the VP marketing: 'I would say another one of our brand attributes is first class. We try to do everything the right way – how we communicate to people, how we put on things, how we invite them to places. That relates to the recruitment of athletes because our general manager wants to bring in class individuals that want to get involved with the community, that are leaders, have experience, and are people who are eager to go out and work with others. We try to stay away from potential issues or trouble'. In addition to the entertainment, professional and social positioning adopted, the Thrashers also hope to transfer this professional approach to their on-ice product in order to become more competitive and to develop expert fans. For instance the VP marketing mentions that 'we hope to make it one of the elite teams in the league, so to do that, we're really trying to promote who our players are, who our coach is, and educate our fans to show that we are legitimate Stanley Cup contenders'.

If the branding goals are similar to other teams', the Thrashers' approach to effective branding really stands out compared to other teams in the league. For instance, the Thrashers have a very proactive approach to branding. They carefully studied the existing brands and their positioning in the league before deciding who they wanted to be. The VP marketing mentions 'we've gone through all sorts of brand analyses. When we started out we were trying to capture some of what the NHL had to offer and how they defined it with aggressive, fast and exciting … we had a company come in, a year and a half ago to do this brand study for us, and they had just finished doing it for the Pistons and the Lightning. For Detroit, they had found a platform that worked in that city – everyone bought into it, including the GM, the President and the players started buying into it and now it's something that the fans talk about, AND THEY WIN … so it gets magnified … that was the same model we wanted to build'.

In addition to these benchmarking studies, the Thrashers re-immersed themselves in marketing research as soon as the franchise was bought from Time Warner. They focused then on the consumers and tried to capture their perception of the franchise and their wants and desires. The level of sophistication of their marketing research is very impressive and in line with what is being done by marketing giants in goods and services industries. For instance, the VP marketing describes their approach to market research: 'We started small a couple of years ago, trying to capture as much information as possible about our fans. Over the last few years, we have really ramped it up to the point where everything we do now is a component of database generating … Two years ago, there was extensive research done with our brand study. We found out what people feel about the team, how they relate it to other teams, how they feel about our players, what about our game experience, our ticket prices, the time of the games, the price of the food … All that stuff is constantly looked at. We have a whole database management department. We also hired a research analyst and we have a group of 10 people who work on random games with handheld devices. We looked at the results that week or the next day so we periodically see what our fans think and our brand evolves. We also want to do more on focus groups'.

This precious information, coupled with an innovative spirit, allows the Thrashers to take a set of new decisions to give life to the brand the team and the fans were looking for. For example, they have dedicated staff to their cutting-edge website and customer service to develop and nurture relationships with consumers using new media technology and database. They hold city-hall style meetings for their GM, Bob Hartley, to meet with fans and season ticket holders to develop hockey expertise and community ties. They offer an incredible on-site experience with their state-of-the-art arena which has a unique design 'it's unlike any other arena – it doesn't have your typical row of suites that goes around between the concourses and on top of your upper bowl. One side is club side only, it has seven sections of club seats, above them it has a wall of suites, where it's four levels of suites, it kind of resembles a European opera house'. The very colourful arena is also totally interactive with thousands of TV sets and interactive games provided by Philips, owner of the rights for the arena. The interactive arena offers fans, young and old, the chance to play and feel like an athlete, creating an amazing game day experience.

In order to intertwine the game day experience and the sense of community, the team followed leads from their research results to develop a rally territory in and outside the arena. They introduced their fans to a section of the arena that they named 'Blue Land' territory in which special activities and songs were performed to support the team. The result was amazing as fans, young and old, embraced the concept and took it to another level with hats, shirts and flags. Everybody wanted to be in the 'Blue Land'. It was the ultimate communion between the team and the fans and it was developed following models of supporter communities in other teams and sports. This approach was adopted from the very top-down as described by the VP marketing. 'We tried to lead our fans toward a direction, but only to a point and then let them take it to another level. So we were very careful when we came out with this concept. We purposely weren't trying to ram it down their throats, we were trying to introduce it and hopefully it would grow. The team, up until recently, was on a roll, so the place was getting very loud and very exciting, and the media was starting to pick up – Bob Hartley (coach) had been our best scorer so every press conference he does he talks about getting people down to "Blue Land". And I think that is very important when you're coaching staff and your general manager can buy into what you're doing, and it's not just the ads you're running, and the things you're saying at games, but it's your broadcasters, your coaches, your players'.

The only area in which the team lacks evidence of success is merchandising. Even though the Thrashers are really creative with the introduction of different logos for games at home and abroad as well as products to tie in with their 'Blue Land' community, they still limit their control on the merchandise sold at the arena and they do not have their own store in the city. They still rely on a network of external retailers to push their products to the consumer which often leads to inconsistency in the way the brand is presented. As suggested by the VP marketing, 'obviously we want to create more excitement, sell more merchandise, become one of the cooler looking jerseys in the league, but you know I don't think we do a lot of our logo design based around merchandise. You know it's a small portion of the overall revenues. We realize that we are still a new team and until we win a few rounds in the playoffs, it's not gonna be a huge national success'.

Conclusion and Diagnosis

The Montréal Canadiens and the Ottawa Senators are two Canadian hockey teams with obvious weaknesses in their brand strategy, which actually takes the form of a combination of different actions rather than a formalized strategy. While the Montréal Canadiens have been going through a deep rebuilding process, the Senators have dealt with a fragmented market: their absence from Canada between 1934 and 1992 made the team original fan base disperse among other clubs. Yet, the fact remains that most of the strategy and the means used to revive both teams' brands are questionable. Indeed, a striking reality is the fact that neither team relies on a formalized brand strategy. In fact, managers from both teams have underlined that 'being a brand is a result of our marketing actions'. In fact, it should be the other way around: marketing actions are supposed to reflect and enhance both the identity and positioning of the team. On the contrary, the Atlanta Thrashers, who evolve in a non-traditional hockey market in Southeastern United States, implement innovative tactics in order to reach the positioning (first class, entertaining, community-oriented team) carefully chosen after a thorough study of the league, the teams and their market. Moreover, they acknowledge the ever-changing environment and the nature of a brand and they have implemented a set of market studies to help them monitor consumers' perceptions and desires. In addition to historical and cultural variables that may explain the discrepancies between teams in their branding approach, several key structural explanations can be suggested.

First, it is only recently that Canadian hockey teams have appreciated the importance of branding, and branding initiatives are still under construction. Second, Canadian teams are facing major economical constraints (exchange rate, small markets and heavy tax burden). That is why the six Canadian teams (among the 30 that are part of the NHL) were quite vocal when it came to negotiate a new collective bargaining agreement (CBA), in order to implement a new economic model in the NHL (among others, a salary cap based on the league revenues), which was finally negotiated after a lock-out that led to the cancellation of the 2004–2005 season. Up until now, it was very difficult for Canadian teams to allocate resources to branding when they were fighting for their survival. Third, the NHL controls the marketing and branding of the teams beyond a 100-mile radius. In other words, individual teams cannot seal agreements with licensors for national coverage and it often discourages their commercial initiatives. Truly, it is often not profitable enough for teams in small market or with limited brand equity to launch local marketing actions because of the relatively small attractiveness (profit and volume) of local markets. Also, being confined to a pre-defined territory, small market teams do not have the ability to put their brand out and make it visible on a larger scale, allowing them to become part of the consideration set of customers across North America. This means that the sales of their products are generally marginal outside of their local market. As a result, the NHL wants to safeguard the integrity of its own brand. Centralization provides homogeneity and strengthens the overall quality of the league itself. However, the league brand being as strong as its weakest team brand, this strategy may backfire and be damaging; the realities of the 30 markets that compose the NHL are very different,

Table 2.1 Highlights specific brand tactics used by Atlanta, Montréal and Ottawa

Criterions	The Canadiens	The Senators	The Thrashers
What the team wants to be	■ A Canadian brand. ■ A young, professional and dynamic brand.	■ A regional then a national brand. ■ A team involved in its community.	■ Provide first-class entertainment. ■ Become an elite team in the league: classy with fun.
Perceived strengths by the managers	■ Impressive record: 24 Stanley Cups; history and tradition of success. ■ Authentic and dynamic. ■ Professional: qualified general manager (Bob Gainey) who has managed the restructuring process.	■ On the ice performance: since 2000, the team is a legitimate Stanley Cup contender. ■ Increasing involvement in the community. ■ Good entertainment for the money.	■ Doing things outside the box in order to grab people's attention. ■ Affordable entertainment experience. ■ Good coaching and involvement of the staff in the community: players, managers, etc.
Perceived weaknesses by the managers	■ Relatively poor on the ice performance in recent years (restructuring process). ■ Conservative image of the club.	■ Fragmented market since the moving of the franchise in the 1930s; it may slow down the process of winning new fans. ■ Small market and limited resources to allocate to branding.	■ Non-traditional hockey market. ■ Not enough exposure on national TV.
Marketing objectives	■ Focusing on younger customers to revive the brand. ■ Capitalizing on their glorious heritage to promote the team to the traditional hockey fans.	■ Building the Senators brand according to the cognitive retention process: building brand awareness through social conscience, thus enhancing brand image and brand personality. ■ Building a solid fan base over time in the Ottawa region (Ottawa and Gatineau).	■ Planning and meeting fans' expectations in terms of entertainment experience. ■ Becoming a forerunner among hockey teams on and off the ice (e.g. making the team jerseys the coolest in the league).

(Continued)

Table 2.1 (Continued)

Criterions	The Canadiens	The Senators	The Thrashers
Attributes of the brand	■ French Canadian. ■ History and traditional success (100 years in 2008). ■ Authentic: same logo and colours since its creation.	■ A young and talented team: Stanley Cup contenders. ■ Dynamic and entertaining. ■ Part of the community: care for the Ottawa community (importance of arousing the sense of belonging to the team among fans).	■ First-class organization/brand. ■ An arena (Philips arena) that showcases and leverages the brand. ■ Professional and entertaining (state of the art Philips arena).
Plans to expand the brand	■ Entertainment experience is seen as a powerful catalyst tool. ■ Targeting younger customers. ■ A reference among professional teams in the province of Quebec, with a strong French Canadian identity.	■ Offering an entertainment experience through the game and the animations around the game. ■ Capitalizing on the winning record to strengthen the Senators visibility. ■ Creating an emotional connection with the fans in Ottawa, Ontario and then Canada.	■ Engaging the fans at the arena who become creators of their entertainment experience. ■ Capitalizing on the hard-core fans who become ambassadors of the Atlanta Thrashers in order to attract and engage other potential hockey fans. ■ Recruiting hockey players who have the potential to become leaders in the community.
Community involvement	■ Nurturing the sense of belonging and commitment of the fans: players' involvement and new mascot (Youppi!).	■ Increasing the sympathy fans have for the players and their sense of belonging to the team: for example, Practice on the Rideau Canal.	■ Involving players and coaches in the community.

Key merchandising actions	▪ Lack of coherence with the history and traditional image: for example, selling bright orange and yellow caps with a black logo in the team boutique. ▪ No new jersey offering to the fans (lack of novelty).	▪ Introducing different lines of products: babies, children, teenagers, men and women. ▪ Introducing a third jersey with a Canadian symbol on the shoulders; this reflects the team's ambition to position itself as a national brand in the long term.	▪ Launching a home, road and third jersey with a unique design. ▪ Strong focus on the stores at the arena; also, trying to get more visibility among sports fans in Atlanta through team merchandise.
Promotional campaigns	▪ Positioning the team as the reference sport franchise in Montreal: 'the city is hockey' slogan. ▪ Key players (Huet, Koivu, Kovalev) and mascot (Youppi!) used as spokespersons in the community. ▪ Building and fostering a fan community on line (website).	▪ Initiating activities in the community: for example, team practice on the Rideau Canal, GM Senators Street Tour. ▪ Inserting colour posters of each Ottawa Senators player in the Ottawa Citizen. ▪ Involving the fans online: contests, interactive options (game highlights) on team website.	▪ Capitalizing on the 'Blue Land' concept: the Atlanta Thrashers hockey fans Community. ▪ Cheerleaders team: Dream Machines and Blue Land Babes. ▪ Capitalizing on the website as a promotional and sales tool.
Competition from other entertainment offering	▪ In any major city, profusion of entertainment options that are in competition for the disposable income customers. ▪ In Montreal, the Canadiens remain the only real major league franchise since the departure of the Expos in 2004.	▪ The Senators are the key entertainment offering in the city. ▪ Problems in attracting fans to the arena.	▪ In a major city, profusion of entertainment options that are in competition for the disposable income of customers. ▪ Atlanta is a non-traditional hockey market: the right positioning is crucial in attracting fans to the arena.

(Continued)

Table 2.1 (Continued)

Criterions	The Canadiens	The Senators	The Thrashers
Key variables to leverage the team brand	■ History and tradition. ■ Entertainment experience at the arena. ■ Increasing the visibility and involvement of the team in the community.	■ On the ice performance (Stanley Cup contenders). ■ Good entertainment experience at the arena. ■ Strong involvement in the community.	■ Quality of the entertainment experience at the arena. ■ Web platform: frequent updates to the team's website, understood as a real sales tool, and continuous marketing research on consumers (satisfaction, feelings about hockey teams, recommendations, etc.).
Hurdles in leveraging the team brand	■ Risk of alienating fans by promoting both the entertainment and the love of the game. ■ No formal brand strategy: incoherence in merchandising actions, which should be seen as a component of an integrated marketing strategy. ■ The team relies too heavily on history and tradition, which are not enhanced by actual team performances.	■ Fragmented market place. ■ No formal brand strategy. ■ Contending team but no Stanley Cup championship yet.	■ Not enough exposure on American national TV. ■ Need to break through in a non-traditional hockey market. ■ First Stanley Cup playoff appearance in April 2007.

and a team brand should have the flexibility to transcend the sport arena beyond its original market and to explore the national or international levels. Finally, it appears that internal factors, more specifically human factors, may also explain the branding strategy level chosen by franchises in the NHL. Based on extensive interviews performed with executives in the NHL and other major US sport organizations, it appears that the background (education and professional) of decision-makers affect their inclination and focus toward marketing actions, with a limited but growing number focusing on branding and strategic issues, whereas others focus more on short-term items such as ticket sales and game day experience. As suggested by one of the VP interviewed for this study: 'The secret is in the appropriate balance between strategy and implementation ... the best plan poorly executed has literally no chance of success but ignoring strategy and data would be suicidal'.

Table 2.1 in Appendix highlights specific brand tactics used by Atlanta, Montréal and Ottawa.

Case Questions

1 How does the misconception of a brand strategy manifest itself in the marketing actions undertaken by the Montréal Canadiens and the Ottawa Senators?

2 Referring to the three specific cases presented in this paper, how could a team manage merchandising actions and community involvement in the context of an integrated marketing strategy?

3 Comparing the Canadiens', Senators' and Thrashers' strategy, how could entertainment activities be orchestrated by a professional sports team in order to leverage its brand equity?

4 How could we compare and assess the relevance of the communication strategies followed by the three hockey teams? How would you compare the importance of communication for selling tickets versus developing fans' allegiance to the team?

5 Taking the Atlanta Thrashers as a case in point, how could a sports team capitalize on the Internet as a platform in order to:
   (a) Increase its visibility and leverage its brand?
   (b) Be a forerunner in market research to anticipate and satisfy the needs and wants of its fans?

6 How would you compare the strategic construction of the brand in hockey versus other sports teams, soccer for instance (e.g. FC Barcelona)? To which extent do you think that the context (sport, country of origin, team involved) influences how the team can leverage its brand?

Case Resources

Reading

Bobby, D. (2002). Can a sports club be a brand? *Sport Business International*, April, http://www.wolff-olins.com/sportsclub.htm (Accessed September 2002).

De Chernatony, L., Drury, S. and Segal-Horn, S. (2005). Using triangulation to assess and identify successful services brands. *Service Industries Journal*, Vol. 25, No. 1, pp. 42–54.

Gladden, J.M., Milne, G.R. and Sutton, W.A. (1998). A conceptual framework for evaluating brand equity in division I college athletics. *Journal of Sport Management*, Vol. 12, No. 1, pp. 1–19.

Kapferer, J.-N. (2001). Is there really no hope for local brands? *Brand Management*, Vol. 9, No. 3, pp. 163–170.

Muniz, A.M. and O'Guinn, T.C. (2003). Brand community. *Journal of Consumer Research*, Vol. 27, No. 4, pp. 412–432.

Richelieu, A. (2004). Building the brand equity of professional sports teams, Chapter 1, in *Sharing Best Practices in Sport Marketing*. Fitness Information Technology Inc., Morgantown, WV, pp. 3–21.

Richelieu, A. and Pons, F. (2005). Reconciling managers' strategic vision with fans' expectations. *International Journal of Sports Marketing and Sponsorship*, Vol. 6, No. 3, pp. 37–57.

Richelieu, A. and Pons, F. (2006). Toronto Maple Leafs vs. Football Club Barcelona: How two legendary sports teams built their brand equity. *International Journal of Sports Marketing and Sponsorship*, Vol. 7, No. 3, pp. 231–259.

Shank, M. (2002). *Sports Marketing: A Strategic Perspective*. Prentice-Hall, Upper Saddle River, NJ.

Websites

Atlanta Spirit (Trashers and Hawks parent company, 2007) – www.atlantaspirit.com/

Montreal Canadiens (2007). http://www.canadiens.com/eng/index.cfm

Ottawa Senators (2007). http://www.ottawasenators.com

NHL – www.nhl.com/

Further Information

Users of the case may want to take a look at the Wikipedia entries for the following:

Atlanta Trashers – http://en.wikipedia.org/wiki/Atlanta_Trashers
Montreal – http://en.wikipedia.org/wiki/Montreal_Canadiens
Ottawa Senators – http://en.wikipedia.org/wiki/Ottawa_senators
NHL – http://en.wikipedia.org/wiki/nhl

Case

3

ESPN STAR Sports

James Santomier

Case Focus

The case examines the important accomplishments, issues, and challenges facing ESPN STAR Sports as it adjusts its business strategy of broadcasting a diverse array of international and regional sports to the unique economics and demographics of the Asian market.

Keywords
• Broadcast rights • Broadcast sponsorship • Business strategy • Strategic partnerships • New media platforms • Global brands

Case Summary

ESPN (Entertainment and Sports Programming Network) STAR Sports (ESS), a partnership between two global media giants; the Walt Disney Company and News Corporation, currently operates across Asia and across multiple media platforms. The rapidly developing markets of Asia have presented significant opportunities and challenges to ESS, and it has adjusted its core business strategy to take into consideration a multitude of issues, including a rapidly growing and diverse media market; increasingly sophisticated consumers interested in a variety of international sports; development of local and regional broadcast partnerships; involvement with local federations in the development of sport across the region; the interest of global brands in Asian sport; increasing broadcast rights fees and intensifying competition; and the political dynamics of the Asia-Pacific region.

Case Elements

Asian Sport

The rapidly maturing markets of Asia, with over 3.5 billion people, are progressively more important for the continued growth of sport worldwide. This is due, at least in part, to the rapid growth of the economies of China and India, the significant influence of Korea and Japan on the global digital revolution, and the emergence of Singapore, Qatar, and the UAE as global business centres. In its Global Entertainment and Media Outlook: 2006–2010, PricewaterhouseCoopers (PwC) forecast rapid growth in Internet, mobile, TV distribution, and casino and gaming revenues in the Asia-Pacific media/entertainment industry. The Asia-Pacific sport market will also experience rapid growth due to a rejuvenated television rights market and enhanced revenues from sponsorship and merchandising. According to PwC's Entertainment and Media Group, projected revenues, including ticket sales, will increase from $11.2 billion in 2003 to $15.8 billion by 2008. A significant part of this growth will come from major sport events held in the region. Korea and Japan hosted the 2002 FIFA World Cup, Thailand holds a world-class golf tournament annually, and Beijing will host the summer Olympics in 2008. According to Michael Mellor of IMG Media, the Beijing Olympics, in addition to being the most important investment ever made in Asian sport (US$230B), is an important psychological moment: 'I don't think people have fully comprehended yet how significant this is. China has never before opened its doors to the rest of the world on this scale – in sport or any other cultural sphere'. The concept of sport as a driving force in Asian economies is important because it is being replicated across the region. In China, Japan, Korea, India, Malaysia, Singapore, Hong Kong, Qatar, Dubai, and Bahrain, investment in sport has become one of the most visible symbols of how economic power is gradually shifting toward Asia.

In West Asia, Bahrain has invested heavily in Formula One (F1) and Dubai currently is building a 'sports city', which may lead to Dubai being involved in a joint Olympic bid with Qatar and Bahrain. In Asia-Pacific, Shanghai has developed Qi Zhong, the largest new tennis stadium in the region, and has launched a new International F1 circuit. Malaysia also has an F1 circuit while Singapore has manoeuvred its Golf Open into an event that is comparable in quality and prize money to most competitions in the USA and Europe. Whether it is football in Southeast Asia, cricket in India, baseball in Japan/ Korea, or basketball in the Philippines, Asia has a very large consumer base that is knowledgeable and passionate about a variety of sports. The quality of Asian play is not always comparable to play in highly developed economic markets such as North America and Western Europe. However, there is avid consumption of sport on TV and at venues, and economic growth in Asia has generated activity and excitement around hosting important international sport events. In addition to the Beijing Olympics, Asia has been a target for expansion by F1, the US-based National Basketball Association (NBA) and Major League Baseball (MLB), Association of Tennis Professionals (ATP) Tennis, and European football franchises. There is not only a strong desire among Asian countries to host international sport events, but a willingness among international brands to sponsor them. From the media side, most Asian countries have at least one public broadcast station, a minimum of one commercial network, and a pay-TV platform, such as ESS.

ESPN STAR Sports

ESPN Inc. is a pioneer among basic cable television networks because its entire programming is dedicated to sport. It was founded in 1978 by William Rasmussen with the intention of broadcasting sport events to cable television operators via satellite. ESPN started broadcasting in 1979 and by 1980 was broadcasting 24 hours per day, seven days per week. By 2002, ESPN reached more than 87 million households in the USA and televised the major US professional leagues: baseball (MLB), football (NFL), hockey (NHL), and basketball (NBA). It is considered to be one of the most successful basic cable networks, in part, because ESPN is able to deliver the 18–35 years old male demographic to a variety of advertisers. Included among the numerous ESPN business units are ESPN2 (sporting events, news, and original programming), ESPN Classic (historical sports footage), ESPN HD (high definition), ESPN360 (Internet), ESPN Deportes (Spanish language), and ESPNEWS (24-hour news and information). ESPN is currently reaching more than 97 million US homes as well as another 190 countries through ESPN International. ESPN creates content for TV and radio and operates one of the most popular sports sites on the Internet. ESPN also has a magazine and a chain of sports-themed restaurants (ESPN Zone).

In 2005, George Bodenheimer, ESPN and ABC Sports President and co-chairman of Disney Media Networks, reorganized ESPN and into six business units: content, technology, sales and marketing, international, finance, and administration. Bodenheimer stated that 'aggregating all our creative energies in one division; placing all sales and marketing in one area to sell our growing menu of services; consolidating oversight of all technology; and affirming the centralized management of all international businesses are powerful statements'. ESPN International began operating in the early 1990s with the objective of taking advantage of the growing satellite markets in Asia, Africa, and Latin America. Russell Wolff, currently the Executive Vice President and Managing Director of ESPN International, is responsible for all of ESPN's international business initiatives across television, radio, publishing, wireless, broadband, and ESPN Enterprises operations. According to Wolff, the company's strategy in the USA, and globally, is based on its commitment to technology and live sport. The international market is very important for ESPN and, according to Wolff; ESPN intends to increase the value of television, radio, and mobile by serving customers – affiliates, advertisers, and consumers by continuing to produce content across multi-platforms. ESPN also plans to increase its appeal to advertisers and sponsors for all of its offerings.

STAR, which is based in Hong Kong, is a subsidiary of News Corporation and the leading media and entertainment company in Asia. STAR broadcasts over 60 television services in nine languages to over 300 million people in 53 Asian countries. The network controls over 20,000 hours of Indian and Chinese programming and owns the world's largest contemporary Chinese film library. STAR businesses include filmed entertainment, television production, cable systems, direct-to-home services, terrestrial TV broadcasting, and wireless and digital services. STAR is India's second-largest media company after Bennett, Coleman & Co., which is the publisher of the *Times of India*. STAR's primary source of revenue is India, with 80 per cent of Indian viewers watching STAR channels. There is some speculation that News Corporation may eventually merge STAR with BSkyB and DirecTV (its UK and US satellite businesses) to form a global satellite TV company. STAR, which was launched in 1991 with five television channels, pioneered satellite television and was a major catalyst for the significant growth of the media industry across Asia. Concomitant with the development of Asian economies, increasing access to satellite television has redefined the viewing experience of Asian consumers and STAR has set new standards in content, production, and variety.

ESS, a 50/50 joint venture between ESPN and STAR, was created in 1996. ESS owns 11 television networks including ESPN Asia, ESPN India, ESPN Taiwan, ESPN Singapore, ESPN Philippines, ESPN Hong Kong, STAR Sports Asia, STAR Sports Hong Kong, STAR Sports India, STAR Sports Taiwan, and STAR Sports Southeast Asia. ESS is aggressively pursuing markets in Asia and as part of this strategy, is 'localizing' production and various 'SportsCenter' franchises. It recently launched its 10th international version of the popular TV show in Japan. ESS depends heavily on a variety of major international sports to maintain the interest of its Asian consumers, who are avid consumers of the English Premier League (EPL) football. ESS' live coverage of Wimbledon, the F1 circuit, and the US Masters Golf Tournament also attracts large audiences across Asia. According to Wolff, as the business continues to grow, the greatest challenge for ESS is escalating broadcast rights fees.

Broadcast Rights

Broadcast rights agreements with US-based MLB and F1 have strengthened significantly the ESS franchise in Asia. In March, 2007, ESS and MLB agreed to a new three-year deal for comprehensive cable and satellite broadcast packages. According to the agreement, ESS maintains cable and satellite television rights in 29 countries and territories across Asia (with exclusivity in all, except China) through the 2009 MLB season. ESS has expanded its inventory in Taiwan specifically to include the right to broadcast up to seven regular season games per week (up from four games), any and all games featuring a Taiwanese player, and the entire MLB postseason. ESS, which has been an MLB broadcast partner for the past 10 years, considers the key to the success of MLB on ESS will be showcasing all 30 MLB franchises and international baseball stars from the Asia-Pacific region.

According to the F1 agreement, the F1 World Championship will be broadcast across all of ESS' major territories in Asia (excluding China), and ESS will have exclusive TV rights for India, which is a critical market. This rights agreement represents a 14-year partnership between ESS and F1 that has increased the number of affluent well-educated motor racing viewers in Asia to approximately 85 million. In addition to live broadcasts of all Championship races, ESS has created a range of support programming to provide consumers with a comprehensive package of news, analysis, and commentary. According to Rik Dovey, Managing Director of ESS, ESS 'was the first to deliver such intense and expert programming for F1 in Asia and this has broadened the support for the sport among the world's biggest populations and converted casual viewers into dedicated fans'. Bernie Ecclestone, CEO of F1, stated that 'we are delighted to be able to renew our long-standing relationship with ESS and together we hope to be able to continue to grow the popularity of F1 in Asia'. It is estimated that F1 is watched by a global audience of over 500 million, which makes it the second most popular TV sport after football. ESS broadcasts approximately 250 hours of F1 coverage across Asian markets. In China approximately 117 million unique viewers watched F1 coverage in 2006, while in Japan, the audience approximated 38 million unique viewers.

In India, with over 90 television channels broadcasting over 800,000 hours of uninterrupted telecasts to millions of consumers, ESS is one of the premier channels. ESS essentially has redefined the concept of sport broadcasting in that country. At one point, broadcasting was limited to national cricket and some additional local sports. Currently, however, a large variety of national and international sports is being broadcast to over 30 million consumers. ESS has created 'intelligent viewing', where the passion and excitement of a sport is supported by stimulating information. Indian viewers are among the most sophisticated and demanding worldwide, which has contributed to ESS' high level of penetration in the Indian market. ESS has set new standards for broadcasters in India and introduced Indian consumers to sports other than cricket and field hockey. In 2004, ESS and the Indian Hockey Federation (IHF) created a partnership to systematically and scientifically develop Indian field hockey.

ESS also has received practically all of the sport broadcasting awards in the country, including the 'Best Sports Channel', and the 'Best Anchor'. In a deal with Infront Sports & Media, ESS acquired the exclusive rights to broadcast the 2006 FIFA World Cup for the Indian subcontinent. During the 2006 FIFA World Cup ESS broadcast matches live to more than 25 million households in India, Pakistan, Bangladesh, Bhutan, Nepal, Maldives, and Sri Lanka. In addition to live coverage of all 64 matches (accompanied by English and Hindi commentary), daily pre-shows during match days, a daily review show and special lead-in programming were aired. Oliver Seibert, Executive Director of Infront, stated that 'ESPN STAR Sports is a great soccer supporter and this agreement will continue the process of developing football across the Asian region'. In India, overall interest in international football is growing tremendously and ESS provides the most comprehensive programming to consumers in Asia and the Indian subcontinent with properties that include the EPL, FA Cup matches, England Home Team matches, UEFA Champions League, the Asian Football packages, and the Spanish Primera Liga among others.

More recently, ESS announced the launch of a dedicated cricket channel that is specifically geared to Indian consumers. STAR Cricket will begin broadcasting in June, 2007, and represents the 15th network spawned by ESS in the Asia-Pacific region. This announcement follows ESS' successful bid for the broadcast rights to the International Cricket Council (ICC) for the next eight years, for which the reported price ESS paid was US$1.1 billion. Included in the agreement are 18 ICC tournaments with two ICC Cricket World Cups (Asia, 2010 and Australasia, 2015), and a minimum of three ICC Champions Trophy Tournaments. Davis stated: 'This acquisition affirms our commitment to the Indian subcontinent and the world and we are absolutely delighted to bring the exciting line-up of ICC Events to millions of cricket fans globally. Our company has done pioneering work in showcasing cricket in an entertaining and informative way and we will continue to innovate and extend the excitement of cricket through to 2015'. STAR Cricket will feature live Indian cricket and international cricket, especially from test-playing countries such as the UK and Australia. It will also feature programming on cricket including reality shows, archival programming, and magazine shows. Ravi Shastri, ESS expert commentator, stated that 'cricket is a religion in India – the interest, passion, and emotion this game evokes will remain unmatched for all times to come. With cricket being an integral part of our lives, a dedicated channel with the right mix of live, non-live, and feature programming was always needed'.

New Media Platforms

ESPN first offered mobile content-based service outside of the US in 2004 with the X Games Mobile in Japan. X Games Mobile offered X Games-branded content including news and information, screensavers, ring tones, wallpaper, photos, logos, and streaming audio and video highlights to Japan's leading wireless carriers including KDDI and Vodafone. ESS also delivers data applications, video, wallpaper, ring tones, games, WAP, and SMS throughout the Asia-Pacific region. Asia is perhaps the world leader in the diffusion of new media and Korea, Japan, and Hong Kong are world leaders in broadband connectivity and 3G mobile phone usage. Currently in Japan there are between 50 and 60 million 3G subscribers and another 20 million in Korea. In 2002, the FIFA World Cup dramatically increased Korean sales of T-DMB mobile TV handsets. In June, 2002, 127,000 units were sold, compared with 84,000 in May of 2002. ESS also has started to develop the new media space, which will be used to offset some of the problems and issues related to TV rights revenues in Asia. Currently, ESS has launched ESPN Mobile, espnstar.com, espnstar.com.cn, and espnstar.com.tw. Davis: 'we need to get to fans wherever they may be – whether via TV, mobile, or PC'. ESS is trying to capitalize on the international sport appetite of a billion consumers who are, technologically speaking, quickly catching the developed markets of the world. Millions of Chinese consumers skipped the phase of having a landline telephone connection – they have gone from having no phone to having the latest in wireless technology. Davis stated that 'for us to be able to capitalize on this and create innovative content is a huge opportunity'.

Online, espnstar.com, espnstar.com.cn, and espnstar.tw offer information and interactive opportunities for millions of users providing them with in-depth sports news, results, and competition. This multi-lingual online platform, which is closely integrated with ESPN and STAR Sports on air networks, has established the sites as the number one online sports destination in their respective markets. Mobile ESPN is a specialized feature service from ESS, which offers unique sports content to consumers on their mobile phones, delivering not only wireless voice service, but also applications such as easy to access sports news, information, commentary, analysis, and statistics. Related to enterprise technology, ESS currently is using SPSS Software to identify the preferences of millions of Asian consumers and then developing sport programming based on those results. ESS already was measuring exposure, both continuously and electronically, across various Asian markets, however, with the new SPSS platform it is now measuring 'engagement', including attitudes and perceptions. ESS is able to survey Asian viewers simultaneously, regardless of location (home based or mobile), in different languages, going directly into multi-level probing of what they saw, liked and interacted with, as well as measure their resultant attitudes toward brands associated with the broadcasts. Anand Rego, ESS Director of Research, stated that 'we turned to SPSS' enterprise feedback management software to get this picture consistently and simultaneously across the diverse Asian geography, along with the ratings'.

On the other side of the technology equation is the Chinese version of *ESPN the Magazine*, which has a circulation of 40,000 per month. The Chinese version, which is heavier, larger, and more durable than the US version, was created to take advantage of the high pass-along rate for magazines in China. Davis stated that 'we can no longer think of the fan as sitting at home and that being the only place to get content. There are 1.3 billion people there, and our potential is probably about 1 billion of them. We can't reach all of them right now, but we can probably reach the majority of them one way or the other'.

Strategic Broadcast Partnerships and Sponsorships

Most recently ESS has partnered with NOW Broadband TV and IPTV service, which is owned by Pacific Century Cyberwork's (PCCW). NOW, which has a flexible pay-per-channel model that has been successful in Hong Kong, currently has 650,000 subscribers using a selection of over 70 channels. NOW benefited significantly when ESS joined its platform in 2004. The switch to NOW broadband was precipitated by the loss of the TV rights to the EPL to HKCTV, which has them through 2007. Although PCCW and ESS have had issues in the past, their partnership in Hong Kong was an important shift in the balance of power, with PCCW adding over 300,000 thousand subscribers. As part of the deal, ESPN and STAR Sports are broadcasting Cantonese-language content together with English language. As part of the partnership, ESS brought with it the FA Cup, the UEFA Champions League, the NBA, F1, the Masters, and the British and US Open golf championships. In addition, it brought the Australian, Wimbledon, and US Open tennis Grand Slams. Since the agreement with PCCW, ESS has added the Paulista League (Brazil), the Brazilian Cup, and Brazilian Championship. PCCW outbid I-Cable for the EPL rights for 2007–2008 to 2009–2010 seasons, which cost US$200 million. This leaves PCCW in a strong position to renegotiate its carriage deal with ESS channels, for which it is now paying approximately US$8 million per year.

ESS Event Management Group manages and promotes premier sporting events across Asia. The ESS Event Management Group is responsible for organizing, managing, and promoting a variety of ESS' proprietary sporting events across Asia, including the Asian X Games, Thailand X Games Cup, KL World's 5s, and the San Miguel Asian 9-Ball Tour. The Guinness sponsorship of the 9-Ball Tour has resulted in the doubling of the total prize money to US$320,000. The Guinness 9-Ball Tour is the only ranking tour in Asia for players to qualify for the WPA World Pool Championship. It also staged the first Thailand X Games in 2005, which was an event that helped to support tsunami relief efforts. ESS, and the athletes competing in the event, donated a portion of the proceeds to the Rajaprajanugroh Foundation, which is associated with the Thailand Royal Family. The 2005 X Games Cup was hosted by the Tourism Authority of Thailand, included sponsors Powered by True and Orange; Official Mobile Handset, Motorola; Official Automobile, Kia Motors; and Official Television Platform, UBC.

ESS has created important partnerships with local rights holders as well and this dimension of ESS' growth strategy apparently has become a priority. As previously stated, in India, ESS is involved in the development of a professional field hockey league and anticipates creating more co-ventures that focus on developing local franchises. In addition, ESS has broadcast sponsorships agreements with four of Asia's most recognizable global brands (Tiger Beer, Toshiba, Toyota, and Nokia) for the EPL. All four brands are associated with the EPL though a combination of multi-level integrated benefits. These include on-air and online entitlements around all 'live' matches and repeats on ESPN and STAR Sports as well as marketing and online benefits. The EPL is broadcast to 210 million homes across Asia live and exclusive on ESPN and STAR Sports. ESS has doubled its coverage of the league, which includes new programs intended to engage and involve viewer participation, taking football entertainment to a new level in Asia.

In 2005, Malaysia Airlines and ESS agreed to a two-year broadcast sponsorship (the campaign is themed 'Taking You There') that gives the national airline significant visibility during two seasons of the EPL. As part of the agreement, ESS will air 'Malaysia Airlines Football Extra' on Sunday mornings. This platform provides features from the previous day's EPL games as well as phone-in and email reactions. More recently, ESS and Malaysia's Ministry of Youth and Sport (KBS) announced the launch of the Malaysian version of SportsCenter. The localized version is produced in Malaysia, presented by Malaysians and covers international and local sports. This initiative is part of a multi-year strategic partnership to raise participation and interest in sport in Malaysia. The Minister of KBS stated that 'we are confident that the Malaysian version of SportsCenter will have a positive impact on all sports-loving Malaysians who will enjoy following their heroes on a show with renowned high standards'.

Special Olympics

In 2006, ESS announced that 'the full might of its Asia-wide organization' was committed to help promote the Asia-Pacific Special Olympics. Troy Greisen, Managing Director of Special Olympics Asia Pacific, stated that 'we are absolutely thrilled about this partnership with ESS as it is a great opportunity for us to spread the word and inspire people throughout Asia to get involved and support Special Olympics. ESS is the most powerful medium for us to achieve this as the premier sports network in Asia. Not only does ESS reach millions of viewers whose lives can be touched by our message and hopefully become supporters, it will also create a great platform to showcase the ability of our Special Olympics athletes alongside other world-class athletes'. Davis stated: 'special Olympics is indeed a very special organization. Its ideals are something we are very attracted to and something we want to fully support. Nothing will be more satisfying than to be able to play a small part in changing the lives of these special athletes'. The ESS commitment to the Special Olympics includes producing and broadcasting the flagship events as well as running public service announcements to increase the awareness of people with intellectual disabilities and the ESS staff will actively work with the Special Olympics athletes through volunteer coaching programs.

Case Diagnosis

The combination of rapid and sustained economic growth, political objectives, and an increasingly larger nucleus of well-educated and passionate consumers, has made Asia an appealing opportunity for global media corporations and major international sport federations, leagues, and franchises. The rise of China, India, and the Middle East as major economic powers has resulted in a change in strategy and resource allocation for global media and sport enterprises. Many Asian countries already possess the core elements, although at different stages of development, for creating and sustaining sport-generated revenues: (1) educated consumers with a high degree of fan identification; (2) a public/private strategy for developing infrastructure and hosting world-class sport events; (3) media companies with capabilities to provide exposure for sport; and (4) sponsors and advertisers interested in creating and sustaining a presence for their brands in the Asian marketplace. For the past 25 years most of the growth in the sport industry has been focused almost exclusively on North America and Europe, with the exception of Japan. The growth has definitely shifted toward Asian and at a pace that is unprecedented.

Although Asia is an immense and culturally diverse region, football and basketball are widely played and watched. Motor sports, especially F1, and golf also have a dedicated consumer base that spans national borders. While many other sports do not have pan-Asian appeal, they have substantial support in specific regions and countries – cricket in India and the Middle East; baseball in Japan, Korea, and Taiwan; horse racing in Hong Kong and the UAE; and badminton in China and South East Asia. These regional differences appear to be one reason why ESS is focused on developing and emphasizing localized TV programming and sponsoring regional and local sport development. This strategy may lead to the emergence and prominence of 'regional sports networks' (RSNs) across Asia, similar to those that span the US media market. In the USA, RSN stations are important strategic assets for ESPN and consist of live broadcasts of professional and intercollegiate sport events as well as talk and highlight shows.

An important issue for ESS in terms of increasing its broadcast reach in Asia relates to the nature of the population itself. For example, India and China each have over 1 billion people; however, active consumers probably number only 50 million in both countries. Many people actually live below the poverty line and large parts of Asia remain undeveloped in economic terms (low per capita income, low TV penetration, etc.). This means that for ESS is that the major revenue generating opportunities exist primarily in the larger urban areas. This demographic situation places serious limitations on ESS in terms of its potential growth. This is why it is important for ESS to not only acquire the rights to the most popular Asian sports, such as Indian cricket, but to be able to sell on those rights to non-Asian broadcasters.

In comparison to US and European markets, the Asian sport market has, up until very recently, placed emphasis on sponsorship rather than TV rights. ESS and the Asian-Pacific Broadcasting Union (ABU) continue to argue that rights holders are too optimistic about revenues that can be generated in Asia. Given the US$1.1 billion rights fee that ESS recently paid for the ICC, it appears that this is an attempt to downplay the rapid growth in broadcast fees in the region. Interestingly, ESS now wants changes in the terms of that agreement before it signs a long-form contract. ESS is seeking the changes to help it sell on the rights to broadcasters outside of India. Apparently, ESS already had deals with two News Corporation broadcasters: Fox in Australia and BSkyB in the UK. These broadcasters indicated that the deal with ESS is dependent on changes in the contract that relate to a variety of issues, including whether or not the broadcasters have to pay for matches if they don't actually take place. ESS also faces issues in the US market due to competition between DirecTV and Echostar, two satellite broadcasters interested in the South Asian expatriate market. DirecTV is now less interested in broadcasting cricket because Echostar has acquired the rights to the Indian and Pakistan boards. DirecTV has more than 200,000 South Asian subscribers, while DirecTV has only 10,000. Therefore, Echostar is very likely to offer a much lower bid to ESS for the rights to the ICC. The current view in Asia is that rights holders should focus less on TV rights valuations and more on securing exposure, which can then be used as a bargaining tool when negotiating with sponsors. However, with increased rights fees and competition from media companies such as Nimbus, Setanta, ITV, StarHub, and others, rights fees are positioned to escalate drastically.

Presently China Central Television (CCT) has a virtual monopoly on TV rights in China and is slowing the emergence of a competitive TV sports rights market. However, a recently developing digital pay-TV market may help to reduce CCT's control of the rights market in China. Another problem related to the Chinese rights area is the significant financial investment in the Beijing Olympics, which has precluded investments in other sports. In order to stabilize the sports rights area in that country, there is a need for more coordination and consistency among the Chinese government, national sports bodies, and local media and sport power-brokers. Although ESPN cannot obtain broadcast rights to the Olympics, which go to terrestrial stations, it is planning to create Olympics-related programming. Davis, of ESS, stated that 'Beijing 2008 presents a huge opportunity for us to create programming around the Olympics'. However, ESS and ESPN have been removed from the list of foreign broadcasters that may be distributed to hotels and high-end housing compounds in China. According to a report in the *Financial Times*, they are not among the 31 channels approved for broadcast in 2007 by the State Administration of Radio, Film, and TV (SARFT). *Hollywood Reporter* claimed that the move followed the failure of ESS to attend a licensing meeting with Chinese regulators last year about the extension of 'landing' rights. It was reported recently that negotiations are continuing and that ESS expects to be broadcasting in China sometime in late 2007 or early 2008. A recent Chinese government ruling decreed that Chinese TV and radio stations can no longer form new partnerships with foreign media companies and in response to this, ESPN's Wolff stated: 'We have to adapt our model to do business anywhere'.

Adding to ESS' problems, within some federations in Asia there is resistance to losing control to Western sport and media interests. For example, the Asian Football Confederation is concerned that consumers in some regions of Asia are watching the EPL on ESS rather than attending a local league match or participating in sport themselves. In addition, the Chinese Basketball Association is concerned about the drain of basketball talent to the NBA, and Japanese baseball officials are reluctant to allow MLB to take too much of a leadership role in the global development of baseball.

Conclusion

The diverse and rapidly emerging markets of Asia provide unique opportunities for global media corporations and sport enterprises, however, serious exigencies exist. ESS is adjusting to the shifting of geopolitical power in the direction of Asia, increasingly fragmented media landscape, and introduction of new broadcast players and platforms, by developing an integrative approach to the market through the establishment of critical partnerships and broadcast sponsorships. Digital media is now main stream in Asia and the rise of broadband and mobile opportunities portend a difficult navigation for ESS going forward. Broadcast rights valuations across all platforms will continue to increase and competition for those rights will continue to intensify. Sports rights holders are beginning to understand the importance of maintaining as many touch points with consumers as possible and they are engaging their sponsors in helping them drive consumers back in the direction of TV and the Internet. With its integrative approach and use of appropriate new media metrics, ESS is able to implement such a strategy, which provides a value-added benefit to rights holders and strategic local and regional partners. Although significant issues exist related to the Chinese market, escalating rights fees, and competition, ESS is navigating the swiftly moving, and often turbulent current of the Asian sport market, with an apparently steady hand, at least for now.

Case Questions

1 What do you consider to be the most important strategic reasons why ESS is developing partnerships with local and regional sport federations?
2 ESPN and Fox Sports are competitors in the USA What do you believe are the major reasons that ESPN and STAR, a subsidiary of News Corporation, developed a 50/50 joint venture in Asia?
3 What are the reasons that global sport federations, such as the NBA, MLB, FIFA, and F1 recently have focused so much of their efforts on the Asian market?
4 What do you believe are the most interesting opportunities and the most significant threats to the development of the sport market in Asia?
5 Why do you think Asian consumers have developed such a dynamic and serious interest in Western sport?
6 Why do you think the Chinese government has taken such a strong position against ESS? Do you think that this will ultimately benefit or harm the development of sport in China?
7 Do you think that Asian sport federations and rights holders should feel threatened from ESS?

Case Resources

A mission to serve (2006). *SportBusiness International*, October. Retrieved 12 April 2007, from Sports Business Research Network database (www.sbrnet.com).

Asia: Opportunities in the business of sport (2007). SportBusiness Group, London.

Asia: Understanding the Eastern Promise (2006). *SportBusiness International*, March. Retrieved 12 April 2007, from Sports Business Research Network database (www.sbrnet.com).

Asian growth fuels sports sector expectations (2006). *SportBusiness International*, July/August. Retrieved 12 April 2007, from Sports Business Research Network database (www.sbrnet.com).

Bodenheimer restructures ESPN business units (2005). *SportsPipe*, October 6. Retrieved 12 April 2007, from Sports Business Research Network database (www.sbrnet.com).

China halts distribution of ESPN, STAR Sports Channels (2007). *Sport Business Newslines*, March 2. Retrieved 2 March 2007, from http://www.sportbusiness.com.

ESPN (2003). *Super Brands India*. Retrieved 19 March 2007, from http://www.superbrandsindia.com/superbrands2003/espn/index.htm.

ESPN expands international mobile initiatives (2006). *SportsPipe*, March 14. Retrieved 12 April 2007, from Sports Business Research Network database (www.sbrnet.com).

ESPN Inc. and ABC Sports to provide multi-media coverage of the 2006 FIFA World Cup (2006). *SportsPipe*, June 6. Retrieved 12 April 2007, from Sports Business Research Network database (www.sbrnet.com).

ESPN to stage first-ever Thailand X Games Cup March 24–27 in Bangkok (2005). *SportsPipe*, March 2. Retrieved 12 April 2007, from Sports Business Research Network database (www.sbrnet.com).

ESPN STAR Sports announces launch of 'STAR Cricket', a dedicated 24×7 cricket channel (2007). *IndiaPRwire*, April 24. Retrieved 25 April, from http://www.indiaprwire.com.

ESPN STAR Sports deploys SPSS Software (2006). *Business Intelligence Network*, July 10. Retrieved 14 March 2007, from http://www.b-eye-network.com.

ESPN STAR Sports embraces Special Olympics (2006). Espnstar.com., August 29. Retrieved 12 April 2007, from http://www.espnstar.com.in.

ESPN STAR Sports flags Formula One agreement (2005). *SportsPipe*, July 26. Retrieved 12 April 2007, from Sports Business Research Network database (www.sbrnet.com).

ESPN STAR Sports launches SportsCenter in Malaysia (2007). *SportBusiness Newslines*, 2 February. Retrieved 2 February 2007, from http://www.sportbusiness.com.

ESPN STAR Sports renews and expands MLB coverage (2007). *SportBusiness Newslines*, 8 March. Retrieved 12 April 2007, from http://www.sportbusiness.com.

ESPN STAR Sports scores with EPL broadcast sponsorships (2004). *PR Newswire*, 24 August. Retrieved 12 April 2007, from http://www.xprn.com.

ESPN STAR Sports strengthens its events division with appointment of new head. Espnstar.com. (2005). Retrieved 12 April 2007, from http://www.espnstar.com.

ESPN STAR Sports wins exclusive broadcast rights for 2006 FIFA World Cup for Indian Sub continent (2005). *SportsPipe*, 3 February. Retrieved 12 April 2007, from Sports Business Research Network database (www.sbrnet.com).

Malaysia Airlines & ESPN STAR Sports Pact (2005). *Asianet*, 5 August. Retrieved 12 April 2007, from http://news.xinhuanet.com/english/2005-08-05/content_3324451.htm.

Nethery, R. (2005). The China opportunity: ESPN faces rapidly changing market. [Electronic version]. *SportsBusiness Journal*, 28 November, p. 23.

One-on-one with Russell Wolff, executive vice president and managing director, ESPN International (2005). [Electronic version]. *SportsBusiness Journal*, 6 June, p. 34.

Pickles, J. (2007). ESS wants ICC to agree changes in eight-year deal. *TV Sports Markets*, 23 February.

Reassessment in the face of revolution (2006). *SportBusiness International*, March. Retrieved 12 April 2007, from Sports Business Research Network database (www.sbrnet.com).

Reading

Curtis, B. (2006). Adrift on the sea of ESPN.com. *The New York Times*, 4 June.

Evey, S. and Broughton, I. (2004). *Creating an empire: ESPN*. Triumph Books, Chicago, IL.

Fatsis, S. (2006). Fans say ESPN's World Cup coverage deserves penalty. *The Wall Stree Journal Online*, 5 July, p. A15.

Freeman, M. (2002). *ESPN: An Uncensored History*. Taylor Trade Publishing, Lanham, MD.

Hill, L.A. (2004). Building a TV sports empire; How ESPN created a model for cable success. *Television Week*, September.

In the Zone – http://www.businessweek.com/magazine/content/05_42/b3955001.htm.

Slicing and Dicing in Asia – http://www.businessweek.com/magazine/content/05_42/b3955014.htm?chan=search.

Welcome to next generation sponsorship. (2006) *SportBusiness International*, May.

Websites

ESPN – http://www.espn.com
ESPN (Wikipedia) – http://en.wikipedia.org/wiki/ESPN
ESPN STAR – http://www.espnstar.com
ESPN STAR Sports – http://answers.com/topic/espn-star-sports
News Corporation – http://newscorp.com

4

The challenges of modernizing a professional sport: a case study of professional road cycling

Stephen Morrow and Catharine Idle

Case Focus

In 2004, the world governing body of cycling, the Union Cycliste Internationale (UCI), replaced its World Series of race events with a new competition, the UCI Pro Tour. This has resulted in major conflict between the main stakeholders in the sport: the governing body, race organizers, sponsors, teams, riders, the media and the public. The case illustrates the challenges involved in modernizing and restructuring a professional sport.

Keywords
• Professional road cycling • UCI Pro Tour • Governance • Modernization • Power • Stakeholder conflict

Case Summary

Professional road cycling is a sport founded on commercialism. Since the first races of the late 1800s, the sport has maintained a close relationship with commercial companies and sponsors. This case study examines the challenges faced by a sport trying to restructure and modernize to retain its contemporary relevance. In 2005, the Union Cycliste Internationale (UCI) Pro Tour was established. Based on models common in American professional sports, it created a super league of 20 licensed teams, obligated to contest all 27 Pro Tour races per season. Its creation has been controversial. The case focuses on the power play that has taken place between stakeholders in the sport – the governing body, race organizers, sponsors, teams, riders, the media, the public – and the conflict between stakeholders keen to protect their individual financial interests.

Case Elements

Professional road cycling has a long history and remains one of the most popular sports in Europe. Arguably, one of the most physiologically demanding of all athletic disciplines, road cycling is also renowned for one of the highest-profile annual sporting events in the world – the Tour de France.

But beyond these facts how much do most people know about professional road cycling and about how it operates? Test yourself. Below are pictures of three prominent professional road cyclists – before starting the case you should make a note of what, if anything, you already know about each cyclist.

Despite the visual spectacle of some events, the mass publicity and heroic displays of strength and endurance by riders in physically exhausting races, for many people professional road cycling has become synonymous with drug-taking. After several high-profile drugs raids involving well-known cyclists and prominent events, the sport has been widely dismissed as unethical and unclean. With many fans disenchanted by the current state of the sport, road cycling is losing its credibility fast and, critically, sponsors are becoming more reluctant to offer funding to teams taking part.

| Lance Armstrong | Floyd Landis | Alejandro Valverde |

Of the main races which take place in the professional cycling calendar, most media focus and public interest centre on the Tour de France, a three-week stage race that takes place in July every year on public roads across France. The race was won in seven consecutive years from 1999 to 2005 by the American cyclist, Lance Armstrong. In doing so, he beat the previous record of five consecutive wins, held by Spain's Miguel Indurain and five non-consecutive wins shared by Bernard Hinault (France), Eddy Merckx (Belgium) and Jacques Anquetil (France). More remarkable still, his victory run began just 18 months after battling against life-threatening testicular cancer.

Following Armstrong's retirement, there was great expectation about the 2006 Tour de France as no individual rider was an obvious favourite to win. But sadly for the sport, the eventual race winner, the American Floyd Landis, became a household name as much for the announcement of his positive drug test result, as his spectacular, against-the-odds win in stage 17. Eight months on, the 2006 Tour still has no official winner.

While doping indisputably presents a huge challenge for professional cycling, paradoxically this is not the issue which looks set to drive the sport to complete implosion. Instead, the demise of road cycling in its present format looks set to be the likely outcome of an increasingly bitter power struggle between major race organizers (such as the Amaury Sports Organization (ASO), organizers of the Tour de France) and the international governing body, the UCI. Their argument centres on the setting up of the UCI Pro Tour; a super league of cycling, made up of 20 licensed teams, obligated to contest all 27 Pro Tour races per season, including professional road cycling's most prestigious events – the three 'Grand Tours': the Tour de France, the Giro d'Italia and the Vuelta a España. While both factions claim to hold the interests of professional cycling at heart, their dispute has been described as more of a clash of egos, driven by financial considerations rather than a quest to modernize the format and organizational structure of the sport.

And Alejandro Valverde? Just how many people knew that the Spanish cyclist was the 2006 UCI Pro Tour Winner? Probably very few, clearly demonstrating the challenges faced by the UCI in trying to promote a new cycling brand in a marketplace of such long-established and iconic brands as the Tour de France.

The History of Professional Cycling

Professional cycling has its roots firmly in Western Europe. Amateur competitions began in France with the Paris-Rouen road race in 1869, followed by Bordeaux-Paris in 1891. Due to the spectator appeal of these events, the sport quickly won a dedicated public following and before long, the commercial potential of staging road races had attracted the attention of business sponsors. Indeed, from its outset through to its current format, road cycling has always maintained a commercial link – a factor which differentiates it from other sports.

The development of professional cycling began with the birth of the Belgian and French 'Classic' races such as the Liège-Bastogne-Liège (first staged as a professional event in 1894), Paris-Roubaix (1896) and Paris-Brussels (also 1896). Around this time, many new races were launched by enterprising newspapermen to bring the latest technology and a new competitive sport to the general public. The races were seen, both literally and figuratively, as a vehicle for increasing the sales of newspapers of the organizers behind the events. This same business logic lay behind the creation of higher-profile events: the Tour de France (1903) was used to increase sales of the French daily newspaper '*L'Auto*'; the Giro d'Italia (1909) was used to promote sales of the '*Gazzetta dello Sport*'; the Vuelta a España (1935) was used to increase circulation of the Spanish '*Informaciones*'. Known as the three Grand Tours, these three-week stage races are widely regarded as the foundation upon which modern day professional cycling is built. However, for the organizers, the nations which stage the events and for the sport itself, the events have come to represent much more than simply cycle races. Recognized as the ultimate endurance events, the three main tours are celebrated as social and cultural tributes to their host countries and are subjects of intense national pride and prestige.

To understand the history of cycling, some awareness of the history of cycling organizations is also necessary. The first international federations were founded in the late 19th century and the UCI, the international federation of cycling, was founded as a non-profit making organization in Paris in 1900. While cycling specific, its aims are very similar to those of many global sporting organizations (GSOs):

- regulating cycling at international level;
- promoting cycling in every country throughout the world and at all levels;
- organizing the World Championships for all disciplines;

- encouraging friendly relations between members of the cycling family;
- promoting sporting ethics and fair play;
- representing the sport of cycling and defending its interests on national and international bodies;
- collaborating with the International Olympic Committee with respect to Olympic cycling events.

Historically, the UCI and the national federations only exercise a regulatory function, for example setting up the race calendar, establishing the rules of competition and the distances of races. They play no direct role in the organization and management of major stage races like the Tour de France or one day races like the Liège-Bastogne-Liège. As an international federation, the UCI acts as the representative of all national cycling federations and as the regulatory body for all cycling disciplines including mountain biking, track cycling, cyclo-cross, BMX and para-cycling. Professional road cycling is the oldest of these disciplines – and by far the most commercial.

The Organizational Structure of Professional Road Cycling

Figure 4.1 sets out the organizational structure of professional road cycling. The UCI represents the interests of more than 170 National Federations,

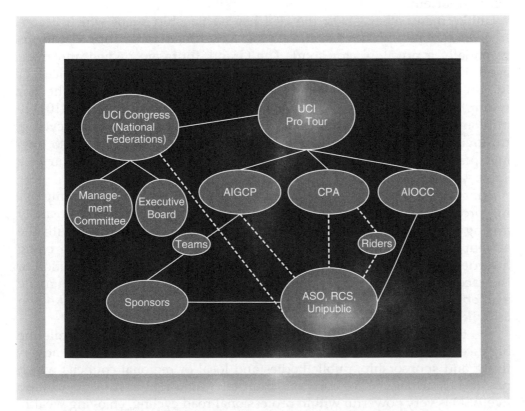

Figure 4.1 The organizational structure of professional road cycling

five Continental Confederations, 1,200 professional riders, 600,000 licensed riders, millions of cycling athletes who train regularly and more than a billion recreational cyclists. The UCI Congress is made up of representatives of the recognized national federations and is the supreme controlling body in cycling. The Congress elects a Management Committee to which it delegates, under its supervision, the management of the UCI. Consisting of 15 members, the Management Committee is empowered to take decisions and to act immediately where events require intervening action. The Management Committee's decisions are operationalized by the UCI's administrative staff.

In terms of elite level professional road cycling, the UCI Pro Tour Council manages the Pro Tour on behalf of the UCI. The Pro Tour Council is made up of representatives of the UCI, the race organizers (International Association of Organisers of Cycling Races, AIOCC), the riders (Associated Professional Cyclists, CPA) and the teams (International Association of Professional Cycling Groups, AIGCP), with a small number of administrative staff managing the Pro Tour. But the organization, management and governance of professional road cycling is more complex and fragmented than this would suggest, given the influence and power that resides with individual race organizers in particular, as well as within team sponsors, teams and riders. Moreover, the relationships between these groups can be very important.

Unlike many other GSOs, the UCI has no flagship event which it controls and from which it benefits financially. Professional road cycling is essentially a private sector sport. The Grand Tours are owned and managed by commercial organizations such as ASO (Tour de France) or RCS (Giro d'Italia) and are financially significant in their own right. For example, 70 per cent of ASO's annual turnover of approximately €110–120 million is derived from cycling, with about 70–80 per cent of this cycling turnover coming from the Tour de France. These organizations also own and manage several other cycling races in the professional calendar (see Table 4.1).

Prior to the Pro Tour, race organizers invited private teams employing professional cyclists to take part in their events; the invitation usually arising from an evaluation of the team's sporting achievements. With the advent of the Pro Tour, race participation is now dependent upon being awarded a licence by the Pro Tour Council. In addition, at the discretion of the race organizers, a small number of supplementary places can be made available to teams not holding a Pro Tour licence. These places are known as 'wild cards'.

The teams are funded by professional sponsors (see Table 4.2), while the big races gain revenue from various sources: commercial monies from advertising and sponsorship, public bodies and local or regional councils which pay to host a stage of the race and from television rights. An organization like ASO is very powerful within professional road cycling, enjoying wealth, celebrity, status and influence on a scale that few other sporting bodies enjoy.

Table 4.1 Organizations involved in cycling races

| Race organizer | Grand tours | UCI Pro Tour races | |
		Other Pro Tour races	Other races
Amaury Sports Organisation ASO	Tour de France	Paris-Nice Paris-Roubaix La Flèche Wallonne Liège-Bastogne-Liège Paris-Tours	Critérium International Tour de Picardie
RCS Sport	Giro d'Italia	Tirreno-Adriatico Milan-San Remo Giro della Lombardia	Milan-Turin Giro del Lazio Giro del Piemonte
Unipublic	Vuelta a España		Trofeo Luis Puig Vuelta a la communidad Valenciana Seman Catalana Vuelta a Murcia Vuelta a Aragon

Table 4.2 Team sponsors

Team	Country
Ag2r Prevoyance	France
Astana	Switzerland
Bouygues Telecom	France
Caisse d'Epargne	Spain
Cofidis, le Credit Par Telephone	France
Credit Agricole	France
Discovery Channel Pro Cycling Team	USA
Euskaltel – Euskadi	Spain
Française Des Jeux	France
Gerolsteiner	Germany
Lampre-Fondital	Italy
Liquigas	Italy
Predictor-Lotto	Belgium
Quick-Step – Innergetic	Belgium
Rabobank	The Netherlands
Saunier Duval – Prodir	Spain
Team CSC	Denmark
Team Milran	Italy
T-Mobile Team	Germany
Unibet.com	Sweden

The Tour de France is a sporting institution which is the subject of intense social and cultural pride in France. Organizers of historical stage races like the Tour and the Giro see themselves as having a moral duty to retain the integrity of both the race and sport for the benefit of their nation and each sees its individual race as synonymous with national identity. Over time there has been little evidence of individual race organizers acting together in pursuit of shared objectives.

The Birth of the Pro Tour

Since 1984, the UCI had maintained a ranking system which was based on the result of 10 major one day races. In response to widespread calls for more structure within the sport, the UCI then brought about a more radical change in 2005 when the World Cup series of races was replaced by a new annual event, the UCI Pro Tour. The UCI saw the Pro Tour as the means to modernize professional cycling, using it to develop the highest-level international circuit in cycling which would bring together the best teams, the best riders and best races in the world.

The UCI Pro Tour series is made up of 27, mainly classic races within the European professional road cycling calendar. Most prestigious events, such as the three Grand Tours, are included in the Pro Tour, in addition to some lesser-known races. To take part in Pro Tour events, cycling teams must apply to the UCI for a Pro Tour licence, which is ordinarily valid for four years. In 2006, the cost of this licence was €100,000. However, the cost to the team of taking part in the Pro Tour does not end with the licence payment. Teams granted a Pro Tour licence are obliged to send riders to compete in all 27 Pro Tour races, although they are allowed to draw on different riders for different events. Many higher-profile riders target the most important races – in particular the Tour de France – as the pinnacle of their season and do not compete in all events. In addition, the timetabling of the Pro Tour series is such that some race dates clash. This effectively means that teams need to have a larger pool of riders to draw on in order to maintain their competitive presence at the other Pro Tour races throughout the racing season. Prior to the inception of the Pro Tour, teams had a pool of 22–23 riders: now they retain a pool of approximately 30 riders. Teams pay more not only in employee costs to cover the contracts of more riders, but also in terms of ancillary costs like medical and mechanical support for their riders.

The Pro Tour has three main objectives:

1 To make cycling more attractive to the public, especially by improving participation levels at key events of the season.
2 To increase the interest that cycling generates with investors, by offering teams, organizers, broadcasters and their main partners, guarantees as regards the profit that they will make from their investment.
3 To contribute to the development of cycling on all continents.

In terms of organizational structure and governance, ostensibly, professional road cycling is not dissimilar to other sports in which governing bodies, event organizers and athletes all play a role. Perhaps the most interesting example is tennis. The International Tennis Federation (ITF) is the world governing body of tennis. Its objectives include:

* to further grow and develop the sport worldwide;
* to develop the game at all levels at all ages for both able-bodied and disabled men and women;
* to make, amend and uphold the rules of the game;
* to promote the International Team Championships and competitions of the ITF;
* to preserve the integrity and independence of tennis as a sport;
* to perform all its objectives without discrimination on grounds of colour, race, nationality, ethnic or national origin, age, sex or religion.

The ITF has 205 member National Associations and six Regional Associations. It sanctions and works closely with the four Grand Slams (Wimbledon, the US Open, the French Open and the Australian Open) through its presence on the Grand Slam Committee, and supports each event with administrative, officiating and media services. Like road cycling, professional tennis has undergone change. In 1988, a player uprising resulted in the Association of Tennis Professionals (ATP) assuming control of men's professional tennis. Between then and the ATP Tour beginning in 1990, tournament directors representing many of the world's leading events voiced their support for the players and joined them in what was to become a partnership unique in professional sports – players and tournaments, each with an equal voice in how the circuit is run. This parity of influence is not mirrored in professional cycling.

There are key differences between road cycling and other sports. The first thing to note is that it is an individual sport which is practiced in teams. Cycling teams have a particular social structure and there is a high degree of dependency between members of a team. In a major race, a team will have an identified leader who is supported by the other riders in the team – 'domestiques' – whose job is to do everything they can to help him win. By tradition, the winner of a major race splits his cash prize with the members of the team and its staff. For the most part, domestiques ride in front of the team leader, this strategy being based on the idea that it is easier to pedal when there is someone in front of you to cut the wind. Another key difference is that cycling events are not homogeneous. Individual races vary in the physical and technical demands made on riders: some events call for huge endurance and hill-climbing stamina; others require sustained speed or technical expertise to deal with difficult terrain. Riders have different skills and specialities to match and teams are made up of riders selected to cover particular race requirements.

The economics of professional road cycling are also quite different from other sports. One important difference is that as races are run on public roads, no revenue is made from ticket receipts; another, that despite being an individual sport, in professional road cycling it is the teams rather than riders which are sponsored. Perhaps the most important difference, however, arises from the presence of stakeholders like ASO, whose commercial earnings provide it with considerable influence and power as to how the sport is run. ASO's single most important event – the Tour de France – enjoys such reputation as to be known simply as 'The Tour', granting it higher status than the other Grand Tours. It is the race all riders want to compete in and the race that all advertisers want to be seen in.

Grand tour organizers receive approximately 40–45 per cent of their revenue from television rights, 40–45 per cent from sponsorship and advertising and 10–20 per cent from public funds – the fees paid by local and regional councils to host a stage of the event. Until the launch of the Pro Tour, obtaining a place in the Tour de France or, to a lesser extent, one of the other major tours (the Giro or the Vuelta) was fundamental to the sporting and financial viability of the cycling teams. Without the promise of a Tour start, attracting sponsors was very difficult and hence paying riders was impossible. The power of an organizer to dictate who is invited to its event is clear to see.

Case Diagnosis

So everyone is a winner in the Pro Tour? Yellow jerseys all round in the 'peleton'?[1] Perhaps not …

Prior to the inception of the Pro Tour, there was consensus from stakeholders that a fundamental change to the structure of professional cycling was necessary to ensure that the sport retained its economic and social significance. Given the surplus of cycling competitions available, race organizers accepted that a proper hierarchy of events within the sport was now called for. Competition for media coverage is very fierce between sports, particularly during summer months: for cycling to increase its public visibility and its attractiveness to broadcasters there was a recognized need to improve the coherence and presentation of the product. To do this, it was essential to attract the top riders to the big races.

Yet while agreeing on the overall need for change, it is apparent that the stakeholder groups had different priorities. One key factor in explaining events surrounding the Pro Tour is the importance of personalities among the various stakeholder groups. Like many sports, cycling has its share of charismatic individuals who wield considerable influence within the sport. One such individual was Hein Verbruggen, President of the UCI for 15 years until October 2005. He championed the idea of the Pro Tour

---

[1]The various teams in a race tend to ride in a tight bunch, called a peleton. The aim of this is to minimize the wind resistance for the cyclists. The leading rider overall in the Tour de France wears the yellow jersey. The yellow jersey was introduced as a promotion tool in 1919 and was selected to match the colour of pages of *L'Auto* newspaper.

as the way of modernizing cycling and succeeded in selling this vision to other stakeholders in the sport. Between them they agreed that such a system could be introduced in 2006. However, Verbruggen's decision to introduce the Pro Tour prematurely prior to his retirement in 2004 prompted angry protest from race organizers, and in particular from Patrice Clerc, President of ASO. The difference of opinion between these two individuals had a very negative effect on relations between the UCI and the ASO, which in turn has influenced relations with other race organizers. Subsequent meetings between the stakeholder organizations became heated rows between individuals seemingly caught up in the personal politics of the situation. Following Verbruggen's retirement, Pat McQuaid was appointed as UCI President. In spite of continued opposition from stakeholders, McQuaid staunchly defended the Pro Tour and relations continued – and continue – to deteriorate.

Ostensibly, the approach adopted of identifying a fixed number of races to be included in the Pro Tour, along with a fixed number of four-year team licenses, has provided a structure for longer-term security within the sport. Teams know that the award of a Pro Tour licence provides them guaranteed entry to the Pro Tour events, making it easier to secure sponsorship and recruit and pay for riders. Organizers know that the top teams are required to take part in their event and this is something they can sell to television companies and other sponsors.

The security provided by the structure actually raises another key issue in understanding the dispute, namely the perceived conflict between sporting and financial objectives. Some of the race organizers have argued that the Pro Tour is effectively a closed shop and actually stifles competition: once licences are awarded, there is at present no mechanism to ensure that teams holding a licence merit their continued status as a Pro Tour team over the four years. Instead organizers argue that what is required is a system of promotion and relegation which incentivises all professional cycling teams – not just those awarded a Pro Tour licence. In response to this claim, the UCI have pointed out that the 20 teams are chosen from an unlimited number of candidates; that new teams have been awarded Pro Tour licences in the last two years; and that as an individual sport, the riders can be employed by a Pro Tour team or 'leave at any time' and presumably try to sign with another team.

Turning to television rights, the 27 Pro Tour events cover different commercial properties and are not sold a single product. ASO generates the greatest sum from television rights both because it has the most attractive product (the Tour de France) and because it can bunch its events together and sell them as a package (see Table 4.1), in much the same way that television rights are sold collectively for football competitions like the FA Premier League in England or the UEFA Champions' League. While the UCI is keen to encourage greater pooling or bunching of individual races to ensure the best possible financial benefit from marketing and television for all of cycling's stakeholders (including allowing the UCI to promote its wider cycling developments projects), this viewpoint is not necessarily shared by race organizers like the ASO which believes that individual events have more worth if sold separately.

Moreover, race organizers interpreted the UCI's behaviour as being acquisitive; the push for improved television rights being little more than a poorly veiled attempt by the UCI to gain access to the huge earnings made by events like the Tour de France. In other words, why should a commercial race organizer like ASO give up any part of the rights that it has worked hard to develop in the preceding 100 years or more, especially given the cost of staging such a large-scale "moving" event?[2] Another argument put forward by race organizers is that the UCI should concentrate on more urgent matters, such as dealing with the fight against doping and the sport's poor public image, rather than becoming so overtly concerned with more commercial matters. Other arguments centred on which events should be included in the Pro Tour and race organizers social responsibilities to smaller events in their own countries.

The dispute came to a head spectacularly when ASO announced that having made no application to the UCI for its races to be licensed as Pro Tour events, ASO was at liberty to make the decision regarding which cycling teams would be invited to its races, rather than being obliged to invite all 18 Pro Tour teams and only two wildcard options. The two other main tour organizers, RCS and Unipublic, quickly followed the ASO lead which resulted in direct confrontation with the UCI, which accused all three main organizers of acting as a cartel and began legal proceedings against them. Efforts made by the UCI to exercise regulatory control, which included issuing several robust press releases accusing the organizers of unethical and unsporting behaviour, resulted only in a hardening of positions. While the dispute raged – and continues to rage – caught somewhere in the middle are other stakeholders, namely teams, riders, sponsors, media and the public. Having initially thought that the Pro Tour would provide them with some financial security and return on their investment, teams and sponsors are faced with a problematic situation. If race organizers choose not to invite a team to their event, then the sponsor is given no opportunity to advertise. However, having paid a licence fee to the UCI entitling them to participate in Pro Tour races, understandably teams take the view that compensation is due to them should a major race no longer be included within that Pro Tour!

Another factor which helps understand this case is the changing nature of GSOs. In recent years the UCI has undergone substantial organizational change. Having moved from a small-scale office in Lausanne, Switzerland, with a workforce of 14 people, the UCI now employs around 70 staff and operates from the high-tech and cutting-edge design premises of the UCI

---

[2]Unlike sports events such as football matches or the Olympic Games, professional road cycling races are 'moving events', staged on public roads and covering thousands of kilometres over several days. As a result safety costs and costs of televising an event like this can be very high.

Aigle World Cycling Centre. While continuing to work as a public interest, not-for-profit international federation, the organization has necessarily become more professional and commercially efficient, reflecting a general shift in the nature of GSOs.

Historically, the UCI has been funded largely through membership fees and contributions from its member national federations which it has used to further its broad objectives of promoting cycling worldwide and at all levels. But similar to other international sports federations, the UCI's recent behaviour can also be interpreted in part as trying to assert its independence as a regulatory authority. A particular challenge for the UCI in achieving greater financial independence is that unlike many other GSOs, it does not own or control cycling's hallmark events.

Postscript

The first event of the 2007 UCI Pro Tour, the Paris-Nice race, took place on 11–18 March 2007. Only days before the race was due to start, it seemed certain that the event would not take place at all after race organizers ASO refused to allow all of the Pro Tour licensed teams to participate. This decision resulted in the UCI instructing Pro Tour teams not to participate in ASO events. The cycling teams then issued public statements calling for the organizers and UCI to resolve the dispute for the good of cycling. But as each party hardened its stance, there seemed little prospect of a positive outcome to the dispute and the row seemed almost certain to destroy professional road cycling in its current format.

As late as 5 March 2007, following mediation by the AIGCP (Figure 4.1), a temporary compromise was reached between the race organizers and

UCI – with one exception. Pro Tour race team Unibet.com have been excluded from the starting line of all ASO events. As the Pro Tour gets under way for the third year, Unibet has accused UCI of taking money under false pretences and plans to take the international federation to court to recoup some of the €32 million invested in its cycling team. The scale of this investment indicates the commercial contribution made by sponsorship and adds some weight to the view of many teams that it is time they had more say in how their sport is structured. This is very much an on-going story.

And finally back to the picture board. What do you know about David Millar (pictured above)? Praised some years ago by Lance Armstrong who spoke favourably of his cycling prowess and positive future, sadly Millar was outed as a drug user and underwent a two-year ban from the sport. Now back on his bike riding for French team Saunier Duval and vehemently anti-drugs in his public pronouncements, it was Millar who raced to the sun, winning the Prologue stage of the first Pro Tour event, 'Paris-Nice'.

Case Questions

1 From a financial perspective, what differentiates road cycling from other professional sports?
2 What is unusual about the organizational structure and governance of road cycling compared to other professional sports?
3 Discuss the factors which have driven change within professional road cycling.
4 What have been the barriers to change?
5 Explain the distribution of power among cycling's stakeholders.
6 Is the UCI Pro Tour model fit for purpose?

Case Resources

Reading

Dauncey, H. and Hare, G. (Eds.). (2003). *The Tour de France, 1903–2003: A Century of Sporting Structures, Meanings and Values*. Frank Cass, London.

Desbordes, M. (2006). The economics of cycling, in Andreff, W. and Szymanski, S. (Eds.), *Handbook on the Economics of Sport*. Edward Elgar, Cheltenham, pp. 398–410.

Fife, G. (1999). Tour de France. *The History, the Legend, the Riders*. Mainstream, Edinburgh.

Forster, J. and Pope, N.K.Ll. (2004). *The Political Economy of Global Sporting Organisations*. Routledge, London.

Hoehn, T. (2006). Governance and governing bodies in sport, in Andreff, W. and Szymanski, S. (Eds.), *Handbook on the Economics of Sport*. Edward Elgar, Cheltenham, pp. 227–240.

Palmer, C. (2000). Spin doctors and sportsbrokers: Researching elites in Contemporary Sport – A research note on the Tour de France. *International Review for the Sociology of Sport*, Vol. 35, No. 3, pp. 364–377.

Rebeggiani, L. and Tondani, D. (2006).*Organizational Forms in Professional Cycling – Efficiency Issues of the UCI Pro Tour*, University of Hanover. Working Paper, available at http://econpapers.repec.org/paper/hand-paper/dp-345.htm.

Reed, R. (2002). The economics of the tour. *International Journal of the History of Sport*, Vol. 20, No. 2, pp. 103–127.

Slack, T. and Parent, M. (2005). *Understanding Sport Organisations: The Application of Organisation Theory*, 2nd edition. Human Kinetics, Champaign, IL.

Websites

Cycling magazines – www.cyclingweekly.co.uk; – www.procycling.com
ASO – www.aso.fr
RCS – www.rcsmediagroup.it
The Union Cycliste Internationale – http://www.uci.ch
Unipublic – www.unipublic.com

Further Information

Users of the case may want to take a look at the Wikipedia entries for the following:

Cycling teams – http://en.wikipedia.org/wiki/Professional_cycling_team
Giro d'Italia – http://en.wikipedia.org/wiki/Giro_D%27Italia
Road bicycle racing – http://en.wikipedia.org/wiki/Road_bicycle_racing
The Tour de France – http://en.wikipedia.org/wiki/Tour_de_france
UCI Pro Tour – http://en.wikipedia.org/wiki/UCI_Pro-Tour

5

sweatyBetty: by women, for women

Leigh Sparks

Case Focus

Retail sports goods shops can be intimidatingly masculine. This case examines the origins, strategy, development and operations of sweatyBetty, a small women-only 'activewear boutique' retail chain. It addresses some of the distinctive and innovative factors in the business and invites consideration of its past and future development.

Keywords

- Retailing
- Women
- Branding
- Activewear
- Market strategy
- Clotted cream

Case Summary

The retailing of sports goods tends to be focused on the male market with, until recently, female customers treated as an afterthought, if thought about at all. Fed up with the inadequacy of the retail offer for women, Tamara Hill-Norton set up sweatyBetty in 1998. sweatyBetty is a women-only high street retailer ('activewear boutique') best described as retailing a contemporary fusion of sportswear, swimwear, outdoorwear and gymwear. This case examines the rationale behind the establishment of the business concept, the stores and the company's subsequent expansion in the UK. The case encourages consideration of aspects of business development and strategy, market analysis and marketing, retailing and shopping, branding and ways of having and generating fun, commitment and community in a business setting.

Case Elements

Retailers attempt to encourage customers to visit their stores, make purchases and to keep returning to shop. There are many ways to do this. Not all customers will be attracted to stores by the same stimuli. Indeed, some customers will actively be turned off by some retailers by their approach, for example the in-store environment or the type, range, price, quality and display of the merchandise. Sports goods retailers often seem to be guilty of a degree of marketing myopia, particularly in how they (don't) see the changing market. Despite substantial evidence of the rapid growth and considerable scale of the female sports goods market (amongst other expanding markets and niches), many mainstream sports goods retailers appear determined to relentlessly pursue a particular and singular view of the sports goods consumer and retail markets.

Mainstream sports goods retailing has not been a particularly female friendly sector, on many levels. Many sports shops are perceived as threatening environments, viewed negatively by women, being seen as overly male and aggressive. A not untypical female opinion is 'Most sporting goods stores smell of stale sweat and old rubber and have techno booming loud enough to vibrate your diaphragm. They display their wares inelegantly, not to say indifferently, stacking them by activity; golf, jogging and swimming. A man's shopping environment if ever there was one' (http://www.cadaengine.co.uk/files/WEB_PDFs/PR-SexShopping.pdf downloaded 27 February 2007). Such stores do not meet the aspirations or requirements of many women in terms of sports goods products, shopping environments and customer service, nor do they fit with how women wish to shop generally, nor perhaps their perception of 'sport'.

It was such a viewpoint that in the mid-1990s encouraged Tamara Hill-Norton to research, develop and then open a new sports goods retailing business. Her frustration with a high street sports good retailing sector, staffed by young boys only interested in football, with a women's section as a 'pathetic' offering in the back of the store, often consisting of mismatched products, so-called 'unisex' garments and/or down-sized men's clothing, set the scene for a business opportunity. As she asked 'why should women have to get advice on, or buy a sports bra from a spotty male teenager?' Previously a buyer for Knickerbox, Tamara Hill-Norton and her husband Simon believed that there was a gap in the market for women-only activewear. They argued that current sports retailers were not meeting women's needs and that women wanted particular things from a sports store. As Tamara Hill-Norton viewed it, there was no one catering for women properly in the sports market, even at current levels of demand, let alone in terms of the potential female growth in health and fitness and other sport and exercise related activities. For many women, she felt, the feel-good factor and the overall health and well-being aspects of keeping fit were more important than competition and 'winning'. Manufacturers too, she felt, were missing the point about what women wanted out of exercise and needed from clothes for exercise. Tamara Hill-Norton suggests that even Nike did not quite understand the female psyche, with many women put off by the sporty, aggressive, 'just do it' ethos. Her market research identified that current retailers were indeed not meeting women's needs, but also established just what it was that many women were looking for in a sports goods shop.

The research suggested that the shop had to be better and different than other sports stores, particularly mainstream ones. Instead of equipment and replica football strips, snow wear and bikinis were to be added to gym and yoga clothes. These products were to be presented in an aspirational female environment. Preferably, the operation would become a brand in its own right and act (given their general neglect in the sector) as a focus for women helping women. But what to call it? The decision to change from the working title of 'Women's Activewear Retailer' to sweatyBetty took some thought and red wine, but sweatyBetty it was, despite its sexually polarising potential (women loved it and men hated it, so given the target market, what's the problem?).

In November 1998, the first sweatyBetty store opened in London's Westbourne Grove, in a unit that had previously been a Cobra Sports shop (the retail chain had gone into receivership and folded). sweatyBetty was positioned as an 'activewear boutique', perhaps best described as retailing a highly targeted contemporary fusion of sportswear, swimwear, outdoorwear and gymwear. It was designed for, and targeted at a women's only market, and in particular at an affluent upmarket clientele with a core emphasis on women aged 25–34 years and ABC1 in socio-economic terms.

In direct contrast to mainstream sports goods retailers, sweatyBetty put considerable initial emphasis on getting the design right in terms of its appeal to women and the target market. The initial store did not look like an average sports shop. It was designed to be intensely feminine with soft lighting, a spacious environment, with fixtures and fittings more synonymous with an upmarket clothing store than a sports goods shop. The aim was to create a pleasant boutique shopping experience. The colours were distinctive with high white ceilings and loads of pink. The mood was intended to be seductive rather than hard sell. Changing rooms were prominent and large with flattering mirrors and lighting, and enough space to enable mothers to manoeuvre a child's buggy. This deliberately and carefully designed environment focused on the feel-good, health and well-being aspects of keeping fit. Products were high quality and well presented as fashion, with music not overly dominant and an atmosphere that was supportive and non-aggressive. Being targeted at women, the store staff were all female and shared the brand vision. Externally, the window displays were dramatic in pink and white and aspirational in character, seeking to draw people in to the shops, where the environment, products and staff service would deliver the brand and encourage both return visits and word-of-mouth recommendations.

The initial development steps were typically fraught, as with many business start-ups. Finance is always a concern in such circumstances and with the sweatyBetty emphasis on store design and getting the design right for the target market, sufficient finance was a significant developmental factor. Major manufacturers such as Adidas and Nike were initially sceptical of supplying the business, both due to its scale, lack of track record and its not obviously sporting approach. sweatyBetty was perceived as a risky business in a market dominated by larger male oriented, clearly sporting goods shops.

However, the initial store was a success and proved the concept. The approach was refined and developed further, with store expansion adding to the confidence of suppliers, landlords and the company itself. Knowledge of the company was strengthened by store expansion within London to for example Kensington, Richmond, Soho, Hampstead, Clapham and Canary Wharf, as well as an in-store concession in Selfridges. Considerable PR was obtained through celebrity clients such as Elle Macpherson, Emma Bunton, Davina McCall and Nigella Lawson. By 2004, there were eight stores across London, all approximately of 700 ft² (70 m²) sales area. The concept and the brand were well established, particularly amongst its core target market. sweatyBetty had a 'buzz' about it. Tamara Hill-Norton had by then won the Harpers and Queens Entrepreneur of the Year award and been named by the CBI and Real Business magazine as one of Britain's most 'remarkable' women. She was also later named by Management Today as one of the nation's brightest businesswomen and began to be used as a consultant by major sportswear brands keen to focus better on the female market.

Whilst the store design was fundamental to correctly hitting the target market, the product selection, staff recruitment and the business ethos all combined to differentiate sweatyBetty. Rather than being comfortable with the tag of 'sports goods retailer' (despite being named the 2001 Sports Goods Retailer of the Year), sweatyBetty prefers to be described as a niche activewear chain, selling clothing and footwear for yoga, the beach, skiing and the gym in addition to exercise-related accessories. The highly targeted offer provides a stylish, attractive, feminine range of clothing that is intended for exercise but looks good generally. The core target market remains the busy young mum with an active home life and the young professional woman who works hard, but has a highly disposable income to spend on looking and feeling good. sweatyBetty sells activewear combining fun with fashion and fitness, using superbrands such as Nike, Adidas (including now the Stella McCartney designed range) and USA Pro and niche brands (including own brands and exclusive brands) such as Pure Lime, Venice Beach, Fuerteventura and CandidaFaria. The products are not cheap, but offer value through their high quality, fashion and performance.

A vital aspect of the store offer, which brings together all components of the retail brand, was customer service. Rather than conjuring up images of a typical sportswear store sweatyBetty aimed to position itself as a confidant or friend, someone to provide advice and guide exercisers in the right direction. Staff were carefully selected to reflect their target customers. The staff have a passion for the products and the lifestyle and communicate this in the stores and their wider interests and activities. The company has tended to recruit outgoing characters with backgrounds such as dancers, actors and personal trainers. As the target customer is likely to recommend stores by word of mouth, service provision is paramount. sweatyBetty staff are important to the store atmospherics, being sport and/or exercise enthusiasts themselves, keeping fit and leading active lives. They are personified as 'Betties', a device prominent on the website, where their stories feature heavily. The staff (store and central) know their products and their uses. Exercise is seen as fun, and stylish fun at that, but it is recognized that there are more important things in life as well. With the exception of Simon Hill-Norton all sweatyBetty employees are female and all are expected to share the brand vision.

This vision is encapsulated in the sweatyBetty brand, which is built on a concept, focused on a character (Betty) and has a core set of beliefs that emphasize a fun, irreverent approach to life and to business. This is typified by the company's values and beliefs statement, designed after a brainstorming session on a beach in Cornwall:

- We believe in healthy living, having fun, Cornish clotted cream and cool tracksuits.
- We welcome customers to share the sweatyBetty experience with us and to become our friends.
- We give our customers trusted advice and will deliver the perfect solution or even a magical transformation.
- A visit to sweatyBetty is sometimes unexpected, often memorable but always satisfying.
- Our products look gorgeous and perform well. We like comfort, great value and the WOW factor!
- We work with friends, we give each other support and achieve a balanced life. We aim to keep things simple and to stay in control.
- We value financial stability and growth so that we can share the sweatyBetty experience as widely as possible.
- We are building an amazing company, run by women for women to be the best!!!

With these beliefs, sweatyBetty has to live the brand in the stores, online and wherever the consumer comes across them. The website is both a transactional engine (though currently sales are c5%) and an informational resource. The personification of the brand in the form of 'Betties', whether online or in-store, enables some distance for the business from the founder, yet also focuses the brand in consumers' minds. Information is provided about typical 'Betty' interests, including local store links to gyms, ice-skating evenings, running and walking clubs and other social, but exercise and health-related activities. The stores and the website are designed to enhance a sense of female solidarity, community and belonging, including enabling and encouraging events and activities to occur. Exercising alone for anyone can be boring, so the stores and clubs aim to enhance motivation, provide exercise tips and help women meet new like-minded friends. Each store has a community area to focus these activities, making the brand a living experience, rather than simply a place to buy clothes (though that is alright too). Online advice on exercise and health care adds to the community feeling, even where there are no local sweatyBetty stores.

The sense of community extends to both staff and customers. The all-female staff are encouraged to be active and to enjoy exercise and shared activities. Many may have originally been friends. The website takes pride in featuring collective 'Betties in action' including summer retreats, sponsored bike rides, the running and walking clubs, ice skating and a bra amnesty for breast cancer. For customers there is a sweaty Club Card (in pink naturally) available in-store and online, which provides standard 'loyalty' benefits such as promotions, newsletters, competitions, special deals and discounts as well as shop-based events such as shopping nights, previews and parties.

sweatyBetty is also concerned about the wider world. In addition to the charitable acts and sponsored events, 'Betty's planet' features recycling shredded paper, wooden not plastic hangers, bags made from recyclable paper and a ban on an office photocopier. Staff get a contribution (£50) towards buying a cycle for use to travel to work and it is claimed that 50 per cent of staff either cycle or walk to work!

sweatyBetty has continued to expand. Sales to the financial year ending 2006 doubled to £9 million, based on existing store sales increases and an aggressive new store development programme. Moving outside London and the south-east for the first time, stand-alone stores have been opened in places such as Bristol, Cambridge and Brighton, and in-store concessions in Selfridges in Manchester and House of Fraser in Reading, Cardiff and Norwich have also been developed. An in-store concession in Harrods and a stand-alone store in Bluewater have added to the coverage in London and the south-east.

Table 5.1 details the store portfolio as of February 2007. The focus on particular towns and areas characteristically containing high numbers of the target market is clear even from this simple listing.

Table 5.1 sweatyBetty store locations

Stores in London	Stores in London	Other UK stores	Other UK stores
Battersea	Kensington	Bluewater	Manchester
Canary Wharf	Kings Road	Brighton	Nottingham
City	Notting Hill	Bristol	Reading
Chiswick	Richmond	Cambridge	Wilmslow
Fulham	Selfridges & Co	Cardiff	
Hampstead	Soho	Guildford	
Harrods		Kingston	

Source: www.sweatybetty.com/Stores/Stores.asp accessed on 29 January 2007

The table however does not show the degree to which the stand-alone stores are able to be located slightly away from the most expensive retail high streets. Rental is a major cost for many retailers and being able to operate as a destination that consumers will seek out can allow sweatyBetty to reduce its rental and property costs. For example, rather than Kensington High Street their store is on Kensington Church Street at reduced cost, but apparently without affecting consumer willingness to find the store. This approach allows for an interesting list of potential main (but expensive) target locations including Bath, Cheltenham, Winchester, Harrogate and York as well a possible niche opportunities such as Marlow or Padstow where affordable sites with high-target market potential can be found together with a degree of exclusivity.

sweatyBetty though is still a small, but expanding chain, which in the coming years will face all the issues that normally confront such businesses.

Store expansion is needed to generate scale and improve profitability of the company, yet control issues will arise over a larger more dispersed business. Moreover, with its distinct culture, the company is a reflection in part of the founder and the staff, and it is unclear how this ethos would survive a large expansion or even a takeover. Such issues have come particularly to the fore with the October 2006 purchase of sweatyBetty by private equity investment firm Wittington Investments Ltd. Whilst more finance may be available for expansion as a consequence, the risks to the culture and the brand may have increased.

Case Diagnosis

There are many issues raised by the sweatyBetty case. It can be discussed through a variety of topics or lenses. Here, five such themes are developed to assist in the understanding and discussion of the case. These are:

- business start-up,
- out of the mainstream,
- brand building,
- growing the business,
- reactions and the future.

Business Start-Up

sweatyBetty is a classic business start-up, being an innovative concept reacting to a perceived problem. The origins of the perceived gap in the market are discussed below, but it is one thing to identify an opportunity and another to capitalize on it. The gap identification arose due to a combination of personal circumstances, including private consumer frustration and working business realization of the issues in the market. Being a Knickerbox buyer gave Tamara Hill-Norton the knowledge and some contacts, but it still required the development of the concept and then the management of the start-up process. Simon Hill-Norton's experience as a consultant and at Whittard's helped in this process.

The keys to the successful start-up are clear identification of how the gap could be filled, together with a well defined and concentrated focus on the attributes of the business (the products, stores and staff). Finance and security of supply are always small business problems and act as constraints on the delivery of the vision. These could have derailed the project or at least compromised the vision and brand statement.

Out of the Mainstream

Mainstream sports goods retailing is something of a peculiar business in the UK as it seems to be inherently self-destructive and narrowly focused. This does not seem to happen to the same extent outside the UK. The focus on male products and sports and the switch from equipment to clothing and particularly leisure focused wear have tended to emphasize price over all other aspects of the business. With low price a key business driver, the market over the last decade has tended to narrow its focus and strip out many costs. Product selection remains male oriented, football dominates, staff are often the archetypal 'spotty male teenager' and any sense of merchandising is lost in a sea of discontinued product in a shabby environment with stark lighting and loud music. Yes, this really attracts a core market, and particularly one that shops solely on price, but it puts off many more.

There are two clear consequences of this pattern of development. Firstly, there has been a classic dogfight with scale, the key component of delivering low price. The long-time market leader, JJB Sports, has been seriously challenged and overtaken by Sports World International (previously Sports Soccer and also trading as SportsDirect.com and now renamed Sports Direct International and floated on the Stock Exchange in February 2007). These two leading businesses have in their expansion taken over much of the rest of the mainstream market including Sports Division and the Hargreaves and Gilesports regional chains and through their competitive power aided the collapse of All:Sports. Only JD Sports really remains as an alternative mainstream retailer. Some local chains are still trading and can have a very strong and loyal following for example Greaves Sports, but they are in the minority and are small. Whilst the coverage of the women's market has improved in these mainstream channels, the overall effect has been minimal. Mike Ashley, the founder of Sports World in the UK has been accused of irrevocably changing sports retail in the UK in the last 15 years, turning a brand and marketing led mainstream sector into a price driven commodity sector.

Secondly, however, the narrowing of the mainstream market has provided other opportunities. sweatyBetty has exploited one of these by being female focused. The outdoor market has Blacks and Tiso. Niche and specialist/ specialized markets are served by businesses such as Snow+Rock and many Internet sites, as well as licensed merchandise outlets including clubs (e.g. Manchester Phoenix Ice Hockey), events (e.g. Flora London Marathon), sports bodies (e.g. Wimbledon) and individuals (e.g. Andy Murray). The question posed by sweatyBetty is the extent and attractiveness of opportunities and niches out of the 'narrow mainstream'.

Brand Building

sweatyBetty is a brand that has been set up to appeal to a particular target market. The brand building started from the outset and encompassed a range of elements. Some of these are visual in the sense of the stores, colours and products. Some are far more subtle through the staffing of the business. The alignment between the stated values and the lived experience of the stores, website, products and staff has to be complete if the brand is to be believable. The use of 'Betties' in this regard is interesting, offering a personification of the brand concept. This lived experience is fundamental to the success of the brand. The staff have to live up to the ideals and perhaps even more have to encourage others to do so as well. Clubs, advice, community and ethics feature heavily in this, as well as aspects of charitable and sponsored contributions. The potential for this to go wrong is quite considerable.

One aspect of this to date is that much of the brand 'buzz' has been contributed not by advertising but by public relations, celebrity product exemplars (usage rather than endorsement) and word-of-mouth recommendations. This of course may be linked to a lack of finance for huge advertising spend, but is also a strong indicator of people buying into what sweatyBetty stands for. This may have to change as the business expands further.

Growing the Business

The business has grown rapidly in the past couple of years as store development has been speeded-up, though it is unclear if that rate of store-opening growth can be sustained. The concept has proven itself and the question thus becomes one of finding appropriate locations at affordable rentals where the target market can be encountered in considerable volumes. Locationally, the stand-alone stores seem to be of a number of forms, but the overall strategy appears clear, as does the in-store tie-up with major department stores. The pace of the development however runs the risk of putting a strain on the business systems and approach. However, too slow a development misses opportunities and opens the door to other potential operators. This is a typical retail expansion conundrum, particularly in successful start-ups. One solution often adopted is some form of licensing or franchising, but this can affect the control of the business and upset the company ethos.

It is also notable that despite the emphasis on the website to provide information and to develop the community of 'Betties' and the sense of the brand, there has been comparatively little transactional business, despite the rate of growth of Internet sales generally and in some parts of the sports goods market. This is one area where there would appear to be more scope to make the website more engaging and more successful in selling both products and the brand. Currently it appears to be pink and light-hearted which has some strengths, but could run the long-term risk of appearing insubstantial and possibly dated.

Reactions and the Future

Markets of course do not stand still and it is probably fair to say that women have been 'discovered' in sports goods retailing. For example, Nike, initially criticised by Tamara Hill-Norton amongst others recognized the issues that are raised by these 'standard' environments and by the growing demand from women for sports products. Nike operates Nikewomen which focuses exclusively on the female sports product market. These stores look and feel different to standard Nike stores, having different colours, layout, changing rooms, lighting, product presentation, etc., as well as a dedicated website.

Reebok in developing its new women's sports clothing range chose to partner Top Shop, a retailer that has a huge young following from its knack of producing good value high street fashion from celebrity and catwalk creations. For Reebok the tie-up adds youth/street/female credibility and is symptomatic of a realization that women are sensitive to the environment in which they buy sportswear and of the product itself. Next and Marks and Spencers have had some success in this market in the mainstream. Footie Chick, a women's sports football brand, pulled out of JJB Sports in favour of Asda amongst others, which it believes offers a more female friendly environment.

These examples are illustrations of this 'discovery' of the female market. They do not argue for different treatment for women, but simply appropriate proper treatment for this market.

Whilst it would be wrong to see the market as being completely met, there has been an overall change, though its embeddedness does tend to vary by retailer. For sweatyBetty this is an opportunity in that the market is more recognized generally, but it is a threat in that the competition has increased.

The idea behind sweatyBetty is also to a degree transferable, though the outcomes may vary considerably. In other countries, there are examples of a similar market being targeted, though often with particular emphases. For example in the USA, Paiva (part of The Finish Line) claims that it is 'a unique, inspiring, premium athletic store created exclusively for active women who demand an elevated level of service and style. It offers an integrated presentation of branded and private label apparel and accessories, as well as branded footwear blending performance with style to fit her active lifestyle. The Paiva store design exudes energy through its materials, design, layout and product assortment. The stores are inviting and comfortable, providing an ideal shopping environment for our customers' (www.paiva.com).

For sweatyBetty the future will be interesting. The buyout raises its own issues, but whatever the future control and development, care will have to be taken to maintain the brand strength and to develop further customer loyalty. sweatyBetty need to be able to be differentiated in the minds of the consumers and this needs to be maintained despite any pressures to become more effective and efficient. This is a difficult balancing act for any retailer.

Case Questions

1 What do you believe are the origins of, and reasons for the persistence of, the gap in the market identified by Tamara Hill-Norton?
2 To what extent do you agree or disagree with the notion of significant differences in male and female shopping requirements in the sports goods industry?

3 Critically evaluate the approach adopted by sweatyBetty in meeting its target market's needs.
4 To what extent do you believe that a retail brand can be a living experience? How is such a concept operationalized and sustained as a business grows and matures?
5 Attempt to develop a business strategy for the further retail expansion of sweatyBetty. What do you believe are the most significant problems likely to face the business in the future?
6 If the company shares were available on the Stock Market, and you had both the money and the inclination to invest in shares, would you invest in sweatyBetty? What issues informed your decision and why were they significant?

Case Resources

Reading

Anderson, D. (undated). *Sex and Shopping – Gendered Consumption in Sports Retail*. Cada Design Group, London. Downloaded from http://www.cadaengine.co.uk/files/WEB_PDFs/PR-SexShopping.pdf on the 27 February 2007.

Business Europe (2004). *SweatyBetty – shaping up for a peak performance*, 4 February 2004. Downloaded from http://www.businesseurope.com/cmn/viewdoc.jsp?cat=all&docid=BEP1_Feature_0000061983 on the 20 December 2004.

Marketing (2005). Sportwear gets fashionable. *Marketing*, 19 January 2005, p. 18.

Retail Verdict (2004). SweatyBetty expands to tone up financial muscles. *Retail Verdict*, 20 February 2004.

Retail Week (2006). Sweet smell of success. *Retail Week*, 17 November 2006, p. 37.

Retail Week (2007). Sports Direct: on top of the world? *Retail Week*, 23 February 2007, pp. 16–17.

SGBUK (1999). Sisters are doin' it for themselves. *Sporting Goods Business UK*, 14 October 1999, p. 43.

Sparks, L. (2007). Sports good retailing, Chapter 17 (pp. 365–396), in Beech, J. and Chadwick, S. (Eds.), *The Marketing of Sport*. FT Prentice Hall, Harlow.

Telegraph (2004). The shops we can't do without. *Telegraph*, 24 January 2004, p. 4 (weekend).

Times (2006). Reaching out to women who keep fit in style. *The Times*, 4 March 2006, p. 6.

Websites

Adidas by Stella McCartney – www.adidas.com/com/stella/,
  www.stellamccartney.com, www.adidas.com/women
Clotted Cream – http://en.wikipedia.org/wiki/Clotted_cream
Decathlon – http://www.decathlon.com/
Footie Chick – http://www.footiechick.com/
Footlocker – http://www.footlocker-inc.com/,
  http://www.ladyfootlocker.com/
Greaves Sports – http://www.greavessports.com/
JD Sports – http://www.greavessports.com/,
  http://www.jdsports.co.uk/womens.aspx
JJB Sports – http://www.jjbsports.com/
Nike Women – http://www.nike.com/nikewomen/
Paiva – www.paiva.com
Snow+Rock – http://www.snowandrock.com/
SportsWorld – http://www.sports-world.com/
sweatyBetty – www.sweatybetty.com
Top Shop – www.topshop.com

6

University College Dublin Association Football Club: putting an appropriate strategy in place

Anne Bourke

Case Focus

This case sets out the unique situation and issues pertaining to UCD AFC – a university soccer club which competes in the Republic of Ireland's Football Association (FAI) League of Ireland.

Keywords

- Strategy
- Resources
- Sports scholarships
- Elite sports participation
- Service
- Provision
- Strategic planning

Case Summary

This case study provides brief background details on University College Dublin Association Football Club (UCD AFC) which participates in the top Division of the Football Association of Ireland (FAI) National League of Ireland. Currently, it is at a crossroads in that to continue to offer its core service (football to elite and non-elite players within the university and the local community) it will need to re-arrange its governance arrangements, extend its resources (human resources and finance) and shift to new home grounds (Belfield Bowl). The club has undertaken a strategic review and part of the findings are incorporated into this case study to facilitate student and tutor understanding of the nature of a football club and the demands which management/owners/sponsors encounter in getting the service package in place to satisfy customer expectations.

Case Elements

UCD: Brief Profile

UCD is Ireland's leading university in terms of student numbers (approximately 22,500 students) and comprises 5 Colleges with 35 schools. It offers programmes across various disciplines such as medicine, veterinary medicine, science, law, business, arts and social studies.[1] UCD was founded

---

[1] There are seven universities (all state funded) in the Republic of Ireland three of which are located in Dublin: Dublin City University (DCU), Trinity College (TCD) and UCD. Other providers of higher education include the Dublin Institute of Technology; National College of Ireland; 18 Institutes of Technology and various other professional training colleges such as teacher training. A number of private colleges offer degree programmes in Ireland. These are accredited by HETAC or by UK universities.

in 1854 by Cardinal John Henry Newman and was originally located in Dublin's city centre – Earlsfort Terrace. In the early 1970s the main campus was relocated to Belfield (4 miles south of Dublin city centre) – at the time of writing all disciplines are on the one site apart from the Graduate School of Business.

Students attending UCD have a wide choice of sporting pursuits along with access to good quality sporting facilities. In the current academic year (2006–2007) two new clubs (Dodgeball and Kite) were established in the university giving an overall total of 59 – (see Table 6.1). The Director of Sport co-ordinates sporting matters in the University and acts as a bridge between the college authorities and UCD Sport. In 2002, UCD sport established a High Performance Centre (HPC) designed to offer training and support facilities to elite athletes – such as members of UCD AFC squad, AFC Women's squad, the Rugby squad and a number of Track and Field Athletes. While UCD sport offers a variety of sports facilities (all weather

Table 6.1 UCD Sport clubs: 2006–2007

Aikido	Archery	Athletics	Badminton
Basketball (Men's and Ladies')*	Boat (Men's and Ladies')	Boxing	Camogie
Brazilian Jiu Jitsiu	Caving and Potholing	Cricket	Cycling
Canoe	Equestrian	Fencing	Gaelic Football (Men's and Ladies')
Dodgeball	Handball	Hockey (Men's and Ladies')	Hurling
Golf (Men's and Ladies')	Karate	Kickboxing	Kite
Judo	Lacrosse	Mixed Martial Arts	Mountaineering
Kung Fu	Ninjutsu	Olympic Handball	Orienteering
Netball	Rifle	Rugby (Men's and Ladies')	Sailing
Pool and Snooker	Softball	Soccer (Men's and Ladies')	Squash
Ski and Snowboarding	Sub Aqua	Surf	Swimming and Waterpolo
Tae Kwan Do	Tai Chi Chuan	Tennis	Table Tennis
Trampoline	Ultimate Frisbee	Volleyball	Windsurfing
Wrestling			

*Where Men's and Ladies' clubs are listed, they operate independently and are counted as separate clubs.
Source: University documentation

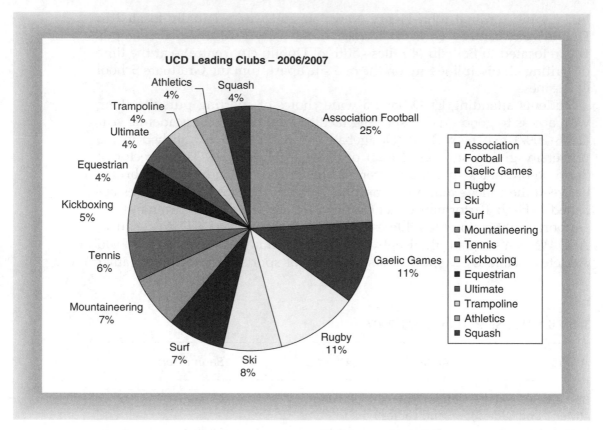

Figure 6.1 Leading clubs in UCD (membership of 200+) 2006/2007
Source: University records

and grass playing fields, a fully equipped gym) the development of athletes is somewhat restricted by the absence of a swimming pool but there are plans to rectify this.

According to university records, student clubs' overall membership for 2006/2007 is 8730 – however, this number may include individuals who are members of a number of clubs. Drawing on University data, 13 clubs have a membership of 200 or more (see Figure 6.1). Interestingly, the club with the greater number of members is the Association Football club (1280 members for 2006/2007). Numbers for Gaelic games[2] and Rugby are combined (women's and men's).

One of the unique developments within UCD sport over the years was the introduction of the sports scholarships scheme in 1979 by the soccer club under the direction of the late Dr Tony O'Neill (then an executive with the UCD AFC). The main purpose of the scheme was to allow students play football and pursue further study, but it was also introduced to halt

[2]The figure for Gaelic games includes Gaelic football (men's and ladies), hurling and camogie.

or curb the outflow of talented Irish youngsters to English Professional Football Clubs, many of whom left home aged 14 years without completing formal second level education. Following the appointment of Dr O'Neill as Director of Sport at UCD in 1990 the scheme was extended to include other sports such as cycling, athletics, basketball, ladies and men's Gaelic football, hurling, rowing, rugby and table tennis. The criteria used by the University in awarding sports scholarships include the profile of the particular sport at UCD; the university infrastructure for that sport; the club's development plan for the sport. Ultimately, sports scholarship decisions are made in conjunction with the relevant sports clubs depending on the availability of funding.

The more common entry route to university undergraduate education in Ireland is via the Central Applications Office (CAO). This office allocates students (using their college and programme preferences) to institutions based on Leaving Certificate (second level terminal examination) results. To gain a UCD sports scholarship, students must satisfy academic requirements and also have attained a high standard in the chosen sport (Football, Gaelic Football, hurling, rugby, track and field, etc.). Also, students awarded sports scholarships at UCD, must be prepared to commit themselves to involvement in the respective UCD sports club and agree to represent UCD and only UCD in competition.[3] In conjunction with UCD Sport, sports clubs are responsible for setting the criteria for awarding scholarships. The scholarship financial package is relatively small amounting in some cases to €4000 per annum and is renewable each year. In some instances part of the package comes in the form of *'benefits in kind'* (accommodation, academic fees, academic books, equipment, membership of the gym, etc.) rather than a sum of money. For continuing students, a satisfactory level of academic and sporting progress is essential, if the scholarship is to be renewed. From the UCD AFC's perspective, this scheme has been very successful and attracted many players who have gone on to gain international recognition as U18, 19, 20 and 21 levels. It is also the cornerstone for the First/U21 team squad. Students can pursue further study in any discipline (for which they have the admission standards) and in recent years, academic programmes have been introduced which focus on sport.

Football in Republic of Ireland

Among team sports, football (soccer) has the highest participation rate in the Republic of Ireland. However, from an attendance perspective, Gaelic games (Gaelic football (men's and ladies') and hurling/camogie) are more popular.[4]

---

[3] There are exceptions as Gaelic games scholarship students are permitted to play with their home county and club should they so wish.

[4] Attendance figure for two key Championship games in September 2006 are as follows: the All Ireland Hurling Final – 82,276; the All Ireland Football Final – 82,300 – www.gaa.ie.

Table 6.2 Clubs in the FAI Eircom League of Ireland – 2007

Premier division	Division 1
• Bohemians FC	• Athlone Town FC
• Bray Wanderers FC	• Cobh Ramblers FC
• Cork City FC	• Dundalk FC
• Derry City FC	• Finn Harps FC
• Drogheda United FC	• Kildare County FC
• Galway United FC	• Kilkenny City FC
• Longford Town FC	• Limerick 37
• Shamrock Rovers FC	• Monaghan United FC
• Sligo Rovers FC	• Shelbourne FC
• St Patrick's Athletic FC	• Wexford Youths FC
• UCD FC	
• Waterford United FC	

Source: www.eircomloi.ie

Other team sports played at various levels (largely part-time and amateur) include rugby, hockey, basketball and netball. In Ireland, football is played on a semi professional and part-time basis. The majority of national league players are likely to have part-time jobs to supplement their club salary. In recent years, there is much competition for sports sponsorship funding – football has drawn a considerable amount, often sourced locally. The Republic of Ireland National Football Team (men's and women's) are deemed attractive by corporate sponsors, but in recent years other activities/events have been sponsored such as women's and youth's football leagues, coaching and the provision of summer camps. It must be noted that the amounts (cash) for football sponsorship deals are small in Ireland when compared to European standards.

The FAI is the governing body for soccer in the Republic of Ireland. It oversees the activities of the national team and now organizes the Eircom National League and various Cup competitions (FAI Carlsberg Cup; FAI Intermediate Cup; FAI Statoil Junior Cup; FAI Inter League Cup; FAI U17 Cup and Setanta Sports Cup (a north/south inter league competition reintroduced in 2005). In organizing its activities, the FAI operates through its affiliates – the Junior Council; the Schoolboys FAI; the FAI Schools (FAIS); the Women's Football Association of Ireland (WFAI); the Irish Football Referees Society (ISRS); the Colleges Football Association of Ireland (CFAI) and the Defence Forces Athletic Association.

Twenty two clubs compete in the Eircom National League of Ireland,[5] 12 in the Premier Division (until 2009, when it will be reduced to 10) and 10 in Division One (see Table 6.2). The League clubs are dispersed throughout

---

[5] This is the Republic of Ireland's new national football league system which was created following the merger of the FAI and Eircom League.

the country with four located in the Dublin area and a further eight located in the Eastern (Leinster) region.

Derry City is located in Northern Ireland and joined the Republic's league at second level in 1985 on getting a special dispensation from the IFA[6] and UEFA[7] (Union of European Football Associations).

In 2003, it was decided to change the football season in the Republic which previously ran from August to May to the current arrangement March to November. According to the FAI (www.fai.ie) changing the season dates has contributed to increased attendances (almost half a million in 2005) particularly during the summer months. The 'summer' arrangement applies only to National League fixtures – other leagues operate under the 'old' calendar (August–May). There are 96 football leagues in the Republic of Ireland with women's football comprising over one-fifth.

To attract participants to any sport it is essential to provide a modern infrastructure (playing fields, training facilities, social amenities, etc.). Many sports clubs and organizations in Ireland are organized and managed on a voluntary basis with few having full time administrators and/or commercial personnel. The Irish sports infrastructure is relatively poorly endowed when compared with that of other countries, particularly for association football. One area where progress is evident is in the area of player coaching and development. Ownership details pertaining to Irish football clubs are difficult to establish – the majority of clubs are private companies while a small number operate as co-operatives. Many clubs operate with very limited resources (finance, personnel) and UCD AFC is no exception. In addition, it has a broad remit in providing football to individuals who wish to acquire an academic qualification and also who may/may not aspire to being an elite professional footballer.

UCD AFC

UCD AFC is the only university team to compete in the top division of the national league in Western Europe. The Club was founded in 1895 and is the oldest club in University College Dublin. Meenan (1995) documents the club's progress over the decades from being the Catholic University AFC to the mid-1990s highlighting the centenary celebration game with Liverpool FC. In 1970, the club took a decision to join the League of Ireland 'B' division. At that time, new competitions were evolving through the Irish Universities and Colleges Football Union and the Harding Cup was introduced to cater for first year (freshers) students. The substantial shortfall in the club's budget to finance the efforts of its first team (in what could be

---

[6] The Irish Football Association (IFA) is the governing body for association football in Northern Ireland.

[7] The remaining clubs are located as follows: two in the West (Connaught), two in counties Monaghan and Donegal and three in Munster (Cork City Cobh Ramblers and Waterford United).

termed 'professional' sport), was made up by the club imposing a higher annual subscription than that of any other College Club and various fund raising activities. In those days, UCD club players were not afforded the privileges which certain others may have regarded as 'divine rights' however, by 1976 international tours to the USA, Canada and China had been undertaken.

In 1979, the club joined the 'old' League of Ireland and since then has spent approximately 20 years in the Premier Division winning several competitions including the FAI Cup in 1984; the Leinster Senior Cup (1981, 1995, 1996); the FAI Super Cup (2000). Also, in gaining promotion to the Premier League in 1995, UCD AFC won the First Division title. By lifting the FAI Cup in 1984 UCD AFC qualified for the 'old' European Cup Winners Cup and was drawn to play Everton in the first round. The home leg was played in Home Farm FC grounds (attended by 9000 people) and ended in a 0–0 draw. UCD lost the away leg (1–0) which was remarkable as Everton went on to win the competition (defeating SK Rapid Wien in the final) as well as the League title that season. In 1999/2000 UCD finished fourth in the League (Premier Division) and qualified for the Inter Toto Cup. The home leg against the Bulgarian side Velbazhd Kyustendil was a 3–3 draw while the away leg was also a draw (0–0) – UCD was eliminated on the away goals rule. The Club came 6th in the Premier Division in 2006 and reached the quarter finals of the FAI Cup (beaten 2–0 by Derry City). For the past two seasons (2006/2005) the U21 team has won the Eircom National League.

UCD AFC fields teams in various universities and higher education competitions – Harding Cup, Collingwood Cup and the Universities League. It organizes its own internal league UCD Super league which consists of 72 teams and has approximately 1200 registered players. This league attracts past and current students from all disciplines at undergraduate and post-graduate level.

The club makes every effort to develop close ties with the local community groups by organizing summer camps for youngsters (boys and girls) aged between 7 and 14 years. It also provides summer camps in socially deprived areas in South County Dublin and invites the participants to attend Club home games from time to time. It also strives to develop closer ties with administrators, coaches, members and players of Mount Merrion Youth's Football Club. To that end it organizes youngsters to play short games during home League matches at half time. On 1 March 2007, UCD AFC held its first Open Day inviting attendees to join UCD Junior Blues Club – members will be informed about home games and other AFC activities/events of interest. The event was held in St Raphaela's Secondary School (one of the local secondary schools) and featured coaching, games, photo and autograph opportunities – first team players and management attended. The club plans to introduce a new Academy structure as detailed in its strategic plan 2007–2009 – outlined later.

Governance of sport within UCD is not clearly defined or easily understood. As mentioned earlier, the Director of Sport has overall responsibility for the development of UCD Sport. To understand further how UCD AFC (or any UCD sport club) operates within the university structure, it is necessary to highlight the role of two bodies – the Student Consultative Forum (SCF) and the Athletic Union Council (AUC). The allocation of grants by the University to clubs and societies is monitored by the SCF. This body consists of representatives of the AUC, Students Union, Students Club (old Bar) and is chaired by the Vice President for Students. The AUC oversees the allocation of university capitation grants to sports clubs, arbitration and the awarding of colours. All sports clubs have representatives on the AUC Executive who are elected on a constituency basis – there are 13 constituencies. The AUC Executive is elected during the Annual General Meeting each year which is held during Semester 1. The Executive normally meets at least once a semester. The Development Manager is responsible for the operations within the AUC and also acts as Executive Secretary.

Club development officers are employed for a small number of clubs – Gaelic games, association football (men's), rowing, basketball (men's) and rugby but employment arrangements vary. Two officers are employed by UCD (Gaelic games and association Football) whereas the remaining three are employed by their respective clubs with UCD making a contribution towards their salary. All sports clubs must apply for grants each year. To gain funding, each club's completed application form must provide details of the previous year's activities along with details of finances and accounts. Each club must include a description of the planned projects and activities for the current year along with associated costs. Grants are assigned for coaching and training expenses, intervarsity competition costs, affiliation fees and equipment costs.

Each sports club within the university is managed by its own committee. Guidelines compiled by the AUC are provided to assist club personnel in relation to roles and responsibilities. Over the years a small number of committed individuals have been associated with the operation and management of UCD AFC. The Executive Committee currently comprises of the following officers and members: Chairman, Honorary Treasurer, Honorary Secretary, Development Officer (full time employee) and two other members. The FAI's recent initiative to appoint (and partially fund) *club promotion officers* have allowed the club to appoint a second full time employee.

UCD AFC's annual turnover is small (€530,000 in 2006; €460,000 in 2005) in the context of professional football today. The university provides an annual grant which in 2006 amounted to approximately one-fifth of the club's turnover. Other sources of revenue for UCD AFC include the FAI contribution; gate receipts (first team games), sponsorship; subscriptions from UCD Super league; player subscriptions; Subscription from Affiliated club (Pegasus); Alumni Association; UEFA Grant; Summer Camp (in partnership with Dun Laoghaire Rathdown County Council); and various social events and activities. The clubs main expenditures consists of players' payroll costs; funding scholarships; graduates who stay with the club when their studies are complete; management/coaching; travel; league entry fees.

Belfield Park (located on the university campus 4 miles south of the city centre) has been the home of UCD Soccer since the 1970s. The University authorities plan to further streamline existing association football facilities by organizing UCD Rugby and Soccer clubs to engage in ground sharing. This arrangement is scheduled to commence in March 2008 when the re-development of the Rugby Ground (Belfield Bowl) is complete and the ground meets the UEFA Licensing[8] requirements.

The Strategic Plan

In July 2005, it was decided to undertake a root and branch review of UCD AFC. This review would cover many of the items specified for UEFA Licensing requirements and also focus on the club's current position, arrangements in relation to personnel and finance, identify the club's strengths and weaknesses with a view to providing pointers for its future strategy, management and development for the period 2007–2009. The exercise was undertaken by a group of people (which for the purpose of this case study will be referred to as 'the Review Group'), who know and understand the world of football in the Republic of Ireland. These individuals were also prepared to commit time, energy and reflection to the task as they have close ties (as distinct from direct links) with the club for a number of years.

The Review Group (which was independent of UCD AFC Executive Committee) consisted of individuals with the following profiles:

- UCD AFC's first scholarship player.
- Former player (now director of a sports-related business).
- Managing director of a leading auctioneering firm.
- Former county manager of Dun Laoghaire Rathdown County Council – now a property development executive.
- Former chair of the Eircom League – now a solicitor (Chair).

The Review Group commenced its deliberations in September 2005 and met on 25 occasions. The final report was completed in December 2006.[9] Data (primary and secondary) were gathered from various sources (reports, publications, journals, etc.) and stakeholders. The stakeholders who contributed to the research endeavour (mainly through personal interviews) included current players (first team and U21); coaching/management staff;

---

[8] For the 2007 season, UCD AFC was deemed to have satisfied the UEFA licensing requirements and will play home games in Belfield Park.

[9] Part of this report was used as a submission to the Independent Assessment Group (IAG) who adjudicated on the FAI National League of Ireland structure for 2007. UCD AFC retained its Premier Division status.

members of the Executive Committee; personnel attached to UCD Sport; representatives from the FAI; commentators from the media (newspapers and television); UCD academic staff and a limited number of individuals who currently play football in UCD's Super League.

Based on the data gathered, Table 6.3 presents in summary form the main strengths and weaknesses identified for UCD AFC. As is evident from the data gathered, two major restrictions exist for the club – funding and poor attendance figures. The club's strengths include good coaching and management reputation and prudent financial management. But for a club aiming to provide *elite* and *football for all* opportunities for students/graduates, it is essential to reduce the weaknesses and develop further the club's strengths. Consequently, the Review Group identified various strategic issues and detailed specific plans to address them.

Table 6.3 UCD AFC strengths and weaknesses

Strengths		Weaknesses
• Well run club with values and integrity • Players treated well and appreciate efforts of club personnel • High level of commitment by Executive Committee and volunteers (small number) • First team and U21 players – highly motivated • Coaching and management structure – highly regarded • College authorities committed to club development • Good training facilities and good high performance unit	• Operates with prudent financial management • Strong intermediate and fresher sections • Super league is very successful • Improved relationships with college authorities and UCD Sport • Scholarship programme attracts able students – sporting and academic • Good club reputation and respected externally • Met UEFA Licensing requirements	• Limited resources – financial and human. Expectation by UCD that AFC club should fund scholarships • Weak committee and governance structure • Financial management on a reactive basis • Attendances very low at League fixtures • Executive Committee does not have time to engage in planning for the future • Reduced number of pitches in UCD • Need to foster stronger ties in the local community • Poor quality of Sports Management Diploma

Source: Strategy Review Group (2007)

For the purpose of this case study the focus will be confined to (i) governance (ii) human resources/career management; (iii) sales and marketing and (iv) finance.

Governance

The Review Group proposals in relation to UCD AFC governance are presented in Appendix 1. It is recommended to introduce a Supervisory Board and Executive Committee. Under this structure, the Supervisory Board would engage in policy development and implement the business strategy. It would oversee the club's compliance with UCD's ethos and the general direction of the club. The Review Group proposed that the Supervisory Board consist of 10 members – 6 non-executives, 1 UCD nominee and 3 Executive Directors. The Board's function would also include developing operational links with UCD authorities (through the UCD Director of Sport) and to establish and maintain appropriate links with the FAI. The role and responsibility of the Executive Committee are not outlined in the strategic plan and the organizational chart sheds little light on its position. Governance specifications for the elite (First and U21) teams, other college teams and the proposed youth academy are also set out in the report.

Human Resources/Career Management

Football Clubs are service enterprises providing a service experience for individuals/supporters/members. To deliver a quality service package[10] service managers are advised to focus on the five features as illustrated in Table 6.4.

Currently, UCD AFC relies on voluntary efforts for many of its services (including coaching; training for certain teams) particularly management. There are two full time employees (Club Promotion Officer and Football Development Officer). While funding these positions is possible due to a subvention from the FAI, the job specifications need to be clearly stated and targets set for each position holder. The Club envisages the appointment of a General Manager who will take care of day-to-day management and organize appropriate support structures. He/she will also have responsibility for managing club resources. A major part of the HR function deals with team management and playing personnel. With respect to the First and U21 teams, manager and player contracts have to be drawn up. Personnel in a university football club are constantly changing – students graduate and move to another club or gain full time employment, consequently, assessment policies for new players need to be developed along with career and academic (study rooms, tutors, etc.) supports. While the club's mission embraces *elite* football, the *football for all* aspect is very important. UCD AFC is the largest club (in terms of membership) in the university due mainly to the existence

---

[10]Service package has been defined as the bundle of goods and services which are provided in some environment (Fitzsimons and Fitzsimons, 2004).

Table 6.4 The service package

• *Supporting facility*	*Physical resources that must be in place to offer the service. Football grounds; training facilities; supporter accommodation, etc.*
• Facilitating goods	Materials purchased or consumed by the buyer, or items provided for the customer. Examples here include match day programme; catering goods and services.
• Information	Operations data provided by the customer to enable efficient or customized service. This would include ticket requirements
• Explicit services	The benefits readily observable by the senses and that consist of essential or intrinsic features of the service
• Implicit service	Psychological benefits that the customer may only sense vaguely or the extrinsic features of the service Attending a game at a particular stadium (Nou Camp/Old Trafford) may confer on an individual a certain status.

Source: Fitzsimons and Fitzsimons (2004) modified

(and success) of the Super League. This League consists of 72 teams which cannot accommodate any more teams due to a shortage of playing fields.

The strategic plan notes that in future UCD AFC will need to target talented youngsters (aged 15+ years) who are interested in attending university but may not have academic support/s. To facilitate this, detailed proposals for setting up and operating such an academy are outlined. The academy will offer scouting, coaching and player development programmes along with generating an awareness of the possible player pathway on offer at UCD. To develop the academy, UCD AFC personnel will need to be assigned to particular roles and linkages with the First and U21 teams are essential. Youngsters in second level schools (local and regional) will be targeted and given additional coaching, player development techniques and academic/career support while continuing to play with the local club. The extent to which this can be realized depends largely on the availability of personnel and effectiveness of club HR policy. It is envisaged that the academy would feed into the existing scholarship programme whereby youths will progress to the UCD First Team while pursuing further study.

Sales and Marketing

Apart from international matches (men's senior) attendances at national league and cup fixtures in the Republic of Ireland are low. During the 2005 season almost half a million people attended domestic football games. The

FAI has taken control of the National League and has commenced a radio and television campaign for its competitions. Many Irish football fans support English Premiership clubs (Manchester United, Arsenal, Liverpool, Chelsea) – evidence of this can be gleaned from supporter club notices inserted each week (Thursdays) in Dublin's only evening newspaper *The Evening Herald*. These notices provide information about fan club personnel (secretary) and also detail ticketing and travel arrangements for club games in England and availability of club official merchandise.

It is acknowledged in the strategic plan that UCD AFC has been unable to sustain a marketing plan aimed at students/graduates/community to increase attendances at home games and stimulate interest in the club. UCD AFC has one of the smallest fan bases among the National League clubs. While Belfield Park can accommodate 1500 fans, it has rarely been at capacity. It is estimated that the average attendance at home games during 2006 was 543, while in 2005 it was 653. Many students attending UCD are from areas outside Dublin and tend to go home each weekend. As club home fixtures are played on Friday evenings – this begs the question if games were scheduled mid-week would there be an increase in student attendees. With a large number of past players and alumni, UCD AFC has an untapped network in relation to club developments. Possible initiatives to draw on this untapped fan base include the appointment of a past players co-ordinator who would update the records and put in place a programme to involve this group in club affairs. Further research is needed on this aspect of marketing and the urgency of developing a marketing and sponsorship plan is acknowledged. Two other matters needing immediate attention are the design and content of the match day programme and the club web page. The latter has improved in that it is now updated regularly, but its design is quaint and not user-friendly.

Finance

According to details provided in the strategic plan, UCD AFC finances have been managed in a prudent manner todate with financial decision-making being more reactive rather than proactive. Given the limited availability of funds and the low attendance at home games, the approach to date has been short term with little attention given to long-term financial planning. Gate receipts, university funding and shirt sponsorship together represent approximately 30 per cent of the total annual funding, with the remaining proportion being funded from donations, grants, sponsorship and fund raising events. It is expected that income and expenditure will increase considerably in the next two years – by 2009, turnover should have reached the €1 million.

Concluding Comments

In the United States' university and college system the performance of sports teams and individuals is frequently used as a marketing tool by the institution. Many European universities while placing particular emphasis on sport and sporting achievement operate and manage sporting endeavours in a different way. As detailed in this case study, UCD has a strong reputation in the provision of sport (and football in particular) but to continue to do so for football particular changes in governance and organizational structures are necessary. Will the implementation of the UCD AFC strategic plan 2007–2009 bring about the desired changes or will there be unintended outcomes?

Case Questions

1 According to Payne (1996) there are four keys to successful management of sport organizations (i) total control; (ii) mutual integration of all different programmes; (iii) a positive environment with the community environment and (iv) professionalism. How does UCD AFC score on such criteria? Please explain.

2 UCD has a student body of 20,000 plus yet few students attend UCD AFC home league games. If we could tap into 10 per cent of the student population it would yield a huge increase in attendance. What factors in your view contribute to the low attendance each week during the season (ignore the summer months)? You have been appointed as soccer development officer at UCD, what would you do to generate some excitement among university students and increase student attendance at League games?

3 This case provides details of UCD AFC's strategic plan for 2007–2009 and the methodology used to document it. Comment critically on the (a) methodology employed and (b) the proposals. Do you anticipate that UCD AFC will have all its structures in place by 2009? Give reasons to support your view.

4 According to Grant et al. (2007) effective strategy is about being different and anticipating future events in order to react and respond proactively. Drawing on the summary strategy detailed in this case, to what extent will it allow UCD AFC anticipate future events and react proactively? Give reasons to support your view.

5 The UCD AFC Review Group proposes a two tiered governance structure which is common in some European countries (Germany and France).
  – Comment critically on the role of governance in the management of a sports club (use a football club). Do you agree that the UCD AFC governance structure proposed will facilitate the club achieve its targets? Why? Why not?

6 Based on your understanding of a service package (detailed in this case) identify the key features of it. How can club management ensure that the quality of the service delivered meets consumer expectations?

Case Resources

Readings

Blake, B. (2007). Total Re Vamp for UCD soccer. *College Tribune*, Vol. 20, No. 7, p. 23.

Bourke, A. (2006). Marketing football in the Republic of Ireland, in Desbordes, M. (Ed.), *Marketing and Football: An International Perspective*. Butterworth-Heinemann, London.

Fitzsimons, J. and Fitzsimons, M. (2004). *Services Management*. McGraw-Hill, Boston.

Grant, J., McKechnie, S. and Chinta, R. (2007). Using the business s-word – strategy – for sports. *The Sport Journal*, Vol. 10, No. 1, pp. 1–10.

Meenan, P. (1997). *St Patrick's Blue & Saffron: a Miscellany of UCD Sport Since 1895*. Quill Publications, Dublin.

Payne, M. (1996). Sport organisation marketing, Presented at the *European Master in Sport Organisation Management Research Seminar*, Dec. 13, IOC, Lausaunne.

Schmenner, R. (1986). How can service businesses survive and prosper? *Sloan Management Review*, Vol. 27, No. 3, p. 25.

UCD Club Operations Manual, 2006/2007. Athletic Union Council.

University College Dublin AFC Strategic Plan 2007–2009 (unpublished).

Websites

www.ucd.ie/soccer
www.gaa.ie
www.irfu.ie
www.eircomloi.ie

Further Information

http://www.ucd.ie/sport/scholarships.htm#About

Appendix 1

Where we want to be: structure and responsibilities – overview

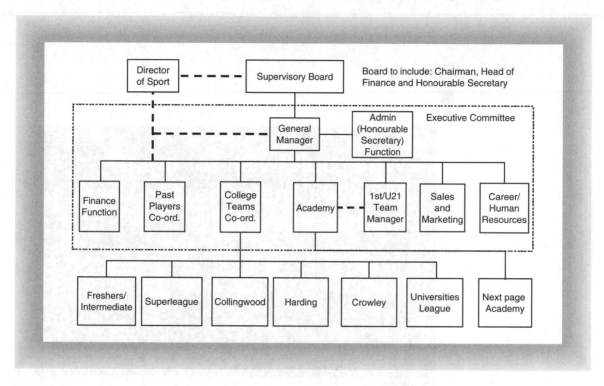

Case

7

Who could wish for more? New Zealand's Coast to Coast multisport event

Geoff Dickson and Sean Phelps

Case Focus

This case examines the variety of unique challenges faced by the organizers of the multisport event known as the Coast to Coast; challenges not faced by traditional sport managers operating in a specific venue. Also addressed are issues which both bolster and restrain the event and multisport in general.

Keywords
• Multisport
• Governance
• Sponsorship
• Brand position
• Endurance athlete

Case Summary

Multisport events are typically comprised of a variety of outdoor disciplines such as paddling, mountain biking, running, cross-country skiing, and snow shoeing. Depending upon the course and format, participants may take from several hours to an entire day to complete the course. Individuals and teams may travel hundreds of kilometres over rugged terrain. There are no standardized distances as in triathlon, and there is no international federation and only a few self-proclaimed national sport organizations. New Zealand's Coast to Coast event, introduced in 1983, provides a one-day format for individuals and two-day option for individuals and two-person teams covering over 240 km. Organizers face a myriad of possibilities that can maintain the status quo, hinder development and growth, or increase the event's status both domestically and globally. This case study explores issues such as permits, brand extension, role of elite athletes, and the potential formation of a national sport organization for the sport.

Case Elements

The Speight's Coast to Coast is arguably one of the world's premier multisport events, and is the self-proclaimed World Multisport Championship. The Coast to Coast is so named because participants race from the west coast of New Zealand to its east coast. Kumara Beach on the Tasman Sea is the starting line and Sumner Beach on the Pacific Ocean is the finishing line. There are three different events operating under the Coast to Coast name. The two-day version of the race may be contested by individuals or two-person teams. In the team competition the runner and the kayaker both do cycling stages. A one-day event, popularly known as 'The Longest Day', is an individual only contest. The Longest Day also acts as the World Multisport Championship, a self-proclaimed title. In 2007, Coast to Coast celebrated its 25th anniversary with over 900 competitors.

Multisport may be defined as a genus of sports events rather than being a single type of event. New Zealand's Sport and Recreation Commission

(SPARC), the government agency responsible for sport development defines multisport as 'less structured' and having 'more variety and flexibility' compared to triathlon. Common to all versions of the sport are a continuous series of stages, also known as legs, which require competitors to transition from one athletic discipline to another to achieve the best overall time. For example, different disciplines may include, but are not limited to, any combination of running, cycling, and kayaking. Unlike triathlon, there are no standardized distances. As endurance events, multisport races can take athletes many hours to complete the course, rivalling ultra-distance triathlons in duration. Adventure Racing is similar, but ultimately different, to multisport because of the variety of activities incorporated into a single competition. However, Adventure Racing is characterized by longer races, that may take days to complete, climbing and other rope-related skills, and the need for map reading and other navigational skills involving several team members.

The Coast to Coast requires competitors to cycle a total of 140 km over three stages of 55, 15, and 70 km. There is a total of 36 km of running including a 33 km mountain stage that crosses the Southern Alps. Also incorporated into the event is 67 km of kayak paddling down the Grade 2 (some rapids, small waves) Waimakariri River. The finishing times for men competing in the individual event range from 11 to 12 hours for the winner to 15 to 17 hours for the final competitor. Over the years various stages of the course have been shortened or lengthened to accommodate growing field sizes, different transition locations, and an increased emphasis on competitor safety. Weather, road, and river conditions also greatly influence the time taken by participants. It takes place in early February, in the middle of New Zealand's summer. A 'how to' book has even been published about the event; *Conquering the Coast to Coast* describes the course and what is necessary to compete. The event's website proclaims: '$150,000 worth of prizes and race pack goodies, finishers medals, two outrageous dinners, a quality event branded shirt and a cold can of Speight's for finishers. Who could wish for more?' In a testament to both the worthiness of the participants and the preparation, and luck, of the organizers, there have been no fatalities at the event and only eight participants have had to go to hospital out of 17,500 total competitors.

Coast to Coast is owned by Robin Judkins and his company Ironman Productions (which is not associated with the Ironman triathlons). Its origins can be traced back to 1980 and the Alpine Ironman, staged by Judkins, a three-day race that combined skiing, trail running, and kayaking. Judkins stumbled into the multisport business after a career in sales and marketing, and a five-year stint running his own house-painting businesses in Australia and Wanaka, Central Otago. A reformed alcoholic, known for his penchant for Hawaiian shirts, his own larger-than-life presence is very much an indelible brand on his company's flagship event. Judkins' autobiography is titled *Mad Dogs: A Life on the Edge*, further illustrates his disdain for bureaucracy, a proclivity for caustic comments, and 'becoming one of New Zealand's genuine larrikin cult figures' as described by his publisher.

As part of the mythos of Coast to Coast, Judkins is said to have had his 'Eureka!' moment while paddling on the Clutha River with a mate. The two determined it was possible to race from one side of New Zealand's South Island to the other using both natural and man-made routes. In 1983, 79 competitors entered the inaugural Coast to Coast. By 2002 the race had grown to over 900 participants. Men typically comprise 78 per cent of the field and the two largest age groups, 30–39 years and 40–49 years, make up 55 per cent of the total entries. Since 1987, the men's race has only been won by a non-Kiwi four times while the women's race has never been won by an international competitor. Gone are the days where participants showed up using bicycles with baskets and tennis shoes for the run. Equipment used now includes carbon fibre bike frames and paddles, titanium componentry, sport specific shoes, wicking and fast drying clothing, and various types of kayaks. High-end race kits can total more than $10,000 and even entry level gear can set back a competitor several thousand dollars. This equipment is simply the tools of the trade as today's elite competitors compete for a first place prize of $10,000 in both the men's and women's Longest Day category. Elite athletes chasing the cash prize are required to do so with competing sponsors on their clothing and equipment. The entry form states that all participants agree to 'not be sponsored by any company in competition with Lion Nathan products in beer'. In addition to the gear, all entrants must include a Grade 2 kayak certificate with their entry form to ensure at least basic paddling competency, water skills, and rescue techniques. Furthermore, there are mandatory items that each person must carry during each stage of the race. Helmets are required during all cycling legs and kayaking sections. A first aid kit, extra clothing for outdoor and extreme weather conditions, water bottles and hydration packs, and a survival bag are just some of the items required by race management for all competitors to have.

This event utilizes both public and private lands. Permits for the race to operate must be sought from local and national governmental agencies as the organizers are operating a for-profit experience using public lands. For example, New Zealand's Department of Conservation (DOC) has permit jurisdiction over much of the area in which the Coast to Coast operates. In addition to the normal considerations involving the permitting process (i.e. number of people, dates and times, trash removal, risk management) a threatened species, the Blue Duck (also known as the *Whio* in Maori), has its habitat in the river area of the course. In its recovery plan for the Blue Duck, the DOC cites as a possible threat to the species and its breeding the frequent use of rivers by endurance and multisport athletes for training. When the organizers apply for a concession to operate in areas managed by the DOC, they must be cognizant of the impact the event has on the natural environment. They must justify to the DOC what they plan to do to avoid, or at the very least, minimize the impact on the local environment. Failure to do so could result in loss of the concession and the event having to relocate or cease operations. To avoid this scenario, Coast to Coast organizers are a financial contributor to the Blue Duck Recovery Programme. The race website shows another 15 groups and organizations that are involved with the race and supported by over $150,000 in contributions since the creation of the Coast to Coast. Another area of concern for organizers and competitors is the microorganism Didymo. Biosecurity New Zealand suspects that the organism is most likely transported by people, moving from one water source to another without properly cleaning their equipment (i.e. kayaks, running shoes). All participants must sign a form indicating they have abided by Biosecurity New Zealand's protocol for cleaning equipment. Fines for knowingly spreading an unwanted organism range from fines and/or imprisonment.

Dove-tailing with the expenses associated with being a good corporate citizen, the ever changing legal landscape impacts Coast to Coast. As expectations for risk management and safety compliance increase, so do the associated costs. Traffic management plans, insurance premiums, permits, ambulance service, and other related items swelled compliance costs to $160,000 in 2005 for the event according to published materials. According to newspaper reports, the event costs associated with Transit New Zealand have gone from $5000 in 2000 to $60,000 in 2007. Judkins has indicated to the media that he has as much as $4.5 million in uninsurable risk with the event. He also derides 'nanny state' mentality that exists because of these regulations. To recoup some of these costs, the entry fee for Coast to Coast rose from $565 in 2000 to its present price of $835 in 2005. Teams comprised of school-aged competitors age 16 years and older pay $625 person as do individuals who are over the age of 65 years. The Coast to Coast entry fees are some of the most expensive in the entire country.

Even with the numerous costs associated with putting Coast to Coast on, its economic impact on the communities surrounding the course is substantial. A 2003 economic impact study commissioned by the Christchurch City Council placed the value of the race between $3.8 and $6.2 million dollars on the region. Nearly 3000 participants, spectators, and support crew descended upon the race spending an average of $3629 per person. New Zealanders spent 5–6 days in the area, Australians one week, and other international visitors stayed two weeks.

The race has been sponsored by New Zealand Breweries Ltd since its second year in 1984. Naming rights for the event were granted to Speight's in 1990. Speight's have become largely synonymous with the event and the event is sometimes simply referred to as 'The Speight's'. One of the race's traditions is for Judkins to shake the hand of every athlete crossing the finish line and provide them with a can of Speight's beer. A New Zealand Breweries sponsorship manager says the event is made for Speight's. He indicated 'we have been involved in the event since day one. It has reflected the growth Speight's has been going through and coincided with our 'Southern Man' campaign and a conscious decision of ours to align Steinlager [another New Zealand Breweries product] with international events such as the All Blacks [men's national rugby team] or the America's Cup'.

In 1983, according to the sponsorship manager, New Zealand Breweries' involvement was '12 trays of beer'. The following two years it was the Lion Brown Coast to Coast. From 1986 to 1988 the sponsorship passed to Steinlager and then Speight's became the title sponsor in 1990. Since then, with the restoration of regional beer brands and the growth of Speight's as a national brand, the southern brewery's long-term backing of the Coast to Coast has become very prominent. 'Are you going to do the Speight's this year' is a common question among Kiwi endurance athletes.

In 2005, the event has received funding from the New Zealand Government, via the Inter-Agency Events Group and its 'Major Events Development Fund'. Major events are said to be those which are of 'national cultural, social, and economic significance that has benefit for New Zealand' according to the government's website. The funding is designed to help promote the event internationally by subsidising the production and distribution costs of a television highlights package. Coast to Coast is broadcast live in New Zealand and the highlights package is distributed throughout 32 countries as well as on Air New Zealand international flights. Encouraging participation by multisport athletes from outside New Zealand is a deliberate effort by the event to attract more interest from overseas television networks to screen footage of their competitors.

The 2005 event also witnessed the introduction of the World Teams Challenge event. Each team consists of two men and one woman and all members of the team must finish the One Day race. Team members are also eligible for individual awards in the Longest Day event. Unlike Adventure Racing, where there is normally a requirement for the team members to stick together, there was no such requirement in the Coast to Coast. In this way, the athletes still completed the course individually, but also doing the best for your team means doing the fastest possible individual time you can. The winner of the World Teams Challenge was the team with the lowest combined time. Eight teams competed in the Speight's Coast to Coast 2005 World Teams Challenge. The countries participating were Australia, Canada, China, France, Japan, New Zealand, Scotland, and Sweden. The World Teams Challenge represented a team concept in the race. Invitations were issued to elite international competitors. The World Teams Challenge was not continued after 2005.

Unstructured and fragmented are terms that have been used to describe the state of governance within multisport. Harkening back to triathlon's creation in the early 1980s, a counter-culture mentally exists amongst both competitors and organizers. This lack of formalized structure is part of the attraction of multisport; flexibility and freedom are available to participants, event organizers, and the events themselves. Credibility and legitimacy issues do not rely on a regulatory agency, but with the event organizers and participants.

For many sports there exists some type of governing body responsible for the wellbeing of a particular activity. The International Olympic Committee (IOC) recognizes such organizations as the international federation for a sport. IOC recognition may or may not mean inclusion on the Olympic Games competition programme. Each international federation is then made up of member organizations known as national sport organizations, national federations, or national governing bodies. Once recognized by the IOC, an international federation must then abide by specific rules and regulations such as adopting the World Anti-Doping Agency's (WADA) code of conduct and accepting the Court of Arbitration in Sport (CAS) as the forum to resolve grievances.

Sports operating outside of the Olympic family also have some type of governing structure. Australian Rules Football, International Rugby Board, Professional Golfers Association, and Association of Tennis Professionals are examples of associations which provide governance for their respective sports at a non-Olympic level. Multisport has no official international federation and, perhaps, few self-proclaimed national sport organizations (i.e. USA and Canada). The International Triathlon Union, the international federation for the sport, incorporates a winter triathlon (run, mountain bike, cross-country ski) under its auspices but does not address other multisport events. At the national level, Triathlon New Zealand's website indicates that it provides endorsements and sanctioning for triathlons (including winter), duathlons (run-bike-run), and multisport events but the forms used for endorsements and sanctioning are geared towards triathlons. USA Triathlon, the world's largest national governing body for triathlon in terms of number of members with 100,000, defines multisport as triathlons (including mountain-bike), duathlons, aquathlons (swim-run), and aquabike (swim-bike) but also does not address other multisport events.

In its 2005 review of multisport and triathlon, SPARC discusses the pros and cons of multisport following under the auspices of either a new governing body or an existing governing body such as Triathlon New Zealand. The latter is disregarded due to Tri NZ's own growing pains and a lack of credibility within the multisport community. A new governing body for multisport could be created with assistance from SPARC, but with limited and clearly defined facets for SPARC so as to not smother the freedom which participants, organizers, and stakeholders seem to cherish. Any multisport governing body, according to the SPARC document, would need to be staffed and led by someone deeply involved in the sport; an outsider would more than likely be viewed suspiciously.

Coast to Coast's success has created a variety of competitors in the multisport arena looking to tap into the marketplace. Through in a few multi-day adventure races in New Zealand and the event has a wide range of rivals vying for the dollars of multisport competitors. Part of its mystique is the natural setting, which is its venue or facility, and that setting can change for the worse concerning the weather but also the accessibility of the public lands impacted by the race. Its safety record has been impeccable, but its entire risk management structure could change dramatically if a fatality were to ever occur during the event. On the upside, Coast to Coast has demonstrated itself to be an economic engine not only for its owner but also for the surrounding region. This type of economic might translates into some political capital as well. Overall, Coast to Coast, although well established and entrenched in the multisport scene in New Zealand, still must face a growing list of threats and opportunities.

Case Diagnosis

Unlike football stadiums, basketball arenas, or tennis complexes, the Coast to Coast 'venue' is the region between the Tasman Sea and the Pacific Ocean. Hundreds of kilometres of river, trails, and roads incorporating thousands of hectares of public land are the facility for this sporting event. Additionally, the 'field of play' involves 900 competitors, hundreds of race support people and hundreds more of volunteers. Moving this many people over 240-plus km in a seamless and environmentally responsible manner, through both public and private lands and thoroughfares, means cultivating a positive relationship with local and national governmental agencies. Alienating the DOC through ignorance, omission, or commission could mean a loss of the concession that allows the Coast to Coast to operate. Damaging the environment (i.e. littering, cutting new trails), negatively impacting the breeding grounds of the Blue Duck, and simply being a poor corporate citizen are ways that could damage the event's relationship with all the permitting agencies and communities along the course.

One way to increase Coast to Coast's race inventory, and its brand exposure, without having to add more competitors on the actual race day would be to create a series of qualifying events throughout New Zealand. Multisport races, operating under the Coast to Coast banner, would allow the possibility of more people participating in Coast to Coast branded events. Ironman, owned by the World Triathlon Corporation, has created a highly successful qualification system for its premier event Ironman Hawaii. To get to Hawaii, a triathlete must win a 'qualifying slot' at an appropriate event or be fortunate enough to win one of the 150 US or 50 international lottery slots. Ironman's lottery system is a revenue generator as it costs $35 to enter the lottery. Several 'community' slots are typically auctioned off for several thousand dollars each with the proceeds benefiting local charities.

A similar system could be established for Coast to Coast, either creating new events or selling an existing race a 'qualifier endorsement'. The qualifying system ensures that the best of the best are in attendance at the premier event while the lottery system allows for the average person a chance at competing with the best. Increased brand exposure, for Coast to Coast and its sponsors, potential increased brand awareness among consumers, and increased revenue streams due to more entry fees and/or qualifying sanction fees certainly exist. A downside to this scheme is that it risks alienating the 'weekend warrior' by forming an elitist caste. The 'Southern Man', as advertised with Speight's beer, might not be able to participate because he cannot qualify. Also, if new races are created then the workload for Ironman Productions would rise dramatically while selling the qualifying status to existing events would mean some type of review or oversight to ensure that these qualifying races uphold the standards of Coast to Coast.

Coast to Coast has had a long and productive relationship with Speight's beer. As alluded to earlier, the event has become known as 'The Speight's' in some circles. A symbiotic relationship of sorts has developed between the two businesses. The identities of the two are tied to one another. However, should the relationship change and either one decide that it is time to 'go in another direction' a potential problem for a new sponsor would be how to become associated with Coast to Coast in a manner that would eliminate it being referred to as simply 'The Speight's'. While the Coast to Coast brand would remain, and along with it peoples' perceptions of a unique Kiwi sporting activity, a new sponsor would be faced with the notion of changing the brand of 'The Speight's' to its own brand.

Multisport events, such as Coast to Coast, are not subject to established criteria and guidelines by some sort of regulatory agency. Coast to Coast does not have to implement drug testing or abide by the results of drug testing by other organizations, does not need to use a standardized rule book, and could offer unequal prize money based on gender. In the case of Coast to Coast, Judkins himself has an expressed disdain for bureaucrats and there exists, according to SPARC, within multisport athletes' attitudes about the 'freedom provided by the lack of structure and bureaucracy within the sport and they demonstrate faith that the multisport "community" will ensure sustainability of the sport'.

Within the Coast to Coast entry information it is stated that the race director's decision is final with regards to any complaint initiated by athlete against another. This places the event organizer in the position of being judge, jury, and executioner in terms of enforcing rules, rules which are not specifically defined. For example, the entry information indicates that drafting is allowed on one leg of the bike but not the other two. Drafting occurs when one cyclist follows immediately behind another to gain an advantage because the leading cyclist breaks the wind. No mention of the penalties are mentioned if one is caught drafting. The possibility of a conflict of interest arising is also present when the 'officiating' is handled by the race organizer. Officials are usually presumed to be impartial in their decision-making. In this instance, the race organizer for Coast to Coast has a vested interest, on a variety of levels, regarding the outcome of the race.

The previous two paragraphs highlight the potential downside of not having a standardized rule book, independent officials, and a sanctioning process which includes oversight by another entity which incorporates a template for risk management plans not to mention the possibility that a governing body *may* provide credibility and legitimacy in the eyes of those who grant permits and permission. SPARC has identified the possible reluctance of multisport organizers and participants to form a national sports organization. A loss of freedom and flexibility is said to be feared by the formation of such a bureaucracy. For a multisport governing body to develop, event organizers and multisport athletes would need to assume the various leadership categories required. Outsiders to multisport might be viewed warily by those heavily involved in multisport if they were to take the reins of a fledgling sport organization. Organizers of multisport events would certainly want some type of representation within the new governing body. Elite athletes could be expected to want representation. However, ethical dilemmas are a distinct possibility when you place individuals on a board of directors who will be voting on items that directly impact their financial wellbeing as is the case for event organizers.

Creating a national sport organization/national governing body/national sport federation is country dependent. How a national governing body forms in the USA is different from how one develops in New Zealand. The role, or non-role, of the national government, power of the National Olympic Committee, funding entities, and whether or not an international sport federation already exists are some of the factors which influence how an emerging sport's governance structure evolves for those sports following the Olympic model.

Coast to Coast has been successful, on a financial level as well as on a participatory level, without the intervention of SPARC or the formation of a national sport organization. The freedom of not having a regulatory agency and entrepreneurial attitude held by organizers allows for nimbleness in the marketplace that might not be present if a governing process existed. Then again, Coast to Coast calls itself the World Multisport Championship. This is a self-proclaimed title with no formal acknowledgement. Any other multisport race could claim the same designation and organizers of Coast to Coast could do little to defend their assertion that they are the Multisport World Championship. Coast to Coast has secured its position in the New Zealand multisport marketplace and in the end, who could ask for more?

Case Questions

1 What are the key factors behind the success and popularity of the Coast to Coast?

2 What are the advantages and disadvantages of a national sport organization forming to govern the sport of multisport racing in New Zealand? What impact would this organization have on Coast to Coast?

3 How might qualifying standards (i.e. qualifying events) impact the event in terms of participation, legitimacy, quality, and brand extension?

4 A symbiotic relationship is characterized by each partner to the relationship adding value to the other partner. Why would the strategies of attracting overseas participants and seeking international television exposure be described as symbiotic strategies?

5 An athlete is serving a suspension for a positive test for performance enhancing drug in another sport. How do the organizers of Coast to Coast respond when this athlete registers for the event?

Case Resources

Reading

Brown, M. (2007, January 28). Robin's nest. *Herald on Sunday*. p. 34.

Judkins, R. (2000). *Mad Dogs: A Life on the Edge*. Hazard Press, Christchurch, New Zealand.

No coasting for juggernaut Judkins. (2006, October 3). The Dominion. Retrieved January 31, 2006 from http://www.stuff.co.nz/stuff/0,2106,3817102a1864,00.html

Nutsford, D., Artus, J. and Blight, M. (2005, August). *Review of multisport (including triathlon) in New Zealand*. SPARC.

Still crazy (2007, February 9). *The New Zealand Herald Super Sport*. pp. 2–3.

Websites

Canadian Adventure Racing Association – http://www.canadianara.com/
Coast to Coast – http://www.coasttocoast.co.nz/
International Olympic Committee – http://olympic.org
International Triathlon Union – http://www.triathlon.org/
Ironman – http://ironmanlive.com
New Zealand Major Events – http://www.majorevents.govt.nz/
SPARC – http://www.sparc.org.nz/
Speight's – http://www.speights.co.nz/Sponsorship/Speights-Coast-to-Coast.aspx
Triathlon New Zealand, Inc. – http://www.triathlon.org.nz/
US Adventure Racing Association – http://www.usara.com/
USA Triathlon – http://usatriathlon.org

Further Information

Users of the case may want to look at other entries for additional information:

Multisport – http://en.wikipedia.org/wiki/Multisport

Case

8

Twenty-20 and English domestic cricket

Paul Kitchin

Case Focus

This case examines the brief history of the Twenty-20 Cup in English domestic cricket. From the outset the tournament was seen by managers and stakeholders as an important marketing tool for the repositioning of the sport to connect with new audiences.

Keywords
• Innovation • Market research • 'Match-day experience' • Repositioning

Case Summary

This case examines the brief history of the Twenty-20 Cup in English domestic cricket. It considers the state of English cricket prior to 2003 when attendances were stagnant and participation in the game was extremely low. The England and Wales Cricket Board (ECB) undertook a significant piece of market research in 2000. From this research it was revealed that the current format of most cricket matches was inaccessible to many and did not appeal to their leisure needs. The introduction of a new competition called Twenty-20 based on this research was extremely popular among general sports fans new to the sport of cricket. The coordinated planning, promotion and management of the event were reasons for this success but it is clear that these competences need to be applied in other areas of the sport for long-term success to be achieved.

Case Elements

Domestic Cricket Pre-Twenty-20

Since the end of the Second World War consumer tastes and the time available for leisure time have changed. The attraction of a six-hour sporting event requiring a competent understanding of a complex rule system does not easily sell in a competitive sport-entertainment market. In the past 20 years a general reduction in leisure time for adults has led to greater competition for the leisure pound. Sporting practices and consumer tastes are becoming more fragmented the rise of extreme sports, informal sport and increases in personal fitness have made a more individualistic sports market. Although still a leading summer sport the increasing competition from an ever-expanding football season, which has major summer tournaments every two years, has encroached on cricket's traditional season. The performance of the English team has been inconsistent, rarely capturing new segments of sports fans. McDonald and Ugra (1998) stated that cricket's traditional values of civility, country pride and gentlemanliness are still associated with the game but create a situation where

English cricket strongly identifies with certain demographic groups; where white, ABC1, males aged over 50 years dominate support.

The sport is governed by the ECB who are responsible for the development of the game of cricket in Britain. The cricketing regions under the ECB, the County Cricket Associations,[1] compete in a number of domestic competitions. In 1997, the ECB launched an ambitious strategic plan that would provide a clear direction for the sport. *Raising the Standard (1997)* set the importance of improving the performance of the national team. To do this the ECB aimed at making the game more attractive to a wider audience through improvements to the domestic competition in the hope that it could make the Counties more financially independent and also encourage new talent into the sport.

The 18 County Championship[2] is the traditional domestic cricketing product, consisting of four-day matches (expanded in the 1980s from a three-day competition). The Country Championship was joined by limited over cricket in the 1960s in the form of the Gillette Cup, the John Player Sunday League and the Benson and Hedges (B&H) Cup. Initially designed as one-day limited over competitions they consisted of a variety of guises and schedules some which have, at times, caused great confusion among cricket fans and the general sporting public. However, on an international scale this limited over format proved successful in the 1970s and its popularity was enhanced with the staging of the first Cricket World Cup in 1975. The commercial benefits of the popularity of cricket was reinforced by the lengths Kerry Packer went to in order to obtain the Australian television rights for his Channel 9 broadcasting station.

Packer's cricket revolution changed the way the game was broadcast and picked up the best attributes of the limited over cricket and marketed them successfully. Only a few spectators attended the inaugural matches of the World Series Cricket competition, it should be noted that the competition was created for television without any market research being carried out. The basic premise was fast bowlers versus cavalier batsmen. Action and excitement were clear messages in the game's promotion and a culture that welcomed any business innovation that could increase the potential for commercial revenues.

Innovation on the field throughout the 1980s to 1990s adapted the concept to the game's detriment. Bowlers realized that not only were wickets important but economical bowling also. The introduction of medium-slow, accurate bowlers took the pace off the ball making it more difficult for the batsmen to hit boundaries. These tactics dominated the middle sections of most 50 over innings. Batsmen responded to this realizing that they need not risk hitting boundaries, instead they paddled the ball around the field and managed to score 5–6 runs per over creating large competitive scores.

---

[1] Each County, prior to 2005, held a seat on the management board effectively steering the ECB's direction.

[2] Durham was admitted to the competition in 1992, before that the competition involved 17 teams.

By the end of the 20th century domestic cricket was engulfed in an image problem. The product offerings to the public did little to capture their attention or enthusiasm. The audience figures of the Country Championship and the one-day competitions were extremely low, the B&H Cup was dissolved in 2002 due to poor support and a general lack of interest.[3] County cricket enjoyed loyal support from an ageing (84 per cent over 34) male dominated (male: female, 85:15) target group but has not been able to connect with target segments from alternative audiences. The Counties found themselves making little, if any, revenue from these products and creating little value for sports fans.

The major source of revenue for the Counties was international test match cricket. Revenues generated from international test matches were distributed by the ECB to the Counties (approximately £34 million in 2004). International test matches attract large crowds and depending on the competition, for example Australia in 2005, can reach maximum stadium capacity. The problem lies at the domestic end of the game. This is because the pool that all the Counties receive is technically biased in favour of the test match hosts who accrue income directly from staging the test match events. This has created great discrepancies in County revenues having the potential to destabilize the competition.

An analysis of the strong support for the international game also revealed a different audience demographic than the County game. Interestingly, one grassroots movement that had emerged through the tumultuous period of the 1990s was the Barmy Army. This was a group of supporters who would follow England on their international travels. It revealed that there was a demand for support from younger non-traditional target groups. According to Malcolm (2006) this group was positioned in opposition to the traditional notions of cricketing support. The Barmy Army's members were characterized by three key features: to desire to have fun, to exert an influence on the game and to express their English identity. All focused on an active support more akin to football than cricket. The existence of this support provided an opportunity for the sport's managers. Hence, while the domestic game may have been struggling the success of the international product, the fans that supported that level indicated a potential that could be exploited.

The Development of the Twenty-20 Cup

The concept of Twenty-20 cricket originated from research commissioned by the ECB in 2000. The research examined the cause of falling domestic audiences and worrying participation figures, such as the 40 per cent drop in participation among children of school age. The Cricket Foundation (quoted in Mintel, 2006) believed the DfES' (the Government Department for Education in Britain) statistical figures of 85 per cent of schools offering cricket was in reality more like 10 per cent when accounting for definitions

---

[3] The support of a tobacco sponsor was instrumental in the Cup's existence. With the toughening of legislation concerning the use of tobacco sponsorships this support was withdrawn, which could have been a contributing factor in its demise.

on 'offering' were analysed. Even here at the junior levels there was very little support or development opportunities available.

One of the foci of the market research was the importance placed on customer views (Hopwood, 2006). In the past sporting organizations have been slow to become customer-facing firms. The customer issues raised by the research acted as a wake-up call to the administrators. The general knowledge of the average sports fan was low concerning cricket and therefore was acting as a barrier to participation and spectating. Also the games were too long in duration and played at inconvenient times, many of the matches in the domestic timetable took place when potential audiences were either at work or at school. Importantly, Harrison (2004) revealed was that cricket was perceived as a low-value option for leisure spending, thus positioning cricket as economically unattractive.

Nevertheless, the research revealed that despite the low domestic attendances and lack of interest in the sports products offered at the County level there was still a healthy percentage of cricket 'tolerators' in Britain, revealing the existence of market potential. Hence, if management could create a cricket product that delivered value and entertainment there could be support for it. Cricket had proven its ability to adapt previously with the advent of limited over cricket, hence this flexibility was seen as one of its unique selling points (Harrison, 2004).

The Twenty-20 product was launched in 2003 and was aimed at new segments that may not have seen much appeal in attending the game of cricket. The management believed that the new product should be communicated to two target groups. The primary target group were members of the sporting public aged 16–34 years, families and those who were general sports fans. The second target group mainly focused on women, members of the office crowd and children. It was felt that these groups if attracted to the event could provide the best possibility of developing to the sport over the long term. In order to attract these groups it was determined that the event should be created to be appealing to the novice cricket fan. The competition would follow a regional format and be played quickly. The match itself would incorporate music and general entertainment options for fans, not just relying on cricket, it would also use innovative match presentation features while maintaining the spirit and laws of the game (Harrison, 2004).

The regional format was played over two weeks at the height of summer. To contribute to an increased sense of spectacle the format allowed for derbies between regional competitors, designed to increase the local stakes and hence match attendees. The short timeframe meant that spectators could leave work or school and head to the ground for the match. The three-hour competition proved popular with fans as the format included a guaranteed result. The advent of a finals day containing both semi finals and the grand final at the one venue created a showpiece event that transcended cricket and captured the public's, and importantly the media's, attention (Mintel, 2005).

The provision of music and general entertainment meant the competition produced a broader entertainment product that appealed to a larger variety of new customers. This is important as it did not rest solely on getting people in for a cricket match, the entertainment options increased the sociability of the event. Counties used reflexology tents, face painting and even a Jacuzzi to offer that extra special experience. Technologies such as players 'miked' into the ground's tannoy and the television broadcast for ongoing comments allowed viewers at home to hear interactions between players and commentators. All of these innovations were designed to increase the experience for those spectating.

Mullin et al. (1993) stated that the core product should not be altered and focus should be placed on delivering value to the customer through product extensions. The use of the existing laws of cricket kept the matches true to the core product of the cricket match. Although the Twenty-20 product is quite a change from former cricket offerings the maintenance of these laws and regulations used in the longer form of the match provided it with credibility. Earlier innovations in the one-day game, such as the International Super 8s in 1996, failed to take this into consideration and never gained a successful support base.

An attempt to make the game 'more understandable for those not born into it' (ECB source quoted in Mintel, 2006) meant that the tournament relied heavily on marketing and promotions. A carefully managed integrated marketing communications mix operating nationally and locally supported this unique match-day promotion. The marketing of the competition nationally by the ECB, with the assistance of the marketing agency WSM, focused on the dissemination of the tournaments key values and messages (exciting, social, accessible, inspirational and educational). The reinforcement of these values aimed to appeal not only to the desired target market but also to commercial organizations that could provide important resources as customers or sponsors. Central to the spread of these brand values were agreements with national broadcasters on terrestrial and satellite television (C4 and Sky), on radio (BBC 5 Live Radio), online (ECB website, Play-Cricket.com) and through a coordinated press campaign (Harrison, 2004). All these media sources were carefully managed to present a coordinated message to the sporting public about the differentiated product that was Twenty-20.

At a local level the creative direction for the tournament was set by WSM but the Counties determined local manipulation. This allowed the messages to be adapted to each County's unique conditions. This working arrangement was seen as both positive and novel, the scale of this mutually beneficial relationship had not been seen before from the Counties and the ECB and was clearly a factor in the overall success of the tournament. The Counties were given the autonomy to create their own Twenty-20 experience. Hopwood (2006) noted Durham's successful integrated marketing communications approach to merge the Durham experience with the over-arching brand values of the tournament. Britcher (2003) notes that Surrey appointed a PR company, Bite, to drive activity in the lead up to the tournament. Surrey were successful in their PR drive and used their media partners to promote the event in return for cross-promotions on match day, and given the subsequent interest in Twenty-20 this was a successful strategy followed at a minimum cost

(Groves, Personal Communication, January 2006). The local promotion of the tournament also benefited Counties like Sussex who already had existing local initiatives where Twenty-20 could be incorporated into their existing strategy.

The results of the inaugural competition in 2003 were extremely successful and have continued to improve over the first three years of the tournament. The initial season's attendance was up 245 per cent generating an overall tournament attendance of 255,000, 40 per cent of these spectators attending a cricket match for the first time. The tournament culminated in a sell-out crowd of over 15,000 for the finals day at Trent Bridge, a marked success on the B&H Cup held the year previous (Henderson, 2003; Rawling, 2003). Worchester's first game against Northants attracted more spectators than the all of the matches of the previous season combined. The story was the same in amongst other Counties, Surrey attracted 20,000 spectators for the first time since the 1950s, while Hopwood (2006) noted that Durham's ground occupancy figures for the tournament was over 88 per cent with attendance for the competition averaging 5300 per match resulting in 'huge' increases in revenue for the club.

The new audience demographics were also promising, despite the capacity crowds the scene was 'liberally sprinkled with women and children' (Hopwood, 2006, p. 225). These new audiences were just what the cricketing authorities were looking for. Table 8.1 contains some statistics on the breakdown of live attendance figures that are extremely positive for the sport.

The attendances at the ground were not the only success story. Despite the attention to the live match-day experience the television viewership is important to cricketing authorities also. Mintel (2006) found that one in three people watch cricket on television but do not attend the matches; 60 per cent of these viewers are aged between 24 and 64 years while 75 per cent of all viewers fall into the ABC12 classification which presents the cricketing authorities with an indication of some new segment possibilities. Interestingly, the gender ratio of watching cricket is closer on television than it is live attending, the ratio for female to male viewership was 31:69 (Mintel, 2006). Television viewing figures

Table 8.1 Live attendance demographics 2003 Twenty-20 competition

Factor	Ratio of attendees
Age – under 34:over 34	62:38
Gender – female:male	23:77
Percentage of spectators who said Twenty-20 had altered their opinion of cricket (%)	
Under-25	42
Women	58
Men	36

Sources: Harrison (2004); Mintel (2005)

from the Twenty-20 tournament were up by 62 per cent to 3.57 million viewers, which was very encouraging since only 6 of the 45 matches were broadcast live. Gillis (2005) commented that the sport had tapped into a significant vein of latent demand resulting from great amount of attention in a short timespan, Hopwood (2006) even stating that it was the sporting success story of 2003.

The advent of the Twenty-20 competition has impacted on English cricket and the wider British sporting landscape since its inaugural year. Tournament wise the second season in 2004 was always going to have its results closely monitored. The competition was plagued by poor weather but remarkably the attendance figures increased by 12 per cent on 2003. The first Twenty-20 match to be held at Lords between Middlesex and Surrey drew a crowd of 26,500 breaking all previous one-day attendance records. The 2004 season culminated with a finals day attendance that topped 18,000 at Edgbaston, generating nearly £400,000 from the one event (Mintel, 2005). The significance of this revenue cannot be easily understated, the combined revenues from three full one-day international matches in the Nat West Series, not involving England, did not generate this level of revenue. In 2005, overall attendances were up by a further 70 per cent on the previous year. The finals day, held at The Oval in London set a new record for finals attendance by drawing a crowd of 20,160.

This injection of these new revenues into the coffers of the game began to provide certain Counties with a strong source of independent revenue, providing a viable alternative from relying solely on the central allocations of the pre-Twenty-20 years. In 2004, Somerset, a non-test match County, generated £2 million of its £3.3 million in revenues from match-day hospitality (Mintel, 2006). Since hospitality demand depends on the exclusivity of the event then attributing a large percentage of this to the Twenty-20 competition is not beyond the realms of possibility.

Another factor that encouraged the success of English cricket occurred later in 2005 when England reclaimed the Ashes from Australia after 19 years. The series finished culminating in a draw at The Oval to a sell-out crowd and very high final day viewing figures (7.4 million[4]) on terrestrial television and receiving 3.3 million hits on the BBC website. Mintel (2006) reported this effect meant cricket was actively followed during that summer by over 8 per cent of the UK population.

Research conducted after the Ashes series revealed that 46 per cent of parents 'actively encouraged' their children to take up cricket (Mintel, 2006). This positive image is fostered by the new 'star' players such as Kevin Pieterson, Michael Vaughan and Andrew Flintoff provided clean, fresh sporting role models. Despite losing the return series in Australia in the English winter of 2006/2007 the market for cricket is expected to grow. This factor is in no small part to the Twenty-20 competition and the coordination of action between the ECB and its Counties.

---

[4] The record for cricket broadcasting was actually set on the final day of the 4th test match at 8.4 million viewers, this was due to the England win to go 2–1 up in the series.

Case Diagnosis

The success of the tournament from this case appears to be endless, nevertheless there are a few issues that can be drawn from the case that can provide insights for future management actions. Twenty-20 cricket has been hailed as a saviour of English county cricket but the introduction of the competition should be seen as part of a wider repositioning of the sport first initiated with the release of *Raising the Standard*. Even when publishing *Raising the Standard* the problems with County Championship were clear and the performance of the international team, at the time 'the' revenue source for English cricket, was of concern. The establishment of Cricketing Centres of Excellence across England acted to acquire the talent from the junior system into the academy and then direct to the national squad, with the County a secondary option. The elite players were put onto central contracts to allow easier access for international tournaments and to ensure that their skills and talents were not overused by the Counties. This move represented a shift away from reliance on club and Counties to foster and develop talent and meant that the ECB, through its academies, could effectively control the supply of potential international players. While the central contracts were beneficial for the players and the ECB does take away the possibility of using English players as star attractions at County matches.

In the 1990s, the County Championship was reformatted into two divisions with the intention of creating a better standard of play. Unfortunately, the three-up and three-down relegation system led to too much movement between the Counties and was effectively reduced to a two-up and two-down system to make it simpler and cause less confusion (Hignell, 2004). Nevertheless, the interest the divisional structure was intended to create did not occur. In light of the Twenty (20) case careful management of the sport and good market research can provide some insight into what can be done, but some big questions remain for the Counties. What purpose does the County Championship serve? With the success of the academies in developing talent is the four-day game still relevant as a viable product? County cricket suffers from a litany of players who may never make it to the international elite level or even players who remain employed beyond their use by date because they offer a safe performance. Although the traditionalists may prefer the four-day contest a return to the three-day competition may reduce the number of total days played and in effect lower total operating costs. To be more revolutionary should county cricket consider using the long form of the game as an under-19 or under-25 competition? Lewis believes this would provide the traditionalists with a competition based on the best talent in their County associations while fostering an avenue for development for those who do not make, or wish to join, the academies (Personal Communication, January 2007).

The domestic one-day competitions offered have also been repositioned, but in their case from regional formats to divisions. The cricketing authorities attempted numerous changes to reinvent their various products. It could be argued that these changes have cluttered and confused the domestic schedule, creating a weaker product overall and one which is less attractive to the new enthusiast provided by the Twenty-20. At the time of writing the failure to source a tournament sponsor for the 50 over competition (formerly Gillette/Nat West/C&G Tournament) for 2007 shows that the general upsurge in cricketing interest does not always lead to difficult business tasks becoming simple.

Hignell (2004) even proposes a move away from the county format to a series of city-based teams. The formation of county cricket is a bygone product based around demarcation lines that have shifted and lost relevance in modern Britain. Although revolutionary, this idea may take into better account the changing customer needs, with the increasing importance of the customer as a stakeholder these changes may be sensible. However, the structural changes required would mean the Counties agreeing to their discontinuance and after the success of the Twenty-20 competition this seems unlikely. The task for the managers in this case is to increase their levels of market research. What do the traditional members want? What policies on the blooding of young talent would they accept? As with the inception of the Twenty-20 competition involving stakeholders in the future of the game could be beneficial in the long term.

The case highlights a very successful initiative that has gone from strength to strength since inception in 2003. There are many benefits that have accrued to English county cricket but importantly the organization and their customers have been able to share the value created, reinforcing this success. Counties have gained new crowds, renewed interest in the sport and sports fans have gained a new, highly sociable, form of sporting entertainment. The benefits of effective market research were clear, where World Series Cricket opened to low crowds and minimal support the foundation of the Twenty-20 has been strong support and interest from the outset. The lesson here is that the former was created as a product-led initiative whereas the latter was consumer-led from the outset.

The main challenge facing the County associations is converting those attracted to the sport through Twenty-20 into other forms of the game. The conversion of new fans and supporters has created a wealth of academic research in the past, the consideration of some of this research would be beneficial to the County associations. The change in audience may warrant a fresh look at the communication media available to do this. The increasing number of ticket sales for Twenty-20 matches from the County Internet sites suggests an audience competent and highly trusting of information technology. Media campaigns in partnerships with popular cricket websites such as www. cricinfo.com or www.stickcricket.com may be useful for convincing those that have experienced Twenty-20 to partake in the other cricket products on offer.

There has been evidence provided by various sources within the Counties that traditionalists are staying away from the Twenty-20 Cup. Although the invention of limited over cricket in the 1960s created similar concerns among traditionalists, some facts are quite interesting. Essex has noted that only 10 per cent of the crowd for Twenty-20 matches are members, whereas Nottinghamshire noted 33 per cent of members attending the matches. It has also been noted that the matches are characterized by a 'kind of football mentality'. Although the new market segments are extremely valuable to the County coffers it is very early to be dismissive of traditional supporters.

Indeed recent research by Bennett et al. (2007) confirmed that nostalgia and patriotism are still strong motives for the support of English cricket, expressed through viewership of the 2005 Ashes series. Interestingly, these motives were consistent across age highlighting that traditional motives may not yet be obsolete. It would also be unwise to think that new methods of media communication cannot be used for traditional supporters, especially those who qualify as silver surfers. This group have proven their continued loyalty to the sport, commercial business sensibilities may deem the longer game unworkable but rejuvenation of an old product may reduce its over-heads and provide an attractive offering for an important stakeholder group.

Since 2005, there has been a proliferation of international Twenty-20 matches being staged. These matches have been very successful around the world in terms of gate receipts and television broadcasts. Connor (2003) states that such a proliferation is in the fans interest but while it may work very well for Women's cricket in general terms the game was 'invented'[5] for English domes-tic cricket as a way of increasing the County revenues. By increasing the supply of matches internationally this may reduce the demand for the domestic com-petition and the Counties may revert to their pre-Twenty-20 positions where there is an over-reliance on central funding. The International Cricket Council (ICC) is even considering a Twenty-20 World Cup. The ICC's move to formal-ize this will add another property to their existing portfolio but there must be consideration placed on preventing an over-supply of the game. In Australian and New Zealand domestic cricket there are successful tournaments featuring the Twenty-20 format. The possibility of a County/District Twenty-20 World Cup might prevent this saturation from occurring and provide the funds for continued County development. Failure to address this may devalue the domestic competitions and slay the goose that lays the golden egg. In the inter-ests of sustainability this needs to be addressed.

A key factor contributing to the success of the Twenty-20 was the increased profile the tournament received through multiple media chan-nels and partnerships. This success of local and national initiatives also fos-tered the creation of a winning mindset within county cricket. This wining mindset should not be dismissed too lightly. For the first time in recent his-tory the cricketing authorities were seen as innovative and flexible in their management approach. Centrally determined guidelines were laid down allowing for a great deal of local innovation in what was an unapologetic approach. They realized that the Twenty-20 game would disenfranchise some traditionalists but a policy of 'for the greater good' determined the strategy.

---

[5]The advent of a 20 over a side competition is actually nothing new in local club cricket, but as there is more to the event than the match itself hence the term invented can be adopted.

Furthermore the success of the Twenty-20 has also proven that the Counties can revolutionize the way they manage their regions. Studies investigating innovation have found that less direct, centralized controls can lead to a greater capacity for innovation. The local level campaigns designed to suit local needs have been highly creative and successful. Counties are now even looking to diversify their revenue sources. Cuff (2006) commented that Kent were holding an Elton John concert that was expected to add £50,000 to the County's coffers, this combined with their successful sporting goods shop allow Kent to draw revenues from their own initiative, not ECB hand-outs. The importance of this diversification cannot be over-stated as the ECB's 2005 strategic plan (*Building Partnerships*) stated that over the next few years the Counties would see a reduction in the overall percentage of revenue being distributed to the regions. Hence, the future for the Counties is to innovate or to stagnate, but with the examples seen so far it appears as if the former will prevail.

Case Questions

1 How can the cricketing authorities actively encourage Twenty-20 spectators to consider the other sporting products that it offers, that is how can it convert Twenty-20 fans to other forms of the game?
2 Should the cricketing authorities act to bring traditionalists 'into the fold' of Twenty-20 cricket?
3 Do you agree with sporting organizations offering concerts and non-sporting entertainment as ways to increase revenue? Would it alter your perception of the organization? In what way?
4 What implications do you feel the proliferation of international Twenty-20 matches will have on the domestic cricket?
5 Will the sale of the broadcasting rights to a satellite broadcaster be detrimental to the general interest in English county cricket? Try to detail for and against arguments to consider this point.

Case Resources

Bennett, R., Ali-Choudhury, R. and Mousley, W. (2007). Television viewers' motivations to follow the 2005 Ashes Test Series: Implications for the rebranding of English cricket. *Journal of Product and Brand Management* (in press). **16**(1), 23–37.
Britcher, C. (2003). Bite's Twenty-20 vision. *Sport Business* [Online]. Accessed at http://www.sportbusiness.com/news/index?news_item_id=151197 on 1 August 2003.
Connor, C. (2003). Shortened game can reap reward in long run. *The Observer* [Online]. Accessed at http://observer.guardian.co.uk/print/0,,4823907-102283,00.html on 15 May 2006.

Cuff, A. (2006). Is Elton John the saviour of county cricket? *The Guardian* [Online]. Accessed at http://sport.guardian.co.uk/print/0,,329471194-108356,00.html on 5 May 2005.

England and Wales Cricket Board (1997). *Raising the Standard*. ECB, London.

England and Wales Cricket Board (2005). *Building Partnerships*. ECB, London.

Gillis, R. (2005). Cricket moves up the order. *Marketing*, 20 July, pp. 30–32.

Harrison, T. (2004). Twenty-20 cricket. *From Conception to Reality: A Marketing Challenge*. Paper presented at Think! Sponsorship Seminar, 13 May 2004.

Henderson, J. (2003). Instant cricket takes off. *The Observer* [Online]. Accessed at http://observer.guardian.co.uk/print/0,,4823937-102283,00.html on 15 May 2006.

Hignell, A. (2004). England and its cricketscape: In decline or on the up? in Majumdar, B. and Mangan, J.A. (Eds.), *Cricketing Cultures in Conflict: World Cup 2003*. pp. 33–50. Routledge: London.

Hopwood, M. (2005). The sport integrated marketing communications mix, in Chadwick, S. and Beech, J. (Eds.), *The Marketing of Sports*. pp. 213–238. FT Prentice Hall: London.

Malcolm, D. (2006). *A New England? Cricket, the Ashes and National Identity*. Paper presented at Birkbeck Sport Business Seminar Series, 8 February 2006.

McDonald, I. and Ugra, S. (1998). *Anyone for Cricket? Equal Opportunities and Changing Cricket Cultures in Essex and East London*. Centre for Sport Development Research, Roehampton Institute, London.

Mintel (2005). *Spectator Sports – April 2005*. Mintel Market Research, London.

Mintel (2006). *Cricket and Rugby – February 2006*. Mintel Market Research, London.

Mullin, B.J., Hardy, S. and Sutton, W. (1993) *Sport Marketing*. Human Kinetics Publishers, Champaign, IL.

Rawling, J. (2003). Too many games are seen only by a few pensioners. *The Guardian* [Online]. Accessed at http://sport.guardian.co.uk/print/0,4740144-108356,00.html on 15 May 2006.

Further Information

General Cricket Websites of Relevance
http://www.ecb.co.uk
http://uk.cricinfo.com/db/NATIONAL/ENG/Twenty20/
http://en.wikipedia.org/wiki/Twenty20

Twenty-20 Websites of Note
http://www.cricket.com.au/default.aspx?s=kfcTwenty20bigbash0607
http://en.wikipedia.org/wiki/Stanford_20/20
http://en.wikipedia.org/wiki/Twenty20_World_Championship

Case

9

Manchester United: the commercial development of a global football brand

Sean Hamil

Case Focus

The case examines the history and commercial development of Manchester United Football Club in the UK as it has developed into the world's leading international football brand.

Keywords

- Operating environment
- Commercial strategy
- Marketing strategy
- Brand management
- Sponsorship

Case Summary

Manchester United is one the greatest club names in world football. Its reputation derives firstly from its formidable record of achievement on the field of play from the early 1960s onwards. In 1968 it became the first English club to win the European Cup; and in the more recent era has won the English Premier League 9 out of 15 times since the competition's inception in 1992/1993, also winning the European Champions League in 1999. Secondly, Manchester United enjoys an iconic status with its supporters. The origins of this status lie in the way in which it's most celebrated manager, Sir Matt Busby, rebuilt his team after a tragic air crash at Munich Airport in 1958 that left eight players dead and many others seriously injured. Busby's re-fashioned team then become associated with the free spirit which characterized the liberal social changes in Western Europe and North America of the 1960s, notably embodied in the playing style of the team's flamboyant and mercurial forward George Best; a spirit which was reflected in the team's, the so-called Red Devils, buccaneering attacking style of play which saw Best supported by other equally extraordinary, attacking players such as Bobby Charlton and Denis Law. The name of Manchester United continues to be associated with the romance of the team of that period, and this has become a critical factor in the make-up in the modern Manchester United brand. Many would argue that this is in fact one of the key reasons why it remains England's best supported team with average attendances in the 2006/2007 in excess of 75,000 for every league game. Thirdly, since it became the first English football club to float on the London Stock Exchange in 1991, Manchester United has consistently been Europe's most innovative club in terms of the development of its commercial strategy, and continues to be its most profitable. The BSkyB pay-TV broadcasting company unsuccessfully tried to take over the company in 1999. In 2005 it was these successful commercial attributes which led the Glazer family, owners of the Tampa Bay Buccaneers National Football League (NFL) American football franchise to buy Manchester United and de-list it from the stock exchange. This case examines how this successful commercial strategy was developed by the Board of Manchester United Plc from the mid-1990s onwards, and examines its prospects for continued success given that under the ownership of the Glazers, Manchester United has moved from being debt-free to carrying very significant borrowings on its balance sheet which demand very high interest servicing payments each financial year; and has adopted an aggressively commercial approach to its relationship with the club's supporters which critics argue may erode the traditional strength of the brand in the medium term and ultimately threaten revenues in the long term.

Case Elements

A Short Sporting History

The key starting point in the modern history of Manchester United is the tragedy of the Munich air disaster of 1958. The team, along with their Manager Matt Busby, were returning from a European Cup match in Belgrade (in the part of the former Yugoslavia that is now Serbia) when their plane crashed during a re-fuelling stop in Munich, Germany, in bad weather. Eight members of an exciting and promising young team, the so-called Busby Babes, died in the crash along with 15 other passengers, with many others seriously injured including the manager himself Matt Busby. The manner in which the mercurial Busby, out of this extraordinary tragedy, then refashioned his playing squad team to produce the iconic United team of the 1960s captured the imagination of the English footballing public but also their sympathy, as Busby triumphed over adversity. The team went on to win the fore-runner to the Premier League, the Football League 1st Division, in 1964/1965 and 1966/1967; and then became the first English team to win the European Cup in 1968 against Benfica of Portugal who included the great Eusebio amongst their players. Earlier in 1966, leading Manchester United players Bobby Charlton and Nobby Stiles had been key figures in England's World Cup winning team becoming national heroes in the process.

So, in the 1960s Manchester United were winning, but they were also winning with some style. The team was packed with exciting attacking players such as Bobby Charlton, Dennis Law, and George Best, all three of whom won the European Footballer of the Year award during this decade. And this was reflected in a buccaneering style of play full of flair which contrasted strongly with the defensive-minded 'catenaccio' approach favoured by the leading Italian teams of the era. Perhaps partly as a result of their style of play Busby's team also became associated with the free spirit with which the liberal social changes of the 1960s are associated in Western Europe and North America. However, another critical factor was the extravagant 'film star/pop idol' lifestyle of George Best, who became known as the 'fifth Beatle' and was the first footballer to cross over into the realm of popular entertainment, as well as sporting, icon making front page as well as back page news with his off-the-field exploits. The 'fifth Beatle' observation was a reference to the world's first global pop music phenomenon, the Liverpool band the Beatles, and illustrates the scale of Best's impact beyond the purely sporting arena. Blazing a trail that would later be followed much more successfully and lucratively by David Beckham, Best, for example, dabbled in fashion modelling and retailing.

Because of his extraordinary ability on the football field, Best created a bond with the Manchester United supporters that was never broken. And his mentor Matt Busby enjoyed a similar place in the heart of supporters' affection and respect. Knighted for his services to football a statue to Sir Matt Busby was erected outside United's Old Trafford ground and a road leading to the ground renamed Sir Matt Busby Way as Manchester United as an institution paid homage to their great manager following his death in 1994. To this day the statue is focal point for fans attending the stadium, a place where families of supporters gather to have their pictures taken. Critically, this serves to illustrate that the Manchester United 'brand' does not derive from a purely sporting or entertainment root, but has much more complex origins in how supporters define themselves and their club in social identity terms, which both make the brand much more difficult to replicate by competitors but also much more complex to sustain in the era of increasing commercialization at the beginning of the 21st century. A significant advantage of the special loyalty engendered towards the United brand by the hard core of its supporters, the so-called 'fan equity', is that it does not require consistent success on the field to sustain it. It therefore works to ensure a consistent income stream from match-day attendance even when the team is performing poorly. By way of example, after Busby's retirement in 1969 (he briefly returned as manager in 1971) the club's performance on the field of play went into decline, and United were actually relegated to the Football League 2nd Division in 1973/1974. Despite this, the club's grip on the loyalty of its supporters remained un-eroded and the team continued to attract average crowds of over 50,000 throughout this period. Manchester United returned to the 1st Division at the first attempt, but they were not to enjoy significant on-field success again until the 1990/1991 season when they defeated FC Barcelona in the final of the European Cup Winners Cup. In 1991 the owners of the club also floated it on the London Stock Exchange in order to raise new capital to develop the company (also laying the ground for the enrichment of many of the existing owners, notably Martin Edwards the company chairman, in the process); this also allowed supporters of Manchester United to buy shares in their club and many thousands did.

In 1986 United appointed a new manager; Alex Ferguson. Having at his disposal much more constrained resources than his main rivals Ferguson had enjoyed much success in Scotland as manager of Aberdeen, where he had succeeded in three times breaking the stranglehold on the Scottish 1st Division by Glasgow giants Celtic and Rangers, and had also achieved European honours winning the Cup Winners Cup in 1982/1983 against Real Madrid. Ferguson struggled in his first years in charge at United. However, in November 1992 the inspired transfer of the totemic Frenchman Eric Cantona provided the spark which saw United win their first top division English championship (now re-branded the FA Premier League) in the 1992/1993 season since 1966/1967. The temperamental but flamboyant and highly gifted Cantona drew immediate comparisons with the playing personality of George Best. Cantona thus fitted immediately into the buccaneering playing myth with which United are associated, the myth which has come to influence so strongly the romantic dimension of the Manchester United brand.

Manchester United then embarked on an unprecedented period of dominance on the playing field in English football. Since the 1992/1993 season they have won the Premier League nine times, the FA Cup four times, and the European Champions League once. In that time they have never featured outside the top three in the Premiership, thus guaranteeing permanent entry into the lucrative European Champions League. Whilst Ferguson's teams have been characterized by well-organized and disciplined team performances, individual and iconic performers have emerged in the manner of Best, Law and Charlton; notably Ryan Giggs, Roy Keane, and most critically David Beckham. Whether by accident or design the success of United as a sporting brand has benefited in this most recent era not just from the playing success on the field, but also from the intense non-sporting media attention which has developed around individual players in the team, but most notably around Beckham (who has gone on to become a global entertainment brand in his own right) and which has served to reflect back positively on Manchester United as a sporting brand. But the images of these players have themselves benefited from playing in the Manchester United colours, because of the iconic status of Manchester United as not just an English footballing institution but also a global one; an institution that stands for all that is exciting and great about the game of football in the popular sporting imagination.

It is interesting to note that Beckham, though he came from East London, came from a Manchester United-supporting family. This underlines how the qualities of sporting excellence and romance that United as a football club, and by extension as a commercial business brand, had acquired in the years following the Munich air disaster in 1958 exercised a pull on football supporters, and potential players, well beyond United's Manchester, or indeed north west of England, base. So whilst these qualities might be intangible and thus difficult to define, their possession by Manchester United did deliver very tangible benefits in regard to its ability to attract and retain key sporting talent.

In parallel with its sporting success over the 1992–2005 period Manchester United enjoyed a period of unprecedented commercial success as it became the world's most profitable football club. This financial success was underpinned by the historic strength of its brand going back to its roots in the Munich air disaster and the iconic team of the 1960s, by 13 years of consistent success on the field of play at the highest level, and by continuing to play a style of attacking football which could accommodate gifted individualists like Cantona, Keane and Beckham which was popular with the wider football watching public and not just supporters of United. However, a fourth critical element in United's success over this period was that, since it had become the first English football club to float on the London Stock Exchange in 1991, Manchester United had consistently been Europe's most innovative club in terms of the development of its commercial strategy. In 2005 it was these successful commercial attributes which led the Glazer family, owners of the Tampa Bay Buccaneers NFL American football franchise, to buy Manchester United Plc and de-list it from the stock exchange.

A Short Financial History[1]

Since the foundation of the Premier League in the 1992/1993 season Manchester United has consistently been the strongest English club financially both in terms of financial turnover and pre-tax profit, and amongst the top five clubs in Europe. In fact it is one of only four clubs who were in the Premier League in the 2005/2006 season who have made a cumulative pre-tax profit over the previous 10 seasons; the other clubs are Arsenal, Tottenham Hotspur and West Bromwich Albion. What this illustrates is that despite the phenomenal success of the English Premier League as a sporting spectacle and as a generator of revenues it has signally failed to deliver pre-tax profits for the majority of the owners of its clubs. Even allowing for Chelsea's huge pre-tax losses the majority of Premier League clubs are either losing money or marginally profitable. The key exceptions are Manchester United and Arsenal who made cumulative pre-tax profits for the two-year 2004–2006 period of £41.6 million and £35.2 million, respectively (Table 9.1).

Manchester United derives its income from three key sources: match-day (attendances and related expenditure), broadcasting (mainly revenue derived from BSkyB's collective selling broadcasting deal with the Premier League; and revenue derived from United's share of broadcasting income from the European Champions League administered by European football's governing body UEFA), and commercial (mainly sponsorship and related

Table 9.1 Pre-tax profit of the combined Premier League clubs and Manchester United

	2005/2006 (million)	2004/2005 (million)	2003/2004 (million)	2002/2003 (million)
Premier League clubs total	−£69	−£78	−£128	−£153
Manchester United Plc	£30.8	£10.8	£27.9	£39.3

Source: Deloitte (2002–2007) *Annual Reviews of Football Finance*

---

[1] The following analysis draws extensively on statistical analysis contained in various recent editions of the Deloitte *Annual Review of Football Finance*. The *Review* should be compulsory reading for anyone, student or otherwise, seeking to understand the financial dynamics of the English and European football industry.

commercial activity). Prior to the inception of the Premier League in 1992/1993 the critical source of revenue for all English football clubs including United was matchday income. However, since that time English football's leading clubs, and particularly Manchester United, have dramatically increased income from the latter two sources. Table 9.2 illustrates the split between the three revenue streams in the 2004/2005 and 2005/2006 seasons.

What this illustrates is that all three sources are now of great importance in driving club revenue and so to remain commercially successful Manchester United must be constantly seeking to improve performance in each area. Over the last 15 years Manchester United has been able to achieve this. The key factors that have driven this success are as follows.

Firstly, it has been the most successful club on the playing field, never having been out of the top three places in the last 15 seasons. The next most successful clubs are Arsenal, Liverpool, Chelsea and Newcastle United. None of them can match this level of consistent achievement.

Success on the field directly drives higher income because United take a greater share of TV revenue awarded on the basis of higher league placing. And of course higher league placed clubs get larger TV appearance money through the BSkyB broadcasting deal because their games are broadcast more regularly. Since its inception Manchester United has been the highest grossing club in the Premiership from the BSkyB broadcasting deal. Table 9.3 illustrates their revenue from the deal in the last two seasons (2005/2006 and 2006/2007) when compared to their main competitors.

Table 9.2 Manchester United sources of revenue

	2005/2006	*2004/2005*
Matchday	£71.3 million – 43%	£69.3 million – 42%
Broadcasting	£45.5 million – 27%	£48.4 million – 29%
Commercial	£51 million – 30%	£48.7 million – 29%

Source: Deloitte (2006 and 2007). Football Money League

Table 9.3 Premier League TV income

	2006/2007 (million)	*2005/2006 (million)*
Manchester United	£32.1	£30.7
Chelsea	£30.9	£30.4
Arsenal	£28.9	£28.7
Liverpool	£28.4	£28.8
Newcastle United	£21.2	£24.2

Source: Deloitte (2007). *Annual Review of Football Finance*

In addition Manchester United derives significant TV income from participating in the European Champions League. Even in a disappointing season such as 2005/2006 when United failed to graduate from the qualifying group stage the club still derived £9.6 million from its participation in the competition. By way of comparison, Arsenal, who reached the final against Barcelona, derived £24 million. This serves to underline the critical importance of first, qualifying for the Champions League; and secondly, progressing to the knock-out stages of the competition, in terms of driving TV broadcasting related revenue. It also serves to underline the critical importance of maintaining a strong playing squad led by an effective manager. Reducing the wage bill too significantly in the pursuit of profit can undermine playing performance and hence financial turnover leading in turn to the erosion of any available financial surplus.

And of course success on the field drives the price that the club can generate from corporate sponsors as playing success also drives the level of exposure on TV, which is a key factor for consideration by potential sponsors.

The second key factor driving Manchester United's financial success, as Table 9.4 illustrates, is that it has consistently enjoyed a higher financial turnover than its main rivals, a reflection of its greater commercial strength and the unique attractiveness of its brand. It is the differential in turnover rather than the absolute amount which is of critical importance as is explained below.

In part Manchester United's persistent success in enjoying the highest financial turnover in the Premiership reflects the fact that the club has a much higher ground capacity which it consistently fills with sell-out crowds. In the 2006/2007 season, after the latest ground expansion was completed, it had a stadium capacity of 76,000, well ahead of its nearest rival Arsenal who had a capacity of 60,000 in the new Emirates stadium at Ashburton Grove in North London. This allows United to drive a much higher matchday income than any other club in the Premier League.

It is also the case that United's ability to fill its ground is a reflection of the historical strength of its brand going back to Sir Matt Busby's team of the 1960s. This is reflected in the fact that the club draws spectators from

Table 9.4 Average league attendances

	2006/2007	2005/2006
Manchester United	75,826	68,764
Chelsea	41,541	41,901
Arsenal	60,045	38,184
Liverpool	43,561	44,236
Newcastle United	50,686	52,032

Source: http://soccernet.espn.go.com/stats/attendance?league=eng.
1&year=2006&

across the UK as well as abroad in addition to those from its North West of England base.

As outlined above, Manchester United is also the biggest net beneficiary from the BSkyB TV deal in the English Premier League; and turnover is also driven by consistent participation in the Champions League.

Critically, Manchester United has also consistently had the highest commercial income of any English club. For example, it generated £51 million from this source in 2005/2006 compared to £42.5 million at Chelsea, Liverpool at £39.3 million, Arsenal at £34 million and Newcastle United at £27.9 million. A key sponsorship relationship is with sportswear company Nike, who manage the club's merchandising operation as part of a £303 million 13-year partnership deal established in 2002. The size of this deal is in itself a reflection of the market power of Manchester United's brand; and the perception that it has global brand recognition. Again the roots of this brand recognition lie in the 1960s in the Busby-managed team of Best, Law and Charlton; in a perception that Manchester United embodies what is best about the beautiful game in terms of the style of play they adopt and the cultural roots from which the club was formed.

And finally, Manchester United has, since the foundation of the Premier League, had the ability to pay the highest wage bill and spend the most on player transfers of any Premier League club until the takeover of Chelsea by Roman Abramovich led to a dramatic acceleration in that club's expenditure in the 2004/2005 season. United has been able to do this because it has had a much higher financial turnover than any other Premiership club. For example, the financial turnover of United in the five years from 2001/2002 to 2005/2006 was 30 per cent higher than that of its nearest rival Chelsea (see Table 9.5). This extraordinary ability to drive revenue again reflects the underlying strength of its brand; its ability to drive the highest attendances in the league, attract a fanbase which is increasing global and not just English or indeed Mancunian, secure the most lucrative sponsorship contracts in the Premier League, and attract the best playing and managerial talent which in turn drives success on the field of play. And of course

Table 9.5 Financial performance 2001/2002–2005/2006 complete pre-tax profit

	Turnover (million)	Total wages/ wages-turnover ratio (million)	Net transfer income (million)	Pre-tax profit (million)
Manchester United	£821.6	£389.6/47.4%	−£78.6	£141.2
Chelsea	£631.4	£448.1/71%	−£372.5	−£351.4
Arsenal	£557.4	£340.9/61%	−£52.6	£27.9
Liverpool	£539.9	£309.2/57%	−£84.3	−£4.9
Newcastle United	£428.1	£224.5/52%	−£55.4	−£5.9

Source: Deloitte (2002–2007). *Annual Review of Football Finance*

consistent success on the field in itself drives a virtuous circle as playing success means a higher return from TV income, larger and more extensive sponsorship and merchandising deals and sales, consistent sell-outs at home fixtures, and finally a continued expansion in the potential global fanbase whose interest may be converted into potential future revenues through sales of Manchester United-branded goods and services.

Critically it allows United to fund expenditure on wages and transfers out of income, thus ensuring a pre-tax profit can be made, and not out of debt or the personal resources of shareholders, the latter being the case at Chelsea where Roman Abramovich has been running Chelsea at a very significant loss since he took over the club. By way of example, in the two-year period 2004–2006, whilst Manchester United made a very respectable pre-tax profit of £41.6 million, Chelsea made a pre-tax loss of –£220.7 million.

The critical advantage of having the highest financial turnover in the Premier League is that United is able to outbid all the other clubs (with the current exception of Chelsea) for playing talent (most recently over the 2001/2002–2005/2006 period.) This ensures that a very competitive playing squad is maintained, which is essential to ensure continued success on the pitch, and yet still retain a conservative wages-to-turnover ratio of 45 per cent over the period. A true measure of this achievement is that the leading sports business consultants Deloitte recommend a ratio figure of no more than 60 per cent. It is only by maintaining a disciplined approach to the wages-to-turnover ratio that any profit can be retained after expenditure on players' wages and transfer fees. It is exactly this ability to make significant pre-tax profit whilst remaining competitive on the field of play, a unique combination of attributes in the Premier League, that attracted the interest of the Glazer family. The critical achievement of Manchester United, first over the 1992–2005 period, and at least for the first year under the Glazer takeover in 2005/2006, is that it has been able to attain the holy grail of being both successful on the field of play whilst also delivering a healthy pre-tax profit; a feat that has been rarity in the football industry across Europe. It has achieved this because of the sophisticated way it has developed its brand since the establishment of the Premier League; but also because, due to an accident of history, the board of Manchester United Plc inherited an extraordinarily valuable sporting asset from the Busby era in the late 1950s and 1960s strongly rooted in the hearts as well as minds of its supporters. The 'brand' of Manchester United has been as much about romance as it has been about playing prowess.

Case Diagnosis

Strategic Development

Manchester United has been unusual in the context of football clubs globally, in that since its stock market flotation in 1991, it has explicitly focused on building a business in addition to the traditional focus of pursuing success on the pitch at any price. Whilst all football clubs in England are structured as limited companies, historically very few have made a profit at the pre-tax level; in fact the industry is characterized by chronic loss-making. It was this phenomenon that led multi-millionaire businessman Sir Alan Sugar (now made famous in the UK by his role in the hugely popular *The Apprentice* TV reality show) to sell his controlling interest in North London's Tottenham Hotspur, notoriously referring to football's 'prune juice effect' where increasing revenues from television deals went straight through the company balance sheet to be paid out in increased players' wages as club managements chased success on the field by bidding for new playing talent. (Though, as noted above, Tottenham have been one of only four clubs to have been in the Premier League to at least break-even over the 1995/1996–2005/2006 period). The reason for this is that almost all have historically prioritized success on the field (utility maximization) over profit maximization. By contrast Manchester United has consistently made a pre-tax profit over this period whilst also being successful on the field.

Manchester United has been able to achieve the very difficult task of being consistent profitable by building on the traditional strengths of the United brand through a commercial development strategy with five key sub-strategies which the board of Manchester United Plc identified in the company's 2004 *Annual Report*:

1 Maintaining playing success.
2 Treating fans as customers.
3 Leveraging the global brand.
4 Developing media rights.
5 Maximizing the use of Old Trafford football ground.

Each sub-strategy interacted with and re-inforced the others to influence the overall direction of the company. The five sub-strategies worked as follows.

Maintaining Playing Success

Success in professional sports is ultimately determined by winning on the field of play. Playing success underpins all other strategic plans as it is success on the field that drives customer interest outside the core fan group amongst (1) occasional match attendees, (2) television viewers both domestic but particularly international and (3) critically sponsors. Whilst the hard core of any English football team will tolerate short periods of poor team performance, as when Manchester United were relegated to the Football League 2nd Division for the 1974/1975 season and crowds were unimpaired, in the medium term it is critical that any team which wishes to build a growing supporter base must enjoy a consistent level of success of playing success. It is also the case that in European football it is absolutely critical that any club wishing to compete at the highest level must consistently qualify for European club competition. And in professional sport the likeli-hood of success is critically dependent on the quality of the playing squad of an individual team, and in turn by the quality of its manager and his coaching staff. However, because the labour market for talent in football is highly competitive the danger for all football clubs is that they may over-pay for talent in an auction to the extent that they become unprofitable. This was the case with one of the great names of English Football Leeds United, who won the English 1st Division as recently as 1991/1992, and were European Champions League semi-finalists in 2000/2001. Leeds sub-sequently stumbled into financial collapse as poor performance on the field of play and consequent decline in revenues meant that they were unable to cover the cost of loans taken out to acquire and retain underperform-ing playing talent. Leeds United started the 2007/2008 season in Division 1 of the Championship, two divisions below the Premier League, following another financial collapse at the end of the 2006/2007 season and a conse-quent spell in financial administration.

Manchester United was able to address the challenge of sustaining the quality of the playing squad whilst remaining financially disciplined in five key ways:

1 The club developed an excellent youth development structure from which key players like David Beckham, Paul Scholes, Ryan Giggs and Gary Neville graduated to the first team. This had the effect of signifi-cantly reducing the size of the transfer budget necessary to augment home-grown talent in the playing squad.
2 The fact that United had the highest financial turnover of any English club due to its strong domestic gate receipts, consistent qualification for European club competition, high media and commercial receipts reflect-ing its consistent playing success and the overall strength of its brand, meant that United could (as was discussed above) both outbid most other English clubs for talent where necessary, as in the case of Wayne Rooney and Ronaldo, but still remain profitable at the pre-tax level.
3 United remained committed to a disciplined approach to wages policy aiming to pay no more than a ratio of 50 per cent wages to turnover. But because United had the highest financial turnover of any club in the Premier League, even at a conservative 45 per cent wages-to-turnover ratio over the 2001/2002–2005/2006 period its salary packages for key playing staff remained competitive against other Premiership clubs with the possible exception of Chelsea.
4 United constructed a training facility at Carrington in Cheshire which set new standards for an English club.
5 Critical to the maintenance of playing success in any football team is the role of the manager. In Sir Alex Ferguson Manchester United have clearly had one of the greatest of his generation and have worked hard to retain his services. A critical strategic challenge will come when he decides to retire.

In addition, and tellingly, Manchester United explicitly acknowledged that playing style remains an important element in the brand mix, as is noted in the 2004 *Annual Report*:

> *'Going forward we will continue to invest in our squad and play our sport in the proper spirit and style for which the Club has become famous'*.

This was not mere rhetoric. In fact it was a formal recognition by the board of directors that a flamboyant attacking style of play was a critical element in the successful dynamic (i.e. the Manchester United brand). This legacy of the Busby era remained a key factor which continued to draw new supporters to the football team 40 years on at the beginning of the 21st century.

Treating Fans As Customers

One of the greatest strengths of Manchester United has been the fact that it has been the best supported team in England both in terms of the numbers attending live matches, but also in terms of the number of 'armchair' fans who claim some kind of affinity with the club. The leading consultants to the sports industry Deloitte estimate that Manchester United have 75 million fans worldwide. A key element of Manchester United's strategy has been to find ways in which to encourage both groups to spend more on United-related goods and services in a way which enabled them to demonstrate their affinity with the club. Manchester United was able to address this challenge in the following key ways:

- By expanding the range of goods and services available for purchase on matchdays.
- By developing a membership scheme – 'One United' – through which anyone with an affinity to the club could purchase United-branded goods and services, or those from partner companies of United, notably financial services products (through Manchester United Finance supporters can purchase products such as credit cards) and mobile phones.
- By selling members of 'One United' subscriptions to a range of Manchester United-branded media services such as the club's dedicated TV channel MUTV, text messaging services, etc.

Through the ongoing development of a Customer Relationship Management (CRM) system (which had 25,88,000 records in 2004) United saw opportunities to grow its relationship with its millions of fans worldwide and sell them products and services. Whilst many of these services are embryonic the Board of Manchester United Plc believed that they did offer the hope of significant revenues in the future. And it is has been reported that it was a confidence amongst the Glazer family that they could drive this particular revenue more aggressively, particularly in the various markets of the South East Asia pacific rim and China, which was a key element in the business plan that underpinned their takeover of Manchester United in 2005.

Leveraging the Global Brand

A critical source of commercial revenue for Manchester United comes from sponsorship from major companies who wish to partner with Manchester United in order to leverage off the United brand. In 2007 the two key sponsors were Nike and the AIG insurance company; there are also a tier of lower level 'platinum' sponsors. As mentioned above, Nike manages United's merchandising operation and this would appear to have been particularly successful, for example United reported in its 2004 *Annual Report* that it had sold 3.8 million replica shirts in the first 22 months of agreement with Nike. In 2006/2007 AIG replaced Vodafone as United's main shirt sponsor in a four-year deal worth a reported £14.1 million a season, an increase of over 50 per cent compared to the previous deal with Vodafone, and the most lucrative sponsorship deal in the Premier League by a wide margin.

Once again it is important to remember that the underlying strength of the United brand has its origins in the Busby team of the 1960s and that this brand has now been developed and extended through the extraordinary success on the field enjoyed since the inception of the Premier League. Sponsors want to be associated with winning teams with global reach. For the last 15 years United has offered both attributes.

Developing Media Rights

The key source of revenue from media rights continues to be derived from United's share of the BSkyB Premier League broadcasting deal and Champions League participation.

From 2007/2008 a new three-year Premier League broadcasting deal commences which guarantees all participating clubs a significantly higher income. BSkyB no longer has a monopoly with Setanta Sports winning the rights to a minority of the broadcasting rights. Between them BSkyB and Setanta paid a total of £1.7 billion, a two-thirds increase on the previous deal. The BBC also paid a 63 per cent increase for the right to broadcast highlights (£171.6 million). BSkyB and BT agreed to jointly pay £84.3 million for delayed television rights to 242 games (i.e. the right to broadcast them in full on television and over the internet).

Moreover, as Deloitte outlined in their 2007 *Annual Review of Football Finance*, a critical aspect of the deal was the almost doubling of annual rights values for TV markets outside the UK and Ireland to £208 million per annum over the 2007–2010 period from £107 million per annum over the 2004–2007 period. Fifty-five per cent of this revenue is derived from broadcasting rights in Asian TV markets, and 9 per cent in the Middle East. This underlines the growth in popularity of Premier League football in these markets, and by extension the growth in popularity of Manchester United which is one of the most heavily featured clubs in the broadcasts to these markets. Nevertheless, it should be acknowledged that Manchester United has been a huge beneficiary of the success of BSkyB in promoting Premier League football as a sporting and entertainment spectacle across the world.

The overall size of the Champions League broadcasting deal is also expected to rise thus benefiting United as long the team continues to qualify for the competition.

Separately United continues to try to develop more sophisticated media products such as interactive websites which drive revenue through sponsorship, e-commerce, betting and on-demand services. It is also seeking to build subscriptions for MUTV, its in-house TV company, which is a joint venture with BSkyB and ITV.

Maximizing the Use of Old Trafford Football Ground

United's Old Trafford ground has now been expanded to become the biggest club ground in Britain with 76,000 seats. An additional 2400 corporate seats were added to the ground bringing a total of 8000. In 2006/2007 it enjoyed 99.5 per cent stadium occupancy throughout the season. The stadium also offers extensive conferencing facilities. There is also a Museum and stadium tour service.

Strategy Summary

Table 9.6 taken from the 2004 Manchester United Plc *Annual Report* provides a useful summary of how the various sub-strategies fitted within the overarching macro-strategy.

Strategic Challenges

There is no doubt that Manchester United has been an outstanding success both in playing and commercial terms over the last 15 years. However, it does now face a number of very significant strategic challenges. How the new owners of the club deal with these challenges will determine whether or not it continues on its upward curve of development, or goes on a 1970s style detour.

The Glazer Takeover and the Implications of Its Debt-Driven Structure

In 2005 Manchester United ceased to be a public limited company quoted on the London Stock Exchange following a successful takeover bid by the family of Malcolm Glazer. The multi-millionaire American businessman's takeover was achieved in the face of a very public campaign by a coalition of fans' groups that included the main United fanzines, notably *Red Issue*, the Independent Manchester United Supporters Association (IMUSA), and most critically, the independent Manchester United Supporters Trust (then known as Shareholders United – SU). The latter organization, which by the end of the campaign had over 30,000 United supporters and shareholders

Table 9.6 'Our strategic focus'

	Matchday	Media	Commercial
Maintaining playing success	League and cup success fuels demand for membership and tickets	Playing success guarantees a greater share of media pools and drives supporters to our own media business	Provides a strong foundation for relationships with our commercial partners and increases our future value to them
Treating fans as customers	Improving customer service focus in order to increase appeal of Old Trafford matchday and stadium experience and stadium expansion to provide more opportunities for fans to attend	Development of a range of integrated cross-platform media products enables fans to keep in touch with United wherever and however they want	Focusing on key markets, a set of new products and services will be developed for fans, to match their needs and requirements
Leveraging the global brand	Sell-out crowds, a world class venue, together with the new LED perimeter advertising displays, provide the strongest platform for our partner's brand presence	Global media exposure through TV, websites and mobile supports partners and develops brand awareness with fans	Our worldwide fan base underpins the value of our commercial rights and enables us to develop deeper relationships with our fans
Developing media rights	Matchday experience enhanced by exclusive content in award-winning programme, concourse TV's and stadium announcements	Exclusive club content and archive material increase appeal for our cross-platform media businesses to our global fan base	Exposure of partner's brands through club channels provides effective targeted messages to our fans internationally
Maximizing the use of Old Trafford	Implementation of electronic point of sale equipment to speed up service and increase stock and cash control in stadium	Concourse TV and radio encourages fans to spend longer at the stadium and enhances the experience	Improved food and customer service supports marketing of Old Trafford as the venue for conferences or events

Source: Manchester United Plc (2004). *Annual Report*

in membership, had started life in 1999. It had been established to represent small shareholders in the company in fighting the proposed takeover of Manchester United by the BSkyB broadcasting company. Largely due to the joint efforts of SU and IMUSA, the bid was referred to the Monopolies and Mergers Commission and ultimately rejected, an extraordinary achievement for a campaign run by a small group of volunteer football supporters on a shoestring budget. That Manchester United supporters could mobilize in this way around the issue of club ownership says a lot about the nature of the emotional investment the hard core of United supporters have in their team.

Following this victory Shareholders United decided not to disband, but rather establish a platform through which ordinary supporters of United could buy shares in the club, with the ultimate aim of acquiring control. A share-save scheme was established and several million pounds worth of investment was raised which was used to buy shares in United on behalf of supporters. Critically they feared that a new owner might fail to respect the cultural and sporting traditions of the club embodied by Sir Matt Busby and George Best. The emergence of the Glazer family, owners of the Tampa Bay Buccaneers NFL franchise, as bidders, crystallized these fears.

Moreover, it was the structure of the Glazer takeover vehicle which raised particularly heightened concerns for the independent Manchester United Supporters Trust (MUST). For the Glazer family intended to conduct a 'leveraged' buyout of the club. In layman's terms this meant that they would borrow the money to buy the club, transferring a significant proportion of the debt onto the balance sheet of the previously debt-free United after purchase; in effect they were using the future revenue streams of United to finance their own purchase of the club. The Glazers were successful in buying United using this highly debt leveraged method. But the high price they ultimately paid only served to inflate the size of the £660 million in loans they had to take on, many of which are at penal rates of interest. MUST feared that this would have the following consequences. Essentially, in order to cover their debt payments the Glazers would have to significantly curtail the budget available to the manager for playing staff, while at the same time significantly increasing the prices that United supporters would have to pay to watch their team. Even more of United's traditional supporters would be priced out of the ground further eroding the club's historical core of support who, as is widely acknowledged, drive the atmosphere at the ground; a fact recognized rather eloquently by former team captain Roy Keane who, when complaining about a lack of atmosphere at a particular game, stated that there were too many of the 'prawn sandwich brigade', shorthand for new higher income fans, in the ground there for the event rather than through their love of the team; there to be entertained rather than to invest their emotions in supporting 'their' team.

Under the new financing arrangements Manchester United are committed to paying at least £62 million a year to service the debt. This is £62 million which will not be going towards strengthening the playing squad. This can only be paid for by driving revenue at the club. In the two years since the Glazers took control of Manchester United season ticket prices have risen by 11 per cent and 14 per cent, respectively. In 2007/2008 every season ticket holder will also have to buy a ticket for every cup match, a possible extra £300 per head. As long as United continue to enjoy success on the field it is possible that they may be able to continue to drive revenue through increased ticket sales at Old Trafford. The extraordinary feat of Sir Alex Ferguson in leading United to yet another Premiership title in 2007 demonstrates that this is not impossible. The scale of his achievement is all the more impressive given he made only one significant squad signing for the 2006/2007 season; Michael Carrick from Tottenham.

However, such are the demands on revenue from the debt requirements it is clear that the challenge for even a manager of the extraordinary talent of Sir Alex Ferguson got a lot more difficult with the imposition of the Glazer's debt-financed ownership structure. This requirement to find £62 million every year to pay debt interest before any other expenditure can take place does raise a series of critical strategic questions:

- What happens when Sir Alex Ferguson retires? Successful succession management of football team managers is notoriously difficult.
- What happens if performance on the field slips? Will the new fans who have been replacing the hard core locals unable to afford a seat at Old Trafford continue to attend when the team is not sweeping all before them?
- If playing performance slips and attendances start to drop, what are the likely consequences for United's financial health? Could the ultimate disaster of a Leeds United-style implosion be a realistic possibility in a situation where, post the retirement of Sir Alex Ferguson, a new manager fails to secure Champions League qualification in a particular season, with all the consequent knock-on effect in reducing media and sponsorship revenues?

These are questions which many, not just amongst fans' groups like independent Manchester United Supporters Trust, are asking.

Football Club United of Manchester: The Real United?

Following the takeover by the Glazer family, such was the sense of disenfranchisement of one group of Manchester United supporters, that they decided that for them the United dream had died. They decided to form a supporter-owned club, Football Club United of Manchester, or FCUM; a club they could really call their own. In the words of FCUM board member Jules Spencer:

'One of the things that took hold of Old Trafford and all top football clubs was a distance between the supporters and the manager and players. As romantic as it sounds, 15 or 20 years ago you did feel a sense of attachment to what your football club was. You were part of it. That's where the sense of disillusionment comes from. It's not just about the Glazer thing'.

For the founders of FCUM the Glazer takeover was therefore simply the culmination of an alienation from their club a decade long in the brewing. Ever higher ticket prices forcing traditional supporters out of the ground, rampant commercialism, and an increasingly anaemic atmosphere at United's Old Trafford ground borne out of too many in attendance with no real emotional investment in the outcome. All contributed to a sense that Manchester United was no longer the club they grew up with. The Glazer takeover was therefore the final straw in a long process; confirmation that any sense that United was an institution that they as supporters could even claim moral ownership over was gone. It was now simply a speculative asset in the portfolio of a family of entertainment industry entrepreneurs.

Two years after they were founded FC United has been promoted twice and has started to move back up the league pyramid towards the Football league. Their strip is the classic red shirts, white shorts and black socks favoured by Manchester United in the 1970s. The club are attracting crowds of up to 3000, mostly disillusioned Manchester United supporters. Ryan Giggs's brother Rhodri was one of their most popular players in the 2006/2007 season. In their two seasons of existence FC United had not only survived, but they had prospered. More importantly, it appears that a special fan culture is beginning to develop at FCUM. As one of the founders of FCUM, Julian Coman, observed:

> *'One of the most frequent comments I hear from older fans is 'It's just like the Seventies all over again.' This is the Red Army, witty and irreverent but without the riots. Freed from the feeling of powerlessness that followed the Glazer takeover; able to stand if they choose and no longer the targets of ruthless commercial practice, the support has come into its own'.*

The founders of FCUM never really wanted to leave Manchester United. But now that they have they seem set on re-creating the soul of the old United. They regard themselves as the true inheritors of the playing tradition of Sir Matt Busby's great team of the 1960s. To some extent they are engaged in a hearts and minds struggle for the allegiance of the hard core of the Manchester United fanbase. For them to succeed in this objective would be an extraordinary achievement. As matters currently stand the odds are stacked against them. Nevertheless, the 'idea' of FCUM does represent a threat to the Glazer business model. For in their search to generate revenue in the short term to pay debt the Glazers are in danger of losing sight of the key attribute of any successful football club; the 'fan equity' investment of their supporters, that special emotional bond that drives interest and so revenues. It was this special emotional bond that helped make Manchester United Football Club the extraordinarily valuable sporting brand it is today, a brand that the Glazers actually wanted to buy. It would be ironic if, in their rush to pay the debt needed to purchase this brand they actually succeeded in destroying the very thing that makes the brand so special, the 'fan equity' in the brand of its supporters. Without this United is just another entertainment brand amongst many, easily substitutable. Only time will tell how effective the Glazers will be in taking forward Manchester United in the next stage of its strategic development. For now, they should be very thankful to Sir Alex Ferguson.

Case Questions

1 Critically assess strategic development of Manchester United as a business since 1992. To what extent has it been critically dependent on the success of manager Sir Alex Ferguson in delivering success on the field of play?
2 To what extent do you agree that the heart of the Manchester United brand lies with the emotional relationship its hard core supporters have with the club?
3 Critically assess the role of Sir Matt Busby's team of the late 1950s and the 1960s in developing the Manchester United brand.
4 Is it realistic to expect that Manchester United can continue to enjoy long-term success on the field of play whilst carrying significant debt on its balance sheet?
5 Critically assess the importance of maintaining a disciplined wages-to-turnover ratio of 50 per cent or less to Manchester United's success as a business.
6 Evaluate whether or not you think Manchester United's commercial strategy is likely to be the most effective for the club.

Case Resources

Reading

Bose, M. (2007). *Manchester United: And the Business of Soccer*. Aurum Press Ltd.

Deloitte (2001–2007). *Annual Reviews of Football Finance*. Deloitte.

Deloitte (February 2007). *Football Money League: The Reign in Spain*. Deloitte.

Deloitte (February 2006). *Football Money League: The Changing of the Guard*. Deloitte.

Manchester United Plc (2001–2005). *Annual Reports*. Manchester United Plc.

Websites

www.thebusbybabes.com
http://fcumfiles.co.uk/index.php
http://www.joinmust.org/
www.manchesterunited.com
http://soccernet.espn.go.com/

Further Information

Users of this case may want to take a look at the Wikipedia entries for the following:

Manchester United – http://en.wikipedia.org/wiki/Manchester_United

10

Something for nothing: the free ticket myth

Paul Muller and Dave Arthur

Case Focus

This case successfully applies a new theory of free ticket potential to a greyhound racing venue.

Keywords

- Greyhound racing
- Free tickets
- Promotions
- Spectator motivation
- Retail sampling
- Attendance marketing.

Case Summary

Despite a wealth of academic literature on sports marketing, scant regard appears to have been paid to an almost inevitable element of the event promotion mix – the distribution of free tickets. The few references tend to be dismissive of it as an old-fashioned, short-term solution to the problem of maximizing stadium attendance for profit. Far greater attention is paid to more sophisticated and exotic promotional tools. Yet the practice of free ticket distribution stubbornly refuses to die out; which begs the question: if benefit remains, how can we maximize it? To answer this, discourse from two distinct marketing sub-disciplines – the study of sports attendance motivation and retail sampling – is drawn together. The conclusions are illustrated in the context of a conservatively conducted field study, demonstrating that the proper application of this new theory does in fact increase attendance and drive profit.

Case Elements

The principle of paying for admission to elite sporting contests is well established and largely unchallenged by the community. The revenue that this generates represents a significant source of income for the host organization, and is justified to off-set the cost of event staging. Yet the majority of expenses incurred in the conduct of events are fixed, as opposed to proportionally variable to the number of attendees. Venue overheads, such as rent, utilities and upkeep, as well as production charges (e.g. player fees) are often the same regardless of whether 100 or 100,000 people attend. Although secondary, retail expenses (such as hospitality and merchandising) vary with patronage, these enterprises can be treated as separate business entities, with their own income that is closely linked to their expenses. It is therefore an economic statement of fact that the more paying customers an event can attract, the more profit it will generate. Indeed, after the break-even point is surpassed, nearly every additional paying patron is 'pure' profit, even before any contribution to marginal income that they might make through participation in secondary activities. Entry charge thus represents the greatest profit potential for an event host, and, as such, is often considered sacrosanct.

Nevertheless, there are a number of ways that a person can gain discounted entry to these same events, which is seemingly at odds with the above proposition. Certain classes of citizen are often regarded as having an entitlement to a discount; namely pensioners and children. Ticket bundling also occurs, with family, group or multi-visit specials on permanent offer. Event sponsors, stakeholders and members of the host body also receive an allocation of tickets that may be worth more than the prima facie financial contribution that they have exchanged. Finally, there are the 'freebies' – an allocation of tickets that have no obviously direct financial utility.

This case closely examines the rationale behind the distribution of these 'freebies'. There has been a surprising lack of research published into this field of enquiry, so it is necessary to draw together two distinct academic philosophies to provide a framework for the study. The first of these, the practice of retail sampling, is a well-founded marketing tenet, which is analogous to the practice of free ticket distribution. Secondly, an appreciation of how sport businesses distinguish spectator motivations is critical to understanding how the theory of sampling can be embraced therein. The application of this scholarship to a free ticket programme conducted at a greyhound racing venue is used to highlight the utility of these theories.

To preface this study, a survey of marketing managers across a broad cross-section of Australian professional sports was conducted. It found that there was a general lack of awareness of the potential benefits of free ticket distribution. For many organizations, the priority was to sell memberships or season tickets. Free tickets were seen as a distraction (at best) and a threat (at worst) to this goal – in fact, most respondents could identify at least two reasons for limiting the same. In order of frequency, the following themes emerged:

- Free tickets diminish the value of full price attendance.
- Free ticket redemption cannibalises paying attendance.
- Free tickets diminish the perceived value of the contest/sport.
- Free tickets are revenue neutral (and, implicitly, not worth the effort).
- Organizations lack the resources to properly employ and measure free ticket schemes.
- Some had poor past experience with free tickets.
- Strong current attendances were cited as a reason to do no more.

The almost universal perception was that free tickets have a positive short term and goodwill effect, contrasting with less-favourable long term and revenue consequences. All responding managers circulated free tickets; yet negligible strategic consideration or systematic review of organizational methodology was apparent. Most made the bulk of their distributions to sponsors, and it was clear that very few organizations had any interest in what happened to these tickets once they left the club's direct control.

Research Methods

The sports venue chosen to test the efficacy of a theory of considered free ticket distribution was Richmond Race Club (RRC), a well-established greyhound racing track in metropolitan Sydney, Australia. Although it has been successfully running greyhound race meetings on site for over 50 years, the Club has recently suffered the malaise affecting many wagering codes – waning consumer interest. The growth of off-course wagering and gaming alternatives, the diversity of leisure options, changing community attitudes and even social urbanization have all contributed to the decline of this once hugely popular blue-collar past-time.

Despite this, there has been almost no academic research conducted on the specific exigencies of greyhound racing. Limited study of the problems faced by the analogous industry of horseracing, however, identifies with some of the issues raised in the general literature on sports marketing. For example, quality of contest is an observable determinant of attendance, and the local presence of other professional sports has a negative effect on the same (Thalheimer and Ali, 1995). Social interaction, too, has been found to be the most influential attendance variable, above and beyond price, quality of contest and service standards (Brindley and Thorogood, 1998). From a marketing perspective, the sport is constrained by tradition and regulation in terms of the product it can offer, so sponsorship and promotional activity are seen as the keys to industry growth (Parker, 2000). Although this is by no means definitive, it all suggests that race wagering is an industry that, for the purposes of this research, will provide data consistent with the experiences of other sports. The only possible divergence is that for racing spectators the admission expense commonly represents only a fraction of their discretionary spending for the day. If anything, this suggests that cover charge is less of a barrier to attendance than it may be in other sports; therefore, free tickets are likely to be less successful here than in other contexts. The true effect of the proportional relevance of entry charge in more passive spectator sports, however, will need to be explored in future research.

At the time of the research, the club was conducting meetings every week on Monday at lunchtime and Friday evenings. A race meeting consisted of 10 races staged approximately 20 minutes apart. Patrons and participants alike were required to pay a five dollar ($5) entry levy, although club members, pensioners and children were admitted for no charge. There was an average of 175 paid admissions per Friday meeting, with just under 100 each Monday in the period of the survey. Once on-course, direct spectator revenue was derived in the main from bar and wagering sales, with incidental streams such as programme sales and vending making up the balance. Food catering leases and bookmaker stand fees (as distinct from totalizer revenue) were contractually fixed, so the club's income from this source was predetermined for the period in question, without regard to turnover.[1]

---

[1] It is nevertheless assumed that should lessee turnover consistently increase as a result of any promotional strategy, then the club can negotiate more favourable terms for future leases. This would effectively 'lock in' the profit potential of, for example, free ticket redemption schemes.

RRC was considered ideal to test the applicability of free ticket distribution theory as it satisfied many of the necessary preconditions for control.

1 The brand (greyhound racing) and the product (meetings at RRC) were both well established within the community. This meant that their attendance was in the low category of spectator risk due to the familiarity of the sport.
2 The quality of contest was uniform from meeting to meeting; although Friday events offered larger-prize money and generally attracted better dogs. During the course of the research there were two feature events run, and the effect of free ticket distribution on popular, well advertised events could also be contrasted.
3 There was no change to the business or marketing activities of the club over the period, or from previous periods, with which the results would be compared. This mitigated the potential for other changes to the marketing mix – such as new (or reduced) advertising, public relations or promotions – to unduly influence research outcomes. The free ticket distribution strategy employed was a new expense of the club, which made it additionally easy to track.
4 There were no capital works or facility improvements programmed for the research period. This implied that there would be no skewing of results due to novelty; although, the substandard quality of spectator infrastructure was widely acknowledged as a disincentive to attendance.
5 All meetings were broadcast on the pay television network, Sky (into homes, totalizers and licensed premises), and free-to-air radio 2KY across the state. Industry and local press also covered events. This meant that feedback – albeit a subjective measure of quality rather than empirical quantity – could be received on things such as ambience, interest and other spectator dynamics. It also meant, however, that the effects of broadcast versus blackout could not be studied.
6 The authors had – with the leave of the Board – unfettered access to the club's financial records (past and present), channels of distribution, business plan and vision, as well as a good understanding of the current and desired demographics.

Strategy

Over 4600 business card sized free ticket vouchers were distributed to 563 businesses across two categories. On 1 February 2006, 478 members of the local Chamber of Commerce received six passes per business, and 86 licensed venues within a similar geographical radius received 20 passes each. A personalized letter was also sent to introduce RRC and invite recipients to either personally redeem or pass on the voucher as a staff or client reward. This was an unsolicited direct mail out to participants. The Chamber of Commerce distribution was seen to be a cost effective way of achieving a random sampling of the community, whereas the licensed venues – hotels and clubs – all had an on-premise totalizer which publicized and accepted wagers on RRC race meetings. It was therefore believed that this market segment might be predisposed to attend. A final 25 double passes were used by a local newspaper to promote one of the club's feature events in the survey period.

Each 'VIP Entry Pass' carried a unique serial number that was used to track the source of redemption, and, despite being valid for only three months, was otherwise unencumbered by restrictive terms and conditions. The reverse of the card demanded of users the most important piece of information for the validation of our theory – when the last time was that they visited Richmond Greyhounds. A first time attendee (one who checked 'never previously attended') was assumed to be someone who would not have come were it not for the fortuitous arrival of the free ticket. Someone who had attended within the last three months was generalized as a regular patron, and those within the 3–12 months band were supposed to be infrequent attendees. The fourth response – 'a long time ago' – implied that the redeemer had not been to the venue for one year or more, and was a lapsed patron. Despite the arguable accuracy of these assumptions, the logic was considered sufficient to advance the purpose of this study.

Each gate attendant was also instructed to gather some basic demographic information about redeeming patrons on the reverse of the card; namely, their gender, age (in the opinion of the attendant), time travelled to the venue, and the number of free and paid entries in their party. The relevance and effective use of this information is considered below in the discussion of results.

Results

Of the 4638 tickets distributed, 211 – or 4.55 per cent – were redeemed in the three-month window of validation. The results per distribution channel are tabulated below.

Chamber of Commerce	88/2868	3.06%
Pubs and Clubs	111/1720	6.45%
Newspaper promotion	12/50	24.00%
Total	211/4638	4.55%

The first goal of any free ticket distribution should be to maximize redemption, and this is considered more fully in the later discussion on profit. Nonetheless, it can be seen that a distribution to a market that is predisposed to attend (Pubs and Clubs) is twice as successful as a random allocation (Chamber of Commerce). This affirms the conclusions of Mullin et al. (1993) that aware non-consumers and media consumers of a sport are more likely to convert to light users – occasional patrons – than non-aware (or adverse) non-consumers, who are going to be better represented in the random sample.

The newspaper promotion, on the other hand, promised a free double pass to the first 25 people to phone the paper on the day of circulation. Mention of the promotion only occurred in the final paragraph of an article on a feature event, so respondents were at the very least media consumers of greyhound racing news, and more probably occasional or regular patrons. Indeed, on learning that the full allocation of tickets was quickly taken up, this author expected that most redeeming patrons would be familiar to RRC. The actual results were, however, surprising – not just because only 24 per cent of people actually made the effort to show up, but because only two redeemers admitted to coming to the venue in the last 3 or 12 months. The rest were evenly split between lapsed patrons – those who had not attended RRC for 'a long time', or first time visitors.

Despite being an almost after-thought in the design of this research, the limited newspaper promotion results point tentatively toward a number of interesting outcomes. Firstly, as sports managers, we often underestimate how many people follow our sport in the media just because it is there. Our readership may not necessarily be loyal, and is unlikely to protest our media absence, but they do represent a predisposed and accessible segment through which we can grow our patronage. Secondly, the framing of restrictions – in this case, by limiting the number of tickets available and linking them to a single event – can accelerate consumer interest and redemption intentions (Krishna and Zhang, 1999; Aggarwal and Vaidyanathan, 2003). Thirdly, the actual 'VIP Entry Pass' used in the newspaper promotion did not differ at all from the others issued, in that it was valid for a full three months; however, none was redeemed except at the meeting with which the article was linked. This is perhaps evidence that customers often assume terms and conditions that do not really exist, and reinforces the need to keep any free ticket restrictions simple and aligned with consumer expectations. Finally, by linking an effort of the customer with the relevant reward (i.e. call in to win), the something-for-nothing risk is mitigated and higher rates of redemption are achieved (Porter, 1993; Kivetz, 2005).

The total results of patrons' visit frequency (self-reported) were as follows.

First time visitor	83/211	39.3%
Within last 3 months	68/211	32.2%
Within 3–12 months	13/211	6.2%
A long time ago	36/211	17.1%
Unreported	11/211	5.2%

This shows that over half of the redeeming patrons were either first time or lapsed visitors to RRC. This is a great result when it is remembered that one of the anecdotally perceived risks of free ticket distributions is that they cannibalise already profitable markets. Multi-layered analyses of these results suggest further strategies to reduce this likelihood.

For Chamber of Commerce respondents, the mix was as follows (with relevant variations from the collated results bracketed).

First time visitor	41/88	46.6%	(+7.3%)
Within last 3 months	27/88	30.7%	(−1.5%)
Within 3–12 months	8/88	9.1%	(+2.9%)
A long time ago	7/88	8.0%	(−9.1%)
Unreported	5/88	5.7%	

The random sample attracted the highest proportion of first time visitors, indicating that a free ticket alone can be sufficient to stimulate an otherwise unenthused potential patron. For a sporting organization hoping to enhance organic attendance growth, a random free ticket distribution may be a viable strategy. However, the high cost of distribution must be considered. Only 41/2868 (or 1.42 per cent) of Chamber of Commerce respondents were first time visitors; whereas 37/1720 (or 2.15 per cent) of Pub and Club patrons were the same. In that respect, a targeted strategy is preferred.

For Pub and Club respondents, the following was observed.

First time visitor	37/111	33.3%	(−6.0%)
Within last 3 months	39/111	35.1%	(+2.9%)
Within 3–12 months	5/111	4.5%	(−1.7%)
A long time ago	26/111	23.4%	(+6.3%)
Unreported	4/111	3.6%	

In this predisposed market, it is not surprising to see higher rates of redemption from frequent visitors; after all, those with a keen interest in the sport will frequent such venues when Richmond is not racing, and will be prominent beneficiaries of free ticket rewards. It is interesting, however, that the Pubs and Clubs achieved better returns from lapsed patrons. The authors assume that this is because those who have lost interest in attendance may still retain an interest in wagering off-course, and only need a gentle nudge to get them back to the venue. A more general conclusion that is supported by the literature reviewed may be that sporting organizations experiencing falling attendances can attract people back to stadia by targeting people with free tickets where they watch the game socially.

Of additional interest was the skewing effect of repeat ticket redemption over the three-month period. In the first month of the promotion, 114 tickets were redeemed, compared with only 97 in the final two months. In that first month, 58.7 per cent of visitors were first time or lapsed patrons, versus 50.5 per cent in the last two months. Patrons who had attended in the last three months (or presumed regular patrons) jumped from 23.7 per cent to 42.3 per cent over the same periods. Is this evidence of some first time or lapsed patrons liking what they saw and using a second free ticket to revisit, thus developing loyalty to greyhound racing? Or does this indicate that the promotional period was too long, and that only already loyal patrons benefited from the extended redemption window? Further research in this regard would be illuminating.

Other lines of enquiry can be compared to the 'base' crowd. Gender, for example, was split 3:1 males to females in redemptions, and there was no significant difference in the rate of gender redemption between the random and targeted distributions. Whereas this doesn't tell us much about free ticket distributions per se, it may indicate a prevailing community perception of greyhound racing as a male friendly or even male dominated past-time. This is despite a much more balanced mix (3:2) in established patronage. In that respect, a free ticket distribution may be a cheap and effective way of identifying general market sympathies – especially those at odds with intuitive or current experience – and direct more detailed research. The greyhound racing industry may in this instance recognize that this perception could be inhibiting attendance growth, look at why this is, and propose solutions for redress.

Useful data was also gleaned from a review of how patrons collectively redeemed their tickets. Of note was the fact that not one 'VIP Entry Pass' user was reported to have brought a paying customer through the turnstiles with them at the time of redemption. Although the reliability of this information is in some doubt – this data set had an almost 50 per cent unreported response by the gate staff – it is not unreasonable to conclude that free tickets on their own do not significantly drive paid admissions at the point of conversion. Despite this, there was a marked difference from the base case in how patrons redeemed their tickets en masse. The Figure 10.1 uses the base case parameters to compare rates of collective redemption.

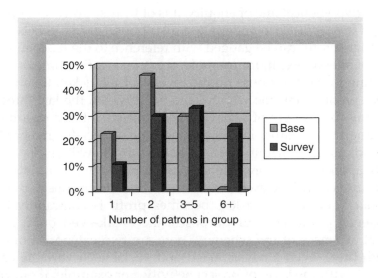

Figure 10.1 Collective rates of redemption.

This shows that, given the opportunity, over 50 per cent of patrons preferred to redeem their vouchers in groups of three or more. In contrast, over two-thirds of paying customers either came individually or with a sole partner. Communal experience as a motivator for sports stadium attendance is thus affirmed (Hocking, 1982; DeSerpa and Faith, 1996), and it is not inconsistent to infer that group attendance may also mitigate the perceived risk of free ticket redemption, and stimulate secondary purchase intentions (Ho and Gallagher, 2005).

Finally, as previously mentioned, the Friday evening greyhound meetings had a higher quality of contest, and were no doubt more convenient for patrons to attend than the Monday lunchtime events. An overwhelming 86 per cent of redeeming patrons chose to use their voucher at the Friday events – this is in contrast to Fridays only contributing 65 per cent of current attendances. Indeed, 97 per cent of first time or lapsed patrons took the Friday option – the distribution of regular and infrequent attendees was much more statistically consistent with existing trends. For RRC the conclusion is inescapable – attendance growth will almost exclusively derive from Friday night racing. For free ticket distribution theory, quality of contest (Mason, 1999) and convenience (Pan et al., 1999) are important predictors of the rate of redemption.

Another interesting sidebar to this study is that free ticket redemption was maximized when supported by other event marketing. The two feature races heavily advertised during this period attracted one-third of all redemptions – the remaining vouchers were converted over a further 17 meetings. A free ticket distribution is therefore best employed as an integrated part of an overall marketing campaign, and is only of limited utility as a substitute for the same.

Profit

Beyond the hypothetical line of enquiry, it is of further practical importance to determine if it is *profitable* to undertake a distribution of free tickets to the market. Patronage 'profit' can be gauged with reference to the redeeming patron's frequency of attendance. If, for example, a patron is a first time or lapsed visitor according to their response on the reverse of the ticket, then they can be considered 'profit'. Someone who has attended within the last three months, however, must be thought of as having been likely to attend regardless of the offer. Although this is rather imprecise reasoning, especially in regard to those visitors who attended within the last 12 months, it will suffice when conservatively applied. Therefore, any redeeming patron who has attended RRC within the last year will be excluded from our final profit consideration.

The dollar value at which loss becomes profit is commonly known as the break-even point. For our purposes, the break-even point is the sum of the total expenses of the scheme. There are two categories of cost associated with break-even analysis: fixed and variable. A variable cost is one which varies with the level of project activity. For example, if our free ticket project demanded hiring casual staff, opening previously unused parts of the venue, or otherwise consuming a proportional share of organizational resources, then they need to be considered in determining the point at which profit is achieved. A fundamental problem with RRC was, however, the under-utilization of necessarily deployed resources. As a case in point, it was necessary to staff both gates for the duration of a race meeting, even though the staff could have quite easily managed two- or even three times the volume of customer traffic. Similarly, the lights and air-conditioning ran at their full capacity regardless of the fact that the main viewing lounge was only half-full. To that end, it was well within the variable cost capacity of RRC to manage even a significant fluctuation in patron numbers. The variable costs associated with this promotion were therefore immaterial to its profit – this point is raised because it is not a universal truth, and may be critically relevant to subsequent applications of free ticket schemes.

This simplifies our ability to measure the profit of the project. The fixed (and total) costs for this project are shown in the following table.

Database acquisition	$150	
Postage and distribution	$350	($500)
Ticket design and printing	$450	
Management labour (20 hours)	$700	$1650

The database acquisition expense is the cost of joining the local Chamber of Commerce, thus gaining access and usage rights to their membership directory. And although the cost of designing and printing 5000 vouchers was met by the sport's peak body in return for their logo appearing prominently on the voucher, it is considered a real cost for the academic purpose of evaluating profit. Nevertheless, this use of co-sponsorship remains a viable means of lowering the break-even point of free ticket distribution strategies. The indirect cost of management labour component is also considered, even though it is an expense that would have been incurred regardless – it is illustrative, however, of the level of effort necessary to deliver the programme. Note, too, that $1650 compares favourably with the cost of other promotions that require a high-incentive giveaway and/or significant advertising media. Although it is beyond the scope of this research to compare and contrast the efficacy of free ticket distributions with other promotional strategies, this is strong evidence of its cost competitiveness.

There are two material streams of secondary (i.e. post-entry) revenue available to RRC – bar and wagering sales.[2] Therefore, over the three-month period of the promotion, bar and wagering *profit* must increase by $1650 or more. It is important to remember that gains in turnover from these sources do suffer from variable cost increases, so this must be factored into any honest calculation. Without going into too much detail about the confidential commercial transactions of the club, it was found that 115 patrons would have returned $15.07 profit per head, or $1733.79 in this period, representing a +7.5 per cent return on total investment, or nearly 3½ times the real cost to the club ($500).

---

[2]Merchandise (race programme, snack vending and other miscellaneous sales) are of limited material relevance to this project, mainly because of their low unit cost, insignificant turnover and very low-profit margins (<10 per cent).

Therefore, without considering the positive effect of unreported patrons who meet our criteria, secondary sales increases across marginal lines, and Monday meetings, the free ticket distribution was financially profitable on its merits. The anticipated but less tangible benefits of potentially loyal patron conversion, intra-audience effect and goodwill should only enlarge the margin of yield.

Case Diagnosis

The unsold seat is an increasingly untenable concept in the business of sports entertainment. For that reason, marketers are altering their selling theories not only to avoid losing unit sales and the supplementary revenue they drive, but also in order to aggressively compete in the broader leisure and lifestyle category (Burton and Cornilles, 1998). Personalized selling to differentiated market segments, novelty in promotion and the add-on stadium experience are *de rigueur* in this age of profit imperative. Yet despite this focus on incremental sales strategy, scant regard appears to have been paid to an inevitable element in the mix – the complementary potential of free ticket distribution.

This paper has challenged the widely held (but apparently unsupported) assumptions of sporting managers that free ticket distribution is either a short-term strategy to 'make up the numbers', a revenue neutral necessary evil, or the desperate act of a drowning organization. And while it is true that – casually applied – such a scheme can be all three things, it seems that many have lost sight of the profit potential, or why sports organizations started these programmes in the first place. To stimulate management action, or even mere diligence, in this regard, a number of recommendations are made for those charged with free ticket distribution. None is individually earth-shattering, and hopefully all pass an intuitive standard of common sense. And each can be applied as an incremental adjustment in thinking toward a more positive application of an established management process, rather than a major cultural shift or resource reallocation. The list – drawn from the indirect academic sources previously referred to – is by no means a finite template, and has only been partially tested by the forementioned case. It is expected that subsequent internal debate would refine these recommendations to suit the organizational circumstance.

When to use Free Tickets

- When a predisposed but dormant market is identified and can be accessed (e.g. media-only consumers, fans of a complementary sport, lapsed patrons).
- To personalize or reinforce an advertised or other promotional message.
- When extrinsic barriers to redemption are minimized; although an appropriate intrinsic challenge may stimulate the same (e.g. an entry form or competitive process to 'earn' the free ticket reward).

- To introduce a new sports product or service.
- When the quality of contest is high and to the slight advantage of the home team (Knowles et al., 1992) – this strategy may be especially effective for building attendance when it would otherwise be negatived by live television coverage (Borland and Macdonald, 2003).
- To increase the convenience of attendance at the expense of other sporting events and leisure alternatives.
- When sponsors' interests can be aligned with the objectives of the scheme, thereby sharing costs and mutually extending profit potential.
- To artificially stimulate hype and subsequent home team advantage, word-of-mouth enthusiasm and player participation (Tapp, 2004).
- Service recovery – free tickets may compensate for poor quality of contest and/or poor spectator experience in spectators with low team or sport identification.

When not to use Free tickets

- Fans of the sport (as opposed to the contest) are predisposed to attend, regardless of the availability of free tickets (Wakefield and Bush, 1998).
- Free tickets should not be regularly or predictably accessible to the same market segments.
- Corporate, premium and other highly inelastic seating (e.g. sold-out segments) should not be given away except in exceptional circumstances.[3]
- New stadia benefit from their novelty and relative quality of facilities (Coates and Humphreys, 2005), and need not rely on free tickets to drive patronage.

How to Convert Free Ticket Redemption into Regular, Paid Patronage

- Encourage group redemption to gratify social need.
- Fans of other sports are more likely to be enticed by free tickets where the perceived quality of contest is high; although, the retention of such patrons is dependent on the on-going satisfaction of that expectation.
- The ability to deliver the same high-quality service received at the visit of redemption to future, paid attendances will predict spectator loyalty (Berry et al., 1990).
- Identification and analysis of redemption 'clustering' – by geographic, demographic and psychographic factors – can focus strategy and indicate future leveraging opportunities (e.g. membership and sponsorship).

---

[3] *Rule of thumb:* If a ticket can be scalped (on-sold, as opposed to passed-on), then it probably shouldn't be free, unless significant public relations value can be leveraged.

- Withdraw free tickets from the market when demand *exceeds* supply (not when supply and demand are in equilibrium).
- Prefer occasional free tickets to frequent discounted offers (Bawa and Shoemaker, 2004; Dawes, 2004).

Future Research

In challenging convention wisdom, one must be mindful of the fact that it remains an earned wisdom – regardless of the scholarly vacuum in which it appears to exist. Therefore, despite postulating some interesting theories, the limited scope of this investigation means that its recommendations are far from definitive. A number of aspects of the free ticket conundrum that invite future academic research include:

- Considering the effect of free ticket distribution schemes across different classes of attendance (e.g. under-subscribed premium seats versus accommodation in the outer/unreserved areas).
- Measuring the profit impact of free ticket distribution on secondary income in other sports, especially where admission is the prime or only source of club revenue.
- Comparing the local results with the experiences of other (international) communities.
- Isolating the effect of free ticket redemption on the future purchase intentions (and actions) of patrons.
- Designing means for assessing and maximizing the goodwill and other intangible benefits of free ticket programmes.
- More detailed analysis of management understanding of the utility of free ticket distribution.

Individual sporting codes or clubs can also experiment to establish important quantitative benchmarks in their own free ticket schemes, such as 'tipping points'. For example:

- What percentage of the promotional budget is an effective spend on free ticket distribution (e.g. 14 per cent in retail marketing).
- How many event tickets should be allocated as free.
- An appropriate length of time for ticket validity.
- When should free tickets be withdrawn, and at what rate.
- What the measurable criteria for success are in free ticket distributions.

The most important conclusion for sporting managers should therefore be that free ticket distribution is as much a science as the other marketing sub-disciplines, and should be subject to the same rigours and scrutiny. Critically, any such strategy should be an evolving, on-going response to how each game is likely to self-satisfy its need to sell out, and be answerable to relevant performance criteria. It is hoped that further academic and organizational research along these lines will promote this aim.

Case Questions

1 Describe the free ticket distribution strategy of a sport or team that you are familiar with.
2 In what way could sponsors be used to leverage the benefits of a free ticket scheme?
3 Critically respond to the reservations of the sports marketing managers identified in the pre-study survey.
4 How could a sports organization use free tickets to promote community goodwill? (Hint: This strategy may differ in some respects from one designed to drive attendance traffic.)
5 Compare the pros and cons of free ticket distribution with discounted entry schemes.

Case Resources

Reading

Aggarwal, P. and Vaidyanathan, R. (2003). Use it or lose it: Purchase acceleration effects of time-limited promotions. *Journal of Consumer Behaviour*, Vol. 2, No. 4, p. 393.

Bawa, K. and Shoemaker, R. (2004). The effects of free sample promotions on incremental brand sales. *Marketing Science*, Vol. 23, No. 3, p. 345.

Berry, L.L., Zeithaml, V.A. and Parasuraman, A. (1990). Five imperatives for improving service quality. *Sloan Management Review*, Summer, p. 29.

Borland, J. and Macdonald, R. (2003). Demand for sport. *Oxford Review of Economic Policy*, Vol. 19, No. 4, p. 478.

Brindley, C. and Thorogood, R. (1998). Attracting the under-30's to UK horse racing events. *Sport Marketing Quarterly*, Vol. 7, No. 4, p. 25.

Burton, R. and Cornilles, R.Y. (1998). Emerging theory in team sport sales: Selling more tickets in a more competitive arena. *Sport Marketing Quarterly*, Vol. 7, No. 1, p. 29.

Coates, D. and Humphreys, B.R. (2005). Novelty effects of new facilities on attendance at professional sporting events. *Contemporary Economic Policy*, Vol. 23, No. 3, p. 436.

Dawes, J. (2004). Assessing the impact of a very successful price promotion on brand, category and competitor sales. *Journal of Product and Brand Management*, Vol. 13, No. 4/5, p. 303.

DeSerpa, A.C. and Faith, R.L. (1996). 'Bru-u-u-ce': The simple economics of mob goods. *Public Choice*, Vol. 89, No. 1/2, p. 77.

Helitzer, M. (1992). What's the big idea? Creating special events, *The Dream Job: Sports, Publicity, Promotion and Public Relations*. Ohio University Press, USA.

Ho, F.H. and Gallagher, M.P. (2005). The impact of wine tasting on wine purchases: evidence from Napa, California. *International Journal of Wine Marketing*, Vol. 17, No. 1, p. 44.

Hocking, J.E. (1982). Sports and spectators: Intra-audience effects. *Journal of Communication*, Vol. 32, No. 1, p. 2100.

Kivetz, R. (2005). Promotion reactance: The role of effort-reward congruity. *Journal of Consumer Research*, Vol. 31, No. 4, p. 725.

Krishna, A. and Zhang, Z.J. (1999). Short- or long-duration coupons: The effect of expiration date on the profitability of coupon promotions. *Management Science*, Vol. 45, No. 8, p. 1041.

Mason, D.S. (1999). What is the sports product and who buys it? The marketing of professional sports leagues. *European Journal of Marketing*, Vol. 33, No. 3/4, p. 402.

Mullin, B.J., Hardy, S. and Sutton, W.A. (1993). *Sport Marketing*. Human Kinetics Publishers. Champaign, USA.

Pan, D.W., Zhu, Z., Gabert, T.E. and Brown, J. (1999). Team performance, market characteristics and attendance of Major League Baseball: A panel data analysis. *Mid-Atlantic Journal of Business*, Vol. 35, No. 2/3, p. 77.

Parker, R. (2000). Problems in the marketing of spectator sports. *Mid-Atlantic Journal of Business*, Vol. 36, No. 1, p. 37.

Porter, A.L. (1993). Strengthening coupon offers by requiring more from the customer. *Journal of Consumer Marketing*, Vol. 10, No. 2, p. 13.

Tapp, A. (2004). The loyalty of football fans – we'll support you evermore? *Journal of Database Marketing & Customer Strategy Management*, Vol. 11, No. 3, p. 203.

Thalheimer, R. and Mukhtar, M.A. (1995). The demand for pari-mutuel horse race wagering and attendance. *Management Science*, Vol. 45, No. 1, p. 129.

Wakefield, K.L. and Bush, V.D. (1998). Promoting leisure services: Economic and emotional aspects of consumer response. *Journal of Services Marketing*, Vol. 12, No. 3, p. 209.

Websites

Greyhound Racing New South Wales – www.grnsw.com.au
Richmond Race Club – www.richmondgreyhounds.com.au

Case

11

Guinness, sport, and the positioning of a global brand

John Amis

Case Focus

This case assesses the global brand positioning strategy of Guinness. The prefigurative importance of sport to Guinness is examined, particularly with respect to the multiple ways in which it is used to bring coherence to the brand across disparate global markets.

Keywords

- Global brand strategy
- Sport
- Guinness
- Local resonance

Case Summary

The purpose of this case is to reveal the ways in which sport is used to help position the Guinness brand. Drawing on an analysis of Guinness' three largest markets, Ireland, Great Britain, and Africa, we explore the ways in which sport is used to help bring coherence to brand positioning initiatives across the world. Of central interest is the way in which Guinness' global strategy was radically transformed from one in which local markets created their own disparate campaigns to one which is highly centralized but that still offers essential opportunities for pronounced local engagement. Sport is central to this multi-layered approach. Sport is used through direct sponsorship agreements, as focal points of advertising campaigns, and as a driver for on-trade promotions. However, by ensuring that these components build towards a Key Brand Benefit (KBB) of 'Guinness brings out your inner strength', Guinness' executives have established a coherent position intended to overcome brand fragmentation caused by rapid flows of media and people across geographic boundaries.

Case Elements

The Guinness name and logo has become synonymous with sport around the world. Whether it is the Guinness All-Ireland Hurling Championship, regularly touted as the most effective sport sponsorship arrangement in Ireland, the Guinness Premiership (rugby union) in England, or the support of football and tennis in Africa, associating with sport has long been a major component of Guinness' global brand positioning. In so doing, Guinness has become one of the preeminent sponsors involved in world sport. The purpose of this chapter is to provide insight into the strategies employed by senior decision-makers at Guinness as they appropriate particular sporting spaces, develop these associations into a coherent brand position, and then use this position to meaningfully engage people in different ways across the world. To this end, the chapter is organized in the following way. First, in order to provide a contextual understanding, we explore the history of

Guinness and its strategic brand architecture. Next, we examine the utilization of sport by Guinness in its three biggest markets, Great Britain, Ireland, and Africa. In so doing, we explore the ways in which sporting properties are secured through traditional sponsorship agreements, how sport is used in media advertising campaigns, and the ways in which Guinness takes advantage of major sporting events through on-trade promotions. We will conclude with a consideration of the implications of the case and some lessons that we can take away.

Developing a Global Brand

The story of Guinness begins with Arthur Guinness who, in 1755, set up a small brewery in the Irish village of Leixlip, County Kildare. From these humble beginnings, the legendary brand was born. Four years later he signed a 9000-year lease on a disused brewery at St James's Gate, Dublin for an initial payment of £100 and a subsequent rent of £45 per annum. This brewery remains a cornerstone of the Guinness empire and is one of Dublin's most famous landmarks. Originally a brewer of traditional Dublin Ale, Arthur Guinness very quickly appreciated the value of foreign markets. In 1769 he made his first export shipment to England. He also became intrigued by a beer that was being imported from England known as 'porter' and decided that this was where the future of his company would lay. In fact, in 1799, Guinness brewed his last batch of Dublin Ale and from this point on he concentrated his brewing efforts on the black beer that would make the firm famous.

Arthur Guinness died in 1803, but under the stewardship of Arthur's son, Arthur II, overseas markets were aggressively pursued. The West Indies, Portugal, Sierra Leone, East Indies, and the USA all became important markets for the firm. Upon Arthur's death in 1850, his son Sir Benjamin Lee Guinness took over the reins of the company. In addition to continued overseas expansion, evidence of a developing appreciation for marketing appeared with the firm's first beer label in 1862. Edward Cecil Guinness, Sir Benjamin's son, became head of the firm upon his father's death in 1868 and, in addition to the registering of its first trademark – the famous Harp symbol – in 1876, he oversaw continued expansion such that by 1886 Arthur Guinness & Sons had become the largest brewery in the world with an annual production of 1.2 million barrels. That same year, the firm became the first brewery to be listed as a public company on the London Stock Exchange.

Throughout the 20th century, the firm invested heavily in a series of technical innovations. These ranged from the commissioning of boats designed to transport draught Guinness around the world to the creation of the 'widget' that recreated the beer's famous creamy head when poured from a can. Such innovations acted to fundamentally alter the nature of the business allowing quality to be controlled much more tightly and thereby enhancing the ability of the firm to transport and sell casked, bottled, and canned beer all over the world. This helped to reaffirm Guinness' position as a truly global brand.

In the early years of the 21st century, Guinness is brewed in 50 different countries around the world, often under licence or through joint ventures, and sold in over 150; over 10 million glasses of Guinness are, according to the company, consumed every day around the world. Two main variants constitute over 90 per cent of world wide sales: Guinness Draught (including Guinness Extra Cold) is sold as traditional poured pints, in cans, and in bottles, and is most popular in Europe, North America, Japan, and Australia; Guinness Foreign Extra Stout is only available in bottles and cans and is sold predominantly in Africa, Asia, and the Caribbean. The remainder of Guinness' sales come from canned and bottled Extra Stout (sometimes referred to as Guinness Original because of its adherence to an 18th and 19th century recipe when it was known as East and West India Porter).

In addition to expanding by introducing Guinness beer to new markets, a strategy that was followed throughout the 20th century was to increase corporate sales by acquiring other brewing and distilling companies. In this way, names such as Gordon's (gin), Bell's (whiskey) and Red Stripe (beer) were brought into the Guinness stable. This strategy reached its ultimate endpoint in 1997 when Guinness merged with the food and drink conglomerate Grand Metropolitan. The outcome of this was the creation of the firm Diageo, listed on the London Stock Exchange, with Guinness becoming one of an array of premium drink brands – including Smirnoff, Johnnie Walker, Bailey's, and Captain Morgan – owned by the firm.

With the loss of its independence, the maturing of the industry in many of Guinness' major markets which led to stagnating sales, and heavily increased competition from other beer manufacturers, Guinness management found a context in which, rather than being the largest beer manufacturer in the world, the brand had slipped in most markets to little more than niche status.

It is against this backdrop that, in 2000, a new Global Brand Director (GBD) for Guinness was appointed. He immediately set about developing a marketing strategy that would re-elevate the Guinness brand to global prominence. He also envisaged that sport, a long-time Guinness affiliate in markets around the world, would play a prominent role in securing this global affirmation. First, however, he wanted to define a global brand position that Guinness could occupy that would draw on the brand's long established values and work to differentiate it against its major global competitors.

Developing a Global 'KBB'

The self-described 'global essence' of Guinness comprises three values – power, goodness, and communion. These are held to have long-underpinned the brand in markets around the world. The famous 'Guinness is good for you' slogan was first coined in the late 1920s and was featured alongside testimonials from doctors as to the medicinal and athletic benefits that could accrue from the product! In fact, according to records held at the Guinness archives, one of Wellington's cavalry officers, severely wounded at the

Battle of Waterloo in 1815, wrote that:

> *it was not long before I sent for the Guinness and I shall never forget how much I enjoyed it. I thought I had never tasted anything so delightful.... I am confident that it contributed more than anything to the renewal of my strength.*

Such stories have helped to reify the brand values of power, goodness, and communion. However, the new GBD wanted something that could articulate the essence of the brand in a relevant and up-to-date manner. Consequently, a survey of Guinness' major global markets was undertaken during 2000–2001 which led to the identification and articulation of a 'KBB' of 'Guinness brings out your inner strength.' This was crafted to fit with the brand essence described earlier, and also the brand identity of Guinness as being 'masculine, strong, genuine, and independent.' As stated in an internal publication, 'The Brand Map' (2001):

> *The Guinness brand positioning has to be something with which our main target audience can identify. Research shows that Inner Strength is a highly relevant and motivating concept to men throughout the world who need to feel strong, assertive and independent. This need, described as 'potency' or 'independence', is the consumer need that Guinness currently meets across the world. This means that it is already a credible positioning from a consumer point of view on which we can build even further. Our global insight also highlights that in a world of increasing speed, disconnection and uncertainty there is a greater need for self-reliance. Inner Strength is a powerful and motivating position because it is seen as the foundation stone of self-reliance.*

Crucially, the KBB, in addition to being perceived as consistent with the long-held values of the brand, was also seen as being a way in which Guinness could mark out its cognitive territory in such a way as to differentiate itself from its major competitors (see Table 11.1).

Table 11.1 The perceived KBB of Guinness and its major competitors

Brand	KBB	Core brand essence
Guinness	Guinness brings out your inner strength	Power, Goodness, Communion
Budweiser	Allows you to be one of the 'guys' (anywhere)	Masculine, Consistent Quality, Ubiquitous
Stella Artois	Gives you a sense of heightened status and discernment	Expensive, Stylish, Worldy
Carling	Allows you to fit in with your mates	Proud, British, Irreverent
Heineken	Creates more memorable experiences	Quality, Respect, Worldliness
Carlsberg	Shows you've got taste/discernment	International, Quality, Experience
Fosters	Helps you lighten and loosen up	Australian, Humour, Masculine

Source: Internal Guinness presentation

While the uncovering of the KBB was clearly a significant step, there was also a strong realization that if the message of 'inner strength' was going to be successfully delivered worldwide, then there needed to be a radical transformation of the global marketing strategy. There were two major reasons for this. First, in addition to the major variations in brand positioning in different countries, there had also been a proliferation of advertising approaches even within single markets. For example, the GBD noted that in 2001, there were five different messages being communicated to the public in Ireland through different advertising campaigns. Second, there were also increasing examples of individual consumers being exposed to advertising messages from different markets, either through the increasing prevalence of international travel for work and leisure, or perhaps more importantly, because of the tendency of satellite television broadcasts to cross national borders. It was felt by members of the Global Brand Executive that this had led to a degree of brand fragmentation that was only going to get worse in the years ahead. In order to address this, the GBD in conjunction with the Global Brand Executive moved to centralize the overall global advertising strategy. Part of this involved paring down from using seven advertising agencies to just two: BBDO was given the brief to develop campaigns in the draught markets, most notably Great Britain, Ireland, North America, Australia, Japan, and Continental Europe; Saatchi & Saatchi was asked to develop the Extra Stout and Foreign Extra Stout markets, particularly Africa, Asia, and the Caribbean. However, the overall brand strategy was set by the Global Brand Executive with members of a Global Brand Team charged with working with local markets to develop campaigns that would articulate the KBB in a locally resonant way. Sport has played a very prominent role, at both global and local levels, because of the perception among Guinness decision-makers that it is a useful vehicle through which to affirm images of inner strength, often in the form of an individual athlete drawing on his/her self-belief to achieve a desired outcome. The Brand director for Great Britain described the thought process behind this to me:

> *David Beckham scoring a free-kick in the last minute against Greece in the [2002] World Cup qualifiers; scoring a penalty against Argentina in the World Cup. Just look at his face as he goes to take it, and he controls his breathing and he settles himself, and its all about self-belief. We believe that there are a huge amount of self-belief moments in sport.*

In order to try to exploit these 'self-belief moments', sport is utilized by Guinness in three ways: direct sponsorship of teams, leagues, and events; as a component of advertisements; and, as a way to drive on-trade sales in pubs and bars.

Direct Sport Sponsorship

Perhaps the most straightforward way for a company to attach itself to a sporting celebrity, team, league, or event is through a direct sponsorship arrangement. In this way, the company provides money, products, and/or services in return for the right to be associated with the sporting entity. Guinness has made heavy use of this form of marketing communication in a large number of its major markets around the world. In Great Britain, for example, Guinness has long been a sponsor of the Cheltenham Horseracing Festival and the London Irish Rugby Union Club. In 2005/2006, it entered the first year of an agreement to sponsor the Guinness Premiership, thus continuing a long-standing association with rugby union that, perhaps most notably, included the 1999 Rugby World Cup.

In Africa, Guinness has sponsored, among other sports, golf, tennis, and rugby. Perhaps most notable has been the continual attempt to leverage an association with football, by far the most popular sport on the continent. Sponsorship strategies have varied widely in scale and scope. For example, in 2006 it was announced that Guinness would be sponsoring the Western Area Football Association in Sierra Leone, in the words of the press release announcing the sponsorship, the first 'community league' in the country. Guinness has also been a sponsor of the Cameroon national team that won the 2000 Olympic and 2002 African Cup of Nations competitions and competed in the 2002 World Cup finals in Korea and Japan.

In Guinness' traditional home country of Ireland, Guinness is a major sponsor of sport and the arts. Its most high profile sponsorship, and indeed the most highly recognized sponsorship of any type in the country according to industry analysts Amárach Consulting, is the Guinness All-Ireland Hurling Championship. Starting with the inaugural 1995 Championship, Guinness involvement has included public relations and advertising campaigns that have taken in print, radio, television, and Internet media. According to Guinness' Assistant Brand Manager for Ireland, the sponsorship was intended to contemporize the brand by linking it to the power, pace, and inner strength required to compete in elite-level hurling, and also to draw upon the tribalism associated with supporting local teams. Further, the Head of Sponsorship for Ireland noted the close match between the values that underpin the Guinness brand and the sport. He suggested that:

> we looked at the DNA of both hurling and Guinness and they are so remarkably similar ... it's 9.9 out of 10. It's so, so perfect .... We've tested it, and it's proven over the last eight years to be a perfect fit.

Irrespective of the location of the sponsorship, the GBD was very clear in his conversations with me that all such arrangements were expected to contribute to the KBB in both conception and execution. This, he held, was central to bringing coherence to the brand across multiple markets. This consistency was also apparent in other marketing initiatives in which the firm engaged during this period. It was clearly stated by several marketing personnel involved in different markets around the world, and in corporate documents, that all advertising – with the exception of some promotions around St Patrick's Day that were intended to drive product trials – should build towards establishing the KBB. This is evident in various media formats, particularly television advertising, in which sport has also played a prominent role.

Sport and Advertising

When considering the different types of advertising that Guinness has utilized, it is quite apparent that there is a clear attempt to provide consistency with respect to delivering a particular message, providing certain imagery, and even utilizing particular sports. For example, the hurling and rugby union sponsorships in Ireland and England, respectively are used to leverage advertisements for Guinness on billboards, print, Internet, and television. However, sport is also used in ways not directly tied to official sponsorships. Two notable examples of this are the development of the global hurling advertisement, 'Free In', and the use of football in African markets.

One of the first executions of the KBB on a global scale was the 'Free In' advertisement that was launched in Great Britain in February 2002 and subsequently rolled out across other major international markets. The narrative below describes the scene:

> *Just one minute of injury time left in a knife-edge match and a vicious foul creates a chance. Over the bar and the game is tied, but into the goal and the game is won. Stepping up to take the free as the crowd go wild, our man's mind spins out of control. With a deep breath the player looks down. He sees himself and the coveted silver cup held aloft on the shoulders of exuberant fans, victoriously sipping a well-earned pint of creamy Guinness beer. Inspired by the vision of success he whips the ball up off the ground. If you want it, you've got to believe.*

While hurling is a sport little known outside of the Irish and Irish diasporic populations, that was seen as irrelevant. The Brand Manager for Great Britain explained the thought process behind this execution as follows:

> *What hurling gave was a generic sport that people didn't necessarily know exactly the rules, but they got the idea that it was a last-minute free-kick [sic], and were therefore able to take out the point of the bloke needing self-belief to score.*

Consequently, the advertisement featuring a little known sport – though of course we should not forget the Irish symbolism that will be important in some markets – and a nameless central character, was able to provide a message that, it was believed, would resonate in markets around the world.

While the 'Free In' advertisement was clearly a global manifestation of the KBB, sport has also been used to reify the message in locally distinct ways. For example, in Africa, football has been seen as a valuable advertising tool that has been integrated into other initiatives, including direct sponsorship. As the Brand Director for Africa suggested to me:

> *The need for self-belief, the need for inner strength is particularly relevant in Africa. The reason for this is that Africans see themselves as coming from a disadvantage. In every way of life, Africa is behind the world. Again Africans believe, because we are Africans we can overcome all of those obstacles and we can achieve things almost of world standard. It comes through in football and we've leveraged it, so one good example will be where we begin to say … if you believe in yourself and your ability you can overcome your obstacles and your disadvantages and perform at a first world class. We have leveraged that during the [2002 football] World Cup with the football ad, where we have shown Africans training on sub-standard pitches, without sports equipment and saying 'Well, because we are what we are, because we believe in ourselves, we can overcome' and then we lead on from that showing national teams, African national teams, that have played in the World Cup and have performed well. So again, it is tying that need of Africans to believe that in spite of our disadvantages we can still be reckoned with at the global stage, and tying that to the brand benefit of inner strength, that it reflects your inner strength.*

Again, we see an attempt to deliver the KBB through the use of sport. However, this time, the execution is locally specific rather than carried out in a way that can interact with different global populations at the same time. This local emphasis is also apparent in the third way in which Guinness uses sport in on-trade promotions.

On-Trade Sporting Promotion

While Guinness has sponsored major high profile events at a local (e.g. All-Ireland Hurling Championships, England's rugby union Premiership) and global (e.g. the 1999 Rugby World Cup) level, it also regularly tries to utilize other sporting events of which it is not a sponsor. This is intended to exploit the propensity that people have for wanting to watch sport 'live', often with other like-minded people. Thus, in recent years, Guinness has designed on-trade promotions in pubs and bars around the football and rugby union world cups, and the international rugby union 'Six Nations' competition featuring England, Scotland, Ireland, Wales, France, and Italy. During such promotions, Guinness will provide extensive in-house 'decoration', competitions, and often offer product promotions. While such campaigns can involve significant investment – Guinness spent £2 million on its 2002 FIFA World Cup promotion in England – the company does not, of course, have to pay official rights fees (about $40 million for the FIFA World Cup) nor does it have to exploit – and protect – its investment in numerous markets around the world. This makes it a much simpler campaign to manage.

Needless to say, Guinness marketers are also keen to maximize the return on their official sponsorship investments, so on-trade promotions also tend to feature as part of this aspect of the brand's marketing mix. A good example has occurred in Ireland as part of the leveraging of the Guinness All-Ireland Hurling Championships. In order to support this sponsorship, and drive trade in pubs and bars, there is a carefully orchestrated series of events that coincide with televised matches. Quiz nights, musical entertainment, and even talent competitions have all featured as part of a strategy intended to encourage individuals to watch the hurling encounters in local pubs and, of course, drink Guinness in the process.

Conclusion

Sport has assumed a prefigurative importance in the marketing strategy at Guinness. While individual emphases will alter over time, the value of sport lies in its malleability to different messages, its inherent global appeal, and its ability to reach individuals in different locales in idiosyncratic ways. As we see in the discussion here, sport has played a prominent role in the attempt by Guinness' marketing executives – those located in the global headquarters and those in local markets – to affirm the KBB of 'Guinness brings out your inner strength'. We see among Guinness executives a recognition of the reality of operating a transnational corporation (TNC) in the early days of the 21st century. Specifically, we can point to a desire to simultaneously provide a brand coherence that will overcome any tendency towards fragmentation caused by enhanced global communications while also being able to engage with individuals in different geographic spaces in locally relevant ways. Sport, as has been shown in this case, can play a key role in helping executives fulfil such potentially conflicting demands.

Case Diagnosis

The purpose of this analysis is to provide some insights into the context in which the brand positioning strategies at Guinness unfolded. It is a truism to say that no organization exists in a vacuum, but too often we tend to view the actions of organizational leaders in isolation from the broader environment in which they and their organizations operate. Thus, if we are to truly gain useful insight from the decisions and actions undertaken by those executives at Guinness involved in the global articulation of the brand, we must consider how they were influenced by, and also influenced, what was happening in the world around them. Central to this are attempts to reconcile competing pressures of being a truly global brand that is also viewed by geographically dispersed consumers as being locally relevant.

In 1983 (p. 22), Harvard Business School professor Theodore Levitt famously entreated senior managers to act 'as if the entire world (or major regions of it) were a single, largely identical entity' and supply the 'same things in the same way everywhere'. Central to this standardization thesis was the idea of a 'global village' in which geographically separated individuals would become increasingly connected through various electronic media, most notably television, and would thus come to exhibit homogenous demands. In line with this thinking, many corporations attempted to rationalize their products and promotional strategies in ways that would both satisfy this perceived homogeneity of demand while also exploiting the massive economies of scale available from the establishment of a global market (Bartlett and Ghoshal, 1989).

While it appeared that some firms were indeed able to establish truly global brands and deliver common products across the world – Coke, Levi Strauss, McDonald's, and Sony perhaps spring to mind – it was also quickly apparent that managers of such global behemoths ignored varying local demands at their peril. Consequently, firm executives began to accord much more attention to meeting demands for local differentiation, even if it was mainly apparent in the advertising and packaging around otherwise seemingly indistinguishable products. More recently, it has been suggested that we are once again entering an era of the 'global brand' (e.g. Quelch, 2003; Holt et al., 2004). However, this understanding of what a global brand is, and how it should be managed, is occurring in a very different historical epoch than when Levitt (1983) made his comments. Specifically, we have witnessed pronounced, and ongoing, transformations of the technological, social, political, and economic contexts within which TNCs now have to operate. For example, technological advancements have altered the ways in which we work, travel, and live; deregulation, free trade agreements, and the spread of market economies have, in many cases, significantly enhanced trading opportunities for TNCs; and accentuated nationalistic sentiments have become key considerations for local and foreign firms in many markets.

Needless to say, Guinness has not been immune from these contextual variations. At the end of the 20th century, the dominant behaviour among Guinness brand executives was to allow geographic divisions to position the Guinness brand in which ever way they thought would best fit local market requirements. As the Brand Director for Africa explained, 'Africa did its thing, Great Britain did its thing, and America did its thing'. While this was successful to some degree, it was also apparent that changes in the technological, social, and economic landscapes were rendering such an approach anachronistic. The Brand Manager for Great Britain explained how such changes were affecting the Guinness brand:

> *Every time we showed an ad on satellite TV [in Great Britain], that ad was also shown to everyone in Ireland who was watching satellite TV at the time, which is a fair audience. And when Ireland and ourselves had very different styles of advertising, which was only say a year ago, then that was becoming more and more of a problem: that consumers would be watching satellite one minute, see one completely different ad with a different strap line and a different idea behind it, to when they switched on to their terrestrial TV. And there are more examples of that, of media starting to cross more countries. Also … consumers moving around from country to country, they would see a slightly schizophrenic brand because in different countries you would see such a different type of positioning around it. And then thirdly, also an element of cost efficiency by the fact that ultimately we can reach the stage where we can show the same advert in different countries.*

Thus, while there was an economic aspect to the decision to replace a decentralized brand positioning strategy with a much more centralized one that was reflective of the intense competition in the global beer industry, the major driver for the revised strategy was the collapsing of time and space precipitated by technological advancements that have allowed media to cross borders in real time, and the increased flows of people for work and leisure from one country to another. Together, these have placed much greater pressure on corporate executives to ensure that there is brand coherence across territories that would have previously been seen as almost entirely unrelated.

While this coherence can provide a consistency that works against brand fragmentation, there is also the undeniable fact that different things matter to different people in different markets. Thus, while the global KBB developed at Guinness can provide a useful touchstone for staff around the world, there is also a need to make sure that it is delivered in a relevant way. This is where sport plays such an important role for Guinness, and of course other brands.

Sport can be useful at the global level because of its wide appeal. Thus, sponsors of the Olympics and FIFA World Cup rely on the fact that millions of individuals around the world will be interested enough to follow the action through different media and in turn – it is hoped – not only recognize who the sponsors are but also transfer some of the positive feelings about the event to the sponsor. At a deeper psychological level, sport also has a widespread appeal because it can throw up situations that individuals can relate to even if they have never directly experienced them. Thus, the 'Free In' advertisement has relevance for people around the world: even if they have never experienced hurling, or even know how it is played, they can appreciate the scenario of a young man under great personal pressure having to overcome self-doubt and draw on his 'inner strength' to succeed. We can readily relate such a situation to other more familiar sporting (e.g. David Beckham scoring a penalty against Argentina in the 2002 FIFA World Cup finals; Jonny Wilkinson kicking a penalty against Australia in the 2003 Rugby World Cup final; our own games played on a local pitch, court, or course) and non-sporting (e.g. having to do a presentation, sitting an examination, interviewing for a new job) events. Thus, while the advertisement is common across different markets, it can be interpreted in a way that is personally meaningful depending upon our own individual context.

Perhaps more importantly than the 'Free In' advertisement, however, is the way in which sport allows Guinness staff to make the brand relevant in an individual context. Key here is that sport is used in such a way that the Guinness brand becomes positioned as integral to local activities and, hopefully, some positive experiences among local people. Further, this must be done in such a way that the KBB is actively reinforced. The use of football in Africa is a good example. As the Brand Director for Africa told me, sponsorship of the Cameroon national team that won the 2000 Olympics and the 2002 African Cup of Nations, and that competed in the 2002 FIFA World Cup finals, along with television advertisements that showed African teams training on pitches and using equipment that put them at a distinct disadvantage to non-African teams, emphasized the way in which Africans, despite some disadvantages, can succeed against better equipped rivals because of their greater 'inner strength.' By locating the Guinness brand within this message, the KBB is presented and reinforced in a locally meaningful way. Similar approaches have been adopted with other sports around the world: the articulation of the message may have been different, but the location of the brand and the KBB within the sporting context provides a local resonance in what is perceived by those at Guinness as being an effective way.

To sum up, in a global age, it has become extremely important that executives at TNCs carry out a difficult balancing act. On the one hand, in an age of rapidly increasing flows of images and people across geographic borders, it has become incumbent upon executives to overcome the potential for brand fragmentation by offering a consistent central message – a KBB – that provides coherence across international markets. However, within this, there must also be space to allow individuals to interpret and consume the brand in personally relevant ways (e.g. consider the differing interpretations of the Guinness brand in Ireland, among the diasporic Irish community in the USA, and among Guinness drinkers in Japan and Jamaica). This requires the creation and active management of polysemic, multi-vocal texts. These are positioned to allow multi-level interpretation of the brand that permit simultaneous engagement with, and negation of, local idiosyncrasies. With worldwide sales increasing between 4 per cent and 6 per cent each year from 2001 to 2005, quite significant for a very mature industry, it appears that those at Guinness have been able to realize an effective global brand positioning strategy in which sport has played a central role.

Case Questions

1 Consider which new global and local sport properties that could be used to help Guinness reinforce its KBB. Explain the logic behind your selections.
2 Using the examples that you developed in response to question 1, explain how you could leverage them in different ways to maximize their impact on Guinness' KBB.
3 Pick a global brand other than Guinness. Outline the properties that you feel it should develop in order to craft an effective global brand position.
4 Research the Guinness personalities Michael Power and Adam King. Explain how they may be used to help Guinness retain its brand position of 'Guinness brings out your inner strength.'
5 Drawing on your research for question 4, explain how you would use specific sports to help further secure the brand position of 'inner strength' in particular markets.
6 Create your own advertisement that features sport and would help further secure Guinness' KBB.

Case Resources

Sources

This case is based upon information that I have collected from a variety of primary and secondary sources. These have included interviews with Guinness executives, company documents, internal presentations, employee orientation materials, videos of advertising campaigns, consulting reports, the official Guinness website, popular press accounts, and academic articles. Some of this material has formed the basis of other articles (e.g. Amis, 2003, 2005).

Reading

Amis, J. (2003). Good things come to those who wait: The strategic management of image and reputation at Guinness. *European Sport Management Quarterly*, Vol. 3, pp. 189–214.

Amis, J. (2005). Beyond sport: Imaging and re-imaging a global brand, in Silk, M., Andrews, D. and Cole, C. (Eds.), *Corporate Nationalisms: Sport, Cultural Identity and Transnational Marketing*. Berg, Oxford, UK, pp. 143–165.

Bartlett, C.A. and Ghoshal, S. (1989). *Managing Across Borders: The Transnational Solution*. Harvard Business School Press, Boston, MA.

Holt, D.B., Quelch, J.A. and Taylor, E.L. (2004). How global brands compete. *Harvard Business Review*, Vol. 82, September, pp. 68–75.

Quelch, J. (2003). The return of the global brand. *Harvard Business Review*, Vol. 81, August, pp. 22–23.

Rines, S. (2001). Guinness Rugby World Cup Sponsorship: A global platform for meeting business objectives. *International Journal of Sports Marketing and Sponsorship*, Vol. 3, pp. 449–465.

Schultz, M., Hatch, M.J. and Larsen, M.H. (Eds.) (2000). *The Expressive Organization: Linking Identity, Reputation and the Corporate Brand*. Oxford University Press, New York.

Silk, M., Andrews, D. and Cole, C. (Eds.) (2005). *Corporate Nationalisms: Sport, Cultural Identity and Transnational Marketing*. Berg, Oxford, UK.

Simmons, J. and Griffiths, M. (2001). *Believe: Six Turning Points for Guinness that Hinged on Inner Strength*. Guinness UDV, London.

Websites

http://www.guinness.com
http://www.sponsorship.com/
http://www.business2000.ie/cases/cases/case413.htm. Sponsorship: A Successful Partnership Between the GAA and Guinness.

Case

12

Sports in the country of a billion: a study of the marketing possibilities and the resulting development of less popular sports in India

K.K. Ramachandran

Case Focus

The case examines the enormous possibilities for sports marketing, as yet untapped, that exist in India, a country with a population of over a billion people. It also highlights the interrelationship that exists between sports marketing, business and the development of sports events which have until now been ignored in this country with a very large rural population.

Keywords

- Indian sports
- Sponsorship
- Sports marketing
- Billion people
- Cricket
- BCCI

Case Summary

The case briefly traces India's long history of sports activities dating back to the Vedic Period, from which games like chess and polo evolved.It examines current popular games and sports events in India and studies the reasons for poor performance and lack of interest in most games and sports events. It offers sports marketing as a useful method of developing these because the generation of funds through promotion and sponsorship depends on the popularity of the event. While pioneers in this area could choose sports and events that were already popular, later entrants can benefit by developing and promoting those less popular. In a country which has divergent cultures, the possibilities offered constitute a wide spectrum. The case also takes into consideration governmental support for sport.

Case Elements

India is a country of a billion people but is also a country which is struggling in the field of sport, surprising, given that many sporting events originated there. Sports can tell us a lot about ourselves as individuals and as a society. Cricket is a religion in the country and the Board of Control for Cricket in India (BCCI) is now the world's richest cricket association despite a deficit of $150,000 in 1992. The BCCI has increased its profits from $1.11 million in 2004–2005 to $7.64 million in 2005–2006. Yet the Indian team was eliminated in the preliminary round of the 2007 World Cup despite all the facilities and support provided by the BCCI. Last year, Forbes magazine attempted a valuation of the different cricket boards. According to its calculations, the BCCI was worth $1.5 billion, the England and Wales Cricket Board $270 million and Cricket Australia $225 million. The International Cricket Council (ICC) was pegged much lower at $200 million. The others were Pakistan ($100 million), South Africa ($65 million), Sri Lanka ($14 million) and Bangladesh ($5 million). 'There are 10 full members of

ICC, but in terms of revenue. India contributes more than 70 per cent to the game', the magazine wrote. 'Most sponsorships and broadcast rights come from India, and Indian tours make foreign boards rich.' As a justification for this case study the following interesting statistical snippets are offered:

- Since its Independence, India has won only four individual Olympic medals (K.D. Jhadav for Wrestling, K. Malleshwari for Weightlifting, R. Rathore for shooting and Leander for tennis).
- India last won a hockey gold way back in 1980!
- Currently India is ranked a lowly 157 in world football.
- India's excellence in swimming is limited to the SAF Games in spite of talents like Nisha Millet and Rohan Poncha.

This case is a study of the marketing possibilities of the development of less popular sports in India.

In the last 11 decades, sport has undergone an immense transformation. Gone are the days, when school teachers, professors and elders in the family drew the attention of the younger generation to the fact that the purpose of games was to inculcate team spirit, improve physical prowess and gentlemanliness. To participate and to meet victory and defeat with equanimity was considered to be the essence of sportsmanship. Every player or athlete was reminded that the prize in the ancient Greek Olympics was a wreath of laurel leaves whose value lay not in its monetary worth but in the effort that earned it.

When sports entered the international arenas of intercountry football, hockey, cricket, tennis and basketball matches and of course the modern version of the Olympics, the important factor of national prestige arose. At this stage, the players and athletes were still amateurs with 'incentives' being given 'off the record' in order to permit sports personalities to retain their amateur status. From this nebulous state professional sports evolved all over the world with India being no exception.

Like much else in India, sport constitutes a complex matter. The single question that nags the minds of most sports enthusiasts is: 'Why is a country, with a population of 1 billion, which is considered to be the possible origin of a number of sports events like polo, judo, karate and games like chess, cards and snakes and ladders unable to produce a large number of medal winners at the international level?'

A backward glance shows us that the history of sports in India dates back to the Vedic Age. A mantra in the Atharva Veda gives a clear definition, that is 'duty is in my right hand and the fruits of victory in my left', which resembles the spirit of the Olympic oath that is 'for the honour of my country and the glory of sport'. Yet our athletes and players have not made their mark in international competition – even in hockey, the national game in which we were unbeaten till the middle of the last century.

In the current scenario, the task of governing and promoting sports is distributed among a number of sports associations and organizations, with the Indian Olympic Association and the Sports Authority of India spear-heading the efforts to raise the standard of Indian sports through a variety of talent identification schemes. Apart from the central governing bodies, another category of organizations viz. the sports academies and institutes are actively involved in grooming Indian sportspersons. The current list of governing bodies for sports, institutes and academies includes:

- The Indian Olympic Association
- Sports Authority of India
- Laxmibai National Institute of Physical Education, Gwalior
- Netaji Subhas National Institute of Sports, Patiala
- National Cricket Academy, Bangalore
- MRF Pace Foundation, Chennai
- Tata Football Academy, Jamshedpur

Unfortunately, despite the existence of these organizations, sport-related marketing is in its infancy and there is much more to be done before sport becomes an integral part of marketing in India. It is also a matter of regret that neither the physical education colleges nor the business management colleges offer a course on sports marketing.

Specialization in Sports Marketing

Ogilvy & Mather (India) Advertising's recent decision to dedicate an entire division to cater to sport marketing and communication indicates that specialization is gaining momentum in the sports business. More and more advertising and media agencies are entering the area of sports business, thereby enhancing levels of specialization. A positive aspect of this entry is the impetus given to sports promotion by these agencies, drawing from the international experience of their parent companies. Currently cricket dominates in India and brands like Pepsi have taken the lead in promoting this particular sport. 'Cricket is now too overheated', says Gupta of SET MAX, referring to the amounts being paid for rights. 'At $1.1 billion (paid by ESPN Star Sports for the audiovisual rights for ICC events up to 2015), it will be impossible to make money.' A decade down the line, he could be proved right, but for a different reason. The game in 2020 is more likely to be Twenty-20. It might make money. But will it be cricket? The forthcoming Commonwealth Games (2010) has also given a fillip to the growth in sports-led marketing.

Current Shortcomings in Sports Marketing

Until recently sports marketing has been restricted to player management in India, in the areas of endorsements and newspaper columns. The focus has mostly been on the individual player especially in cricket. Sachin Tendulkar, arguably India's best-ever cricket player, earns some $30 a minute. India's highest-paid CEO, Mukesh Ambani of Reliance Industries, gets $10, and celluloid superstar Amitabh Bachchan, $8. This trend is spreading to other sports too. If one player – like tennis player, Sania Mirza – shines, everybody wants to go after her. This is neither systematic nor sustainable because companies end up supporting individual brilliance rather than putting money into a system. In Indian sports, the biggest weakness is that whenever money flows into a sport, it ends up with individuals rather than in a system that can help build that sport. It is opportunistic in nature and very, very limited in its scope. Others agree that the focus on individual incentives lies at the root of many problems. Unfortunately, the individual is valued much more than the team sport in India.

Ignored has been the fact that the popularity of other sports is growing and that interest in sport in general is growing gradually among the population. Of course it will take some time before other forms of sport catch up with cricket but the increased interest in watching and participating in them is encouraging. Today, there are alternatives; Vishwanath Anand is the world chess champion. Sania Mirza has been doing exciting things on the tennis court. And, after several barren decades, India has started picking up medals at the Olympics. Indians have long lacked sporting icons. The moment they have others to cheer for, cricket could lose its primacy – and possibly its mass appeal. The process may have begun. 'There is a huge consumer market in South Asia and (Indian) advertisers have plans for this market.' It is a common knowledge that some of the advertising money is also going to football and car racing, even without an Indian team.

The Changing Attitude to Sports Marketing

Despite the fact that sports-related marketing in India still has a long way to go, there is a gradually increasing awareness of the immense possibilities that exist in this area of marketing and brand identification, thanks to a few pioneers in the area. These thought leaders have, by their positive and successful use of sport in their marketing plans, created a new attitude to sports marketing even though the general belief that there is a lack of scientific evaluation and benchmarking in this area. The entry of media and advertising agencies has also positioned sports marketing as an intrinsic part of their media strategies.

Budgets and Sports Marketing

Funds and their proper allocation are the foundations of the super structure of a country's excellence in sports activities and budgets a vital factor are part of this. Currently, cricket is the largest beneficiary of the commercialization of sports in India but the National Olympic Committee (NOC) is also eagerly hoping for a much larger grant than in the previous financial year in the current budget. Other factors, which are expected to give a fillip to India's performance in the Commonwealth Games and the

Asian Games are the opportunity to organize the Commonwealth Games (2010) and bidding, though ultimately unsuccessfully for the Asian Games (2014).

Budgets and taxes go hand in hand. Hence, it is but natural to hope that the tax returns arising from the rapidly increasing sales of sports equipment (consequent to the new interest in and attitude to sports along with taxes from other related factors) will help the formulators of the 2007–2008 budget to make an allocation for sport. It is also hoped that the new attitude to sports would have been noted by the ministry which looks after sports and the politicians who head sports committees. They could also help by sending more players than officials to major sports events! There can be no catalyst more powerful than the supportive policy of government to hasten the development of sports and through it indirectly sports marketing.

Cricket and the Marketing Panorama

Under the existing conditions, cricket provides over two dozen areas for brand placements, which include T-shirts bearing messages, logos and the now ubiquitous perimeter boards. According to estimates, brand visibility generates 520 crore rupees a year, while sports-related products like energy drinks consumed during breaks and which are able to harmoniously blend with a sport also generate sizeable but smaller amounts. Since cricket was the pioneer in building the sports marketing business, it naturally commands the largest proportion of funds. This in turn has had an indirect positive influence. Other companies tried to join the cricket bandwagon and later began to look at other sport events. This is certainly a positive trend for both brands and sports for as increasing numbers of brands enter the fray a wider spectrum of sporting events will benefit by their entry. The set back in Jamaica in the 2007 World Cup at the hands of Bangladesh and Sri Lanka is certainly a stumble during India's efforts but the large panorama of Indian cricket and the spirit of resilience among Indian cricketers will surely tide Indian cricket and relevant marketing ventures well, as was evident in India's convincing win over Bangladesh in both the one dayers and tests.

Swimming and the Marketing Panorama

Virdhawal Vikram Khade is the fulcrum providing leverage for India's hopes for a gold medal in the 2012 Olympics. This child prodigy, who is the fastest in his age group, has been hailed as the Tutankhamen of Indian swimming. Then there is the old favourite Rohan Poncha with his nine gold medals, two silver and as many bronze at the National Games. In addition, there are Twenty-20 other record breaking feats in swimming and one in diving. With India preparing to host the Commonwealth Youth Games in Pune and intending to call in a foreign coach, to help in the participation in

South Asian Swimming in Pakistan and the age group events in Indonesia the swimming segment is an inviting proposition for sports marketers. Whether business houses will use it, remains to be seen.

Formula One and the Marketing Panorama

Ever since the success of Narain Karthikeyan, the number of Indian fans with a passion for Formula One has grown. Currently, the Indian fan has to go abroad to witness this sport live however, it is estimated that by the year 2010, India will have circuits at home, with Delhi the earliest of them. There is abundant interest among leading competitors to participate in Indian events – a fact which is borne out by Bernie Ecclestone's comment to the Bloomsberg News Service, India is a country that is probably going to grow quicker than China. We had to make sure that we find the right places in India.

Hockey and the Marketing Panorama

For a long-time hockey or field hockey as it was formerly known (to differentiate it from ice hockey) was a game at which India excelled as the Olympic champions. In those days we scored many goals against our European competitors and were renowned for our stick work, dribbling and short passing game. Even today Dhyanchand is considered the wizard of hockey and the greatest exponent of stick work. After one of the international matches his stick was split open to see if it contained concealed magnets, which made the ball 'stick' to his stick. After Dhyanchand until the time of his son Ashok Kumar, the Balbir Singhs, Udham Singh and Claudius inspired other players and kept the game going.

From this pinnacle of eminence, India descended to a point where by the last quarter of the 20th century, we were struggling to make the last four in The Olympics and The World Cup. Changing the rules has often proved detrimental to India. A few decades ago, the country had no challengers in field hockey. Then came Astroturf – a faster surface – and rules were changed to make the game more 'exciting'. India just couldn't adapt. It didn't have the money to put up Astroturf surfaces across the country. And the players didn't have the muscle, size and stamina that the new game demanded. Two major factors were responsible for this downfall. First, several changes were made in the game itself. Gone were the bully offs at the centre and the 25 yards lines, the penalty bully and the roll-ins for balls that went out of the side lines. Instead of the tufts of turf the field became a smooth fast game providing greater interest for the spectator and greater facilities for accurate long passes. Second, India did not and has not responded sufficiently to new playing conditions, rules and game strategies. Third, this was partly caused by insufficient marketing and training, which in turn is the result of little interest in the game on the part of the

Indian public even though it is our national game. If business and government are able to sponsor popular national and international events as well as modern training facilities, India will surely make it back to the top and business too will benefit.

Tennis and the Marketing Panorama

Tennis is another game in which India had done well at the international level from the time of Ramanathan Krishnan and later his son Ramesh Krishnan. The Amirtharaj brothers, Leander Paes, Mahesh Boopathy and currently Sania Mirza have kept the Indian flag within the ambit of professional tennis. The new crop of talented probable includes Vivek Shokeen, Somdev Dev Varma, Karan Rastogi and Sunil Kumar Sipaeya. Despite the pioneering efforts at raising the standard of tennis in India, which have been partially successful, we have been unable to make it to the finals of Wimbledon and other major tournaments due to three major reasons.

First, the game is not sufficiently popular in our largely rural population. The achievements of our leading players are largely viewed through the sports columns of newspapers and sports magazines. Since important tournaments are played mostly in cities and large towns the rural population seldom gets a chance to view the game live. Naturally, the game has not caught the attention of the rustic population, where the game is barely kept alive by clubs and a few educational institutions. The second reason is the unfortunate intrusion of unnecessary politics into the higher realms of the game. The Indian debacle in the Asian Games at Doha is still fresh in the mind of many a player. The third contributory factor is the expensive nature of the game. The solution is for both business and government to take greater interest in the game.

Football and the Marketing Panorama

Football has commanded much greater popularity than hockey or cricket from the beginning of the 20th century. However, we have not notched up any notable achievements at the international level in the past apart from the fourth place in the 1956 Olympics and the gold medal in the 1962 Asian Games. Currently, India is ranked 157 out of 199 FIFA members but Indian football has recently received a fillip with India bidding to host the AFC Asian Cup in 2011. This will open up new possibilities in manufacturing and marketing equipment connected with the game, construction of international standard infrastructure and business and brand development opportunities.

Athletics and the Marketing Panorama

Indian athletics declined between the 2002 Busan Games and the Doha events. The chief causative factor appears to be the absence of a foolproof list of entries, which left the officials without a clear picture of the participants until almost the eve of the events. The 33rd National Games, which were held at Guwahati on the brand new Polyton track, was robbed of its glitter by the absence of some of the stars, who could have raised the standard of the events to much greater heights.

The armed forces, the railways, the state police departments, corporate houses and the state athletic associations have been sponsoring individuals and teams in the field of athletics under the overall control of the Indian Olympic Association for quite some time. Milka Singh, P.T. Usha, Shiny Wilson (née Abraham) to name a few came through these channels. However, this is a segment of sports in which marketing has not utilized the ample opportunities that exist and as a result business has not contributed much to the development of Indian athletics.

Water Sports and the Marketing Panorama

Water sports received great encouragement with the launch of Yaka, a Goa based adventure Sports Company, which distributes kayaks manufactured in New Zealand. This marks the recognition of India as a white-water destination with enormous sports marketing possibilities. With its many mountain rivers, rapids, beautiful backwaters and vast, spectacular beaches India presents an ideal destination for kayaking and adventure sports. Arcadia and Contour are the new names in India offering opportunities in kayaking at various levels, water sports and water adventure.

Case Diagnosis

To understand and analyze Indian sports one has to know about India. India is a huge country with many different cultures. To market a new product or to market a product, where products that were early entrants command the lion's share of the existing market, a demand has to be created. In India, cricket had a head start, because it had early sponsors in the British, and the Maharajas. During British rule and for a short time after independence, cricket was a status symbol in which Gymkhana Clubs with a predominantly European membership and the Officer's Clubs with members from the upper segments of society kept the sport alive. At times cricket was used either to gain recognition or to prove the ability to beat the ruling race at the game, which they had introduced.

The advent of professional cricket and tennis turned stadiums into advertising zones opening up the new avenue of sports marketing. The introduction of one-day matches, vastly improved playing areas and stadiums, radio commentaries, live TV – telecasts, sponsorships and brand ambassadors put cricket ahead of tennis. However, the other games and athletics did not receive the same encouragement, though individuals did benefit in a small way.

With more and more businesses trying to enter the cricket segment of sports marketing, new entrants were forced to examine possibilities in other games until India reached the current situation in the first decade of the 21st century. At the root of this slow change lies the increasing interest of the Indian public to various games and events including indigenous games like kabbadi, which has now been included in the Olympics. More important is the role played by the Ministry of Sports.

India needs to rethink the business model for sports. The current model needs improvement in areas such as governance as well as in the way incentives for players are structured. Three problems with the business model of Indian sport, first, the market is not as deep. It allows those who have talent to command a very high price, while those who are not part of that small group don't make money. In India, the money from endorsements exceeds payment for performance by many multiples. We should ask if these incentives are structured the right way. Second, the governance system for sports is not functioning effectively. The third issue is the motivation of the sportsmen. In the past, it was an honour to represent India. Now players look at only money since some cricket players make $30 million to $40 million a year. If you make so much money, to what extent does that take away your motivation for the game? Money has changed the nature of the game.

Where does the money come from? Eventually, of course, it comes from the consumer. In India cricket sells better than anything else, including movies. In a curious sidelight, Bollywood, as Bombay's film industry is called, tried to cash in on World Cup fever with cricket-themed movies such as *Hat Trick, Say Salaam India* and *Meerabhi Not Out*. The first two were released to coincide with the World Cup and have bombed at the box office, in keeping with the Indian team's performance. Earlier movies on cricket have done better. Cricket has been a catalyst for social transformation, which is borne out by the film *Lagaan* (which won an Oscar nomination) and has cricket as its central link.

Some say discipline is a problem area too. Players have been known to arrange their schedules to accommodate their sponsors instead of participating in mandatory practice sessions and coaching camps. The coach and trainer have no authority because the top players never listen to the coach. Another challenge facing not just cricket but also other sports is the severe shortage of sports infrastructure. For long, food has come before football. Though India is no longer a shortage economy, sports and games are still not top of mind at most schools. Even today, if faced with a choice between funding a midday meal programme (which have had remarkable success in improving attendance levels) and investing in a playing field, administrators are more than likely to choose the former.

The cash-rich BCCI, too, has found it difficult to set up the grassroots infrastructure to locate new talent. This is one of its mandates, but it has been largely content with refurbishing old stadiums. In its defense, though, it must be said that all the BCCI's wealth wouldn't make a significant impact. That does not mean that the BCCI is blameless. Cricket may be a gentleman's game, but for its administrators, it is a pugnacious sport. At the BCCI, every election for its office bearers is hard fought, and many election contests end up in court players are stars – and can sometimes act like prima donnas. Fighting often breaks out among different factions. Office bearers sometimes make more news than cricketers do. It is run by industrialists and politicians. A long-term vision for developing the game is not apparent.

Today in India, there are five factors, which must be blended to bring about expansion in sports marketing, bringing more games and sports events into public focus and raising the standard of each to international standards. These are:

1 Greater participation of more business houses in popularizing and developing games or sports events of their choice at the district, state, national or international level.
2 Participation in the training of individual players, athletes or participants using the latest methods and equipment under internationally reputed trainers brought in to India for the purpose.
3 Sending participants and teams to participate in events in other countries.
4 Construction of infrastructural facilities by the Ministry of Sports with corporate cooperation.
5 Overall coordination, supervision and control of all these activities by the Ministry of Sports, which will benefit from the taxes that sports marketing brings in.

At the root of these five factors lies the mantra, which will help Indian sports and sports marketing to complement each other in the future. Sponsorship today is the fastest growing marketing medium in the world. The growth of sponsorship is higher than the expected rates of advertising. India needs to leverage this advantage to bring more funds to those games which needs funds to improve the standards.

Case Questions

1 What do you think are the reasons for Indian sports not being able to perform well?
2 Evaluate the infrastructural facilities of Indian sports.
3 Trace the factors which have improved the marketability of sports other than cricket in India

4 Highlight the relationship between sports marketing, the development of the sport and the development of the individual participant in the game or event.

5 Compare and contrast the marketing challenges of cricket and other sports in the Indian context.

6 Enumerate the different possibilities of other sports bodies adopting BCCI strategies to successfully market other forms of sports.

7 Why is India unsuccessful even in the sports which have originated in the country?

8 How can we encourage India's youth to achieve excellence in sports?

9 Is something amiss in our strength as a nation when it comes to promoting sport?

Case Resources

Reading

Baimbridge, M. (1998). Outcome uncertainty in sporting competition: The Olympic games 1896–1998. *Applied Economics Letters*, Vol. 5, No. 3, pp. 161–164. [Competition]

Barney, R.K. (1998). The great transformation: Olympic victory ceremonies and the medal podium. *Olympika*, Vol. 7, pp. 89–112. [Ceremony]

Georgiadis, K. (1992). International Olympic Academy: The history of its establishment, aims and activities, in IOA, op. cit., pp. 57–61. [International Olympic Academy]

Gillen, P. (1994). The Olympic games and global society. *Arena*, Vol. 4, pp. 5–15.

Shank, M.D. (2002). *Sports Marketing: A Strategic Perspective*, 2nd edition. Prentice Hall Inc., Englewood.

Shilbury, D., Quick, S. and Westerbeek, H. (1998). *Strategic Sport Marketing*. Allen and Unwin, UK.

Websites

Sports Marketing News

http://www.agencyfaqs.com/perl/news/index.html?sid=15717

Sports Marketing

http://www.indianchild.com/marketing/sports-marketing.htm

http://www.indiantelevision.net/headlines/y2k3/jan/jan133.htm

http://www.wharton.universia.net/index.cfm?fa=viewfeature&id=966&language=english

http://www.blonnet.com/2004/09/18/stories/2004091801270700.htm

BCCI

http://en.wikipedia.org/wiki/Board_of_Control_for_Cricket_in_India

Sportsmarketingsurveys

http://www.sportsmarketingsurveys.com/vsite/vnavsite/page/
   directory/0,10853,5045-148760-165976-nav-list,00.html

Indian Cricket: Sports News

http://news.bbc.co.uk/1/hi/world/south_asia/6491053.stm

http://cricketnow.in/cricket-news/official-bcci-website-launched.php

http://www.tribuneindia.com/2002/20020323/spr-trib.htm

13

Developments in web technology: enhancing the viewing spectacle of sport

Paul Turner

Case Focus

The case examines the introduction of technology through the World Wide Web and the impact it has had on the viewing of particular sports, in particular on the way in which this web-based technology is enhancing the television viewing experience. The case has two distinct areas of focus. The first aspect investigates the impact of the Web on creating a broadcast viewing experience for an audience, particularly through the introduction of streaming video, while the second issue addresses the impact of technical enhancements such as motion analysis, graphics enhancement and rule changes on the Web delivery for sport.

Keywords

- World Wide Web
- Sport viewing
- Streaming video
- Motion analysis
- Virtual replay

Case Summary

The impact of technology in sport, while always having had an effect, has in the past 20 years become even more pronounced. The emergence of computer data analysis, increased memory capacity associated with database management systems, developments in broadcasting, graphical representation and re-creation of sport, all coupled with the enhancement and immediacy of information transfer has resulted in a change to the way sport is now packaged and presented to the spectator. While sport has continued to package itself in ways to encourage increased game attendance, it has also sought ways to enhance its offering to the viewing spectator. This case views sport through the elements of enhanced viewing experiences that are being presented to the sport watcher, particularly through the implementation of streaming video on the Internet.

The first part of the case introduces the concept of web broadcasting technology, while the second part examines the introduction of technology through the World Wide Web and the impact it has had on sport, in particular on the way in which a sporting organization might initiate changes to their rules as a result of this web-based technology. The way in which sport is presented through the broadcast to the viewer has become so real, lifelike and 'in your face', that the viewer often now gets a better seat than the spectators at the venue and even the match officials on the field. This leads to potential conflict arising in the situation when the viewer sees an obvious mistake made by a match official. The result has been the introduction of additional referees in some cases, while the addition of virtual and real replays to be reviewed by an official has occurred in other cases.

While the case presented represents a fictional account of a situation, the opportunities and examples are based around a 'real-life' scenario. That said the people and circumstances presented act as a basis for analysis and discussion. The case is not intended to illustrate either effective or ineffective handling of a situation.

Case Elements

Joan Bennett sat in her office at Table Tennis Australia (TTA) and looked at the yearly planner. While the normal daily activities associated with running a National Sporting Federation were listed, the major highlight was the inclusion of an Australian leg of the 2008 Pro Tour Series to be held in July (see Figure 13.1). While table tennis had been part of the Olympic and

ITTF Pro Tour 2008 and Pro Tour Grand Finals
Professional circuit

January
16–20 Croatian Open, Zagreb
23–27 Slovenian Open, Velenje

February
08–11 India Open, New Delhi
13–17 **LIEBHERR** Qatar Open, Doha
19–22 Kuwait Open, Kuwait City

April
12–15 **LIEBHERR** Brazil Open
19–22 **LIEBHERR** Chile Open, Santiago

June
14–17 Volkswagen Open, Korea
21–24 Volkswagen Open, Japan, Chiba

July
01–05 Volkswagen Open, China
013–16 *Australian Open*, Melbourne

August
23–26 Chinese Taipei Open, Taiwan
30/08–02/09 Panasonic China Open

October
18–21 Serbian Open, Belgrade
25–28 **LIEBHERR** French Open, Toulouse

November
31/10–04/11 **LIEBHERR** Austrian Open, Wels
07–11 **LIEBHERR** German Open, Bayreuth
15–18 Swedish Open, Gothenburg

December
13–16 Volkswagen Pro Tour Grand Finals, Beijing CHN

Figure 13.1 2008 ITTF Pro-Tour Series
Source: Adapted from http://www.ittf.com/TMS/PDF/2007Properties.pdf accessed on 20/02/2007

Commonwealth Games for some time now, having a major international tournament as part of the professional circuit presented an opportunity to move Australian Table Tennis into the mainstream in media, sponsorship and sporting terms, both in Australia and internationally. The potential opportunities to grow the sport and attract interest from sponsors and the media would be the challenge for TTA.

Joan knew that this tournament presented an immense opportunity to develop the sport. Table tennis was already recognized as one of the most popular sports in Asia, and in particular within the Chinese markets. It was reported that in China more than 100 million people play table tennis, and the cumulative audience of Chinese adult television viewers of the Volkswagen World Individual Championships was listed at 527 million (ittf.com, 2006). Equally, TMS International reported that table tennis attracted an amazing 255 million television viewers (cumulative audience) during the week of the 2006 LIEBHERR World Team Championships in Bremen. An interesting note about this broadcast was that Chinese fans did not seem to have a preference between men's and women's matches, which is not the case in some other parts of the world where men's matches were predominantly favoured (tmsin.com, 2007). The figures being presented to Joan regarding the interest in table tennis in China was of great relevance to the broader Australian business community. The Chinese interest in the sport presented a great opportunity for sponsors to come forward in order to develop links with potential Asian business and tourism destinations.

While it was great to be part of the International Table Tennis Federation (ITTF) Pro Tour at long last, with the potential to tap into broader international markets through business and sponsorship links that could emerge through this event, this also brought with it many additional complications. While the obligations surrounding the management of the event, attraction of the world's best players, access to world-class venues, ability to host athletes, officials and media, and the capacity to attract sponsorship all brought with them many challenges, by far the greatest opportunity but also the biggest headache in terms of learning faced by Joan and her organizing committee was the 'web-management' of the event.

Joan thumbed through her copy of the ITTF Pro Tour Directives (ITTF, 2006). This document, covering the organizers' obligations, technical implementation of the event, arrival and departure, hotel, meals, transportation, media, results, ITTF Website and spectators was simple enough to follow. It was Section 4.4 however, which referred to the ITTF Website that was of most interest. Section 4.4 stated:

The world wide web will become an universal tool of communication in the future. A lot of information is provided through the web. Now, there is a lot of sports websites and the competition between the biggest of them is very intense. Our target is not to implement a 'showcase website' with static information, but on the contrary an interactive website where the information is permanently 'live'.

Interactivity means that we must allow to all users and fans the opportunity to:

- buy articles and products with a secure payment online;
- give opinion through a forum;
- write and ask questions to the responsible through an e.mail service;
- keep up with the news and keep a close eye to the matches 'live' through streaming video pictures which can also be downloaded;
- live broadcast coverage of events.

The capacity to develop the current TTA website to incorporate e-commerce, enhanced graphics and streaming broadcasts was a step into the iFuture for TTA. Their current information-based website was a long way short of that which was being specified by the ITTF.

The emergence of broadcasting opportunities and in particular web broadcasting was becoming a key direction of the ITTF. Recently, the English Table Tennis Association introduced new technology in order to promote one of its major events of the year. Live streaming was available for the first time from the English National Championships staged in Sheffield, in March 2007 (ITTF.com, 2007).

Joan knew that the developments occurring in the broadcast of international table tennis were presenting great opportunities for the sport, but she had many reservations about the capacity of the local organizing body to move quickly enough to adapt and include the technologies to achieve the opportunities that would emerge. There were potential problems with the actual delivery of broadband services across the country which had the potential to impact on the delivery of a quality live broadcast. While the event would be broadcast live into key Asian and European countries, via the ITTF broadcast partner and in conjunction with local television stations, other countries would only receive the broadcast through the live streaming site on the Internet. There had already been much controversy in the news about the inadequacy of the Australian broadband service. Just recently Joan had viewed a report on the television about the poor quality services being provided to Australian consumers. The speed and quality of delivery were being brought into question. This was potentially creating an external environmental problem to the TTA, in order to maximize the distribution of the Pro Tour event to the world.

Also Joan had recently read that the capacity to deliver this technology to mobile devices such as the mobile phone was not being developed quickly enough. While images were available through the on-demand content provided over a 3G mobile network, the introduction of mobile TV (also known as DVB-H) had already been successfully implemented in the USA and Europe (Moses, 2007). While Joan really did not understand the full implications associated with the technology, she was concerned that these types of problems may jeopardise the delivery of the event, and in the longer term the future of Australia being able to host major international table tennis tournaments.

In discussions with the organization responsible for managing the broadcasting of international table tennis, TMS International, Joan already knew that this organization was clearly stating in its core business distribution that it is 'now very much "on track" to achieve most probably the biggest TV audience than any previous World Table Tennis Championships'. Agreements were already in place to provide coverage to at least three continents (Europe, Asia and North America) plus large geographical areas such as the Middle East (Africa and Asia) as well as high populated countries such as India and China. Eurosport International and Eurosport 2 were contracted to cover 58 countries in Europe, while CCTV were in place to broadcast extensively the event in China. Three additional regional Chinese networks were also part of the distribution network, adding to the TV exposure in that country.

TMS International had also recently negotiated the establishment of a 24 hour permanent Internet TV channel for the ITTF available worldwide to any broadband Internet connection. This new initiative had been established in order to provide worldwide exposure to ITTF events. The service is readily accessible from the ITTF's website and the ITTF's Chinese language website. The 2008 Pro Tour events had been determined as being events that could be web-cast on the ITTF Internet TV channel that commenced web-casting towards the end of 2007. An ITTF official stated that 'This is extremely good news and will help all our members to access our events on their computers as long as they have a fast Internet connection' (tmsin.com, 2007).

While TMS International assumed responsibility for developing international table tennis broadcasts, the actual organization that Joan's event committee would be dealing with was IEC In Sports. With respect to the Oceania region IEC In Sports were the Swedish-based Sports Marketing Agency specializing in television distribution and rights consultancy with a contract to deal with the ITTF, until the end of 2008. Under the terms of the agreement, IEC handled a large number of the international rights agreements for the Federation, with the ITTF themselves handling certain territories in keeping with the previous agreement between the companies. IEC's relationship with ITTF stemmed back to 1996 when the agency was first mandated by Table Tennis' governing body to market their television rights. The agreement between ITTF and IEC includes the World Table Tennis Championships for Individuals and Teams (every other year, respectively), the ITTF Pro Tour, the prestigious World Cups and the European Top-12 tournament.

Having never had any direct dealings with this company was a source of nervousness for the board of TTA. They had just recently entered into discussions over possible production of Australian table tennis with a local distribution company for highlights to be distributed around the country. Bringing an outside company in, notwithstanding their vast experience with distributing international table tennis events, was something that the TTA board was not experienced in dealing with.

While Joan was concerned with the capacity of the Internet to deliver quality images, and her expressed concern over the introduction of an outside broadcasting company, she was less concerned about the quality of the production. Already the ITTF Pro Tour TV Production Guideline had been forwarded to Joan and the people from IEC In Sports had made contact. Their description of the way the broadcast would be managed, including the use of a minimum of six cameras, including a super slow-motion camera would mean the quality of the signal produced would be superior to any provided in table tennis in Australia, bar the 2000 Olympic Games and 2006 Commonwealth Games (ITTF, 2007b).

Even though Joan was satisfied about the capacity of this organization to successfully produce and distribute the broadcast, there were some other considerations that came to mind. Table tennis in Australia had made some great inroads into the sport sciences, and the implementation of computer simulations in motion analysis was one area that was offering great insights into athlete development. Through extensive work with sport scientists at the various Institutes of Sport around the country, the analysis of sport-specific related movements, such as the magnitudes for angular velocities and accelerations associated with sports activities had become a major area of interest for the coaching staff. Motion analysis was providing the tools for the Sports Medicine and Performance professional to perform accurate functional evaluations/analyses for clinical and research-oriented purposes such as:

- performance enhancement,
- injury prevention,
- return to activity,
- effects of orthopaedic/athletic devices (The Virtual Football Trainer, 2004).

But there were also emerging opportunities to include this information into the telecast, not only as an additional support service for coaching, but also to enhance the images that the viewing audience could see. Virtual trainers and virtual replay programmes were becoming readily available and effective in developing the vision that was presented during the telecast. Joan thought that TTA was in a good position to be able to enhance the viewing spectacle by transposing the viewer into a variety of positions in order to be immersed in the game. The opportunity now existed for the viewer to feel like they were viewing the broadcast almost as a participant and no longer just a spectator. The rapid development of virtual reality technologies, delivered through the Internet, opens opportunities for new directions in training and game play viewing by investigating still unexplored areas of virtual simulations.

While TTA had introduced some of these technologies to enhance their internal coaching programmes, Joan was happy to look into developing these technologies further to incorporate them into the telecast. There was a long way to go, but already the ITTF had expressed interest in specific elements.

A further emerging consideration was in the area of graphical enhancement of the broadcast. While the current consideration in production called for the bare basics of the overlaying of the event title, players profile with four best results, players/officials presentation, set and game score, permanent screen score and information notes (such as set ball, time out, etc.) (tmsin.com, 2007), Joan was of the mind that this was one area of the broadcast that could provide significant enhancement and information at minimal additional cost or disruption to the viewer. The difficulty was that there were so many companies providing similar services. Just the week before, Joan had met with one of the Directors of Pineapplehead Sports to discuss possible future broadcasting opportunities and how they might be able to become involved. While Pineapplehead was a company that provided good quality sport-related products for live television, the IEC In Sports people were already identifying their own graphics support activities. Joan's concern was that while IEC In Sports were completely devoted to the Pro Tour Series, their ongoing involvement in TTA was not assured beyond the Pro Tour event. Equally, the opportunity to become involved in a relationship with another organization with vast broadcasting and Internet experience was a step that the sport needed to take in Australia.

The other issue that Joan was not sure about was the implementation of specific rule enhancements to be introduced to the Pro Tour the next year. While the integration of virtual systems such as HawkEye had been successfully implemented in the tennis Grand Slam Tours, international cricket and there was even discussion that it would be trialled in the English Premier League (The Australian, 2007), Joan wasn't convinced that stoppages, challenges and rulings were appropriate for the game of table tennis. Equally, she felt that her conservative Board of management would be against implementing something intrusive like HawkEye. This was one of those issues that would need to be debated further across the range of national and international meetings of delegates. Although Joan had to admit, on the positive side, any technology would have already been trialled in the early tournaments prior to being introduced to the Australian event.

While this all sounded exciting and high tech to Joan it also was an area where she felt that control needed to remain with the organization running the event, so that the dynamics of the event were not highjacked by technology. While the opportunity to be involved in a major international tour event was not to be missed, the management of key activities was significant to the ongoing development of the sport. Joan decided that she needed to become more conversant with the technological developments which were becoming an increasingly important part of delivery of the sport. This included gaining an understanding and insight into the broadcast and Internet requirements. There was a lot of homework to be done prior to the Pro Tour event and in the future.

Case Diagnosis

The case study presents an overview into the impact of technology, particularly relating to streaming on the Internet, on the broadcast delivery of sport programmes. The introduction of the World Wide Web (www) has had a profound impact on the way in which sports now conduct their business. The impact in database management, marketing and information dissemination has been pronounced. What has also emerged is the way that particular sports have embraced the use of technology to alter the way in which they present their sport to spectators and viewers. This presentation is now delivered in a multitude of ways, through television, the Internet, mobile systems and is enhanced with sequences of slow-motion replays, graphics and special commentary.

As a sport manager attempting to understand the various issues and nuances of the technology, while still presenting the core operational activities of the organization or event, is a key requirement. Briefly analysing areas of focus the following summary includes reference to the delivery of sport programmes, and some brief examples of the technological enhancements that are occurring, as well as attempting to shed light on some of the potential pitfalls and problems that emerge.

The traditional approach to television distribution in Australia had been one of trying to develop partnerships with one of the three commercial networks or the two public service broadcasters. Television was only distributed via the terrestrial method of distributing electromagnetic waves to predmoninantly densely populated regions 'free-to-air'. The opportunity for sport to be broadcast was primarily the domain of the most popular professional sports such as cricket and the football codes on the commercial free-to-air networks, and second-tier football codes and other team sports on the often unfriendly late night slots presented by the public service broadcasters. Following the introduction of pay-television through cable and satellite methods in the mid-1990s, greater opportunity for broadcast of local sport was identified through this emerging outlet, but again the more popular professional codes were being sought. Where the local professional leagues were not featured, the remaining time was often allocated to cheaper overseas imported sports programming.

To counter this lack of opportunity available through the traditional television networks, aligned with advances in technology, increasing Internet connection speeds, the number of people online and the decrease in connection costs, traditional television content is becoming more freely and legally accessible over the Internet. In addition, specific broadcast content is now streamed exclusively over the Internet, bypassing the requirement for distribution via the cable, satellite or terrestrial systems.

The benefits associated with streaming broadcasting are many and varied. For example the broadcast can be viewed on a regular television, a computer or even a portable device such as a mobile phone. The broadcast can occur 'live' or be delayed to suit the requirements of the viewer and the event organizer. The quality can be altered depending upon the requirements from presentation via a simple digital camcorder recording through to more elaborate professional post-production technologies. The capacity to incorporate advertisements or other graphics can be easily undertaken. There is also the capacity to provide content either free or via a subscription service.

While the major barriers that are referred to with streaming technology is the poor quality reproduction and download size, coupled with the cost to the consumer, the technology is developing at a rapid rate.

With Internet television becoming more pervasive, efforts are being made by companies to develop the transmission of existing pay-TV channels to regular TV sets over the net, while retaining control over how the media is used. This control is required in order to protect existing subscription and pay-per-view business models (Wikipedia, 2007).

One of the core attributes of a move towards more sophisticated broadband services is that it delivers access to digital content, applications and a range of services, many of which can occur simultaneously. The real advantage of this exponential growth in data speed is that it unlocks more sophisticated capabilities, most notably those featuring audio-visual elements (ACMA, 2007).

While the implementation of successful Internet streaming comes with the accessibility and speed of download, the issue with respect to the speed of broadband Internet services in Australia had been questioned widely in the media in 2006 and 2007. An example of the types of criticisms presented highlighted on the current affairs programme 'The 7.30 Report' on the ABC in February 2007. Essentially, the report referred to the problem that the consensus amongst those in the industry is that, despite government assurances, Australia is very much in the slow lane of the Internet superhighway. The argument over how best to go faster, and who should pay for the new model broadband, had seen major telecommunications companies debate the issue through the media. Australia's largest telecommunications provider, Telstra had launched a vitriolic campaign against the government regulation it says is holding back its plans to upgrade its network. On the other side, a coalition of telcos, proposed its own fibre-optic rollout to fill the gap. The end result is that it was felt that Australia was being left behind in the rush for the rewards offered by the Internet (Hoy, 2007).

Another area providing immense opportunity for the telecast of sporting events has been through the introduction of advanced graphics packages. The graphical representation and interpretation of data, presents the opportunity to implement graphically interesting, 'tell the story at a glance' info-graphics to be superimposed over the live action to heighten the drama of the sporting activity. These info-graphics increase the viewers interest, explain fundamental aspects of the sport and help make sometimes very subtle, arcane rules understandable (one+one=thr33, 2005).

An example of where these graphics have been introduced is in the Australian Football League (AFL) telecast. One way in which this occurs is where the footballer lines up for a goal and a 'super' is transposed on top of the action explaining the probability of the kick scoring correctly. The prospect of successfully making the distance and to which side the kick may swing to if the kick is a poor one (and from which direction the wind is blowing), are graphically conveyed before the kick for 'a major' occurs. If it's a tight match, the suspense is accentuated by the inclusion of 'success rate at 48 m is 32 per cent' – and the wind is blowing from the left (one+one=thr33, 2005).

There are many companies involved in the presentation of graphical information that can be used to enhance the broadcast, as in the AFL case, or to replay aspects of a match through sports visualization. For example, 3D web technologies provide dynamic applications which can recreate a single goal from a football match or an entire cricket test match. Their virtual replays allow web users to view action from any position or viewpoint – even from the position of a player or referee (3dwebtech, 2007).

Another way graphics and technology can be integrated into the telecast is highlighted through the broadcast of the recent Tour de France on German TV station ARD. The graphics presented display cycle and rider-related data overlayed on the live action. Current speed, heart rate, cadence and power output are flashed on-screen. What is reputedly the toughest sporting event in the world takes on a whole other dimension when one is confronted by the live physiological data. He's going that fast? Up mountains? Incredible. Or in the case of one particular rider: His pulse rate won't come back down? (one+one=thr33, 2005).

While these technical enhancements through graphics and commentary enhance the experience to the viewer, one other area which has raised more than its fair share of controversy, is through the way in which technology has encroached on the rules or way in which the game is officiated. While some sports such as American Football have integrated and adapted to these television intrusions rather seamlessly, other sports have struggled with certain aspects associated with the concept. Cricket has successfully integrated video-replay technology associated with close run-out decisions. While this aspect of the technology has been widely developed, one other area of technology support has been somewhat avoided. The support from the International governing body for use of replays in close LBW decisions has been largely avoided. This decision has been left in the hands of the central umpire, even when the television replay shows that the decision was clearly wrong or much closer than that being made. The video decision in this instance is being ignored by the officials running the game. As mentioned in the case, tennis has moved down the path of integrating technology in replays of close line calls, and Premier League football will consider the technology in the future for line-ball goal decisions.

However, as stated by key executives from CBS and Entertainment and Sports Programming Network (ESPN) in an interview conducted for Broadcasting and Cable; 'You do have to be careful that you aren't providing a perspective the core viewer isn't used to,' says sports consultant and former CBS Sports President Neal Pilson. 'You can't surprise them. You can't scare off the current fan base.' This emphasis on enhancement rather than technology for the sake of technology is a key consideration of any sport manager. 'You just want to enhance the game. You can't try to do too much', says CBS Executive VP/Executive Producer Tony Petitti. 'The goal can't be anything more than enhancing the viewing experience', stated ESPN Senior

VP/Executive Producer of Remote Production Jed Drake. 'If it is a marketing exercise, it's not going to last' (Grossman, 2007). The concept of developing and introducing technology to the broadcast in order to develop fancy gadgets, will likely have an immediate impact, but the longer-term effects may in fact be detrimental to the broadcast. It is a fine line that the sport manager must negotiate with their prospective broadcast partner(s).

Case Questions

1 Does sport provide enhanced opportunities to develop business and tourism with overseas companies?
2 In reviewing a 'smaller' sport organization, what is the capacity for most to adapt quickly to emerging technology, particularly with respect to the opportunities presented through Internet streaming? (*Note*: A smaller sport organization is defined here in terms of domestic interest in the sport – which in the case of table tennis in Australia is quite low key in levels of participation and spectator interest.)
3 What are the issues that emerge through having different delivery modes in the broadcast of sporting events?
4 Identify some of the virtual enhancements that have emerged in the broadcast of sport. How effective are these virtual enhancements?
5 As a sport manager faced with the situation now faced by Joan, how do you maximize the value received by potentially competing broadcast/Internet interests given an ITTF obligation to deal with one organization for delivery of a major tournament, while having another partner interested in the domestic delivery of the remaining sport programmes?
6 What sports have enhanced their rules through broadcasting? How could table tennis introduce changed rules to support the broadcast of the sport? What might some of these rule enhancements be?

Case Resources

References

one+one=thr33 (2005, 26 August). The graphic datafication of broadcast sport. *Design, media, culture and more*. Accessed 20/02/2007 via http://www.oneplusoneequalsthree.com/2005/08/the_graphic_dat.html

ACMA (2007). Accessed 25/02/2007 via http://www.acma.gov.au/

Grossman, B. (29 January 2007). High Tech Sports. Broadcasting & Cable. Accessed 30/01/2007 via http://www.broadcastingcable.com/article/CA6410622.html

Hoy, G. (2007). Australia left behind on Internet superhighway. The 7.30 Report. Australian Broadcasting Corporation. TV Program Transcript accessed 25/02/2007 via http://www.abc.net.au/7.30/content/2007/s1853607.htm

ITTF.com (2006, 10 April). TV-ratings on CCTV China: Table tennis in Asia. *TMS International*. Accessed 27/01/2007 via http://www.ittf.com/TMS/PDF/TTinAsia2006.pdf

ITTF (2006a). ITTF Pro Tour Directives 2007. TMS International. Accessed 25/01/0227 via www.tmsin.com.

ITTF (2006b). One of the best advertising medium. Accessed 25/01/2007 via http://www.ittf.com/TMS/PDF/TTinAsia2006.pdf

ITTF (2007a). Table Tennis Available Television Programmes in 2007. Accessed 25/01/2007 via http://www.ittf.com/competitions/competition.asp?Category=pt

ITTF (2007b). ITTF Pro Tour TV Production Guidelines. TMS International. Accessed 25/01/2007 via www.tmsin.com.

ITTF.com (2007). Accessed on 25/02/2007 via http://www.ittf.com/_front_page/ittf.asp?category=General

Moses, A. (5 March 2007). Not coming soon: Mobile phone TV. The Age online. Accessed 06/03/2007 via http://www.theage.com.au/news/mobiles--handhelds/not-coming-soon-mobile-phone-t

one+one=thr33 (2007). The Graphic Datafication of Broadcast Sport (2005). Design, media, culture & more. one+one=thr33. Accessed 20/02/2007 via http://www.oneplusoneequalsthree.com/2005/08/the_graphic_dat.html

The Australian (2 March 2007). Soccer's modern vision to embrace HawkEye. The Australian online. Accessed 02/03/2007 via http://www.theaustralian.news.com.au/printpage/0,5942,21312136,00.html

The Virtual Football Trainer (2004). Accessed 20/02/2007 via http://www.ittf.com/_front_page/ittf.asp?category=General

Victorian Government (2003). Case Study: Pineapplehead Sports. Accessed 11/02/2007 via www.invest.vic.gov.au.

Wikipedia (2007). Internet television. Accessed 20/02/2007 via http://en.wikipedia.org/wiki/Internet_television

Further Information

Delta-stat – http://www.deltacast.tv/GL_Main.asp?Resolve=/Products/DELTA_stat.htm

IEC In Sports – http://www.iec.se/default.aspx?m=4

Gametrak – http://www.videodesignsoftware.com/products/gametrak.php.

http://www.videodesignsoftware.com/casestudies/nba.php

Harris Corporation Graphics – http://www.infocomm.org/cps/rde/xchg/SID-3F57FAC3-1037A046/infocomm/hs.xsl/avindustry_685.htm

Olympic Games Graphics – http://www.apple.com/hotnews/articles/2006/02/olympics

Pixel Power Graphics – http://www.pixelpower.com/PressReleases/press_attheraces.htm

Table Tennis Live – http://www.ttlivpartners.com/de

14

Tribalism: attracting fans in a fragmented market

Rudi Meir

Case Focus

This case examines some of the commercial realities faced by a professional rugby league team attempting to gain a viable foothold in one of Australia's most fragmented markets. The Gold Coast region of south-east Queensland has a chequered history of professional sports arriving in a blaze of glory only to fade away and die. This case examines some of the fundamental issues facing professional sport and discusses strategies for developing a tribal following in fans.

Keywords

- Tribalism
- Market fragmentation
- Tribal marketing
- Marketing strategies

Case Summary

Rugby league is one of Australia's most popular winter spectator sports. Clubs competing in the National Rugby League (NRL) competition can attract substantial support and in the process generate significant sums of money. However, while the professional game has moved towards national expansion by introducing teams in new markets, it has not always done so with success. Most notably has been the tumultuous history of professional rugby league since 1988 in one of the country's most demanding markets, the Gold Coast. This case examines the history of teams in this environment and the issues that need to be considered in attracting and sustaining support for the game's newest venture, the Gold Coast Titans.

Case Elements

The sport market is now more crowded than ever. In decades gone by a relatively small number of sports dominated their marketplace. In England sports such as football (soccer), cricket and netball were the team sports that everyone grew up with and often supported as a fan. In Australia it was sports like Australian Rules Football (AFL), rugby league and cricket. In many cases these were literally 'the only game in town' and they had a captive market from which to draw their support. But the world of sport has changed and while these examples may have been the traditional sports of their respective geographic locations the sport choice landscape in these countries and regions, and many others around the world, has changed dramatically. Gone are the days when the National Basketball Association was solely a North American sport consumed exclusively by North American fans. Gone are the days when teams like Manchester United, Real Madrid and AC Milan were supported by fans of their local communities. Now such sport teams are mega brands delivered to a global market and supported by millions of fans, who form tribes and consume their team via a vast range of mediums never considered possible 20–30 years ago.

Young sport fans in particular have a huge range of options from which to choose and with the growth in extreme sports such as snowboarding, motor cross and surfing, to name just a few, the more traditional sports are having to fight hard to retain market share and fight even harder to achieve any form of growth in this increasingly competitive marketplace. Combined with the enormous variety of other forms of entertainment available and the ever growing range of new distribution challenges, such as the World Wide Web, mobile technology, video and computer games, specialist magazines, daily print and terrestrial TV programming, DVD and online video streaming, satellite TV with hundreds of hours of dedicated sport programming and entertainment per day, all this adds up to a very fragmented market.

For sport organizations it means that none can be complacent about their fans and their ongoing commitment and involvement. This is true for every level of sport, regardless of whether the organization operates on a for-profit or not-for-profit basis. The number of consumers in the marketplace is a finite resource that all sports are trying to vie for; this is particularly true in the relatively small market of a country like Australia with a population of just over 20 million. The fact is that consumers want entertainment 365 days of the year. Yet the problem for many sports is that they operate competitively for only a portion of this time. As a result this means that the committed fan of today has the potential to be seduced by the offerings of other forms of entertainment out there in the market. This has the potential to see fans become defectors as they divide their leisure time and limited disposable income between a range of options on offer.

As identified by Rein et al. (2006) in their book '*The Elusive Fan: Reinventing Sports in a Crowded Marketplace*', there are some fundamental questions to which the sport industry needs answers. Of particular relevance to this case is 'why do fans connect with a particular sport, team or star and ignore others? What are the challenges of retaining core fans and attracting new ones? What are the essential strategies that will enable a sports decision-maker to connect to the fast-changing competitive sports audience that is splintering into numerous groups?' (Rein et al., 2006, p. ix–x). By its very nature sport can only produce one 'winner' on the field but in the context of marketing in a crowded and competitive marketplace it may be possible to be a winner off the field by developing strategies that support and encourage the tribal behaviour of fans.

Nurturing a New Identity in Rugby League's 'Graveyard'

Rugby league in Australia is one of the country's dominant sports and yet it has, as with most professional sports, a very chequered history. In the game's halcyon days, during the 1950s to 1960s, crowds filled various venues to overflowing throughout Sydney, the heartland of the game, and were packed in shoulder to shoulder to watch their teams play. Attracting a capacity crowd never seemed to be a problem. There was no need to spend huge sums of money on advertising and promotional campaigns; it was more a case of 'build it and they will come', and they did. Then during the 1970s rugby league's support took a nose dive with many clubs struggling to attract crowds from a dwindling support base. In particular the game suffered from a major image problem and was seen very much as too 'blokey' and violent with foul play allowed to go unchecked by referees and officials. The net result of this was a drop in crowd attendance, little interest from females generally and parents, more specifically, who did not care for the idea of diverting their sons away from more acceptable pastimes to play such a 'rough' and potentially harmful sport. A 'family sport' it was not. The natural economic impact of this was falling revenues at the turnstiles, major problems in attracting sponsors and falling interest from the media; a triumvirate of woes. However, in the 1980s the game was revitalized by some very innovative marketing and management decisions by the game's administrators.

The turning point in the rugby league's fortunes came in the form of a very slick and creative advertising campaign that revolved around American singer Tina Turner. Turner was the centre piece of a television advertisement that featured her singing her hit song 'What you get is what you see'. While the music and Turner's sensual imagery stressed the inherent sex appeal of the sport it also focused on the carnival-like atmosphere of families, young and old, male and female going to games en masse in the tribal colours of their various teams. The campaign also focused heavily on the athleticism, skills and rugged good looks of the players – after all sex sells, even in a sport like rugby league. It was also saying to the wider sporting public that rugby league was a sport of international significance, illustrated by the fact that it was the first professional sport ever to use an international pop star to deliver and sell its message. The campaign was enormously successful and played no small part in attracting females back to the sport as both fans and spectators. It also played a significant part in the resurgence of young players taking to the game and its overall repackaging as 'family' entertainment. The League went on to use Turner in subsequent campaigns into the early 1990s and with each one there was an ever increasing message of sophistication. Importantly, this new marketing push was also being supported by changes to the rules of the game that stressed its skill and power and moved it away from the images of thuggery that characterized it during the 1970s.

Rugby league in Australia has historically been predominantly played along the eastern seaboard in the states of New South Wales (NSW) and Queensland. Prior to 1982 its premier competition was centred entirely in Sydney with just nine clubs competing in the NSW Rugby League Sydney Premiership. However, in the period 1982–1988 the decision was made to expand the competition and progressively teams were introduced in Canberra, Wollongong, Newcastle, Gold Coast and Brisbane – all strong rugby league areas with vibrant local junior and senior competitions of their own. Of these regions the Gold Coast is the only one to have struggled to establish a commercially viable team.

The Gold Coast region is one of Australia's most rapidly expanding population centres and benefits from its proximity to Brisbane, Queensland's capital city, and the natural beauty of its location on Queensland's south-east coastal strip. The range of recreation and leisure activities on offer is diverse and as one of Australia's most popular tourist destinations residents and visitors alike have no shortage of things to choose from and to spend their discretionary income on. It is a region that has also seen a significant influx of people migrating from Victoria, a cooler and generally less hospitable climate than that in Queensland, and with them comes the southern state's legendary fanaticism for AFL. In addition the AFL has a very clear and aggressive plan for expansion and market development, which has seen it make a significant investment into the promotion and development of the game at all levels in markets such as Queensland.

Given the population of almost 500,000 people and the strong local interest in a range of sports, as evidenced by junior and senior competitions, the Gold Coast has been seen as something of a pot of gold at the end of the rainbow for professional sports. Yet it has had a lengthy history of failed attempts at establishing professional teams in sports such as basketball, baseball, AFL and rugby league. A team from each of these sports has tried in vain to attract the support of local residents, but apart from brief periods of interest, support has been short lived. The result has been teams either folding completely or relocating, as in the case of the AFL team the Brisbane Lions (previously called the Bears when located on the Gold Coast).

Initially the Gold Coast's first professional rugby league team entered the Winfield Cup competition in 1988 as a privately owned licence granted by the NSW Rugby League. Its owners comprised a syndicate of Queensland-based businessmen and retired rugby league international players. The club was called the Gold Coast-Tweed Giants, reflecting the fact that its home ground was actually located just a few minutes over the Queensland border in the far northern NSW coastal town of Tweed Heads. It was hoped that this location would provide the club with much needed corporate support from businesses based on the Gold Coast and easy access to the Tweed and Northern Rivers region of NSW, which had strong rugby league support. However, the consortium struggled financially and reluctantly sold the licence at the end of the team's second season in the Winfield Cup to the Seagulls Rugby League Club, which owned the ground and facilities that the Giants operated from. The club clearly needed a financial benefactor and the Seagulls Leagues club could provide the kind of money that was going to be needed if the team was to survive in the newly expanded NSW Rugby League competition. However, the new ownership felt that a change in identity was needed; a simplistic attempt at casting off the poor image of the team and its performances in the first two seasons. As a result it introduced a new logo and team name, in an effort to also link it directly with the much larger market of the Gold Coast to its north. It also identified the club more intimately with its new owners, which was reflected in the name, the Gold Coast Seagulls.

By linking the team more strongly to the Gold Coast region, even if only by name change alone, it was hoped local residents would see the Gold Coast Seagulls as 'their' team. The perception of club management at the time was that the physical location of the team's playing venue in NSW acted as a form of psychological barrier that residents of Queensland could not relate to. This was also reinforced by the historical animosity that existed between residents of both states and the fact that Queensland was effectively represented by one of the other new expansion teams, the Brisbane Broncos. The Broncos were located in a market of over 1 million people, had the support of corporate Queensland and had a hugely effective marketing campaign that focused on the fact that the team was representing Queensland in the 'fight' against all of the other teams, which were essentially all based in NSW. The Broncos were also led by one of the game's most respected and successful coaches and had a squad of players that included numerous current Australian internationals, who were all Queenslanders.

The Gold Coast's hoped-for fans never materialized and the club continued to struggle for support across the community. Throughout the period 1988–1995 they only managed to fill their 14,000 capacity stadium on a handful of occasions. Crowds of just 5–6000 were the norm and the team's generally poor performances played a large part in it being unable to attract the same level of sponsorship enjoyed by many of the League's other teams. The catch-22 was also that it could not attract quality players and the instability of seven CEOs, four head coaches and two name changes in eight seasons, combined with wholesale changes to the playing squad every year, did not paint a picture of stability. Fans found it hard to warm to 'their' team and in a market that had so much to offer, much of which could be enjoyed for free, such as the area's beautiful beaches and world class surf, the prospect of spending their discretionary income on a team that more often than not would lose was not an appealing proposition.

At the end of the 1995 season the Seagulls Leagues Club decided that enough was enough. It could no longer justify supporting its professional league team, which was reportedly haemorrhaging almost $2 million each year. As a result the club relinquished its licence to operate a team out of its Tweed Heads headquarters. This was a decision that proved to be almost fatal for professional rugby league on the coast as it struggled to fight for existence. Ultimately, after a brief flirtation with transferring ownership to a local Gold Coast businessman, the team's licence was taken over by the Australian Rugby League (ARL) for the 1996 season. However, the game was on the brink of entering the most destructive period in its history as it split into two separate competitions, one owned by Rupert Murdoch's News Limited and the other by the game's custodians, the ARL.

During this period the ARL moved the team from its previous base at Tweed Heads to Carrara Stadium, a bigger more central facility originally designed to accommodate the Gold Coast's first professional AFL team. It was hoped that its location, and yet another name change to the Gold Coast Chargers, would see it enter a new and exciting era. Yet, once again the club struggled to gain the support of the Gold Coast community. The Chargers had a brief period of improved performances in the 1997 split season competing in the ARL's 12 team competition. However, once the ARL and News Limited's Super League competitions brokered a peace treaty, re-forming as the NRL competition, the Chargers were to revisit old habits and spent 1998 firmly entrenched at the bottom of the new league winning just four games all season. Ultimately the ARL agreed to sacrifice the Gold Coast team as part of its new relationship with News Limited and in the rationalization of the 20 team competition down to 14 teams, which was to take effect in 2000. The club was closed down to barely a whimper from its fans.

For the next eight years the Gold Coast became a professional sporting wasteland. However, logic suggested that Australia's seventh most populous region with an annual growth rate of approximately 3 per cent should be able to sustain a professional sport franchise, of some sort! The simple fact was that rugby league on the Gold Coast had a thriving junior competition with over 11,000 registered players and was well known as a breeding ground for senior players who went on to play for professional teams in the NRL competition. The Northern Rivers area of NSW, just over the Queensland border, was a fortress of rugby league support. When considered collectively these two regions, south-east Queensland and the Northern Rivers of NSW, had a potential market of approximately 3 million people being represented by just one NRL club (the Brisbane Broncos). Combined with the fact that there were an increasing number of large businesses interested in supporting a locally based NRL team, it seemed reasonable that a club could and should exist and prosper in the region.

To this end, in March 1999, a group of local Gold Coast businessmen and rugby league stalwarts, some of whom were connected in various ways with one of the Gold Coast's previous attempts at establishing a professional team, set about lobbying the local community, businesses, local and state governments, and the NRL for readmission into the national competition. The group formulated a strategic and financial plan for admission into the national competition and claimed to have secured investors who would back the team to the tune of $15 million. They consistently lobbied the NRL to both expand the competition and in the process endorse the Gold Coast's bid for inclusion in its competition. They presented a powerful case to the NRL and their bid plan was considered to be the most comprehensive and professionally prepared that the NRL had ever reviewed.

Subsequently the bid group showcased a number of professional rugby league 'trial' matches at Carrara Stadium with other teams from the NRL. This was done in an effort to both demonstrate and gauge the level of support for the game, and by extension, potentially a new team on the Gold Coast. According to NRL Chief Executive David Gallop, 'trial games are an opportunity for people to vote with their feet. The response the Gold Coast gets to those games is certainly one of the things we would look at'. Attendances typically ranged from 13 to 17,000 and peaked at 23,000, the NRL could not dispute the popularity of live rugby league on the Gold Coast, and must have been satisfied of the team's ability to fulfil this particular criterion when it finally granted a new licence to the Gold Coast Titans late in 2005. However, there was still one major piece of the jigsaw puzzle to be resolved. The Carrara Stadium was not considered a long-term venue for the team. It was hampered by its ageing facilities, the fact that it was originally designed to accommodate an AFL team, and it lacked the intimacy that most fans wanted in a rugby league venue. Once again the new Gold Coast Titans' administration successfully lobbied local, state and federal governments for funding to construct a purpose built facility at a site in Robina, located in the growth centre of the Gold Coast. Construction of the new stadium commenced in 2006 and will be completed in time for the start of the 2008 NRL season.

Season 2007 marked the commencement of yet another chapter in the ongoing history of professional sport on the Gold Coast. To date professional rugby league has shown signs, albeit weak ones, of being able to support a team. However, the biggest single issue for its long-term survival will be its ability to both attract and maintain a big enough support base from the local community. Fans of professional sport on the Gold Coast have been shown to be a fickle lot and if teams do not perform and provide at least some hope of more than the occasional victory, it is likely that once again they will abandon 'their' team. Winning certainly is not everything in the marketing of professional sport and teams in a variety of sports from around the world have shown that this is not the sole criteria for long-term success. However, the Gold Coast is a vibrant market with lots to offer and entertain its population. This is particularly true of the younger segments of the market, which are drawn to the vast variety of night life, the surf/beach culture and the offerings of new alternative forms of entertainment such as extreme sports, computer games, DVD and satellite television programming, the Internet and mobile technology that provides on demand content directly into their hands. All of these help to describe and define these younger segments of the market and unlike the older generations before them (the 'matures', born 1900–1945 and 'baby boomers', born 1946–1964), who saw supporting a team as a lifelong commitment, generation 'X' (born between 1965 and 1981), net-geners and millennials (born after 1982; also referred to more commonly as generation 'Y') are less interested in the tribal rituals of brand loyal fans of yesteryear. As a result, one of the biggest challenges to face the new Gold Coast Titans may not necessarily be putting together credible on field performances but rather its ability to attract, develop and 'entertain' a tribal following within its support base.

Professional sport generates significant amounts of revenue from a variety of sources. Central to this is the continued support and commitment of fans. Thus, understanding fans is increasingly critical to sport organizations. Increased financial pressure and competition means that sport organizations cannot afford fluctuations in fan support and need to maintain a large base of loyal fans, something the Gold Coast has failed to deliver in the past. Loyal fans have significant value and can increase profitability through increased revenue because they are more likely to attend games, purchase team merchandise, watch games on television, and listen to games on radio and access it through new media forms.

The emotional attachment sport fans have for their team or club is manifested in a number of ways, such as their willingness to purchase season tickets, club membership, attend special functions and wearing clothing sporting the team's logo (brand). With respect to the latter, consumption of branded clothing and accessories acts as an involvement-enhancing link that can assist in the socializing of new fans (tribal members) while also cultivating the commitment of current ones (Cova, 1996). For the sport marketer therefore there is a need to understand those factors which influence tribalism and the impact that these might have, either negatively or positively, on revenue generation. This may be of critical importance to new franchises such as the Gild Coast Titans.

Case Diagnosis

The Gold Coast Titans are located in an increasingly fragmented market. As a result they will need to develop marketing strategies that will attract and grow new fans, ultimately developing the kind of emotional attachment and identification with the team that will see them prosper and survive financially well into the future. Fans express a sense of personal and social identity through the support of their team and it is this type of connection that the Titans must strive to develop within their marketplace. Ultimately, spectators become involved in sport because they are motivated by a desire to confirm their sense of identity. The activities and interpersonal associations that people undertake to give their lives meaning are the most powerful organizing forces in modern life (Schouten and McAlexander, 1995). Therefore, understanding the relationship between personal identity and subcultures may have significant marketing benefits for the Titans.

There are two forms of identity (i.e. self-identity and social identity). Self-identity represents the degree to which a member of a subculture incorporates the subculture's activity into his or her self-concept (Green, 2001). Social identity is described as the individual's knowledge that he/she belongs to certain social groups together with some emotional and value significance to him/her of the group membership (Abrams and Hogg, 1990). Identification takes place when an individual believes they are part of a group. In this context sport team identification signifies the extent to which the individual '...feels a psychological connection to a team, is involved and invested in the team, and sees the team as an extension of the self' (Wann et al., 2004, p. 209). Level of team identification has also been shown to be important in the attendance decision-making process (Murrell and Dietz, 1992; Wann and Branscombe, 1993; Fisher and Wakefield, 1998). Identification might be considered as a feeling of belongingness or 'oneness' with the object of identification or as self-definition in terms of that object. Socialization through sport is a common cultural experience and in many cases indoctrination into brand support of a particular team starts at an early age. In this context the Titans must not underestimate the role of indoctrination and will need to develop a range of strategies within the community that particularly encourage support from younger fans. Notwithstanding this, membership of social groups in sport may take varying degrees of time to attain and in some instances can require a rights of passage before the individual is accepted (Butts, 2001).

According to Donavan et al. (2005), 'when a person identifies with an organization he or she takes psychological ownership of the entity' (p. 31). Fans 'choose' to belong to the group because it can also be socially rewarding for them to engage in behaviour like attending games, wearing team branded clothing and discussing sports in social situations. This behaviour may also provide a real or imagined connection to others. In fact, being a 'fan' may even provide a form of social prestige (Trail et al., 2000), particularly if the team is considered 'successful' – success might be measured not just by the team's on field performance but also by the way it interacts with and supports its local community. This means that in order for individuals to maintain or enhance a positive social identity by their affiliation with the team it will need to be perceived as an 'attractive' group worthy of their support and investment in terms of time and money. This might be achieved in the early stages of market development by focusing on the skill and competitive character of the team, along with its 'star' players, home-grown local talent and its involvement with local charity groups and community 'causes'.

Sport also provides a vehicle for the affirmation of collective identity and geographical antagonisms; the 'local derby' is one of the most fiercely contested events in sport. This can serve to allow both individuals and groups to strengthen their attachment and identification with a particular community. Kwon and Armstrong (2004) suggest that team identification may originate from the identification that a fan has with the geographical region and that from this they are of the view that '...identification with the team, for some sport fans, is a consequence of regional identification' (p. 97). As a result a fundamental aspect of supporting a particular team is the feeling of shared identity with similar supporters. Identification with the Titans as the sole representatives of the region's involvement in a national professional sports competition will be a fundamental connection point for local fans. Such a connection has the capacity to instil a sense of pride and a 'coming of age' that act as totems around which the community can gather.

There is no doubt that there is a strong level of support among the region's residents for rugby league. However, in terms of support for the professional form of the game, it could be argued that most of this is directed towards existing teams competing in the NRL (i.e. support is directed towards teams that fans have followed for many years and possibly generations). These existing rugby league fans are not likely to give up support of their traditional team to support the Gold Coast Titans simply out of a sense of geographical loyalty. Yet, they may well adopt them as their 'second' team, using their association with the club as a means of seeing their first choice team live when they come to the Gold Coast to compete with the Titans. It is also possible that fans, who consider themselves to be followers of the 'game', as well as a particular team, may choose to attend Titans games simply as a way of satisfying their 'need' for live professional rugby league rather than being confined to watching it on free to air or terrestrial television.

These fans of the game will be an important segment of the market that the Titans need to appeal to in the early stages of their market development and they will provide important revenue streams as the team works to grow support throughout the wider community. To this end, providing a valued total sport entertainment experience for the region's rugby league aficionados must be high on the Titans' agenda.

Based on the above diagnosis it is possible to present a set of effects of tribalism and the practical consequences of these that can assist the Gold Coast Titans in the development of a tribal marketing approach for their organization. These are as follows:

- The Gold Coast rugby league follower needs to identify with the Titans and develop a feeling of 'oneness' with the team. This may see them display a personal commitment to a particular line of activity, such as attending games as a supporter of the team and/or other group (tribe) activities (e.g. special functions). This may require them to be indoctrinated into support of the team before being accepted as part of the team. There may also be a particular way of dressing and communicating that distinguishes Titans' tribal members from other groups (e.g. the wearing of branded team merchandise; communicating through fan discussion groups on the WWW; attending exclusive supporters' functions or meetings).
- There needs to be evidence of a subculture that self-selects on the basis of a shared commitment to the Titans brand. This might result in the sharing of a set of identifiable beliefs, values and means of symbolic expression, which can be expressed in a variety of different ways. This commitment sees tribal members motivated to establish and maintain their ties with the group. As a result this involvement and interaction with other group members results in members learning the unique values and beliefs of the group, linking them more closely to the subculture and confirming their sense of identity as a tribal member.
- Tribal members use socialization with other group members to enhance their identity. This sees them developing a sense of enjoyment and identity by associating with the team and its group of fans (e.g. pre- and post-match functions where fans and players can gather and interact). Evidence of a sense of attachment to the team, which may produce a sense of psychological satisfaction (e.g. being linked to a winning team) produced by the team's performance, related media coverage, social events, the wearing of team 'colours', etc., which represent the club's history and tradition and a willingness to support the team through a range of consumption behaviours. This may see tribal members attend sport events, which bring the group together in a communal experience enriching their lives and providing a sense of belonging. Naturally this will take time for the Titans to develop and certainly putting together competitive performances on a regular basis, particularly when playing at home, will play a vital role in this.
- Tribal members perceive the relevance of the group based on their own needs, values and interests. The more important the team/organization

is to the tribal member in their daily life the more involved they are likely to be with it and other tribal members. This might include cognitive consumption of information about the team/organization through a range of media (e.g. all forms of relevant electronic and print media; Internet and SMS updates, etc.).

- Tribal members will use group affiliation to express a sense of community and particular beliefs, such as geographical origins. These feelings of shared identity can also act to differentiate the group. This is manifested in the wearing and display of team branded merchandise, particularly in public, as a means of emphasizing allegiance/loyalty and collective shared identity. This can also be achieved by a focus on the team as representatives and ambassadors of the wider community.

Individuals will define themselves in terms of their group membership – the more 'attractive' the group the more positively one's social identity will be in attributing the desirable characteristics of the group to themselves and they will assume greater similarity with other group members (Fisher and Wakefield, 1998). Individuals might choose a sport team to follow based on the linking value of such characteristics as image, character and spirit – put simply, the team reflects a state of mind (O'Brien, 1995). Ultimately, as fan identity becomes more prominent, there will be an increase in the frequency of specific activities associated with the sport (e.g. attendance at games and cognitive consumption of the sport through a variety of media). By identifying those factors that increase or decrease fan identification with a team the Titans' administration might develop a greater understanding of the antecedents and consequences of team identification – and ultimately contribute to its long-term survival in one of Australia's most challenging sport markets.

Case Questions

1 What types of marketing strategies could the Titans implement to target young fans?
2 How could the Titans facilitate a 'tribal' mentality in its fans?
3 What do you consider to be the biggest hurdles for the team to overcome in terms of its commercial viability in the first season of operation?

Case Resources

Reading

Abrams, D. and Hogg, M. (1990). An introduction to the social identity approach, in Abrams, D. and Hogg, M. (Eds.), *Social Identity Theory: Constructive and Critical Advances*. Harvester Wheatsheaf, London, pp. 1–9.

Butts, S.L. (2001). 'Good to the last drop': Understanding surfers' motivations. *Sociology of Sport Online*, Vol. 4, No. 1, viewed February 5, 2004, <http://physed.otago.ac.nz/sosol/home.htm>.

Cova, B. (1996). The postmodern explained to managers: Implications for marketing. *Business Horizons*, Vol. 39, No. 6, pp. 15–23.

Donavan, D.T., Carlson, B.D. and Zimmerman, M. (2005). The influence of personality traits on sports fan identification. *Sport Marketing Quarterly*, Vol. 14, No. 1, pp. 31–42.

Fisher, R. and Wakefield, K. (1998). Factors leading to group identification: A field study of winners and losers. *Psychology and Marketing*, Vol. 15, No. 1, pp. 23–40.

Green, B. (2001). Leveraging subculture and identity to promote sport events. *Sport Management Review*, Vol. 4, No. 1, pp. 1–19.

Kwon, H.H. and Armstrong, K.L. (2004). An exploration of the construct of psychological attachment to a sport team among college students: A multidimensional approach. *Sport Marketing Quarterly*, Vol. 13, No. 2, pp. 94–103.

Murrell, A.J. and Dietz, B. (1992). Fan support for sports teams: The effect of a common group identity. *Journal of Sport and Exercise Psychology*, Vol. 14, No. 1, pp. 28–39.

O'Brien, G. (1995). Dream teams. *Details*. April, p. 103.

Rein, I., Kotler, P. and Shields, B. (2006). *The Elusive Fan: Reinventing Sports in a Crowded Marketplace*. McGraw-Hill, New York.

Schouten, J.W. and McAlexander, J.H. (1995). Subcultures of consumption: An ethnography of the new bikers. *Journal of Consumer Research*, Vol. 22, pp. 43–61.

Trail, G., Anderson, D.F. and Fink, J. (2000). A theoretical model of sport spectator consumption behavior. *International Journal of Sport Management*, Vol. 1, No. 3, pp. 154–180.

Wann, D.L. and Branscombe, N.R. (1993). Sports fans: Measuring degree of identification with their team. *International Journal of Sport Psychology*, Vol. 24, No. 1, pp. 1–17.

Wann, D.L., Bayens, C. and Driver, A. (2004). Likelihood of attending a sporting event as a function of ticket scarcity and team identification. *Sport Marketing Quarterly*, Vol. 13, No. 4, pp. 209–215.

Websites

http://www.titans.com
http://www.nrl.com
http://www.rl1908.com

15

The internationalization of Club Atlético de Madrid S.A.D.: creating value beyond borders, a differential strategy

Ignacio Urrutia, Germán Robles, Kimio Kase and Carlos Martí

Case Focus

The case analyses the intention of Club Atlético de Madrid to internationalize and delves into its historical heritage and current situation to assess its feasibility.

Keywords

- Football club
- Strategic position and intent
- Marketing strategy
- Resources
- Brand management

Case Summary

Club Atlético de Madrid (ATM) stands for a set of very specific values shared among its supporters and management, which markedly differentiate it from other clubs including Real Madrid, its eternal rival. This case serves discusses the nature of internationalization in the light of these values: What does the internationalization mean for the club and its supporters, how does the intent and its actual strategic positioning fit, what kind of resources should be fostered for the internationalization purpose, etc.? Last but not the least, is such internationalization unavoidable or is it a fad for football clubs?

Case Elements

… To get back into Europe is our most intimate desire.
(Director of Atlético de Madrid)

Introduction[1]

When a club like Atlético de Madrid contemplates internationalisation, it is not sure what to be international means. This is not a trivial matter, as the club feels international and has figures that prove it: we have Atlético de Madrid fans and fan clubs (Annexe 2) all over the world; we are a team that has included international players; the best coaches in the world have worked for us; we have sponsors that are part of multinational strategies; pictures of the club are broadcast on every television channel in the world; this is why it is difficult to answer when we are asked what it means to be international. If you like, we can evaluate who we are, what we have achieved and where we are going.

---

[1] Antonio Alonso is vice-president of Atlético de Madrid and is responsible for the commercial department; the passage is taken from a conversation with Germán Robles, who is in charge of the Club Atlético de Madrid Centre of International Studies. Antonio was answering the question of what Atlético de Madrid's internationalization strategy comprises.

History

Antonio: 'How were we born? It is important to remember that at the head-quarters of the Basque-Navarre Society on 8 April 1903, the first page in the history of Club Atlético de Madrid was written as an initiative of a group of students from Bilbao who were studying to be mining engineers at the university of Madrid. Club Atlético de Madrid was thus born into the university community as a "branch" of Athletic Bilbao and was initially known as Athletic Club de Madrid. The relationship between the clubs was such that they decided not to play official matches against one another because they were considered to be the same club. The club's first president was Enrique Allende, who stepped down within the first year of the club's existence to be replaced by Eduardo de Acha. In 1921, the club severed all ties with Athletic Bilbao after it began to operate independently. In 1923, the club built its first stadium, the Metropolitano.

In the 1939–1940 season, the club found itself in a difficult situation (players dispersed all over Spain, some taken prisoner, others wounded). Furthermore, the club's debt had risen to such an extent that it decided to merge with the Ministry of Air's team (Aviación Nacional), as a result of which its name was changed to Atlético Aviación. The change did the club good, as it went on to win the league in 1939–1940 and 1940–1941 under the guidance of coach Ricardo Zamora. On 14 December 1946, the Ministry of Air decided to request the club to cease using the term Aviación. The communication was read out at a board meeting, at which it was decided unanimously that a letter should be written to the ministry thanking it for the treatment it had received from the air force. There was then a brief deliberation as to what the club's new name should be, during which there was no argument whatsoever; it was unanimously decided that from that date onward, the club would be called Club Atlético de Madrid and the necessary steps to change the name and remove the word Aviación got under way. To summarize, the history of the club's name is as follows: Athletic Club de Madrid (1903 to 1938), Athletic Aviación Club (1939 to 1941), Club Atlético de Aviación (1942 to 1947), Club Atlético de Madrid (1948 to 1991) and since 1992, Club Atlético de Madrid S.A.D.

Our kit (and that of Athletic Bilbao) consisted of a blue and white halved shirt and blue shorts, as the Bilbao club bought Blackburn Rovers kits on their trips to England to use as their own. One day in 1911, a representative of Athletic Bilbao sailed to the south of England to buy new kits for both teams. However, he did not manage to obtain Blackburn Rovers kits and had to return with Southampton kits instead (red and white striped shirts and black shorts). Athletic Bilbao adopted the colours of Southampton as their official kit and Athletic Club de Madrid adopted the red and white shirt but kept the previous blue shorts.

Our birth was closely tied to Madrid, but as you can see, we have been involved in the main events of European football; look into the heart of club to see who we are'.

The Club's Conspiracy[2]

Germán: 'In searching for the club's identity, I came across the comment made by President Enrique Cerezo[3] (Annexe 1) in explaining the club's vision:

> *Sporting institutions are currently a reference point for society, from its youngest members to its oldest; sportsmen are considered true heroes and therefore, knowing the great importance of sport and football in particular and their influence on people. Club Atlético de Madrid understands this and feels bound to go beyond the realm of sport; it is a responsibility, and we want to contribute to the exaltation of the noble task of dignifying the sport on all levels with genuine values. As a basic principle, football should be a nexus between culture and education. ... The world of academia should be closely related to the world of sport. The search for truth, the thirst for knowledge, perfection and effort should be the basic pillars of this new task. As a result of the increase in the requirements that must be fulfilled in order to achieve sporting success, the Centre of Studies wishes to specialise in the area of sports administration in order to approach the topics with the rigour and professionalism they deserve, as well as anticipate future trends.*

> *Today we are testimony to those who devoted so much enthusiasm, hope and noble effort. Back then, many football clubs coexisted in Madrid, but professionalism was a major challenge which caused many smaller teams to disappear; for this reason former players and fans decided to seek refuge with Athletic Club. The city of Madrid and Atlético de Madrid have always been a place of refuge and this explains why Atlético belongs to everyone, a collective feeling, a well of memories and affection, common property. It is also important to remember that the club used to organise various sporting and social activities, not just football, for example, the first ever cross-country race in Madrid was organised by Athletic, starting from the Café Gijón, a meeting point for art and culture. Club Atlético de Madrid does not shy away from the social responsibility that sport engenders and the Centre of Studies and Research is set to be an international reference point for knowledge, projects and ideas and training within sport. By virtue of our modesty, constancy, effort and values, we want to continue to grow and make history so that our fans feel proud to belong to a big club'.*

Sense of Belonging to the Club Atlético De Madrid

Antonio: 'What is not clear to me, Germán, is whether we would be able to maintain the fans' sense of belonging abroad; I have recorded the words of an Atlético fan to help us understand what we mean to supporters: ... to be colchonero [literally "mattress man" because Atlético's red and white stripes resemble a mattress] is to be different, to have a constant desire to improve, the ability to grow in the face of adversity with the sole desire to always be the champion, to understand that Atlético de Madrid is not manufactured but is nurtured. It is moving to know that the club is currently greater than its own history and possesses not only trophies as testament to the victories it has achieved but also a prestige and a trajectory that have earned it recognition beyond our country's borders'.

---

[2] Address by Enrique Cerezo at the presentation of the Centre of International Studies at the signing of the club's historic agreement with the Olympic Academy and the International Olympic Committee (IOC).

[3] Enrique Cerezo is a film producer and has been president of Atlético de Madrid since 2002.

Germán: 'I have read that before, I would also like you to reflect on the results of survey we requested from the consultancy firm Burston, which indicates what people in general think of us'.

Conclusions Strengths	Atlético de Madrid • Charming/Captivating • Direct/Clear • Unpretentious/Established (Strength vis-à-vis FC Barcelona)
Opportunities	• Different (Strength vis-à-vis Real Madrid) • Sociable (Strength vis-à-vis Real Madrid) • Friendly (Strength vis-à-vis Real Madrid)

International Trophies

German: 'We do indeed have a very good support, Antonio, because we have both suffered and triumphed; think of our victories in Europe. Atlético de Madrid began to win international trophies in 1962, winning their only European title in a 3–0 victory in that year's Cup Winners' Cup final against the holders, Fiorentina. The Vicente Calderón stadium was inaugurated in 1966 and named after the club's president at the time. The Cup Winners' Cup win and the signing of Gárate marked the beginning of a highly successful period. The 1960s and 1970s were probably the two best decades in the club's history. Atlético de Madrid reached the 1974 European Cup final against Bayern Munich. The game was goalless at the end of normal time, but Luis Aragonés put the *colchoneros* ahead with a free kick. Thirty seconds from the final whistle, Georg Schwarzenbach brought the match level with a shot from distance which the goalkeeper, Reina, could do nothing about. The Madrid side began the replay completely demoralized and physically exhausted (in those days the difference in physical condition between teams from the north and south of Europe was vast) and were defeated 4–0. That same year the Germans declined to play the Intercontinental Cup against Independiente de Avellanada and were replaced by Atlético. The first leg in Buenos Aires ended 1–2 to the Argentinians, but the second leg in Madrid on 10 April 1975 was won 2–0 by Atlético, with a goal by Abelardo four minutes from time. Atlético's history in the Fairs Cup – currently the UEFA Cup began in 1963. In the 1963–1964 and 1964–1965 seasons, Atlético were knocked out by the same team, Juventus. In the 1966–1967 season, Atlético returned to the European Cup, but their campaign did not last long. The last significant feat by Atlético was the 1986 Cup Winners' Cup final. Atlético travelled to the final in Lyon accompanied by 15,000 fans, but the red and whites had little chance against a great Dynamo Kiev and were defeated 2–0. Atlético's last appearances in Europe date back to their participation in the 1996–1997 Champions League, where they were knocked out at the quarter-final stage by Ajax, and two subsequent UEFA campaigns, in both of which they were eliminated at the semi-final stage, firstly against Lazio and then against Parma'.

The Club's Assets: International Players and Coaches

Antonio: 'But not just the victories, remember that since the 1960s the club has had great players that have been considered reference points in the major countries of the world. In Spain, perhaps the most highly rated were Gárate, Luis and Adelardo, although as you can see (cf. Annexe 5), the club has also had international-calibre players such as Hugo Sánchez, Schuster, Luis Pereira … and in the club's history many coaches have sat in the dugout to direct the team. Some did it better than others, some were more committed than others. Great footballing figures have passed through Atlético's dugout (Annexe 5)'.

The Club's Assets: The Atlético Madrid Brand

Germán: 'Since 2005, Club Atlético de Madrid has been working to define and position its brand in the place it deserves; in order to position it, it commissioned a survey through from the communications consultancy firm Burston Mastellers, some of the main conclusions of which are as follows:

1 Both globally and locally speaking, Atlético de Madrid is one of the biggest clubs in terms of the brand's vitality and dimension, just behind Real Madrid and Barcelona*. Fans have a neutral opinion of the club.

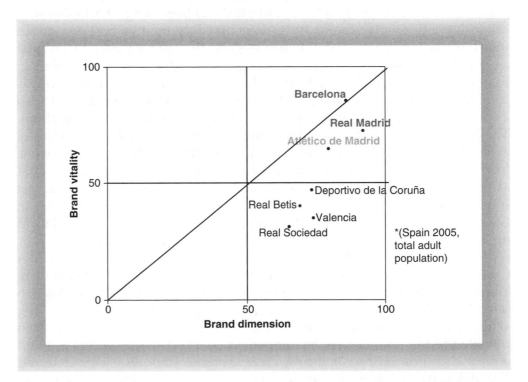

Source: Burston Mastellers

2 At national level, Atlético de Madrid is the team that suggests the most familiarity to fans, just behind Real Madrid and on the same level as Barcelona.* In terms of differentiation, the brand is just behind Barcelona.*

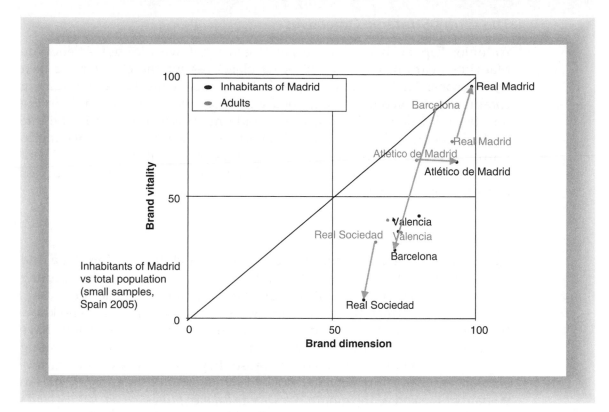

3 Barcelona fans perceive the Atlético de Madrid brand as having a greater dimension than Real Madrid'.

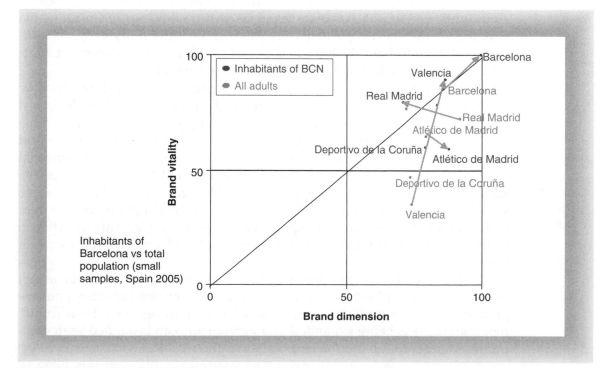

Source: Burston Mastellers

The Club's Strategic Objectives

Antonio: 'Up to this point we have seen what we are, but Atlético de Madrid's board has set the following objectives for the club for the next few seasons: Atlético "need to qualify for Europe, consolidate the training complex in Alcorcón, secure a good television deal and if possible in the mid-term, lay down the terms of the stadium transaction" that is, the sale of the Vicente Calderón. The club's internationalization implies playing in European competitions because although tours are of interest, financial benefits and whether a club is well known or not derive from sporting success in the Champions League'.

Club Tours

'Tours have proved a useful tool for established clubs like Barcelona and Real Madrid, although it is not easy to reconcile them with the sporting side of things because they affect the physical planning of the pre-season, as has been confirmed by the first division's 20 physical trainers, who know that they cannot conduct an ideal pre-season if there are tours. Clubs have a series of commitments with television companies, which the marketing department cannot dispense with because they constitute exceptional revenue in summer. Ultimately, the money is what enables the professionals to be paid at the end of the month. *We have to balance things out so that the club's interests are not damaged*; this is why Barcelona must travel to Mexico and the USA, interrupting their stay in Aarhus (Denmark) and flying more than 20,000 kilometres. This tour will earn the Catalan club €4 million in television rights. Or the €400,000 that we pocketed from our tour of China. China was the springboard for Atlético de Madrid and this market was chosen deliberately to roll out the brand, as one of the club's more important strategies is to improve its results through global expansion'.

German: 'Furthermore, tours help to secure sponsors, which are another of Atlético de Madrid's main commercial objectives. Atlético's board of directors has defended the tours even though they are not profitable (the previous one earned the club €3 million), but I think that in the end they will become profitable because they have facilitated the commercial deals we believe we will be able to close in the next few years and above all, we are investing in territories where establishing the brand can produce very beneficial results, now that competition is increasingly fierce. Kyocera or KIA, two of Atlético's main sponsors, are pressing for visits by Atlético to their countries, but the club must consider in which direction we want to go'.

Antonio: 'Some do what they want and sign footballers in order to sell shirts; we do it to play football. The income is not excessively large, but we give social satisfaction. On a promotion level, sponsors have been found, merchandising is being expanded and agreements can be signed with companies in order to roll out the brand all over the world'.

The 2006–2007 tour?

Antonio: 'Atlético laid the first stone in China and Germany last summer and Atlético's international standing has increased to such an extent that it is coveted in all four corners of the globe, who perceive our brand and our team as very attractive in both commercial and sporting terms. The club is currently considering up to six tour offers for next summer. Asia and America are both interested in Atlético de Madrid and the offers that have reached the Vicente Calderón up to now have been from Japan, Korea, China and the UAE on the one hand and the USA and Mexico on the other.

The success of the Chinese and German tour of a few months ago was illustrated not only by the results on the pitch (the club won the Shanghai International Tournament), but also by the launch of the mark on the Far Eastern market and the opening of business channels with new sponsors and companies.

Having opened the way into Shanghai as a launch pad into the Chinese market, Atlético is now deciding whether to explore and establish itself in other countries. In fact, many of the offers that have reached the club's commercial department come from the Far East. Japan and South Korea tried to entice Atlético last year, but the club opted to lay the first stone in China instead'.

The Asian giant wants to take advantage of the goodwill generated last summer and give continuity to the expansion of business with Atlético in China. Atlético's directors received an approach from Beijing before it left Shanghai with a view to the team visiting the city in 2007 and playing a match to inaugurate the Olympic stadium.

The tour to China last year was dubbed *Los españoles* ['the Spanish'] by journalists, to consolidate the club's image in the USA and Asia (02/08/2006 10:28:08)

The English Premier League was the first European league to exploit the benefits of tours to far-off lands, mainly Asia and the USA: teams such as Manchester United or Liverpool were the first to set foot in Thailand, Los Angeles or Shanghai. Some years later with Florentino Pérez at the helm, Real Madrid broke down barriers for Spanish clubs in those countries. These tours, which receive increasing levels of institutional support, provide substantial exceptional revenue to businesses – football clubs – who are used to living on a knife edge.

Atlético de Madrid were the first to arrive in Asia, after touching down in Shanghai in the early hours of Tuesday, although they are one of the clubs who will spend least time in the Far East, as they are due to return to the Spanish capital the following Monday. During its visit, the club will be supported by Promomadrid, a company attached to the department of economics and technological innovation of the Madrid regional government, which was created in 2004 for the purpose of promoting and developing the Madrid region internationally, and will also play to friendly matches, one in Japan and the other in China.

Barcelona was the second club to embark on a long journey, but in the opposite direction to the club from the banks of the River Manzanares: the Catalan club are repeating the previous year's experience in the USA, a more lucrative market according to the experts, where they will stay for 13 days (1–13 August). As with Atlético, Barcelona's tour is supported by local government, which intends to use the Champions League winners' sojourn to promote Catalonia as a tourist destination. It is estimated that Barcelona will pocket no less than €4 million for their two-week stay in America.

Finally, Real Madrid is going ahead with their summer tours despite changing president. This time, as occurred in previous pre-seasons, Capello's team will travel to the USA on 7 August, where they will play two games in the five days they are scheduled to stay in the USA. However, tours are not the only way to break into new markets: teams such as Real Sociedad and Real Valladolid opted to sign Asian players with the broadcast rights in the Far East in mind, as did Perugia before them when they signed H. Nakata. Other clubs such as Osasuna have opted for more exotic approaches, for example, signing Iranian international Javad Nekouman. As Atlético de Madrid ex-commercial director Guillermo Moraleda previously said, clubs increasingly seek to encourage fans to go one step further and become consumers.

One of the offers being considered by Atlético comes from Dubai in the UAE. Petrodollars carry some weight and the UAE has joined the race to secure the *colchoneros'* presence. However, the club has tremendous appeal on the other side of the globe. Having played in a tournament in Mexico some years ago, the club received an offer from the country from where the current coach hails to go on a tour of various cities. The same has occurred with the USA, which hopes to see Torres, Agüero and co *in situ*. However, the tour will be based on the following clear premise; provided that it does not involve sporting prejudice for the team due to the very long journeys. Furthermore, there will be no final decision until the future is known and the team returns to European competition.

Do Sponsors Make You International?

The commercial department's last meeting, on which occasion the procedure for creating an internationalization strategy for the brand was discussed, many questions were raised once again, including whether these were merely recurring doubts of an already international club. In fact, Atlético de Madrid has managed to attract interest from various different sponsors, some national such as Asisa and Mahou and others international such as KIA, Nike, Coca-Cola, Kyocera and Hugo Boss.

German: 'I have picked up on KIA's presentation as Atlético's new sponsors because I think it gives a good idea of what the club and the sponsor are thinking "from a financial standpoint, the most important in the club's history".

"It is a collaborative agreement that from a financial standpoint is the most important in the club's history and one of the best in Spanish football", said Gil Marín during the presentation at the Vicente Calderón stadium, where he added that the agreement would enable Atlético to enter the "Asian market".

The club's supremo considers the agreement "ambitious" and capable of making a name for Atlético de Madrid in the Asian market. He believes he has sufficient backing from KIA to be able to do it and highlighted the "internationalization of the two brands".

"The new 'sponsor', KIA, is a major car manufacturer in Asia and going on an Asian tour is a good visiting card", said the president, who also pointed out that it is "too soon" to say when it will take place, as "some of the details of the contract are still pending". "I imagine that details of a commitment to travel over there will come later", he said. He was also appreciative of the club's previous agreement with Columbia Tristar over the last three seasons in which they "opted for a different form of advertising on shirts. It was a great experience, both for them and for us", he added.

Kenny Lee, the president of KIA's Spanish subsidiary, explained that it is an "honour" to sponsor "one of the best football teams" and emphasized that his company is the "fastest growing brand in Europe". Lee, who underlined that his company's aim is to become one of the most "important in the world by 2010", said that he was "convinced that the KIA-Atlético de Madrid partnership" will lead to "great successes and satisfaction" for both before departing with an "Aupa Atleti" ["Up Atleti"]'.

Does the Atlético De Madrid Foundation Make You International?

Germán: 'Antonio, the club is full of surprises, look at the following activity by our foundation:

> *Atlético de Madrid footballer Antonio López laid the first stone of the club's Child Development Centre in Nicaragua, which according to Daniela Knorr, the director of Infancia sin Fronteras in Nicaragua, will provide more than 900 boys and girls with medical and sanitary care and educational, cultural and sporting activities. "It's a beautiful project; truly, people in developed countries don't realise what poverty there is until they visit places like this", said Antonio López to the country's sporting press.*

The centre is located in Villa Kokomo in the Quebrada Honda settlement of Matagalpa, 130 km north of Managua, one of the poorest areas in America. "All the work that is done here is a drop in the ocean compared to the existing need", said the Spanish footballer, who arrived in the Central American country on 27 Wednesday during his holidays. Antonio López, who was accompanied by Óscar Jiménez, the head of the Atlético de Madrid Foundation's social department, added that the building of the centre "is a good initiative because it saves many families'.

The first port of call on the trip was Managua, where Antonio López visited the headquarters of Infancia sin Fronteras, where more than 1000 children waited anxiously to meet him. The reception could not have been better and Antonio did not stop signing autographs and handing out toys to the youngest ones. He also took an interest in the problems faced by the staff who work with the children. It was the beginning of an action-packed day, as after this first visit, he went on to visit several schools.

In one of these centres, López, a native of Alicante, expressed an interest in visiting the workshops where the boys and girls learn handicrafts. 'This is really surprising. In a country like Spain, it would be unthinkable for children to learn such wonderful skills. I have been pleasantly surprised', said the player to the Infancia sin Fronteras website.

Atlético de Madrid as of December 2006

In the last few years, Atlético de Madrid has been obliged to develop various strategies following a difficult period resulting from a lack of success on the pitch, the ultimate aim of any sporting institution. The demand by thousands of fans to be Spain's third club behind Real Madrid and Barcelona is both relevant and decisive, as the pressure in the media is extremely significant and affects the whole structure of a football club.

The questions we can ask to help Antonio and Germán are: why should Atlético de Madrid become internationalized? What kind of alternatives exist? What variables need to be managed? How would business, sporting and social strategies be aligned? What relationship would history have with the internationalization? What influence do the city of Madrid and Real Madrid have on this? What role do the sponsors play?

Case Questions

1 What kind of values are shared by the club management and supporters?
2 In the light of the values identified, what does internationalization mean for the club?
3 Can the club's brand image be amenable to brand stretch?
4 From the viewpoint of resources existing in the club, if you are the club's chairman, how would you push the internationalization process?
5 Does internationalization mean a single and unique positioning or can there be variant choices? If so, what are they? Why so?

Annexe 1

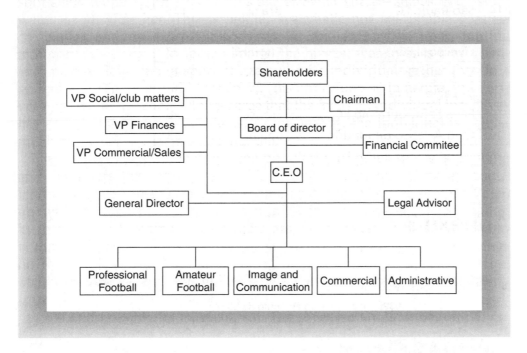

Annexe 2

The International Federation of History and Statistic of the Soccer (IFFHS) analyses all the results of league, it surrounds and continental competitions from 1 January 1991.

Ranking TOP-20:

1	FC Barcelona	Spain	270
2	Juventus FC Torino	Italy	235
3	Milan AC	Italy	224
4	Manchester United FC	England	218
5	Real Madrid CF	Spain	218
6	FC Bayern München	Deutschland	197
7	FC Internazionale Milano	Italy	186
8	Arsenal FC London	England	180
9	CA River Plate Buenos Aires	Argentina	155
10	AFC Ajax Amsterdam	Nederland	126
11	Parma AC	Italy	123
12	FC do Porto	Portugal	122

13	CA Boca Juniors Buenos Aires	Argentina	117
14	São Paulo FC	Brazil	115
15	Chelsea FC London	England	111
16	Liverpool FC	England	107
17	Valencia CF	Spain	99
18	SS Lazio Roma	Italy	98
19	Paris Saint-Germain FC	France	96
20	Club Atlético de Madrid	Spain	83

Annexe 3

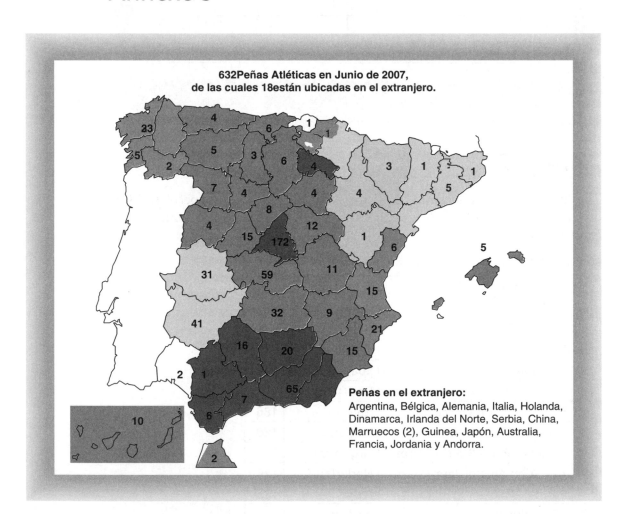

632Peñas Atléticas en Junio de 2007, de las cuales 18están ubicadas en el extranjero.

Peñas en el extranjero:
Argentina, Bélgica, Alemania, Italia, Holanda, Dinamarca, Irlanda del Norte, Serbia, China, Marruecos (2), Guinea, Japón, Australia, Francia, Jordania y Andorra.

Annexe 4

Atlético de Madrid website

DATOS POR MES – MEDIA – Temp 06–07

539.476	Visiting
301.584	IPS unique
34.440	email address
4.767.269	Visiting pages

Annexe 5

The 10 best players of the century

1 Lerby BEN BAREK (1948–1954).
   113 matches/6 seasons/56 goals Titles: 2

2 Enrique COLLAR (1953–1969).
   371 matches/16 seasons/71 goals Titles: 5

3 Joaquín PEIRÓ (1955–1962).
   166 matches/7 seasons/93 goals Titles: 3

4 Jorge MENDONÇA (1958–1967).
   168 matches/9 seasons/59 goals/Titles: 5

5 ADELARDO Rodríguez (1959–1976).
   580 matches/17 seasons/115 goals/Titles: 10

6 LUIS ARAGONÉS (1964–1975).
   265 matches/11 seasons/123 goals/Titles: 5

7 José Eulogio GÁRATE (1966–1977).
   241 matches/11 seasons/109 goals/Titles: 6

8 Luiz PEREIRA (1975–1980).
   143 matches/5 seasons/14 goals/Titles: 2

9 Paulo FUTRE (1987–1993 Y 1997–1998).
   173 matches/7 seasons/38 goals/Titles: 2

10 Francisco Narváez KIKO (1993–2001).
    270 matches/8 seasons/62 goals/Titles: 2

Case Resources

Reading

Barney J. (1991). Firm resources and sustained competitive advantage. *Journal of Management*, Vol. 17, No. 1, pp. 99–120.

Hamel, G. and Prahalad, C.K. (1989). Strategic intent. *Harvard Business Review*, May–June, pp. 63–76.

Kase, K., Urrutia, I., Martí, C. and Opazo, M. (Forthcoming). The proto-image of Real Madrid: Implications for marketing and management. *International Journal of Sports Marketing and Sponsorship* (Special Number on Latin America).

Urrutia, I., Kase, K., Martí, C. and Opazo, M. (2006). El mapa estratégico del Real Madrid: el arte de construir una marca. *www.estratgiafinanciera.es*, Vol. 231, pp. 10–18.

Website

Atlético de Madrid – http://www.clubatleticodemadrid.com/en/index.asp

Case

16

Olympic marketing: the power of the five rings band

Alain Ferrand

Case Focus

The case examines the structure of the Olympic marketing programme addressing the Olympic brand equity as a key success factor.

Keywords
• Olympic movement • Olympic games • Marketing strategy • Brand management • Brand equity • Sponsorship • Ambush marketing

Case Summary

The 6 April 1896, the first modern Olympiad Games opened in Athens. This event is now the most appealing sport event worldwide. According to Sports Marketing Surveys (SMS) 3.9 billion people watched the 2004 Olympic Games in Athens on TV and 3.1 billion watched the Turin 2006 Games. Sponsorship generated 1339 million US$ during the period 2001–2004. According to the Olympic Charter (OC) the Olympic Games are the exclusive property of the International Olympic Committee (IOC). This case study examines how the IOC manages its rights in collaboration with the Organizing Committees of the Olympic Games (OCOGs) and the stakeholders belonging to the Olympic Movement, in order to enhance the Olympic rings brand equity and to develop successful marketing programmes.

Case Elements

In order to understand the Olympic marketing strategy it is important to be aware of IOC mission and goals and to analyze the stakeholders' network forming the Olympic system in relation to the marketing rights.

IOC Mission and Goals

The IOC was founded on 23 June 1894 by Baron Pierre de Coubertin who was inspired to revive the Olympic Games of Greek antiquity. The IOC is an international, non-governmental, not-for-profit organization, of unlimited duration, in the form of an association with the status of a legal person, recognized by the Swiss Federal Council. Its object is to fulfil the mission, role and responsibilities as assigned to it by the OC.

The OC is the codification of the Fundamental Principles of Olympism, Rules and Bye-Laws adopted by the IOC. It governs the organization, action and operation of the Olympic Movement and sets forth the conditions for the celebration of the Olympic Games. It is the codification of the Fundamental Principles, Rules and Bye-laws adopted by the IOC. It governs the organization and running of the Olympic Movement and sets the conditions for the celebration of the Olympic Games. According to the OC the goal of the Olympic Movement is to contribute to building a peaceful and better world by educating youth through sport practised without discrimination of any kind and in the Olympic spirit, which requires mutual understanding with a spirit of friendship, solidarity and fair play.

The Olympic System

The IOC movement should be considered as a large system formed by three main stakeholders[1] defined by the OC. The IOC, the International Federations (IFs) and the National Olympic Committees (NOCs), as well as the Organizing Committees for the Olympic Games, are all required to comply with the OC. In addition to its three main constituents, the Olympic Movement also encompasses the 'OCOGs', the national associations, clubs and persons belonging to the IFs and NOCs, particularly the athletes, whose interests constitute a fundamental element of the Olympic Movement's action, as well as the judges, referees, coaches and the other sports officials and technicians. It also includes other organizations and institutions as recognized by the IOC.

Figure 16.1 presents the IOC main stakeholders according to the OC. This system encompasses athletes which are a fundamental element of the Olympic Movement, judges and referees, associations and clubs, as well as all the organizations and institutions recognized by the IOC.

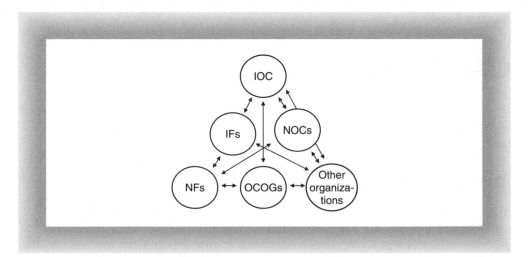

Figure 16.1 IOC main stakeholders according to the OC

---

[1] According to Freeman (1984, p. 46), 'a stakeholder is any group or individual that can affect or be affected by the accomplishment of the objectives of the organization.'

In this system International Sports Federations are divided up between those (35 in 2002) whose sport features on the programme of the Summer or Winter Games, which sanctions their Olympic events, and those (30) whose sport is not included on the programme but is recognized by the IOC. The former contribute to the achievement of the goals set out in the OC (i.e. development of their sports throughout the world; to establish the rules concerning the practice of their respective sports and to ensure their application, technical control and direction of their sports at the Olympic Games; to provide technical assistance in the practical implementation of the Olympic Solidarity (OS) programmes; to spread Olympism and Olympic education). The Olympic federations receive a part of the television broadcasting rights for the Games. Recognized IFs receive subsidies.

There are 205 NOCs recognized by the IOC. They are IOC territorial representatives. Their mission is to develop, promote and protect the Olympic Movement in their respective countries in accordance with the OC. They receive financial resources from the IOC via OS, an organization based in Lausanne and financed, to an extent of approximately one-third, by television broadcasting rights for the Games.

The IOC entrust the organization of the Olympic Games to the NOC of the country of the host city, as well as to the host city itself. In order to fulfil this mission the NOC is responsible for the establishment of an Organizing Committee (OCOG). The OCOG has the status of a legal person in its country and it is based in the city where the Games are to take place. An OCOG usually maintains close relations with the local, regional and national public authorities of a country for numerous organizational dimensions (e.g. constructions, security, transports, diplomatic issues, etc.).

The National Federations (NFs) link up for a given sport clubs and regional associations in their countries and via them, their athletes. To be recognized by an NOC and accepted as a member of such an NOC, an NF must exercise a specific, real and ongoing sports activity, be affiliated to an IF recognized by the IOC and be governed by and comply in all aspects with both the OC and the rules of its IF.

Other organizations and institutions refer to the city where the OG are organized and then to the government of the country. The national government of the country of any applicant city must submit to the IOC a legally binding document which the said government undertakes and guarantees that the country and its public authorities will comply with and respect the OC. The NOC, the OCOG and the host city are jointly and severally liable for all commitments entered into individually or collectively concerning the organization and staging of the Olympic Games, excluding the financial responsibility for the organization and staging of such Games, which shall be entirely assumed jointly and severally by the host city and the OCOG, without prejudice to any liability of any other party.

The Olympic system is made of non-profit organizations according to the law of the country where their headquarters are located, including the IOC in Switzerland. There are other important 'players' in this system which

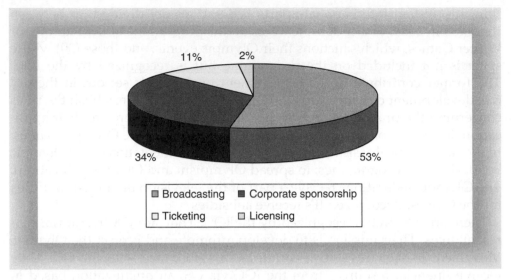

Figure 16.2 Olympic marketing revenues 2001–2004
Source: IOC

have an important economical impact. Olympic marketing revenues are based on four main origins: broadcasting, corporate sponsorship, ticketing and licensing. Figure 16.2 presents the revenue breakdown during the period 2001–2004. It demonstrates the importance of broadcasters (US$2229 millions, 53 per cent) and corporate sponsors (US$1459 millions, 34 per cent). Television networks (i.e. NBC – National Broadcasting Corporation, the channels belonging to the European Broadcasting Union) pay considerable rights to the IOC in order to broadcast the Olympic Games. Sponsors refer to the companies that participate in the IOC's TOP marketing programme.

Consequently broadcasters and sponsors must be considered as primary stakeholders whose involvement is essential to the existence of the organization.[2] Figure 16.3 presents the IOC primary stakeholders and the leading organization that is going to manage its rights and implement a marketing strategy according to this network.

IOC Properties and Marketing Rights

Marketing activities are based on IOC properties and rights. Broadcasters are paying in order to get exclusive diffusions rights and sponsors are paying cash and/or in-kind fee paid to a property in return for access to the exploitable commercial potential associated with that property. Consequently the IOC and the Olympic system must identify and protects its rights.

---

[2] Secondary stakeholders can influence, or be influenced by the organization, but they are not essential to its survival.

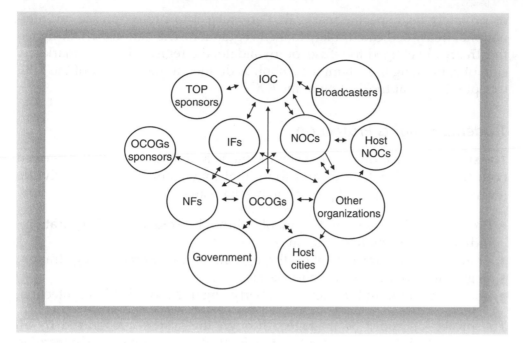

Figure 16.3 IOC primary stakeholders

Camps (2006) stressed the fact that the Olympic Movement is using the three mechanisms available for protecting its names and distinctive marks.

Protection by Law

There are many countries that include in their internal laws (generally laws dedicated to regulating sports) some reference to the idea that the propri-etary names, symbols and emblems of the Olympics (mainly the Olympic rings, the name of the Olympic Games, etc.) are reserved for the exclusive use of the NOC for that country, based on the rules of the OC or as dictated by the IOC. Therefore, there is ex lege protection of the classic symbols which identify all aspects of the Olympic Movement. In addition to this, the OC states that even when the national legal regulations or the filing of a trademark in a registry gives an NOC proprietary right to the Olympic symbol, that NOC may only exercise those rights in accordance with the instructions set forth by the IOC Executive Board.

Conventional International Protection

Through the International Nairobi Treaty (on September 1981) for the pro-tection of the Olympic symbols,[3] the Olympic symbols are the only symbols

---

[3] The Olympic Symbol consists of five interlaced rings: blue, yellow, black, green and red, arranged in that order from left to right. It consists of the rings alone, whether delineated in a single colour or in different colours.

or privately held specific marks that are subject to protection via an international treaty dedicated solely to their regulation. The nations which signed the Treaty are obliged to refuse, or invalidate, the registration as a mark any sign of containing the Olympic symbol, as defined in the Charter of the IOC, except with the authorization of the IOC.

Trademark Rights Protection

The sport organization may register the name and distinctive marks derived both from their legal status and those that may stem from their activities (events). There are several protection mechanisms:

- Protection of names and symbols through Trademark Registration/ Industrial Property Registration.
- Protection of unnamed symbols through Intellectual Property Registration.
- Registration of Internet domain names.
- International World Intellectual Property Organization (WIPO) Protection.

The protection could be managed through the system recognized by all members of WIPO who adopted the Joint Recommendation Concerning Provisions on the Protection of Well-Known Marks.[4] Also be aware that many countries protect unregistered, well-known marks by virtue of the obligations assumed under the Paris Convention for the Protection of Industrial Property and the Agreement on Trade-Related Aspects of Intellectual Property Rights (TRIPS Agreement).[5] These are only anti-piracy protection measures and not direct recognition of the marks themselves.

Beyond any doubt, all those marks that include the names, signs or other distinctive elements of the Olympic Movement would be classified as well-known marks by the competent bodies and therefore the IOC or the NOC could demand the cessation of any piracy by a third party even without a formal registration in its favour.

Nevertheless, there is a potential problem related to the limitation due to rights of third party, individuals and groups (i.e. NOC, OCOGs, Ifs, athletes…). In the Olympic system it is essential to establish the balancing mechanisms among the rights that each stakeholder may have or contribute within the full range of activities developed. The OC defines precisely the distribution of rights and operating regulations.

---

[4] The Joint Recommendation Concerning Provisions on the Protection of Well-Known Marks adopted by the Assembly of Paris Union for the Protection of Industrial Property and the General Assembly of the World Intellectual Property Organization (WIPO) at the Thirty-Fourth Series of Meetings of the Assemblies of the Member States of WIPO. September, 1999.

[5] To find the full text of the treaties, agreements and other WIPO documents see http://www.wipo.int/treaties/

Rule 7.1: 'The Olympic Games are the exclusive property of the IOC which owns all rights and data relating thereto, in particular, and without limitation, all rights relating to their organization, exploitation, broadcasting, recording, representation, reproduction, access and dissemination in any form and by any means or mechanism whatsoever, whether now existing or developed in the future. The IOC shall determine the conditions of access to and the conditions of any use of data relating to the Olympic Games and to the competitions and sports performances of the Olympic Games'.

Rule 7.2: 'The Olympic symbol, flag, motto, anthem, identifications (including but not limited to "Olympic Games" and "Games of the Olympiad"), designations, emblems, flame and torches, shall be collectively or individually referred to as "Olympic properties". All rights to any and all Olympic properties, as well as rights to the use thereof, belong exclusively to the IOC'.

The governance of the Olympic system associated with the revenue generation and distribution related to the application of those rules drives IOC, LOC, host country NOC and NOCs to collaborate in order to protect the Olympic properties. For the Games of the XXIX Olympiad in Beijing the right owners of the Olympic Symbols in these Regulations refer to the IOC, the COC and the Organizing Committee of Games of the XXIX Olympiad (hereinafter referred as BOCOG, Figure 16.4). They have established the following regulations on the protection of Olympic symbols.

'Article 2 Olympic Symbols mentioned in these Regulations refer to:

1 The Five Olympic Rings of the IOC (hereinafter referred to as the IOC), flag, motto, emblem and anthem of the Olympic Games.
2 The special terms of Olympic, Olympiad, Olympic Games their abbreviations.
3 The name, emblem and symbol of the Chinese Olympic Committee (hereinafter referred to as the COC).

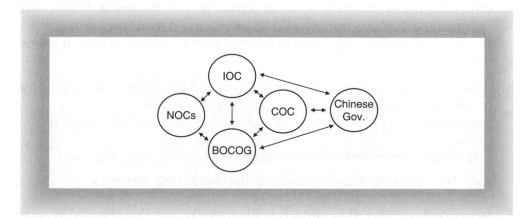

Figure 16.4 Relationship in the Olympic system for the OG in Beijing 2008 (BOCOG = Beijing Organizing Committee for the Olympic Games, COC = Chinese Olympic Committee, Chinese Gov. = Chinese Government)

4 The name, emblem and symbol of the Beijing 2008 Olympic Games Bid Committee.
5 The name and emblem of the Organizing Committee of Games of the XXIX Olympiad; the mascots, anthem and slogans of the XXIX Olympic Games; the 'Beijing 2008', the XXIX Olympic Games and their abbreviations.
6 Other symbols related to the XXIX Olympic Games prescribed in OC and Host City Contract for the Games of the XXIX Olympiad'.

The objective of this programme is to strengthen the protection of Olympic Symbols, thus protecting the lawful rights and commercial and social interests of the owners of the Olympic Symbols to ensure 'the dignity of the Olympic Movement'. The IOC has leadership of the system. It secures the rights distribution and commercialization. The Beijing Organizing Committee for the Olympic Games (BOCOG) is managing its own marketing programme at a national level and collaborates with the COC and the Chinese Government in order to protect the Olympic symbols. Furthermore BOCOG ask COC to stop their marketing activities during the games quadrennial to ensure consistency in these activities. The 202 other NOCs worldwide are protecting these Olympic Symbols on their respective territory.

IOC Marketing Programme

The marketing programme is managed by IOC Television & Marketing Services SA. This company is 100 per cent owned by the IOC. It results from the purchase of 100 per cent shares of Meridian Management SA on June 2005, which was a company owned 50 per cent by the IOC. The name was changed and its offices are still located in Lausanne in Switzerland and Atlanta in the United States of America. IOC Television & Marketing Services SA is responsible for a broad portfolio including the development and implementation of the Olympic broadcast rights and marketing strategy based on the IOC properties. This includes the negotiation of Olympic broadcasting rights and TOP sponsor contracts, and the management and servicing of the TOP Programme and Olympic brand management.

The IOC is developing long-term marketing programmes. It aims mainly at:

– Ensuring the financial stability of the Olympic Movement and supporting the activities developed by each Organizing Committee.
– Promoting the specific Olympic image, values and ideals throughout the world.
– Curtailing uncontrolled commercialization of the Olympic Games.

Table 16.1, presents the evolution of the marketing revenues. We point out that broadcasting was the main revenue source (52 per cent) with a 52.44 per cent increase. It is important to stress the fact that the IOC ensure that the whole world can view and experience the Olympic Games via free-to-air television. LOCOG sponsors, ticketing and Top programme sponsor come second. It is important to highlight the fact that the Top programme

Table 16.1 Evolution of the Olympic marketing revenues

	1993–1996	1997–2000	2001–2004	Evolution (%)	Percentage
Broadcasting	1251	1845	2236	44.05	52.44
OCOG sponsors	534	655	736	27.45	17.26
Ticketing	451	625	608	25.82	14.26
TOP programme sponsors	279	579	603	53.73	14.14
Licensing	115	66	81	–41.98	1.90
Total	2630	3770	4264		

Source: IOC, millions US$

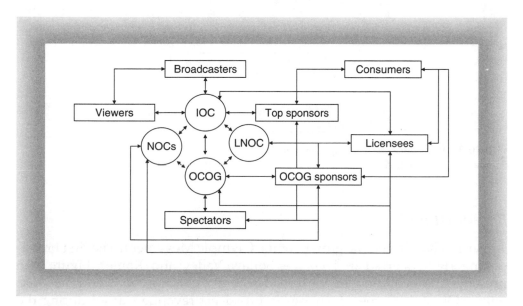

Figure 16.5 Olympic marketing system

revenues increased by 53.73 per cent and during the same period licensing revenues decreased by 41.98 per cent. Those revenues are distributed throughout the Olympic Movement, including future Organizing Committees, NOCs, IFs and other recognized organizations. The IOC Le CIO uses 8 per cent of broadcasting and Top programme revenues for its operating activities.

Olympic marketing structure is controlled by the IOC. The OCOG, host NOC and the NOCs are marketing their respective rights. Figure 16.5 presents this system focusing mainly on broadcasters, sponsors (Top and national) and licensees.

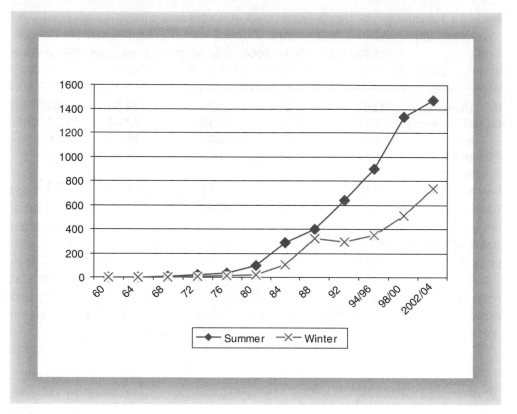

Figure 16.6 Broadcasting rights evolution
Source: IOC, millions US$

Broadcasting

Television has driven the growth of the Olympic Movement. The first broadcasting rights started in 1960 (i.e. Squaw Valley and Rome). Figure 16.6 presents the evolution of the broadcasting rights for both summer and winter Olympic Games. Increases in broadcast revenue started during the Samaranch presidency. NBC and EBU have been retained for 2010–2012 with a 35–40 per cent increase. Nevertheless, the IOC has often declined higher offers for broadcast on a pay-per-view basis or because a broadcaster could reach only a limited part of the population, as this is against Olympic Broadcast Policy. This fundamental IOC policy, set forth in the OC, ensures the maximum presentation of the Olympic Games by broadcasters around the world to everyone who has access to television. The IOC is systematically launching open call for tenders for broadcasting rights. Rights are only sold to broadcasters who can guarantee the broadest coverage throughout their respective countries free of charge.

This strategy allowed the IOC to increase the Olympic Games impact throughout the world. For example, the 2004 Olympic Games in Athens were televised for more than 4000 hours of live Olympic coverage. The winter Olympic Games Torino 2006 got the largest broadcast impact with a 3062 billion potential audience, 200 countries televising the Games, 16,311 hours, 200 of total global coverage and 3.5 hours average potential viewer consumption.

Sponsorship

Olympic sponsorship develops a relationship between the firms intending to support the Olympic Movement and the Olympic Games. Sponsorship contributes more than 40 per cent of Olympic marketing revenue with the Top programme and the OCOG programme. Each level of sponsorship entitles companies to different marketing rights in various regions, category exclusivity, and the use of designated Olympic images and marks. The Olympic Movement works continually to protect and promote the rights of sponsors.

The Olympic Partner Programme (TOP)
Created in 1985, the TOP programme, managed and negotiated by the IOC, is the only sponsorship with exclusive worldwide marketing rights to both winter and summer Games. In Turin the following companies were Top partners: Coca-Cola, Lenovo, Atos Origin, GE, Johnson & Johnson, Kodak, Mac Donalds, Manulife, Omega, Panasonic, Samsung and Visa. These companies receive exclusive marketing rights and opportunities within their designated product category. They may exercise these rights on a worldwide basis, and they may develop marketing programmes with the various members of the Olympic Movement – the IOC, the NOCs and the Organizing Committees. In addition to the exclusive worldwide marketing opportunities, partners receive:

- Use of all Olympic imagery, as well as appropriate Olympic designations on products.
- Hospitality opportunities at the Olympic Games.
- Direct advertising and promotional opportunities, including preferential access to Olympic broadcast advertising.
- On-site concessions/franchise and product sale/showcase opportunities.
- Ambush marketing protection.
- Acknowledgement of their support though a broad Olympic sponsorship recognition programme.

The revenues increase presented in Figure 16.7 demonstrate the success of this programme.

OCOG marketing programme
Under the direction of the IOC, the Organizing Committee (OCOG) manages its own marketing programmes that are targeted for the Olympic Games host country and the staging of the Games. These programmes are negotiated directly with the OCOG and generally limited to the four-year

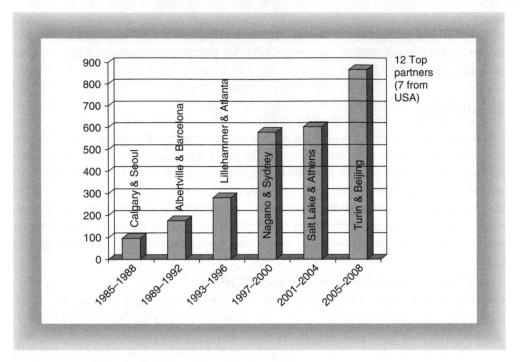

Figure 16.7 Top programme revenues evolution
Source: IOC, millions US$

Games period. IOC is blocking Top programme sponsors products categories. Contracts are generally limited to the four-year Games period and are negotiated directly with the OCOG which receives 95 per cent of the revenue (5 per cent are distributed throughout the Olympic Movement by the IOC).

Suppliers

Olympic Supplier programmes are designed to provide further vital areas of support and services required by the IOC and an Organizing Committee for their operations. Contracts are negotiated by the IOC which ensure product category exclusivity. Marketing rights are more restricted for Suppliers and generally do not include any direct support for the Games themselves. The currents suppliers are Daimler Chrysler (ground transport), Mizuno (clothing), Schenker (freight forwarding and customs clearance services).

Licensing

Licensing programmes produce officially licenced products and merchandise. These items carry the emblems and mascots of the Olympic Games or Olympic teams and are designed to commemorate the Olympic Games and Olympic teams.

Table 16.2 Summer Olympic Games ticketing

Olympic Games	Tickets available (million)	Tickets sold (million)	Percentage of tickets sold	Revenue to OCOG (million US$)
1984 Los Angeles	6.9	5.7	82.6	156
1988 Seoul	4.4	3.3	75	36
1992 Barcelona	3.9	3.021	80	79
1996 Atlanta	11	8.318	82.3	425
2000 Sydney	7.6	6.7	88	551
2004 Athens	5.3	3.8	72	228

Source: IOC

Ticketing

The Olympic Games ticketing programme is managed by the OCOG, with the approval of the IOC Executive Board. Both organizations collaborate in order to enable the public to purchase Olympic event and ceremonial tickets both in the host country and around the world. Table 16.2 provide facts and figures regarding Olympic ticketing programmes, including the number of tickets available, the number of tickets sold and the revenue generated to support the staging of the Games.

Other Programmes

Olympic Marketing also incorporates philatelic, numismatic and other programmes that benefit the Olympic Movement.

Case Diagnosis

To understand IOC marketing programme success despite the strong competition of major international sport events such as FIFA World Cup and IAAF World Championship it is important to stress the power of the Olympic brand and its activation. We stressed some key data about the audience, the broadcasting rights and the sponsorship fees. They are the result of Olympic brand equity. Aaker (1991, p. 15) defines brand equity; it's the set of assets and liabilities that connects 'a brand to its name or its symbols and that brings something to the enterprise and to its clients because they give an added value or a lesser value to the products and to the services'. We are going to analyze Olympic brand assets and liabilities according to the framework developed by Ferrand and Torrigiani (2005) which considers the six following dimensions: foundations, stakeholders, protection, knowledge, experience and value relationship.

Olympic Brand Foundations

Today, the Olympic brand's core attributes are still closely aligned with the Fundamental Principles of Olympism established more than a century ago in The OC. This resonance is a testament to the endurance of the Olympic values and to the timelessness of the philosophy of Olympism.

Olympic rings were designed by Baron Pierre de Coubertin in 1913. He described it as 'a real international emblem', with the five rings representing the five parts of the world that were participating at that time, and the six colours (he included the white background) the colours of the nations represented. Taking the three integral propositions of identity, ownership and origin, the Olympic Games symbol delivers brilliantly. It has lasted through major changes in the world unchanged and still powerful. Depending on the countries, its prompted awareness varies from 85 per cent to 98 per cent (*Source*: IOC, 2005). It expresses the Olympic values such as: heritage, universality, humanity, fair play, peace, equality, loyalty and respect.

IOC promotes the Olympic brand through the Celebrate Humanity global campaign. The campaign for 2006 presented personal interpretations of the Olympic experience, with Andrea Bocelli delivering the message known as 'Heart' and Nelson Mandela delivering the message known as 'Adversaries and Equals'.

Stakeholders in Relation with the Olympic Brand

Stakeholders in relation with the Olympic brand are one of its major assets. We present the primary stakeholders forming the Olympic system. Most of them are powerful players in politics and economy. The IOC develops relationships with a large number of organizations such as:

– the Court of Arbitration for Sport (CAS),
– the International Committee for Fair Play (CIFP),
– the International Paralympic Committee (IPC),
– the World Anti-Doping Agency (WADA),
– World Olympians Association (WOA),
– IFs associations (ASOIF, AIOWF, ARISF, GAISF),
– National Olympic Committee Associations,
– World Olympians Association,
– International Olympic Truce Foundation and Centre,
– Multi-sport events and associations,
– Organization disseminating the Olympic ideals and fair play,
– Sport medicine and science organizations,
– Sport equipment and facilities organizations,
– Media organizations,
– UNESCO (United Nations Educational, Scientific and Cultural Organization),
– United Nations.

It constitutes a large worldwide network, which is activated with various programmes. The IOC and its primary and secondary stakeholders are engaged in cooperative and collaborative activities and programmes in order to strengthen their relationships and to enhance mutual economical and social value.

Olympic Brand Protection

In the first part we stressed the importance of the marketing rights protection and the mechanism used by the IOC. The IOC and its primary stakeholders are continuously developing innovative anti-ambush campaigns. For Torino 2006, the IOC developed for the first time an international anti-ambush[6] campaign implemented by the NOCs on the prevention of ambush marketing for the benefit of the Olympic Movement. The action lines of this campaign were:

- Anti-ambush campaign kit distributed to NOCs providing guidance on local implementation of the campaign. The key messages of the campaign communicated the identities, roles and contributions of Olympic sponsors, defined ambush marketing and the damage it can cause to the Olympic Movement and presented ideas on how stakeholders can combat ambush marketing.
- Broadcast and Internet monitoring aimed at protecting the Olympic Move-ment and the contractual rights of broadcast and marketing partners.
- Standards for proper usage of Olympic marks by the Olympictic movement and its partners through are the Olympic Marks and Imagery Usage Manual.
- Collaboration between the IOC and the Organizing Committee to protect the rights of all Olympic partners.
- Support of venue cities and other non-commercial organizations to ensure a consistent brand image for the Olympic Games which avoided brand dilution and risks for ambush marketing.
- Criminal, financial and civil law enforcement authorities from federal, provincial and municipal levels united forces to combat counterfeit merchandise and ambush marketing.

These collaborative actions are aimed at protecting the Olympic brand and the Olympic partners' exclusive marketing rights. Nevertheless one of the most important aspects refers to the Olympic brand protection itself in

---

[6] 'Ambush marketing is marketing that capitalizes on the goodwill of the Olympic Movement by creating a false, unauthorized association with the Olympic Movement, Olympic Games or Olympic athletes without making the financial investment required to secure official sponsorship rights' (Vancouver: www.vancouver2010.com/en/Look Vancouver2010/ProtectingBrand/OlympicBrandFAQs).

order to preserve its unique identity. The IOC has a strict policy to maintain a commercial-free field of play, with very limited branding allowed. A clean field of play 'emphasises sport over the commercial agenda and protects the Olympic brand. This standard also eliminates distracting messages from the field of play and differentiates the Olympic Games from virtually all other sporting events' (IOC Torino Marketing Report, p. 120).

Olympic Brand Knowledge

Knowledge refers to brand awareness and image. IOC is monitoring the Olympic brand awareness and image. During the Torino 2006 Olympic Winter Games, the IOC conducted research in 12 countries. Results demonstrated that global consumer awareness of the Olympic Winter Games increased from 87 per cent in 2004 to 94 per cent in 2006. Furthermore the Olympic brand image is structured with three dimensions.

1 Striving for Success, which is founded upon the ideals inherent in sport – such as striving, excellence, determination, being the best.
2 Olympic Games as a global festival – such as global, participation, celebration, unity, festive.
3 Celebration of community and positive human values – such as aspiration to universal ideals: optimism, respectful and inspirational.

These three dimensions support a powerful, emotive brand that transcends sport and resonates strongly in people's minds worldwide.

Olympic Brand Experience

The strong appeal of the Olympic brand drives the IOC and its primary stakeholders to use a pull strategy, where organizations and individuals are invited to experience the brand. According to Smith and Wheeler (2002, p. 10), 'experiencing the brand begins with the brand and its desired values, turns these into a promise for target customers, and delivers the promise in a way which brings the brand alive.' Consequently, fulfilling the promise requires an emotional event with unique values, a quality management, an effective teamwork and communication.

Both IOC and LOCOG are managing the operational process in order keep its promises and to fulfil the expectations of individuals and stakeholders involved in this event. This event is dedicated mainly to the athletes and the Olympic Family. Nevertheless, sponsors are one of the main stakeholders. The Olympic Movement manages the Olympic sponsorship in order to enable each partner to derive value from its Olympic association and to ensure that Olympic sponsorship supports the Games and the athletes in a manner that promotes the Olympic ideals. For the Olympic Games 2006 Olympic Movement and the TOROC provided customized services.

– Large account management teams, assistance in activation, resolution of issues and support for maximizing showcasing, hospitality and on-site operations.

- Marketing consultation for strategy and activation.
- Sponsors' activation and information with the Olympic marketing extranet, known as Athena.
- Olympic marketing research.
- Access to Olympic imagery.

Relationship Value

Value is one of the key concepts explaining the relationship between the organization, its brand and its stakeholders and individuals. In the sport context value is based on both functional (i.e. to participate, to improve its business) and experiential motives (i.e. emotional, symbolic and socio-cultural). Furthermore it is experiential because the value can only be derived from experiencing the situation from which the value is created. Several key elements drive consumer interest in the Olympic Games, contribute to the appeal of the event and differentiate the Olympic brand from any other sports and cultural property. Results from 2006 Olympic brand research presented in Table 16.3 demonstrate the elements that drive interest in the Olympic Games.

Table 16.3 Turin 2006 audience motives

Percentage	Motives	Category
77	The Olympic Games are special because they happen only once in a while	Experiential
75	Performance of Olympic athletes encourages children to participate in sport	Functional
73	The Olympic Games are more than just a sports event	Experiential
73	The Olympic Games provide a good role model for children	Functional
70	The Olympic Games are as much about taking part as they are about winning	Experiential
69	There is no better achievement in sport than winning an Olympic gold medal	Experiential
67	No event brings the world together quite like the Olympic Games	Functional
65	The Olympic Games are the pinnacle of all sports events	Experiential
65	The Olympic Games have something for everyone	Experiential

Source: adapted from IOC, 2005

Data presented in the Table 16.3 demonstrates the importance of experiential motives balanced by functional ones related to social benefits. That makes this brand and this event unique and appealing for a large audience. Furthermore, according to the IOC Torino Marketing Report, firms which sponsored the Olympics games in Turin get the following benefits: raised awareness, enhanced brand appeal and image, increased sales, motivates employees, connects with communities and creates legacies, builds consumer relationships and enhances corporate reputation.

Conclusion

Olympic brand equity is one of the most powerful sport brands worldwide and it is a key element of the success of IOC marketing programme. These dimensions are monitored with an Olympic brand research. Data demonstrates that the Olympic Games and Olympic Winter Games enjoy extraordinarily high appeal and awareness among consumers worldwide. Despite major changes in the world since the first modern Olympic Games, the five rings have been strong enough to withstand those changes but also dynamic enough to make the changes work for them – whatever technology or culture throws at them, they will not only survive, they will probably thrive.

Case Questions

1 What are the conflicting areas referring to the marketing rights by IOC, OCOG and NOCs?
2 What do you think are the advantages and disadvantages for a major sport event to have a strict policy in order to have a commercial-free field of play, with very limited branding allowed?
3 Evaluate whether or not you think IOC marketing strategy is likely to be the most effective one for the development of the Olympic Games.
4 Compare and contrast the IOC marketing strategy with another leading international governing body (e.g. FIFA, IAAF...) for a world championship.
5 Which activation strategies are Top programme sponsors implementing?
6 Which co-marketing activities could be implemented between Top programme sponsors?

Case Resources

Reading

Aaker, D.A. (1991). *Managing Brand Equity: Capitalizing on the Value of a Brand Name*. The Free Press, New York.

Aaker, D.A. (1996). *Building Strong Brands*. The Free Press, New York.

Camps, A. (2006). El impacto del marketing en la financiación de los Comités Olímpicos Nacionales. *Revista Apuntes de Educación Física y Deportes*, Vol. 86, pp. 62–73.

Chappelet, J.L. and Bayle, E. (2003). *Strategic and Performance Management of Olympic Sport Organisations*. Human Kinetics, Champaign.

Chappelet, J.L. (2004). Managing the magnitude and complexity of the Olympic Games, in Horch et al., H.D. (Eds.), *Events in Sport*. Institut für Sportökonomie, Köln, pp. 52–62.

Ferrand, A. and Torrigiani, L. (2005). *Marketing of Olympic Sport Organisations*. Human Kinetics, Champaign.

Ferrand, A., Torrigiani, L. and Camps, A. (2006). *The Routledge Handbook of Sport Sponsorship: Successful Strategies*. Routledge, London.

Freeman, R.E. (1984). *Strategic Management: A Stakeholder Approach*. Pitman, Boston.

IOC (2005). Final Report *2001–2004*. IOC Communication Department, Lausanne.

IOC (2006). IOC Marketing Report – Torino 2006. IOC Communication Department, Lausanne.

Payne, M. (2005). *Olympic Turnaround: How the Olympic Games Stepped Back from the Brink of Extinction to Become the World's Best Known Brand – and a Multi Billion Dollar Global Franchise*. London Business Press, London.

Preuss, H. (2006). *The Economics of Staging the Olympics: A Comparison of the Games 1972–2008*. Edward Elgar Publishing, London.

Smith, S. and Wheeler, J. (2002). *Managing the Customer Experience*. Prentice Hall, London.

Websites

International Olympic Committee – http://www.olympic.org
Torino 2006 – http://www.torino2006.org/ENG/OlympicGames/home/index.html
Beijing 2008 – http://en.beijing2008.cn
Vancouver 2010 – http://www.vancouver2010.com/en
London 2012 – http://www.london2012.org

Further Information

Users of the case may want to take a look at some of the TOP programme sponsors:

Atos origin – http://www.atosorigin.com/en-us/Services/Industries/Major_Events/Olympic_Games/
General Electric – http://www.ge.com/olympicgames/

Johnson & Johnson – http://www.jnj.com/our_company/olympics/index.htm

Omega – http://www.omega.ch/index.php?id=102

Visa – http://www.usa.visa.com

If you would like more information that will help you to understand this case, please access the accompanying web site to this book for further resources.

Case

17

To close or not to close: press relations and locker room accessibility in sports

Paul M. Pedersen

Case Focus

The case examines the controversy surrounding opening locker rooms to reporters, addressing some of the factors that influence the relationship in this contested terrain between media professionals and the sports personalities they cover.

Keywords
• Locker rooms
• Harassment
• Sports media
• Accessibility
• Publicity
• Media relations

Case Summary

The locker room in sports often perpetuates the adversarial relationship between athletes and reporters. While reporters find the locker room a pragmatic location to conduct interviews, many athletes consider reporters as invaders of their domain. Although the athletes do not like the arrangement, the open locker room exists for the four major professional sports teams in the USA. The locker room is open to both female and male reporters as sport organizations are required to provide equal access. This case study examines the harassment females have endured in the locker room, their coping strategies, the issues surrounding decisions to open and close locker rooms, and whether or not more stringent policies, procedures, and repercussions need to be implemented to reduce harassment behaviours.

Case Elements

The locker room is a contested terrain in sport. Much of the contentiousness surrounding this location involves journalistic issues such as privacy rights and access. Because of deadline pressures and a desire to get exclusive quotes from players still in the heat of the moment, sports journalists desire access to athletes and coaches as soon as possible after an athletic event. As explained by Christine Brennan (2006), a veteran sports columnist for the *USA Today* – a national newspaper in the USA, 'all I wanted to do was to get the quotes I needed and get back to the press box to write on deadline' (p. 133). Locker room access – and an available and accommodating source – is often considered essential for many beat writers and columnists. The locker room is viewed as the practical and efficient place to get immediate raw reactions and post-game comments while adrenalin-pumped athletes are still jubilant or dejected after a competition. There is, according to one sportswriter, 'an unequaled sense of mood found in a locker room' (Fuller, 1992, p. 39). It is also considered the best place to work sources, discover unique nuggets of information, and obtain story ideas. Because it is the most pragmatic location to conduct interviews, however, does not mean that it is the optimal interview setting. 'People think it's cool to talk to people in a locker room. It's not,' states sports journalist Steve Wilstein. 'It's not my preferred place. We're there only because of deadlines. I don't need to wait an hour in a locker room for a player to come out of the shower' (Fitzgerald, 1997, p. 10).

For athletes, the locker room is often considered a home away from home, with plush surroundings and state-of-the-art designs. Some athletes consider the locker room their domain. Because they believe it is their realm, they consider sportswriters as invading their territory whenever they enter the locker room with their tape recorders. 'The locker room is our safe haven,' explains one professional baseball coach (Sanchez, 2006, p. 1BB). Because of this mindset, the locker room has at times been the source for strained relationships between athletes and sports reporters. Sportswriters have discovered that the result of this adversarial reporter-source association is that the locker room door, according to sportswriter Robert Sanchez (2006), 'is more likely to be slammed shut than swung open, especially if a reporter doesn't know the basics of locker room etiquette. Now, it's about keeping a respectful distance from an athlete – giving the player his space and massaging agents and team officials. And that's before the first question is asked' (p. 1BB). The hostility in the locker room can be partially attributed to competition in sports journalism which has forced some sportswriters to engage in preventative sports journalism. This is where they loiter in the locker room just in case a story breaks or something newsworthy is said, overheard, or noticed. The press–player relationship has changed to a more adversarial association in part because of 'the sheer numbers in the locker rooms. The media mob has become so large and so aggressive that many players feel under siege. So they hide out. On deadline' (Sokolove, 1996, p. 18). For the most part, players – especially high profile and highly compensated professional athletes – feel the press has too much access and they would rather that reporters not be allowed in their locker room. Although the athletes do not like the arrangement and there are occasional verbal outbreaks and physical confrontations, the open locker room has remained in tact in the USA at least in leagues such as the National Football League (NFL), National Hockey League (NHL), Major League Baseball (MLB), and National Basketball Association (NBA).

For over 20 years now, the open locker room policy includes accessibility to both male and female sports reporters. Male athletes, coaches, and team officials have at times had issues with this equal access. This is exemplified by one professional football general manager's comment that a female sportswriter in the locker room 'messes up everything' (Brennan, 2006, p. 165). Studies have shown how the male locker room and other all-male, homosocial environments such as fraternities often have involved male bonding rituals that often degrade and objectify females (Curry, 1991; Messner, 1992; Dellinger and Williams, 2002). This animosity in the locker room has often been directed towards the policies that allow female reporters. 'Male locker rooms are shrines to masculine might,' notes author Mariah Burton Nelson (1994). 'When a real woman does enter this shrine, she automatically challenges the male bonding process' (p. 230). A female sportswriter goes into this male domain as a reporter, questioning the athletes and assessing their on-field accomplishments. Her presence as a professional places her in a position of power and authority, which has at times brought about defensive and sexually violent reactions from – and attempts to make her docile or a sexual object by – some male athletes. The female sportswriter in the locker room, according to sport sociologists Lisa Disch and Mary Jo Kane (1996), 'is an authoritative critic of athletic performance'. The sociologists add that the female sports reporter's 'profession affords her prerogatives over male athletes that exceed those that can be permitted to her as a woman' (p. 281). For instance, legendary NFL defensive lineman Reggie White (1999) once wrote an editorial in the *Wall Street Journal* in which he presented his case against females in the locker room. 'I can't see any legitimate reason for forcing male athletes to walk around naked in front of women who aren't their wives,' noted the hall of fame athlete. 'Most football players I know are as unhappy about this as I am' (White, 1999, p. 1).

Equal access has been obtained through public outcry, legal rulings, and lawsuits that have forced those reluctant sport leagues and organizations to open their locker rooms to female reporters. The landmark decision came in 1978 when the court ruled that *Sports Illustrated* reporter Melissa Ludtke – who had been banned from the New York Yankees clubhouse in accordance with MLB's policy barring female sportswriters from clubhouses – was 'deprived of equal opportunity to interview ballplayers solely on account of her sex ... that the ban substantially and directly interfered with Ludtke's right to pursue her profession as a sports reporter' (Women's Rights, 1979, p. 625). It took several years for many franchises and leagues to open their locker rooms to both male and female reporters. For example, two years after the ruling, sportswriter Christine Brennan entered her first NFL locker room. It was also the first time a female reporter had been in the team's locker room. Brennan (2006), in describing the incident in the chapter 'Welcome to the Locker Room' in her autobiography, noted, 'as soon as I walked into the steamy, overcrowded room, I heard whoops and hollers from distant corners, from players I couldn't see. "We don't go in the women's bathroom!" someone yelled. "What are you doing in here?" "Here for some cheap thrills?" screamed another. I took a few tentative steps into the room, then stopped, not knowing what to do. I was stuck. It seemed like a lifetime standing there' (p. 121). It was not until 1985 that the NFL finally mandated equal access. Although the other major leagues in the USA mandated equal access by the mid-1980s, some university athletic programmes in the mid-1990s still had not opened their locker room doors to female reporters (Bruce, 2002). Often, when closed, the reason is because of equal access. Some have chosen to close the locker room to all media rather than provide equal access. For example, just over 15 years ago Bobby Knight – the coach with the most victories in men's major intercollegiate basketball in the USA – decided to bar all reporters from the locker room instead of allowing access to female reporters. 'We did close our locker room to the press and set it up for players to go to the press room for interviews,' Knight (2002) commented in this autobiography. 'We did it the day after a woman reporter from the Associated Press made a national issue out of being barred from going into our locker room … the only fair thing to do was close the locker room to everybody and bring some players out to our regular press conference' (p. 296). Today, however, if locker rooms are open to the media, they are for the most part open to both female and male reporters.

Granting female sportswriters equal access did not always mean that they were walking into pleasant working environments. With the opening of the locker rooms to female reporters came increased sexual harassment. 'As greater numbers of women invaded the temples of male supremacy – the press box, the sidelines and, most sacrosanct of all, the locker room – a testosterone frenzy erupted in sports venues across the country, igniting the worst rash of sexism ever witnessed against a group of reporters' (Ricchiardi, 2004/2005, p. 55). The watershed incident occurred in 1990 when NFL players harassed Lisa Olson in their locker room. The players taunted and harassed the sportswriter. They exposed themselves to her, thrust their genitals towards her, and made numerous obscene gestures in her direction. Their actions 'came to symbolize the male sports world's resistance to women journalists reporting from the locker room' (Fitzgerald, 1997, p. 11). Beyond this incident, other athletes who have felt the locker room was their male domain have attempted to exert their perceived dominance of this territory through physical and verbal abuse, refusing to talk to a female reporter because of her gender (not because of her position as a reporter), and various sexually suggestive comments, jokes, gestures, touching, catcalls, poses, and other inappropriate behaviours. It is often very hard for sports reporters to challenge the sexual harassment that has occurred because it is often done very methodically and subversively. For example, during his career as a sports journalist the author of this case study once witnessed an MLB superstar – one with over 500 home runs in his career – methodically reveal his genitals to a female sportswriter who had entered his locker room. The naked player sat down and slowly opened his legs in the direction of the sportswriter who was interviewing another athlete in the adjoining locker stall. When the athlete had fully exposed himself and the sports reporter finally noticed (or got tired of being subjected to) the obvious sexual harassment, she quickly finished her interview and left the locker room. If this incident were reported, it would be difficult to prove as the athlete would most likely say that he was simply taking his time getting dressed. Therefore, sexual harassment occurs in the locker room because some athletes feel the need to exert their perceived power and authority over their domain.

Unfortunately, in order to secure access and avoid harassment, female sportswriters are often held to a different standard of locker room behaviour than their male counterparts. Some of the guidelines from their unwritten code of locker room ethics include: 'Give players time to dress and don't linger near the showers; verify with the public relations director you'll be there; use courtesy, common sense, and discretion; and learn to laugh off the inevitable' (Ardell, 2005, p. 208). According to Bruce (2002), female sportswriters categorize their locker room interactions with males as either supportive (accepted, welcomed), professional (viewed as reporters and not as women reporters), teasing (positive relationship), testing (unfamiliar relationship), and hostile (intimidated, degraded). Some of the unacceptable locker room incidents can have dramatic results, including the departure of female professionals from the field of sports journalism. One female sportswriter noted that she left the profession because she 'was, frankly, beaten down by the maleness of the locker room' (Ricchiardi, 2004/2005, p. 56). Although popular press accounts note that sexual harassment has decreased, a recent study was conducted to determine if inappropriate behaviour is still occurring and if the incidents are systemic (throughout the sport organization), situational (specific to the locker room), or dispositional (specific to the individual). There was a need to determine the current status of sexual harassment in male locker rooms. With the watershed moment in locker room harassment having occurred more than 15 years ago, the study sought to determine if sexual harassment of female reporters in the locker room is still occurring. In the past, the philosophy for survival was that female sports reporters in the locker room, according to sportscaster Lesley Visser, 'have to be a little deaf and a little blind' (Brennan, 2006, p. 156). Therefore, the study examined if female sportswriters still believe this is the best way to survive in the locker room. The purpose of the study was to ascertain from female sports newspaper personnel their perceptions of – and advice in handling – sexual harassment in the locker room.

In the study, female sports print media professionals were surveyed in order to determine their perceptions of sexual harassment in the locker room. The survey was designed to explore how they perceived locker room sexual harassment and how they would advise young professionals entering the field. Respondents were asked a series of scale and open-ended questions related to issues concerning the locker room and sexual harassment. Demographic information such as position, age, and ethnicity was also obtained in the survey. The sample was drawn from members of the Association for Women in Sports Media (AWSM). The executive committee chair (and then president) and database manager of this 18-year-old organization approved the distribution of the survey and provided the participant email addresses, respectively. The 263 AWSM members who met the criteria for participation were female, active professionals, and affiliated with newspapers in some capacity. Participants were encouraged to go to the survey website – which was facilitated by the researcher's institutional Center for Survey Research – and complete the questionnaire. Three follow-up email reminders were sent to the AWSM members who fit the study's criteria. Ninety-three active female sports newspaper professionals responded, yielding a final response rate of 35.4 per cent.

The study's findings revealed that the majority of the 93 female sports newspaper professionals were sportswriters (59 per cent), White (94 per cent), and between the ages of 25 and 39 years (57 per cent). Regarding the other positions, 13 per cent of the respondents were copy editors, 9 per cent were columnists, 7 per cent were assistant editors, 5 per cent were editors, and the remaining 7 per cent were in various positions such as management and design. Thirty-six per cent reported they were 40 years of age or older while the remaining 4 per cent noted they were between the ages of 20 and 24 years. In terms of sexual discrimination, 71 per cent of the female sports newspaper professionals believed that women are less likely to receive prime assignments. As one respondent noted, 'As a staff writer, I have felt that at times the better writing assignments have gone to male staff writers covering the largest events in our region – NASCAR, US. Open golf in Pinehurst, the men's NCAA Final Four'.

In relation to the issue of prevalence of sexual harassment, 65 per cent of the respondents stated that they had been sexually harassed at least once (between one and five times) over the past three years. Eight per cent noted they had been sexually harassed 6–10 times over the past three years and 4 per cent noted that they had been sexually harassed 11–20 times over the past three years. Harassment incidents occurred in a variety of sports and levels of sport participation. Regarding the specific sports in which the harassment occurred, football and basketball were mentioned most often with 33 per cent and 30 per cent, respectively. Baseball was listed 22 per cent of the time. Hockey, racing, soccer, and golf were the only other sports listed in which harassment occurred. When specific levels of competition were listed, the general category of major league sports led all categories as it was mentioned 37 per cent of the time. Interscholastic (21 per cent) and intercollegiate (20 per cent) athletics were also frequently listed along with minor league sports (15 per cent).

Regarding where the reporters felt they would more likely face sexual harassment, 23 per cent considered their newspaper workplace while 62 per cent considered the sports environment. In identifying the specific location where they thought the harassment would most likely occur, the participants provided varied responses. Some offered general statements such as 'harassment occurs most in the place each group feels most comfortable – by athletes in the locker room, especially if there's support of a group mentality', 'In the interview setting, whether it's at practices or in the locker room after a contest', and 'Anywhere there exists people who have to prove their power. Board rooms and locker rooms are often the same thing, except for the soap'. Beyond the general comments, their open-ended responses were grouped into four categories: locker rooms, newsrooms, press boxes, and other. The majority (53 per cent) listed locker rooms in their response as to where the harassment would most likely occur. As one respondent stated, 'Locker rooms, definitely'. Workrooms, pressrooms, and newsrooms were listed 33 per cent of the time while press boxes were mentioned in 12 per cent of the responses. The fourth category included a variety of responses such as 'game environment', 'Internet sites', and 'fans at games'. The majority (61 per cent) of the female sports journalists believed there would be a reduction in sexual harassment incidents if the locker rooms were closed.

The female sports newspaper professionals were asked about the advice they would give to new entrants into the field. The suggestions for handling sexual harassment issues fell into three general coping strategies or categories: flight, non-assertive, and assertive. The fewest responses could be categorized as flight. Examples of these responses were 'Get out if you can't handle it' and 'Get used to it or get out of the business. It's sad and upsetting, but it's true'.

The non-assertive category – what some (i.e. Disch and Kane, 1996) have referred to as performing the apologetic – included those who advised avoidance, appeasement, acceptance, and toleration of sexual harassment. The respondents in this category gave advice such as 'Grow a thick skin … day-to-day dirty jokes and such simply have to roll off your back or you'll never get your job done', 'Don't make yourself a target', and 'Shrug it off'. One suggested, 'Don't cry wolf over the little things, because what you may view as a big deal probably isn't in the big scheme of things' while another commented that 'Many times it can be avoided by the way the professional handles herself, by her body language and by the way she dresses when on the job'. Similarly, another respondent advised that female sportswriters not 'wear revealing clothes or act flirty around the athletes'.

The vast majority of responses fit into the assertive category. By refusing to laugh off minor incidents, tolerate unacceptable behaviour, or apologize for their presence in the locker room, these female sports reporters challenge the unwritten codes of conduct for female sportswriters. They are in 'an obvious violation of the apologetic' (Disch and Kane, 1996, p. 303). Their responses could be grouped into the categories of general comments, informing superiors, verbal confrontation, and documentation.

General comments included such statements as 'Stand up for yourself. Don't assume that you must have done something to provoke it', 'Stand up for your rights and have a knowledge of company policies', and 'Don't be quiet because you want to be thought of as "one of the boys"'. Another advised: 'Don't suffer in silence! That was my biggest mistake. Women think we have to bear this cross alone. Nope. You need to tell people, involve as many people as possible'. One respondent simply stated that female sportswriter should 'stay strong, overcome the jerks'.

Several respondents suggested contacting a superior whenever an incident occurred. Some of these comments were 'Go to your boss. If the boss tolerates it, go to the executive editor. If they tolerate it, get a new job' and 'I advise young women to give the guy one chance – be very clear that you're not interested and you want to keep it friendly so you can continue to work together. That usually does it. If not, tell his boss, letting that person know that you don't want a scene, you just want it to stop. That definitely does it. Even at that level, you're considered a bitch'.

Many advocated direct confrontation. Examples of their statements were 'Practice strong retorts', 'Be willing to confront people who harass you', 'Tell people when they say something offensive', 'Don't brush off remarks. Remind people when they are out of line', 'Tell off anyone who makes you feel uncomfortable or gets in the way of your ability to do your job professionally', and 'To inform the harrasser first that what he/she is doing is unwelcome; if it continues, report it'. Another response involved this advice: 'Take care of it personally, quickly, firmly and immediately. You can deal with it quietly, one-on-one, setting the offender straight in no uncertain terms, but without breaking the poor sap's cajones. He's confused enough as it is. Maybe he really likes you and has no social skills – not unheard of in the journalism and sports fields. If he is a real arrogant blockhead, embarrass the hell out of him publicly so he cannot thrive on secrecy'.

A common thread throughout many of the responses was documentation. As one respondent noted, 'Document, document, document … If someone is harassing you, print out any messages they send you … Any time there is an incident that doesn't involve email or messages, document it: Send yourself an email with the time, date and details of the incident'. Another commented, 'Don't let even the slightest incident go by … Most important – document every encounter'. One respondent advised young female sports newspaper professionals to 'Be prepared for it. It's going to happen. Deal with it calmly, professionally and directly. And document everything … More than anything, protect yourself. And don't just accept it. When you do, it makes it harder for other women in the business'.

While there is some evidence that there has been a decrease in locker room harassment of female reporters, the study revealed that harassment continues to exist. Because locker room harassment has not stopped, the question is, given that harassment continues to exist, what should sport organizations do to address this situation?

Case Diagnosis

The findings of the study suggest that female sports newspaper personnel continue to encounter unacceptable sexist behaviours. One participant commented that 'many years ago – before anyone was doing surveys like this – it was open season on us'. Unfortunately, 'open season' still appears to exist as nearly 7 out of every 10 respondents divulged that they had been sexually harassed at least once in the past three years. What is even more disturbing is the frequency in which some of the females have been harassed, with 8 per cent having been sexually harassed between 6 and 10 times and 4 per cent having been harassed between 11 and 20 times over that same time period. Although these numbers are high, they are probably low estimates because, according to Dellinger and Williams (2002), victims often do not consider their experiences sexual harassment and thus they 'rarely answer "yes"' to survey questions asking them if they have been sexually harassed'.

Sexual harassment of female sportswriters can occur anywhere. As the results of the study indicated, sexual harassment is not isolated to a specific sport or competition level. Incidents were reported in sports ranging from football to golf and from professional sports to interscholastic athletics. Incidents happen, as one respondent noted, 'in the places where sources might relax – and cross the line'. The survey results, however, provide insight as to where the most likely locations might be. The female sports newspaper professionals most often pointed to the sport environment (62 per cent) – and within this setting they specifically implicated the locker room (53 per cent) – as the place where sexual harassment would most likely occur. The majority (61 per cent) further agreed that sexual harassment of female sportswriters would be reduced if locker rooms were closed. Overall, sexual harassment incidents continue to occur, the most likely place for harassment is in the locker room, and incidents would be reduced if locker rooms were closed. Do these factors demand, however, that the locker rooms should be closed?

Sports organizations should address the issue of sexual harassment in the locker room by either closing the locker room or refocusing their efforts to eliminate locker room sexual harassment. Obviously, the first tactic – closing the locker room to both male and female sports reporters – would eliminate the sexual harassment of female sportswriters in the locker room. Mariah Burton Nelson (1994), who noted over a decade ago that 'The system should be changed' (p. 233), offered several suggestions, one of which was that interview rooms should be mandated. While locker room access helps to facilitate the work of sports journalists in many ways, a closed locker room is not unheard of as various sports and sports teams around the world have are not open to sports reporters. At the amateur level, the decision to have an open or closed locker room is generally at the discretion of the coach or the athletic administrators in charge. When there are closed locker rooms, quotes are obtained in interview rooms and press conferences. As sports columnist Jay Mariotti explains, 'we interview athletes where we are told to interview them. I have no problem with interviewing someone in a room outside the locker room' (Fitzgerald, 1997, p. 10). Reporters can still do their jobs if some type of access to players, coaches, and managers is provided in a timely manner. Making sport participants available to the media would eliminate the frustration that many sport participants face in dealing with the media in a crammed and combative area such as the locker room.

There are several problems with closing the locker room to eliminate sexual harassment. The first problem is that such action implies that sexual harassment is going to occur in the locker room and such incidents cannot be stopped without separating athletic competitors and sports reporters. Closing the locker room allows sports organizations the opportunity to not have to work and establish a culture where inappropriate behaviour will simply not be tolerated. Closing the locker room to eliminate sexual harassment implies that 'boys will be boys' and the best way to keep them from harassing behaviour is to bar female sports reporters rather than educate and train the athletes, and enforce a zero-tolerate policy. A second problem with closing the locker room involves the unfair accusations and repercussions female sports reporters would encounter. If the locker rooms were closed, according to one of the study's respondents, 'women would be blamed, and all that would do is to bring retaliation against women by fellow media and even fans'. A third problem with closing the locker room is that it would result in even further distance between sports reporters and their sources. 'With casual contact between sportswriters and athletes almost nil, a writer must live on what he can gather in the locker room' (Sokolove, 1996, p. 18). As one respondent noted, 'Closing locker rooms would eliminate a lot of verbal sexual harassment, but that would be ridiculous. That's where we get our stories, talk to our sources. No need to cut that out'.

The second tactic that sports organizations could use to address the issue of sexual harassment in the locker room is to keep the locker rooms open, but take a proactive approach to eliminate inappropriate conduct. This tactic is a more difficult endeavour than closing the locker room, but sports organizations should give this thought due diligence. Research has found that proactive approaches and sexual harassment training can be effective in reducing unacceptable behaviour (Gruber, 1998). The results of the study noted above suggest, however, that sports organizations have yet to embrace such an approach. While many have open locker rooms, the continued harassment of female sports reporters implies that the organizations either do not have a sexual harassment policy or what they have is not effective or enforced. Sports leagues and teams have some difficult decisions to make if they want to reduce, and maybe at some point eliminate, locker room incidents. While closed locker rooms would eliminate the harassment, such a policy would allow sports organizations an easy way out without having to implement and enforce a zero-tolerance policy regarding locker room sexual harassment by their athletes. League and team front office officials 'act peculiarly impotent to convince these million-dollar men to refrain from harassing women' (Nelson, 1994, p. 233). The effectiveness of the second tactic rests on these sports organizations. The benefits of locker room access can be obtained without sexual harassment if a strong policy – including more effective training and stringent enforcement of rules – against any inappropriate statements or behaviour is implemented.

The results of the study revealed that females who work in newspaper sports departments continue to encounter sexual harassment. The most likely location is the locker room. Possible solutions to reduce unacceptable behaviour include the closing of locker rooms or the implementing of more stringent policies, procedures, and repercussions for sexual harassment. If sports leagues and teams have sexual harassment policies and training programmes in place, the results of this study suggest that they are either ineffective or not enforced. Sports organizations need to either revisit or implement their sexual harassment policies and training in order for changes to occur. If they are unwilling to do this, they need to close their locker rooms. Until sports organizations and their stakeholders take a focused and proactive approach to eliminating locker room sexual harassment, locker rooms will remain hostile territories that perpetuate sexual harassment behaviour. Until sexual harassment ends, the advice the female sports newspaper personnel provided in the study will assist young female professionals as they enter this field and the locker room.

Case Questions

1 Is the locker room the domain of the athletes? Are reporters invaders of the athletes' territory?
2 What do you think are the advantages and disadvantages for a sports organization to adopt a closed locker room policy for the sports media?
3 To what extent do you feel sports organizations should accommodate the sports media in their locker room requests?
4 To what extent do you believe sports organizations benefit from locker room access?
5 Evaluate whether or not you think an open locker room policy for the sports media is an effective one for sports organizations.
6 Compare and contrast the locker room access of the major and minor (and/or professional and amateur) sports organizations in your region. Do those with more (or less) media access receive more and better sports media coverage?
7 What are some alternative locker room access strategies that could be implemented by sports organizations that would both accommodate the needs of the reporters and appease the wishes of the athletes?

Case Resources

Reading

Ardell, J.H. (2005). *Breaking into Baseball: Women and the National Pastime.* Southern Illinois Press, Carbondale, Illinois.
Brennan, C. (2006). *Best Seat in the House.* Scribner, New York, NY.
Bruce, T. (2002). Supportive or hostile? Teasing or professional? Women sportswriters categorize locker room interaction. *Women in Sport and Physical Activity Journal*, Vol. 11, No. 2, pp. 49–76.
Curry, T.J. (1991). Fraternal bonding in the locker room: A profeminist analysis of talk about competition and women. *Sociology of Sport Journal*, Vol. 8, No. 2, pp. 119–137.

Dellinger, K. and Williams, C.L. (2002). The locker room and the dorm room: workplace norms and the boundaries of sexual harassment in magazine editing. *Social Problems*, Vol. 49, No. 2, pp. 242–257.

Disch, L. and Kane, M.J. (1996). When a looker is really a bitch: Lisa Olson, sport, and the heterosexual matrix, signs. *Journal of Women and Society*, Vol. 21, No. 2, pp. 278–308.

Fitzgerald, M. (1997). Lisa Olson redux. *Editor and Publisher*, Vol. 130, No. 4, pp. 11–12.

Fuller, L.K. (1992). Reporters' rights to the locker room. *Feminist Issues*, Vol. 12, No. 1, pp. 39–46.

Giobbe, D. (1993). Women sportswriters still face hassles in the locker room. *Editor and Publisher*, Vol. 126, No. 50, pp. 12–13.

Gruber, J.E. (1998). The impact of male work environments and organizational policies on women's experiences of sexual harassment. *Gender and Society*, Vol. 12, No. 3, pp. 301–320.

Kane, M.J. and Disch, L. (1993). Sexual violence and the reproduction of male power in the locker room: A critical analysis of the 'Lisa Olson incident.' *Sociology of Sport Journal*, Vol. 10, No. 4, pp. 331–352.

Knight, B. (2002). *Knight: My Story*. Thomas Dunne, New York.

Messner, M.A. (1992). *Power at Play: Sports and the Problem of Masculinity*. Beacon, Boston.

Nelson, M.B. (1994). *The Stronger Women Get the More Men Love Football*. Harcourt Brace, New York.

Ricchiardi, S. (December 2004/January 2005). Offensive interference. *American Journalism Review*, Vol. 26, No. 6, pp. 54–60.

Sanchez, R. (2006, October 8). Their turf, their rules: Media at mercy of athletes upon entering sacred confines of locker room. *Denver Post*, Denver, colorado, USA. p. 1BB.

Sokolove, M. (1996, December). Across the great divide. *American Journalism Review*. Retrieved on September 5, 2007, from http:// www.ajr.org/ Article.asp?id=824.

White, R. (1999, April 8). Women in the locker room. *The Wall Street Journal*, p. 1.

Women's rights ... access to locker rooms (1979, April). *American Bar Association Journal*, Vol. 65, p. 625.

Websites

APSE – Associated Press Sports Editors – http://apse.dallasnews.com/

AWSM – Association for Women in Sports Media – http://www.awsmonline.org/

ISPA – International Sports Press Association – http://www.aipsmedia.com/

Sports Journalists' Association – http://www.sportsjournalists.co.uk/blog/

Sportswriters – http://www.sportswriters.net/

Further Information

Users of the case may want to take a look at the Wikipedia entries for the following:

Major League Baseball – http://en.wikipedia.org/wiki/Major_league_baseball

National Basketball Association – http://en.wikipedia.org/wiki/ National_Basketball_Association

National Football League – http://en.wikipedia.org/wiki/National_Football_League

National Hockey League – http://en.wikipedia.org/wiki/National_Hockey_League

Sexual Harassment – http://en.wikipedia.org/wiki/Sexual_harassment

Sports Journalism – http://en.wikipedia.org/wiki/Sportswriters

Case

18

"The Game We Love. Evolved.": Cricket in the 21st century

Maria Hopwood and Allan Edwards

Case Focus

This case examines the evolution of cricket from the stages of the sport's early development to the exciting, fast-paced version with which we are familiar today. By exploring some of the issues which have contributed to cricket's evolution and considering what the future might hold, this case deals with the key issues of sport marketing, product diversification and brand relationship management.

Keywords
• Sport marketing • Marketing research • Sports marketing communications • Image and identity • Product diversification • Brand relationship management

Case Summary

Cricket is a sport played and watched by countless millions throughout the world. It is a sport with a long and proud history and one which is imbued with symbolism and values which resonate far beyond the game and which have become powerful cultural statements wherever the sport is played. In recent years, however, cricket's overall popularity has been declining. Spectator attendance figures had fallen to such an extent that as the 21st century began, the England and Wales Cricket Board (ECB) decided that something serious had to be done to reverse this trend and to ensure that cricket remained commercially viable and competitive. Based upon the results of far-reaching market research, the cricket product was extended in 2003 with the introduction of Twenty-20 cricket and since then, a number of other variants including the Stanford 20/20, whose slogan has been used in the case title, have seen the sport continue to diversify and evolve.

Case Elements

Cricket is an almost tangible force that can unify an entire country, an entire group of people, no matter the differences that might exist off the field, in the houses of parliaments or among nations.

Allen Stanford

Modern cricket, perhaps more than most contemporary popular sports, struggles not only with the legacy of its privileged past but also with the fact that it is freighted with extraneous moral overtones (Birley, 1999). The widespread practice of describing unacceptable behaviour as 'not cricket' helps to perpetuate the myth that cricket is the gold standard for the sportsman-like behaviour that belongs to the bygone age of imperialism and gentility. As a direct result of this legacy cricket has struggled to keep pace with the tempo of the age, and has sometimes seemed to be lost in a dream-world of past glories and outworn social attitudes (Birley, 1999). As a result of such enduring perceptions, cricket has found regarding itself as a business particularly problematic. Cricket, like other sports, is a consumer product and it is clear from the comment below that those in the game understand that. Like any similar product, cricket will only survive if it is properly marketed:

> *Let's not mince words. Cricket has an image problem … Like it or not, we are just another arm of the entertainment business and if people no longer enjoy the product we have to offer, we must change.*
>
> Richard Blakey (retired wicket-keeper, Yorkshire CCC and England)

History and tradition, though admirable qualities, do not sell products. Branding, customer relationship building and marketing communications, however, do and the nature of the modern game and the highly competitive business sector in which it operates means that cricket has no choice other than to position itself as a consumer product.

For millions of people across the globe, the crack of willow against leather is one of the most spectacular sporting sounds. Whether in it for the long haul of a five-day test match or enjoying the spectacle of a limited overs contest, cricket conjures up something amongst its fans which few other sports can claim – a sense of history, exclusiveness and immense patriotism. Since its creation centuries ago, the sport of cricket has undergone some shape shifting changes, the most recent of which is the introduction of the Twenty-20 format. In order to predict the success and viability of such innovations it is important to first look back over the development of cricket and then into the game's future in the 21st century.

Cricket, in varying different forms, has been around since the later Middle Ages when the name, if not the game itself, came over to England with the Normans. The sport is a derivative of a number of now defunct, but fascinating sounding, variants such as stoolball, stowball and cat-in-the hole. Cricket's nearest relative was something called club-ball which was banned by Edward III in 1369 as he considered it to be detrimental to his war effort. Records of formally organized cricket matches date from the 18th century. During the mid-1700s, the first explicit rules of cricket were drawn up and the first printed match score was printed. Prior to this, cricket matches lacked articulate regulations and protocols.

Observations on the historical development and progress of the game refer extensively to the gentlemen and players structure of the early game and the aristocratic influences which were responsible for the creation of the MCC and the development of Lords cricket ground. Although cricket was originally a popular spectator sport amongst the lower classes, especially in the 18th century when gambling was as much a part of cricket as it was of racing it became an issue of rising annoyance amongst the aristocratic leaders of the game that spectators were more interested in the potential financial gain than in attending to what was happening on the field of play. During the early stages of cricket's development, the game was believed to instil discipline into the players. For this reason, the English nobility would ensure that their servants and workers played alongside them during cricket matches as a way of training them in moral matters and self-discipline.

Upper class English children would also have these attributes engrained in them, not only at home but also on the school playing fields.

The infiltration of cricket into the English school system during the late 18th century established the sport as the most popular game in England at that time. Eton and Westminster claim to be the first English cricketing schools whose cricket records date back to the mid-1700s. The simmering interschool rivalry and the growing enthusiasm for cricket paved the way for interschool cricket matches during the late 18th century. Debate still reigns about the specific date of the first interschool cricket match, however it is agreed that it definitely occurred during the last decade of the 18th century. The matches were organized by the pupils themselves and played during the school break over the summer. Schools from all over England began to play matches against one another, depending on their geographical location. Cricket soon became regarded as an essential part of education for any upper-class schoolboy who wished to become a part of England's high society. The education system was also imperative for the dispersion of the sport around the globe.

North America was the first British colony to introduce cricket sometime during the 17th century. By the mid-19th century, cricket was immensely popular in both Canada and North America. Astonishingly, the first international cricket match was played between North America and Canada in New Jersey in 1844. Since this time, the popularity of cricket in these nations has declined. However the opposite has occurred to cricket's popularity in other British Commonwealth colonies.

During the early years of the 18th century, cricket was established in the Caribbean and also in South Asia where the sport is now an integral component of those countries' culture and identity. Exporting the game to the colonies was seen as a method of imposing the British moral code onto the new colonial inhabitants. The creation of a British style of secondary education system in these countries bears much of the responsibility for the promotion of cricket to the indigenous cultures. Schools would encourage young boys from indigenous and low socio-economic backgrounds in the Caribbean and South Asia to attend the English modelled boarding schools. These schools would, in turn, introduce cricket to the young boys.

The introduction of cricket into Australian society occurred almost immediately after the colony was established in the late 18th century. Australia's first cricket team to tour England was an all Aboriginal team in 1868. What is now considered the first test match was contested between Australia and England in 1877 in Melbourne. Five years later, a loss by England to Australia gave rise to one of sports greatest competitive series, the Ashes. Cricket's diffusion continued into South Africa and New Zealand in the early 19th century. South Africa's relationship with international cricket has sometimes been strained with the nation being debarred from international cricket indefinitely in 1970 due to apartheid. Since the ending of apartheid, South Africa was reinstated into the international cricketing community in 1991.

The culture and traditions which pervade cricket are undoubtedly responsible for the many challenges that are facing the modern game. Currently, 10 countries belong to the International Cricket Council (ICC). These include England, Australia, South Africa and New Zealand. The South Asian countries involved include Pakistan, India and Sri Lanka. An amalgamation of Caribbean countries is included under the name of the West Indies. Zimbabwe and Bangladesh are the most recent additions. Although there are nearly 100 countries which belong as either full, associate or affiliate members of the ICC, only the 10 countries mentioned above participate in the sanctioned international test matches. Today the ICC fully controls world cricket and many commentators regard that the game's new power base is India; a country of one billion inhabitants where cricket is the sole national sport, but growth is on a global scale; Sri Lanka, Zimbabwe and Bangladesh have all gained test status in the past 25 years.

So what is 'test match' cricket? Test match cricket is the longest, and in the view of many, the purest form of the game. It involves two teams and can last up to five days with each team completing two 'innings' or turns at batting. Long considered to be the ultimate form of cricket, test matches are geared towards the cricketing purists and older cricketing generation. A favourite criticism levelled at cricket today, is that it is an elitist game which is virtually incomprehensible to most ordinary people. Rather unfortunately for the game, the length of time it takes to play some matches, the rules and laws of the game and the fact that nowadays the only schools apparently still playing cricket are the public and private ones, are all factors which only conspire to perpetuate the exclusive image of the game. The long and sometimes monotonous matches have, however, declined in popularity among younger cricket fans who have taken to the more fast-paced and action-packed mode of cricket involving limited overs.

Currently, two forms of limited overs cricket are contested. These are one-day cricket and Twenty-20 cricket which is the most recent extension of the cricket product. One-day cricket involves two teams, as in the test match format, however each team only bats once and the innings are restricted to a limited number of overs, usually between 40 and 60. Other constraints placed on this mode of cricket include fielding restrictions, limits to the number of overs each bowler can bowl and stricter rules regarding wide and bounce deliveries. One-day cricket was introduced in England in 1962 and the first international match took place in Melbourne in 1971. The soaring popularity of this entertaining and succinct format saw the development of the ICC Cricket World Cup and the emergence of a rival, and as it turned out significantly influential entity named World Series Cricket which was owned and run by media magnate Kerry Packer. The arrival of World Series Cricket turned the cricketing world upside down and though it was extinguished in 1971, it has left a lasting legacy on the sport in the form of coloured uniforms, elevated player salaries, white cricket balls and day/night matches under floodlights – all of which have since been embraced by the ICC and have become common features of contemporary cricket.

With the popularity of one-day cricket reaching a plateau, the ECB recognized the necessity for change within the domestic and international competitions. The ECB embarked upon a rigorous five-year-long research project which was concluded in 2001 and which showed that a sizeable gap had opened in the cricket market which needed to be filled by a fast-paced and action-packed format that would attract a new breed of cricket fan. A summary of the findings of the ECB research which eventually led to the creation of Twenty-20 cricket makes interesting reading. Though these statistics specifically apply to the state of the game in the UK, similar findings are evident wherever cricket is being played:

- 47 per cent of the research sample of over 4000 had never attended a live game.
- The image of cricket is that the game is boring, impossible to understand, it takes too long and matches are played during the week while most people are at work.
- Cricket is a sport watched predominantly by an audience whose demographics are white, middle-class, male and over 50 years of age.
- In the five years leading up to the ECB Survey, total attendances at domestic games had dropped by 17 per cent.

It was clear from the research findings that though cricket might be a great sport enjoyed by millions, it needed to evolve to increase its appeal and it needed to be much better marketed. Something clearly had to be done if cricket was to have a viable future both commercially and in terms of the sport's long-term development. The following issues had to be acknowledged and responded to:

- Cricket competes in the very busy entertainment industry.
- Today's younger – and less committed – cricket audiences want a result and excitement from their entertainment.
- Regular audiences recognize the need for change … but want to keep the sport's core values.
- The total cricket offering must compete and justify the significant leisure time and money invested.
- Cricket is capable of being played in many different formats. It is essential to recognize the customer groups who want these different formats and structure the game with them in mind.
- Once customers have experienced cricket for the first time, they come back for more. Getting them to come for the first time is a key.
- Barriers need to be removed through product development and communication.
- The target audience for contemporary cricket is a younger consumer who considers the longer form of the game 'tolerable' but who has never attended a live match.

This new target audience for cricket also includes females and families with young children all of whom would give cricket the opportunity to widen its appeal and broaden cricket's market to compete with other leisure activities.

Sponsors, too, are realizing the importance of engaging non-traditional cricketing audiences and participants. In 2006, npower extended its sponsorship agreement with English cricket and by introducing and supporting such initiatives as Urban Cricket and Kidz@thewicket, which are strategically aimed at getting more youngsters interested in the sport, the changing nature of the sport is further emphasized. Even more recent product extensions than Twenty-20 cricket such as the Twenty-20 Floodlit Cup (UK, 2006) the Stanford 20/20 tournament (Caribbean, 2006) and the XXXX Gold Beach Cricket tournament (Australia, 2007), are further examples of how the sport is responding to global changing audience demographics.

The changing face of cricket is evident not only in product diversification and extension but in the recognition that different formats of the game are continuing to evolve. Each recent innovation has an identified particular appeal for different audiences as illustrated in Table 18.1 which we refer to as A Typology of 21st century cricket:

Table 18.1: A typology of 21st century cricket

Variables	Test matches	One day	Twenty-20
Game, structure and strategy	Emphasis on conservative game plans and cautious scoring	Tactical accumulation of runs through innings	Swashbuckling style of play from outset – 'twice the action in half the time'
Audience demographics	Males 43 years plus	Males 18–27, 34–57 + some families	Males 14–38 and young females
Duration	Three sessions of play per day. Two innings per team	One innings of 50 (six balls) overs per team	One innings of 20 overs per team
Spectator preference	Display of traditional cricket, skill and ritual	Eclectic blend of entertainment, spectacular play and tactical scoring	Fast scoring, entertainment, exciting
Viewing experience	Game of strategy. Moments of boredom and drama	Strategy and drama. Enjoyable	'Not cricket', Innovative. A real 'buzz'
Marketing	Stadiums corporate boxes. Viewing complemented by transistor radio and video replay	Customized seating with reserved sections. Private boxes with customer service. Video screens used to replay critical incidences	Group outings encouraged, fancy dress themes, music, banners and flags. Sport or entertainment?

(Continued)

Table 18.1: (Continued)

Variables	Test matches	One day	Twenty-20
Marketing mix	Product, place	Product, place, promotion, price	4 Ps + People, physical evidence, processes, public relations
Perception	Real cricket	Pyjama cricket	Hit and run cricket
Fan loyalties	Singular loyalty to home team and players	Singular loyalty to home team and players	Personalities/star players/Twenty-20 team identity (e.g. Durham Dynamos, Leicestershire Foxes, Somerset Sabres)

This typology has been developed in order to provide a useful tool with which to segment cricketing audiences and inform targeted sports marketing and communications strategies. By identifying nine key variables and applying them to the three different types of test cricket, one-day cricket and Twenty-20 cricket it has been possible to categorize each variable according to the type of cricket. For example, the perception variable is completely different for each of the three cricket types, immediately emphasizing the necessity for different marketing and promotions strategies according to type. Sports marketing commentators have observed that sports organizations are often prevented from fulfilling their business potential by the symptoms of what Theodore Levitt termed 'marketing myopia'. Marketing myopia in sport can be identified by the following all-too familiar characteristics:

- A focus on producing and selling goods and services.
- The belief that winning absolves all other sins.
- Confusion between promotions and marketing.
- A short-sighted focus on quick return investments.

In sports business terms, no audience or public should be overlooked and by acknowledging the existence of more than one type of cricket consumer, or potential cricket consumer, it is possible to tailor marketing strategies much more appropriately and personally, thus avoiding marketing myopia and creating the foundations for long-term relationship building. Through careful understanding and application of this typology, cricket marketing myopia can be avoided and averted.

Case Diagnosis

Modern spectator sports, of necessity, operate as businesses and therefore have to adopt and adapt to the core business functions of marketing, finance and human resource management. Cricket has traditionally shown a reluctance to express itself in business terms but has come to accept that if it is to survive and compete for media and supporter attention, it has to modernize and behave as a commercial enterprise. In order to maintain its licence to operate, cricket must regard itself as part of the entertainment industry and compete for its share of the global market. A key objective of this strategy is building and maintaining mutually beneficial relationships with a range of publics and audiences, an objective that can only be achieved through the systematic and structured implementation of excellent marketing and marketing communications strategies. Contemporary professional cricket has to face considerable challenges, the most pressing of which is to generate interest in what is seen by many as a game which belongs to a bygone age being played at stuffy and unwelcoming County Clubs. If cricket is to have a viable future, it must address its image problems and must become more appealing to a demographically different audience than has traditionally been the case.

The ECB, as a result of their recent research, knows that modern cricket is part of the entertainment industry and demands that the County Clubs operate as businesses in their own right. Relatively recent initiatives such as the wearing of coloured clothing in one-day matches, playing under floodlights in day/night matches, and the introduction of Twenty-20 kits has done much to help clubs and teams establish their individual identities and attract different audiences. The establishment of 'Lions Dens' at County grounds has been successful in attracting families with small children. Offering reduced price membership for young supporters has increased the number of young spectators at clubs like Essex CCC and test matches, where admission on the last day is often considerably reduced or even free.

There is no doubt that the 2005 Ashes Series had a considerable impact on the popularity of the sport in the UK when, according to Paul Kelso writing in *The Guardian* on 6 January 2007, the sport was bathed in an unprecedented glow of approval and popularity. England winning the urn that year created a level of interest in cricket not seen for many years. During the winter training period of 2006, cricket clubs around the country were reporting increased attendances and Woodworm, the cricket bat manufacturer, could not keep up with the demand from all the budding Flintoffs and Pietersens. However, what happens on the field of play has a direct influence on success off it and the return Ashes Series in Australia in 2006/2007 soon extinguished much of Kelso's glow.

The worldwide interest in cricket is huge and the potential for engaging consumer interest in the game is obvious but evolutions in the sport mean that properly informed segmentation strategies are put in place so that optimum benefits in both marketing and public relations terms can be realized. English marketing executive Stuart Robertson, who is credited with identifying the need for Twenty-20 cricket, made this observation in an article in *The Sydney Morning Herald* in February 2005:

> *It's an old marketing cliche but people these days are more cash-rich and time-poor. They need more instant gratification; more of an instant return. So, while there still is a market*

for the traditional game, if the trend continues you could see things like 50-over games condensing to 40, or Test matches played over three days. Who knows?

Recent trends in cricket viewing and attendance figures further highlight the need for recognizing that the evolving sport is reaching the hearts and minds of consumers and audiences. For example, the ICC Cricket World Cup is one of the world's largest and most viewed sporting events. The 2007 tournament was televised in over 200 countries to an audience of over 2 billion television viewers. Each of the First Class county cricket clubs in the UK have been reporting increased attendance figures and changed audience demographics year on year since the summer of 2003 when Twenty-20 cricket was born. Elsewhere in the world cricket attendance figure records are regularly being broken; on January 9th 2006 the first International KFC Twenty-20 Big Bash played on Australian soil drew crowds of 38,894 which is the highest attendance recorded for any sporting event ever held at The Gabba.

Cricket's appeal is undoubtedly rooted in its history, culture and countless other qualities and characteristics, all of which must be taken into account in its evolution. Maintaining the core product elements is essential in order not to alienate key audiences and stakeholders as realized by the ECB market research team:

> *When we began researching this (Twenty20 cricket), we didn't want the rules to be radically different, because it was intended to be a stepping stone for people to watch the longer versions of cricket. It was more a means to an end than an end itself. It was your fun-size Mars bar; a little taste of cricket that, hopefully, would get people who merely tolerated cricket – rather than those who considered themselves fans of the game – to upgrade to one-day and maybe four- and five-day cricket.*

Evolving cricket is a potentially excellent mechanism for getting audiences and consumers engaged with the sport and moving them up the different levels of the consumer commitment or loyalty ladder so that they become vociferous advocates for the sport no matter what format has most appeal. Whilst still acknowledging cricket's history and traditions, the new shorter product diversifications can reach new market segments and extend the appeal of the sport by creating an active brand relationship. It is suggested that by adopting and applying the brand relationship model used in relationship marketing together with carefully associated marketing communications strategies, cricket can move audiences through the four stages of degree of involvement from raising awareness of its name (e.g. Beach cricket, Pro20 cricket) to bonding a relationship (families looking forward to and planning for the annual mid-summer Twenty-20 extravaganza) (Table 18.2).

Cricket has undertaken a huge journey from its foundations centuries ago. Currently the game infects millions of cricket enthusiasts from all corners of the globe. The sport has clearly evolved and continues to evolve in structure to adapt to the ever changing lifestyles of the world's populations. Cricket is continuing to flourish in more and more countries and with the employment of increasingly innovative and attractive tactics; the game's future has never looked more prosperous than it does now.

Table 18.2 The Cricket Brand Relationship Model

Steps of the process	Levels of degree of involvement		Strategic elements
Naming 'What is this?' (It's cricket but not as we know it!)	Awareness	Progression in Involvement	Advertising
Associating 'Who is it like?'	Character		Positioning
Animating 'Do I like it?'	Personality		Selling
Relating 'How important is it to me?'	Relationship		Bonding

Source: Adapted from Varey (2002)

Case Questions

1 Explore the key factors which have contributed to the evolution of cricket.
2 What do you think are the major challenges that cricket faces in trying to extend and differentiate the core cricket product?
3 Evaluate the impact of the Typology of 21st Century Cricket on cricket's marketing and communications strategies.
4 Analyse any of the new variants of cricket mentioned in the text and evaluate their contribution to contemporary cricket.
5 By applying the Cricket Brand Relationship Model Cricket to any cricket format you choose, devise a marketing and communication strategy by which a consumer could be taken through each of the four degrees of relationship involvement.
6 How do you think cricket should further evolve in order to keep up with future market demand?

References

Birley, D. (1999). *The Social History of English Cricket*. Aurum Press, London, http://www.stanford2020.com/vision.php

The Sydney Morning Herald, "Twenty20 an appetiser for the uninitiated, not a threat" by Alex Brown, 2nd February 2005.

Varey, R.J. (2002). *Relationship Marketing: Dialogue and Networks in the E-Commerce Era*. John Wiley and Sons Ltd, Chichester.

Case Resources

Reading

Bennet, R., Ali-Choudhury, R. and Mousley, W. (2007). Television viewers' motivations to follow the 2005 Ashes Test series: Implications for the rebranding of English cricket. *Journal of Product & Brand Management*, Vol. 16, No. 1, pp. 23–37.

Brown, A. (2006). Bash and dash is the new generation. *The Sydney Morning Herald*, January 9.

Bush, V., Bush, A., Clark, P. and Bush, R. (2005). Girl power and word-of-mouth behaviour in the flourishing sports market. *Journal of Consumer Marketing*, Vol. 22, No. 5, pp. 257–264.

Carter, B. (2004). Cricket puts best foot forward. *Marketing*, 14 July, p. 17.

Gladden, J. and Funk, D. (2001). Understanding brand loyalty in professional sport: Examining the link between brand associations and brand loyalty. *International Journal of Sports Marketing and Sponsorship*, Vol. 3, No. 1, pp. 67–95.

Hopwood, M. (2005). Public relations practice in English county cricket. *Corporate Communications: An International Journal*, Vol. 10, No. 3, pp. 201–212.

Hopwood, M. (2007). The sport integrated marketing communications mix, in Beech, J. and Chadwick, S. (Eds.), *The Marketing of Sport*. Pearson Education Ltd, Harlow.

Murray, I. (2005). Beefburgers, cheerleaders, Zulus, Jools Holland. It's just not cricket. *Marketing Week*, 22 September, p. 86.

Sidhu, G. (2001). Branding a sport: It's just not cricket. *Brand Strategy*, November, p. 12.

SportAustralia (2005). Twenty20 Big Bash set to make a big splash: Inaugural domestic Twenty20 competition starts January 6, 2006, http://www.sportsaustralia.com/articles/dec05/artid4342.html

Websites

Cricket20: The home of Twenty20 cricket – http://www.thetwenty20cup.co.uk/

Cricket Australia: 2006/07 KFC Big Bash – http://www.cricket.com.au/default.aspx?s=kfctwenty20bigbash0607

The England and Wales Cricket Board Twenty20 Cup – http://www.ecb.co.uk/domestic/twenty20-cup/

Further Information

Users of the case may find the following Wikipedia entries helpful:

Cricket – http://en.wikipedia.org/wiki/Cricket
Short-form Cricket – http://en.wikipedia.org/wiki/Short_form_cricket
The KFC Twenty20 Big Bash – http://en.wikipedia.org/wiki/KFC_
  Twenty20_Big_Bash
Twenty20 – http://en.wikipedia.org/wiki/Twenty20

19

Celebrity athletes and athletic clothing design: the case of Natalie Gulbis

Norm O'Reilly and L. Anne Braedley

Case Focus

This is a marketing case about international brands. The subject is Natalie Gulbis, a well-known female star athlete in golf, a global sport of increasing appeal. If viewed as a brand, Gulbis – who is known in addition to her golf prowess for her sex appeal, fashion choices, and media work – provides for an interesting analysis and learning experience in international brands.

Keywords
• Women's golf • International brand • Celebrity athlete • Fashion • Labels • Sport marketing

Case Summary

Branding, one of the most important strategic concepts in marketing, may be applied in international settings for global organizations and/or products. A 'brand' is the representation of the organization or product that is conveyed to the public through their market communications. Marketing scholars have defined it as follows: 'a brand is the company's promise to deliver a specific set of features, benefits, services, and experiences consistently to buyers' (Kotler et al., 2005).

A professional athlete, like any product, is a brand. Interest in celebrity athletes and their lifestyles makes the clothing they wear an important part of their image and consequently their brand. Due to their influence on markets, celebrity athletes are no longer simply fashion product endorsers; many are now also involved in product design. This case study reviews the celebrity athlete–clothing relationship around Natalie Gulbis, a high-profile female golfer, where the important connection between celebrity athletes, their clothing and spectators is emphasized.

Case Elements

Introduction

The dynamics of the athlete–manufacturer–market relationship are changing. The use of celebrity athletes as product endorsers has been a favourite strategy among advertisers (Stone et al., 2003), but it is suggested that celebrity athletes are no longer satisfied with simply licensing their name to be used on products and are getting involved in areas of product development, positioning and brand management (Cleaver, 1998). Michael Jordan's involvement with Nike and Simeon Rice's company, T3K, are two documented cases of this (Stewart, 2003). In the case of athletic apparel, one must now question how athletes, labels, and manufacturers strategize their marketing vis-à-vis how the athlete is outfitted in competition.

A celebrity athlete is defined in marketing circles as 'a name which, once made by news, now makes news by itself ... a person whose name has attention-getting, interest-riveting, and profit-generating value' (Rein et al., 1997). Of particular importance from a marketing point of view is profit generation due to celebrity, which can be discussed in terms of real economic value (Rivers and DeSchriver, 2002), including Nadeau and O'Reilly's (2006) profitability model for professional sports teams which identifies team composition (including the presence of a star player) as a determinant of team profitability through market support. This market support is evident in the segment of fans who follow, admire, mimic and – in some cases – obsess with a given celebrity athlete. It is clear that the involvement of celebrity athletes in marketing efforts has the ability to generate profit for manufacturers of clothing and equipment, and should increase attendance and television ratings at events where the celebrity is competing. For example, it has been shown that, on average, the impact of announcing a celebrity endorsement contract has a positive effect on stock returns (Agrawal and Kamakura, 1995).

The Athlete Brand

A recent development in sport marketing is to consider a sports team or an athlete as a brand. Burton (2004) includes Michael Jordan, Tiger Woods, Anna Kournikova, and David Beckham among the successful athlete brands and notes that athletes as brands have 'combined athletic excellence with partnered sponsorships or endorsements to achieve superior brand equities worth millions of dollars'. The visual representation of an athlete brand is particularly relevant to sports like golf, where a significant portion of camera times involves athlete close-up shots that allow the television viewer to observe both the clothing label brand and the athlete's brand. Typically, this representation is straightforward and recognizes the clothing label as a brand, with its distinct brand name or symbol; well known to consumers (e.g. Nike, Adidas, Reebok, etc.). The clothing label brand provides products to consumers with meanings attached to it that are intended to entice the consumer to purchase so they too can have that meaning. (There is something funny about this sentence as it is. Here are two alternatives I thought might make more sense. (1) The clothing label brand has meanings attached to it and provides products that are intended to entice the consumer to purchase so they too can have that meaning. (2) The clothing label brand provides products to consumers with meanings attached to them that are intended to entice the consumer to purchase so they too can have that meaning.)

When considering the athlete brand, it is also important to consider a few other marketing ideas.

First, the athlete's image – or both the visual pictures/representations and reputation of the athlete (Penfold, 2004) – is conveyed daily through multiple media sources and from many angles and is in a state ongoing change. In fact, it has been noted that 'the public image of female athletes is defined to a large degree by the media' (George et al., 2001). Celebrity athletes, like all other consumers, draw meanings from the objects, people and events around them, and combine them to create their image, which is of interest to consumers as it is unique and 'almost always attractive and accomplished' (McCracken, 1989).

A celebrity athlete strives to differentiate themselves by creating a trademark, which the mass market will recognize as theirs alone (Rein et al., 1997). Tiger Woods, and his (Nike) red shirt on Sunday tradition, provide an excellent example of a celebrity athlete using a trademark to increase the mass market's awareness of a specific product related to his image.

Second, athlete endorsements and sponsorships are an important source of income for athletes and are effective marketing tools for marketers. The exploitation of the celebrity status of athletes and their marketing power is well known to be effective and has thus been heavily adopted in an attempt to attract more consumers to products and brands (Stone et al., 2003).

Third, the performance of the athlete (also known as winning) is also important to the athlete brand. In a study comparing the impact of a celebrity's attractiveness, expertise, and trustworthiness on respondents' intention to purchase, Ohanian (1991) finds that 'in every instance, the respondents' evaluation of the celebrities' perceived expertise with the product was significantly related to the respondents' intention to purchase the product'. Thus, for celebrity athletes it is extremely important to remain competitive in order to provide the most marketing benefit. The fact that winning is more important than look has been supported for both male and female celebrity athletes (Fink et al., 2004). One exception to this is with 'attractiveness related' product such as cosmetics where research has shown that attractive celebrities were indeed more effective endorsers of attractiveness-related products than unattractive celebrities were. Thus, although it is very important for athletes to wear clothing which will allow them to move freely and stay cool, it should also be considered as an attractiveness-related product since the attire may reveal the player's physique, making the perceived attractiveness of the athlete more important to marketers.

Fourth, the cluttered marketplace is a threat to an athlete brand and his/her endorses due to the fact that many celebrity athletes endorse multiple products. Tripp et al. (1994) examined the effect of multiple endorsements by celebrities and found that the number of products a celebrity endorses negatively influences consumers' perceptions of endorser credibility and likeability, as well as attitude toward the advertisement. The results showed no significant effect on the attitude toward the brand, which is significant for companies who hire celebrity endorsers. Bailey and Cole (2004) had similar results with respect to the celebrity's perceived credibility, and found that, contrary to their hypothesis, the purchase intentions increased as the number of product endorsements increased. These results suggest that it is the celebrity endorser who needs to be cautious when entering into more than one endorsement relationships, while the product brand is not negatively affected, the athlete's credibility, or brand image, is vulnerable.

Clothing as a Brand Attribute

As a visual representation of image, appropriate clothing is very important to ensure celebrities portray their chosen image. As Keenan (2001) writes, 'who dresses "best" – where this can be taken to mean not simply the economistic "most expensively" or the aesthetic "most tastefully", but the sociological "most appropriately in role" – impress most'. The meanings present in the clothing, and the overall image of the celebrity athlete contribute to the athlete's brand, and can also be transferred to a brand that the athlete endorses (Ryssel and Stamminger, 1988; McCracken, 1989).

Consumers are fascinated with trademarks associated with celebrities, and while some trademarks are unintentional, such as Monica Seles' grunts, there are others that are 'designed to spawn a fashion rage and propel the celebrity into the audience's consciousness' (Rein et al., 1997), like the clothes worn by Serena Williams. The attention-grabbing black cat suit designed by Puma that Serena wore to the 2002 US Open helped boost ratings during the championship (Cassidy, 2003), and the debut of the Serena Williams Collection by Nike, which Ms. Williams helped design, at the Australian Open in 2005 gained as much media attention as her return after a long absence due to injury (Hodgkinson, 2005).

Due to the importance of the image presented by celebrity athletes, and the role clothing plays in that image, athletic clothing labels have teamed up with athletes to create more fashion conscious options for female tennis players. Examples of athletes involved in clothing design include Venus Williams (Hodgkinson, 2005), Maria Sharapova (Kletter, 2005), Tatiana Golovin (Self, 2005), and Serena Williams (Hodgkinson, 2005). Their involvement in the design process gives the athletes more control over their image, allows them to ensure the apparel fits their style, and demonstrates an interest outside of sports. Involving the athletes in product design is also an important strategy for manufacturers to use as it has been shown that including end users in new product development is a significant factor in determining product success in the market (Ciappei and Simoni, 2005). In all cases, it is also important to note that profit motivations are, of course, important to both manufacturers and athletes.

A Model of Celebrity Athlete–Label–Clothing– Event–Market Interactions

Figure 19.1 presents a model that describes the marketing process of a celebrity athlete wearing the clothing of a given label during a particular event. It is important to note that each of the four aspects (athlete, label, clothing, and event) has an impact on the effectiveness of the marketing effort.

The Case of Natalie Gulbis

Building on the conceptual framework provided previously, this case study explores the role of clothing in the athlete brand of an international celebrity athlete by looking at professional golfer Natalie Gulbis. A recent cover shot of her on *Golf For Women* (GFM) magazine follows here.[1]

---

[1] This cover shot was downloaded from the official website of *Golf For Women* (GFW) magazine in March 2007 from: http//www.golfdigest.com/gfw/gfwcover/index.ssf?/ gfw/gfwcover/gfw200703gulbis1.html – the photo accompanied an article written by Dana White and appeared in the March/April 2007 issue.

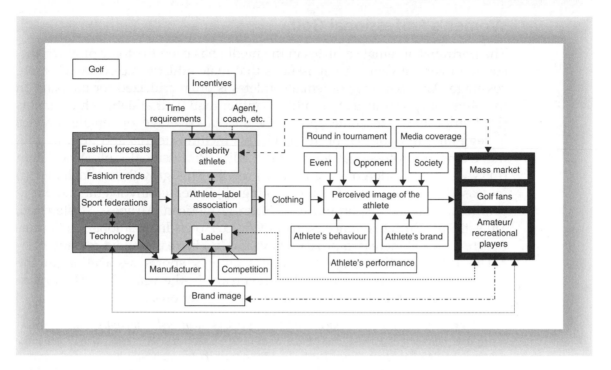

Figure 19.1 Model of celebrity athlete–label–clothing–event–market interactions
Source: O'Reilly and Braedley (2007)

Women's Professional Golf

The portrayal of female athletes in the media has been the topic of much discussion over the years. A key issue is that male athletes receive much more coverage. Also, coverage of female athletes is often criticized for its focus on the physical appearance of the athletes rather than their athletic achievements (Daddario, 1998). In some sports, the media coverage of female athletes is beginning to rival that of the men. This includes tennis and golf. In golf, the women's professional tour – the Ladies Professional Golf Association (LPGA[2]) – has undergone significant growth. This growth has included (i) increased television coverage and ranking; (ii) increased involvement of high-profile/high-quality sponsors (e.g. Rolex, American Airlines, MasterCard, Titleist, State Farm Insurance, Samsun, Choice Hotels International, Anheuser-Busch, etc.); (iii) increased prize money; and (iv) increase media coverage.

The LPGA is the longest-running women's sports association in the world, having celebrated its 50th anniversary in the year 2000. The organization describes itself as follows in its media relations:

> *Featuring the world's best women golfers, the LPGA's membership includes touring, teaching and club professionals. The LPGA tour in 2005 features 34 events, with total prize money of $45.1 million. Since 1981, the LPGA and its tournaments have raised approximately $160 million for charity. From the dreams of its 13 founders in 1950, the LPGA has evolved into the world's preeminent women's professional sports organization. The LPGA has grown from its roots as a playing tour into a non-profit organization involved in every facet of golf. The LPGA Teaching and Club Professional (T&CP) membership boasts a total of nearly 1,200 women golf professionals who serve as teachers, golf professionals, club managers and coaches. Through the LPGA T&CP membership, the LPGA is working to increase the involvement of women and youth in golf, as well as contribute to the growth of the sport overall. The LPGA is headquartered in Daytona Beach, Fla. (www.lpga.com).*

Currently, the LPGA has 117 players representing 27 countries.

Natalie Gulbis

Natalie Gulbis is one of the new stars on the LPGA tour. Following her collegiate career at the University of Arizona, she joined the tour in 2002 and has some solid results but has yet to win a tournament. Her best results include a 4th place finish at the 2005 US Women's Open where she won US$272,723 in arguably the most important tournament in women's golf. More recently, at the 2006 Jamie Farr Owens Corning Classic she lost the title in a playoff to Mi Hyun Kim and won US$106,155. On two other occasions, she has taken home a paycheck of over $100,000. In 2006, she was the only LPGA player to finish in the Top 20 at all four major tournaments. Her career earnings are US$2,490,087 (60th best all-time in the LPGA) and she has notched two holes-in-one.

---

[2]For more information see www.lpga.com.

At only 23 years of age, Natalie also commands expensive appearance fees to play in tournaments. For example, to play in the recent Women's Australian Golf Open, Natalie was paid an appearance fee of $129,300 (Withers, 2007). Many argue that she is worth the money as she attracts considerable media attention wherever she goes, despite not having a professional victory to her credit. Withers (2007) even suggests that she does not attract additional spectators to events and critiques that the 'only thing to have changed about Natalie Gulbis in the intervening four years is the fact that a marketing machine has developed around her'.

Prior to turning professional in 2001, Natalie had a storied amateur career. She began golfing with her dad as a four-year old. As noted on her bio on www.lpga.com, at the age of 14 years, she won the California Women's Amateur Championship. That same year, she became the youngest player to Monday qualify for an LPGA tournament (1997, Longs Drugs Challenge), a record that stood until Michelle Wie Monday qualified at the 2002 LPGA Takefuji Classic at age 12 years. Gulbis represented the state of California in two USGA team championships and was the US. Women's Amateur Championship medalist in 1998. She won four collegiate tournaments while at the University of Arizona, including the NCAA West Regional. She was named a first-team all-American in 2001.

Currently, she has her own website (www.nataliegulbis.com) and calendar and is sponsored by a number of organizations including 24 Hour Fitness, Adidas, Anheuser-Busch, Canon, Life Fitness, MasterCard, RSM McGladrey, SemGroup, Sky Caddie, TaylorMade, The Golf Channel, Winn Grips, and others. She also has her own charitable foundation.

Clothing in the LPGA

Although many golf clubs have their own regulations and rules on sleeves, collars, and short/skirt length for female golfers, the LPGA regulations state that:

> We allow sleeveless and collarless shirts to be worn during play. There is no specific length requirement on shorts or skirts. Denim, cut-offs, workout clothes are not allowed.[3]

The flexibility of the LPGA regulation is evident in the apparel choices of today's female professional golfers. A fair bit of discussion has also developed in the media about the changing fashion sense of the LPGA players and its affect on the marketing of women's golf. Horyn (2006) quotes Susan K. Reed, the editor of *Golf For Women*, who says that the single biggest change in the last few years in women's golf has been the improvement of the clothes. She explains: 'I think it's one of the things that held back women's golf participation … the clothes were ugly'. In her story, Horyn (2006) also quotes Debbie Doniger, the director of instruction at Glen Arbor Golf Club in Bedford,

---

[3]LPGA Dress Code. Retrieved from: http://www.lpga.com/content_1.aspx?mid=0 &pid=56.

NY, who says that her junior girl golfers cannot name another player on the LPGA than Michelle Wie. Wie and other young players, including Gulbis, on the LPGA tour are setting an example for a new generation of fashion conscious female golfers. Doniger is quoted as saying that 'these girls can express themselves. They can be young, in happy clothes, and nobody's yelling at them. If I had worn a V-neck shirt when I was their age, I would have been yelled at'. This newfound freedom is important for players to create their personal image and distinguish themselves from each other.

There is no question that Tiger Woods and his choice of clothing has concurrently helped men's golf transform its image from being a game played only by executives and retirees to the sport every hip youngster should be playing (Dyson, 2006).

This change has attracted large clothing brands to offer golf attire and forced long-term golf labels to re-invent themselves over the past five years. This includes such labels as Ralph Lauren, Bugle Boy, Tommy Hilfiger, Nautica, Brioni, Hugo Boss, Armani, Prada, Froghair, Bunker Mentality, SubSeventy, Difini, Pringle, Lyle Scott, Ferragamo, Burberry, Liz Claiborne, Nike, Adidas, Bogner, J. Lindeberg, Golfino, Birdie, and PinkCaddi. In all cases, the products being offered are newer, sexier, and geared toward the young, fashion-crazed consumer. Of important note for women's golf is that the fashions specific to women's golf convey energy, sex appeal, and femininity and now differentiate them from the men. Dyson (2006) quotes Maria Bovin, Peak Performance's head of design, who says that fashion is 'great with golf because you can really bring fashion to the sport, enjoy the freedom to make really great stuff and be a trendsetter within the sports market without alienating your customers'. The bland history of women's golf wear, has allowed brands the freedom to create new, trendy clothes that appeal to the new, hip female golfers. With a wider range of fashionable options players new to the sport look to their favourite pro players for image inspiration.

The Marketing of Natalie Gulbis

Natalie is the best example in women's golf of the excellence versus attractiveness debate and their impact on the marketability of the athlete. Her website is primarily focused on her as a golfer, while her calendar is about her attractiveness although the fact that she is a professional athlete is certainly an important driver there as well. A recent story of her in FHM, a popular men's magazine, puts the emphasis on attractiveness. A photo from this issue appears below.[4]

---

[4] This photo was downloaded from FHM online magazine's official website (http://www.fhmonline.com/) in March of 2007. There is an ongoing column in the magazine called Gulbis Tips where she provides advise to golfers. The photographer given credit for the shot is Andrew Parsons.

This photo is clearly from a staged photo shoot at *FHM* magazine for an article targeted at male readers. Natalie's normal choice of apparel for golf is practical, comfortable, and more conservative; however sex appeal, fashion sense, coordinated colours, and other important fashion aspects remain evident. A review of Natalie's website and other secondary information suggests that she has no direct involvement in the design of the clothing that she wears in competition and training. However, it can be easily assumed that she takes an active role in the selection of her clothing to enhance both her performance and her image. Recent articles support this assumption. Former professional golfer and now marketing executive for the PGA's European tour, Frederik Lindgren, suggests that 'nowadays, young players look more to fashion and how to profile themselves by what they're wearing' (Dyson, 2006). Further, fashion professionals have been calling on LPGA players to be accountable for their fashion choices, style and look in order to better promote the LPGA (O'Connor, 2002).

In a recent interview with Dixon (2007) of the London Times, Gulbis herself spoke about her image and how she sees herself as much more than a pretty face. Although she indicated flattery about comparisons on 'looks' to tennis star Anna Kournikova, she was strong to defend that she views golf first, fashion second. Dixon (2007), however, points out that she has many detractors who suggest that her calendar, photo shoots and her reality TV show on the Golf Channel are more important to her than practice.

A photo from her in a recent tournament (downloaded from www.sports-wired.com) follows here. Of note is the display of logos on her shirt and hat.[5]

As noted in the photo above, Natalie has an endorsement deal with the Adidas Group (specific brands are Adidas and Taylor Made) and wears their apparel in events and training.

---

[5] This photo was downloaded in March 2007 from http://www.sports-wired.com/women/ a subsite of a website dedicated to various sport trivia, photos, and stats. This particular photo was downloaded from a group of photos of Natalie posted in a section called 'women of sports'.

Business Week Online Story

The respected and widely read business magazine, *Business Week*, published an article about Natalie on 6 December 2004. This article follows in its entirety here.

SPORTS BIZ: She Can Swing A Club, Too – Natalie Gulbis' sexy photo spreads are ruffling feathers in golf – by Mark Hyman (2006).

With rare exceptions, the ladies of the Ladies Professional Golf Association Tour are not the sort of half-dressed hotties who fill the pages of laddie magazines. Then there's Natalie Gulbis. The 21-year-old tour pro steams up the November issue of *FHM* magazine with a photo spread that includes outfits seldom seen on the greens and an interview that poses such burning long-game questions as: 'Can you tell anything about a guy by the length of his drive?'

Gulbis' decision to pose for FHM wasn't one she came to alone, however. A PR firm, retained by the LPGA, aided in soliciting the shoot, as it did an offer for Gulbis to appear on Howard Stern's radio gabfest. (Gulbis turned that one down.) 'As our players become recognizable celebrities, more unconventional media outlets are becoming interested. If Natalie is comfortable (posing in FHM), we're supportive of the decision' says Commissioner Ty Votaw, who has been urging players to leverage their looks and charm, as well as their swings.

FHM isn't the first place Gulbis has bared her navel for fun and profit. In July the 21-year-old golfer's calendar was pulled from souvenir shelves at the US Women's Open when officials of the US Golf Association deemed it too risqué. 'I'm wearing bathing suits and workout clothes, basically. Besides the USGA, I haven't heard the word 'provocative' used about the calendars', says Gulbis, who seems genuinely baffled by the hubbub.

Gulbis and her advisers, led by her dad, John, have turned her sex appeal into one of the more impressive marketing machines on the LPGA tour. Her deals with, among others, TaylorMade-adidas, Titleist, MET-Rx, GeniSoy, and EA Sports will generate more than a half-million dollars this year, according to John.

The attention also has gained Gulbis new cachet with fans. Her website, nataliegulbis.com, where visitors can join a booster club, examine her pinup poses, or buy a calendar, has logged a half-million hits in 2004. She pockets up to $15,000 for about six corporate outings a year. And the LPGA loves to feature her for publicity purposes. This year the tour slapped her likeness, along with those of two other players, on its LPGA-sponsored race car at the Daytona 500. Not bad, considering that in three years on the ladies' tour, she hasn't won a tourney and ranked 42nd on the money list in the 2004 season, with $277,000.

'KEEP IT CLEAN': Gulbis, a golfing prodigy who grew up in Sacramento and won the California amateur title at age 14 years, is undeniably serious about her game. During the off-season she can spend hours in the gym and then end the workout with a 5-mile jog. She sweats almost as much at the course. Her swing coach, Butch Harmon, Tiger Woods's former golf guru, has helped her add distance to her drives, but the analytical Gulbis isn't satisfied. She points out that she ranked a respectable 20th in birdies collected this year but still finished well down the earnings list. 'That's kind of an interesting stat. It tells me I need to work harder on my short game', she says.

Her father gave the nod to the FHM photo shoot but was there to 'keep it clean' and tasteful. 'This is an athlete, an LPGA professional. We're not looking for a 'skin' type of thing', he says. 'No way she's wearing underwear or a negligee.' Still, some of the outfits don't leave a whole lot to the imagination. With Gulbis leading the way, the LPGA seems intent on shedding its dowdy image, even if that means showing off more than a smooth putting stroke.

Golf For Women Magazine Story

The most widely read magazine in women's golf published an article about Natalie in their March/April 2007 issue. This article follows in its entirety here.

Photo Shoots by Dana White, March/April 2007

Golf For Women cover shoots are fun for everyone involved. The subject enjoys getting the glamour-girl treatment especially if she's not used to it the fashion editor enjoys dressing her, the photographer enjoys making her look her best. Our shoot with LPGA tour star Natalie Gulbis was no exception. Of course, we had great material to work with: her legs are endless, her skin golden, her hair long, and blond. A few hot rollers and hair extensions, makeup to enhance her natural beauty, some safety pins to make the clothes fit just right, and we were good to go.

The shoot took place at the Reflection Bay Golf Club at Lake Las Vegas in Henderson, Nevada, where Gulbis has a home. We set up in a conference room in the clubhouse. She loves to multitask, so she conducted an interview and checked her BlackBerry repeatedly while getting her hair and makeup done. A nearby table groaned with cheese danishes and powdered donuts, but Gulbis, who is very disciplined about her diet, stuck to energy bars and a protein shake, which she had brought along. After hair and makeup, she and fashion director Argy Koutsothanasis went to check out the clothes, all by AdidasGolf.

'Natalie has her own personal style', says Argy. 'She was open to trying things, but she knows what she wants to look like. She wanted to look sexy. She wanted her clothes form-fitting and short'.

Gulbis gets her skirts tailored to be shorter, so we ended up using her skirts and the tops we had brought. She wore three outfits that day: the same top and skirt in both black and white, and a brighter outfit for the secondary photos. She wore her platform sandals most of the time, which made her legs seem even longer and leaner, if that's possible.

The photos were taken right outside the clubhouse, on a swathe of lawn in front of a crescent beach on the lake, to the right of No. 18's peninsula green. Gulbis looks taller and prettier in person, so you can imagine the scene she caused. During the shoot, which took about two hours in total, golfers kept driving by in their carts. And driving by again. And hey, didn't that guy just drive by a minute ago?

'Hello, Ms. Gulbis', one older man said as he drove by. It wasn't clear if he knew her or was simply pretending to know her or was just living out some long-held fantasy. Whatever the case, his wife didn't look too pleased.

This guy who worked in the pro shop couldn't stop staring.

A camera crew from the Golf Channel was there to shoot footage of the shoot for Gulbis' reality show. All told, there were a dozen people on set. The shoot went swimmingly, thanks to our enthusiastic and energetic photographer, Jeff Lipsky, and his photogenic subject. Gulbis was never a diva, never impatient, never a 'star' in the unfortunate sense. Afterward she graciously said thank you. She was on to her next appointment – another photo shoot – and we had our cover. The hardest part was figuring out which one to use, so we settled on two: one for newsstand (the white outfit) and one for subscribers (the black).

Case Diagnosis

A number of important issues are brought forward in this case. A few are listed here:

1 International athlete brands – a global brand must be cognizant of cultural, social, technological, political, and environmental difference in each country (region) of the world. This is no different with an athlete brand, particularly an athlete like Natalie Gulbis who is playing all over the world.
2 Brand equity – is the value of a brand, its worth if all of the organizations assets are taken away. For an athlete, like Natalie Gulbis, building this equity is of utmost importance to maintain marketing value even in times of poor performance (slumps, injuries, etc.). In the case of Natalie Gulbis or Anna Kournikova, the equity from their non-sport activities can (or have in the case of Anna) be more valuable.
3 Attractiveness, excellence, and brand equity – as outlined in the case, this is a key consideration for marketers at sponsors, labels, sponsees, events, athletes, etc. as managing the influence of both on the athlete brand is vitally important towards building brand equity.
4 Women in sport – although this case does not get into too much detail on the issue of the objectification of women, this point is implied throughout and is very important to stress. There is a fine line between effective marketing through attractiveness/sex appeal and objectifying women (in this case) in a detrimental way.

Case Questions

1 Using theories of brand, please articulate how and why the Natalie Gulbis brand has become so valuable? Include an identification of the key attributes of the Natalie Gulbis brand.
2 If you were named Natalie Gulbis' marketing manager today, what would you do over the next year to enhance her brand vis-à-vis golf performance, media engagement, and fashion-related ventures?
3 In your opinion, how do the factors of attractiveness and excellence combine to affect an athlete's brand?
4 As a marketer for an international label, what can be learned from this case that could be applied, from a marketing point of view, to other properties (e.g. events, athletes, entertainment stars, musicians, etc.)?
5 Should Natalie Gulbis be marketed in the same fashion in every country of the world? If yes, explain why? If no, explain what needs to be done differently?
6 Explain the role of the media in developing an international brand?
7 Following the reading of this case, how do you feel about the portrayal of sex appeal (male or female) as part of marketing effort?

Case Resources

Agrawal, J. and Kamakura, W.A. (1995). The economic worth of celebrity endorsers: An event study analysis. *Journal of Marketing*, Vol. 59, No. 3, pp. 56–62.

Bailey, A. and Cole, C.A. (2004). The effects of multiple product endorsements by celebrities on consumer attitudes and intentions: an extension, in Kahle, L.R. and Riley, C. (Eds.), *Sports Marketing and the Psychology of Marketing Communication*. Lawrence Erlbaum Associates, Mahwah, NJ, pp. 259–270.

Burton, R. (2004). Teams as brands: A review of the sports licensing concept, in Kahle, L.R. and Riley, C. (Eds.), *Sports Marketing and the Psychology of Marketing Communication*. Lawrence Erlbaum Associates, Mahwah, NJ, pp. 259–270.

Cassidy, H. (2003). This shoe's one cool cat. *Brandweek*, Vol. 44, No. 38, p. M58.

Ciappei, C. and Simoni, C. (2005). Drivers of new product success in the Italian sport shoe cluster of Montebelluna. *Journal of Fashion Marketing and Management*, Vol. 9, No. 1, pp. 20–42.

Cleaver, J. (1998). The Midas Touch: Celebs try hand at building brands. *Marketing News*, Vol. 32, No. 12, pp. 1–2.

Daddario, G. (1998). *Women's Sport and Spectacle*. Praeger Publishers, USA.

Dixon, P. (2007). Gulbis finds difficulty in deciding between pin or pin up, *The Times*. London, UK; February 8, 2007, p. 78.

Dyson, J. (2006). How fashion came to the fore; Golfing chic. Mail on Sunday. London, UK; September 13, 2006, p. 29.

Fink, J.S., Cunningham, G.B. and Kensicki, L.J. (2004). Using athletes as endorsers to sell women's sport: Attractiveness vs. expertise. *Journal of Sport Management*, Vol. 18, pp. 350–367.

George, C., Hartley, A. and Paris, J. (2001). Focus on communication in sport: The representation of female athletes in textual and visual media. *Corporate Communications*, Vol. 6, No. 2, pp. 94–101.

Hodgkinson, M. (2005). Serena: From queen of tennis to catwalk menace. *The Daily Telegraph*, January 14.

Horyn, C. (2006). *Dress, Drive and Putt*. New York Times, New York, NY Jun 22, 2006, p. G.1.

Hyman, M. (2006). She Can Swing A Club, Too – Natalie Gulbis' sexy photo spreads are ruffling feathers in golf. *Business Week Online*, 6 December.

Kamins, M.A. (1990). An investigation into the 'match-up' hypothesis in celebrity advertising: When beauty may be only skin deep. *Journal of Advertising*, Vol. 19, No. 1, pp. 4–13.

Keenan, W.J.F. (2001). Introduction: 'Sartor Resartus' restored: Dress studies in carlylean perspective, in W.J.F. Keenan (Ed.), *Dressed to Impress*. Berg (Oxford International Publishers), New York, NY, pp. 1–49.

Kletter, M. (2005). Sharapova Style At 18. WWD, 189(73, April 7), p. 11.

Kotler, P., Armstrong, G. and Cunningham, P.H. (2005). *Principles of Marketing*, 6th Canadian Edition. Pearson Prentice Hall.

McCracken, G. (1989). Who is the celebrity endorser? Cultural foundations of the endorsement process. *Journal of Consumer Research*, Vol. 16, December, pp. 310–321.

Nadeau, J. and O'Reilly, N. (2006). Developing a profitability model for professional sport leagues: The case of the National Hockey League. *International Journal of Sport Finance*, Vol. 1, No. 1, pp. 49–64.

O'Connor, I. (2002). LPGA is going for the pinups. *USA Today*, 24 July, 2002. Sports Section pg 03c.

O'Reilly, N. and Braedley, A. (forthcoming). Celebrity athletes and athletic clothing design: Branding female tennis players. *International Journal of Sport Management and Marketing*.

Ohanian, R. (1991). The impact of celebrity spokespersons' perceived image on consumers' intention to purchase. *Journal of Advertising Research*, Vol. 31, pp. 46–54.

Penfold, R. (2004). The star's image, victimization and celebrity culture. *Punishment and Society*, Vol. 6, No. 3, pp. 289–302.

Rein, I., Kotler, P. and Stoller, M. (1997). *High Visibility: The Making and Marketing of Professionals into Celebrities*. NTC Business Books, Chicago.

Rivers, D. and DeSchriver, T. (2002). Star players, payroll distribution, and Major League Baseball attendance. *Sport Marketing Quarterly*, Vol. 11, No. 3, pp. 164–173.

Ryssel, C. and Stamminger, E. (1988). Sponsoring world-class tennis players. *European Research*, May, 110–116.

Self, J. (2005). Tatiana dressed to thrill. *The Sun*, June 9, 57.

Stewart, M. (2003). Simeon Rice's T3K tackles the performance apparel category. *Sporting Goods Business*, Vol. 36, No. 11, p. 44.

Stone, G., Joseph, M. and Jones, M. (2003) An exploratory study on the use of sports celebrities in advertising: A content analysis. *Sport Marketing Quarterly*, Vol. 12, No. 2, pp. 94–102.

Tripp, Carolyn, Thomas D. Jensen, and Les Carlson. (1994). The effects of multiple product endorsements by celebrities on consumer's attitudes and intentions. *Journal of Consumer Research*, Vol. 20, No. 4, pp. 535–547.

White, D. (2007). Photo shoot. *Golf For Women Magazine*, April/May.

Withers, A. (2007). Natalie Gulbis: Justified expense or a waste of money? *Fox Sports Online*, 30 January.

Further Information

Following are a few websites related to Natalie Gulbis which may be of interest:

- www.lpga.com
- www.nataliegulbis.com

Case

20

Promoting Pacific Islander rugby in a crowded marketplace: using media relations to overcome the challenge

Dave Arthur and Simon Chadwick

Case Focus

This case examines the challenges of presenting the public face of an international rugby union team (the Pacific Islanders) in the already overcrowded sporting marketplace of the UK. It addresses some of the issues confronting the team management and how they were addressed through the use of media relations.

Keywords

- Rugby union
- Pacific Islands
- Public relations
- Media
- Branding

Case Summary

The nations of England, Scotland, Wales and Ireland have a long tradition of rugby union competition and consequently strong brand recognition in the European marketplace. The English Rose, Irish Clover, Scottish Thistle and the Welsh Dragon are all well-known symbols associated with these countries and their sporting heritage. The Australian Wallabies, South African Springboks and New Zealand All Blacks, through their strong performances over a number of years (between them they have won four of the five Rugby World Cup's (RWC's) contested), have similarly strong brand recognition. However, the Pacific Islanders do not enjoy such an exalted position given their comparative lack of history. In marketing terms generally, and public relations specifically, the 2006 tour to Europe for test matches versus Wales, Scotland and Ireland therefore represented a significant challenge for the Pacific Islanders management team and their constituent nations. Indeed, even the rugby public in the Islands, more used to supporting the individual nations rather than the combined Pacific Islanders side, needed to be harnessed and won over from their traditional parochialism. As 2006 Pacific Islanders coach Pat Lam (2006) intimated:

> There's a lot of expectation back in the islands, he said. They'll all be up until three, four o'clock in the morning watching the games and the boys know that. We realise that there is a responsibility. If we do well there are huge benefits on and off the pitch for pacific island rugby, so it's a great challenge.

This case examines how the vitally important role of media relations as an essential element of public relations was undertaken on the 2006 Pacific Islander's tour.

Case Elements

Rugby union is one of the premier codes of football played around the world. The global peak body for the sport is the International Rugby Board (IRB) with its headquarters in Dublin, Ireland. Current IRB rankings illustrate that the game is played internationally in 95 countries and many others besides that do not compete globally. Every four years the RWC takes place in a country or countries that have previously bid for the event. With a worldwide television audience in excess of 3 billion in 2003 (when the event was held in Australia), RWC has become established as the third most important sporting event behind the Olympics and the FIFA World Cup. In addition to the prestigious RWC numerous fixtures are played between international sides at various levels as organizations seek to maximize revenue in the commercialized world of modern sporting competition. In rugby union specifically it is a similar story, for as well as the various domestic competitive games during November and early December, there is a series of 'autumn' internationals involving touring sides from around the world. Whilst these games are scheduled many years in advance the addition of the Pacific Islanders, a relatively new and unique touring side to this mix is a significant challenge.

Rugby union is played in many places around the Pacific however the three 'powerhouse' international teams are Fiji, Samoa and Tonga. The Pacific Islanders are comprised of the best players available from these 'home' islands. Whilst players are required to be available for their constituent islands, many play offshore in the lucrative competitive fields offered by the Super 14, Guinness Premiership, Heineken European Cup and other quality rugby union competitions.

These three Pacific Island countries have a phenomenal record of producing top rugby players, especially given Fiji has a population of 900,000, Samoa about 175,000 and Tonga just 115,000 (Anon, 2006). Fiji is traditionally viewed as a hotbed for the modified sevens rugby union where the side is seen by many as the 'Harlem Globetrotters' of the abridged version. Their success in the 15-man game has been less high profile however they have competed in every RWC bar one and invariably progress to the quarter-final stage. Samoa suffers greatly from the huge number of players playing professionally abroad, however they have still managed to remain competitive on the world stage. The Samoan side has been responsible for some remarkable upsets at RWC's including two victories over Wales in 1991 and 1999. Similarly to Samoa one of Tonga's main exports is rugby players. Despite this, and a small base of population, they too have recorded upset victories including wins over Australia in 1973, France in 1999 and Italy in 1999 RWC.

There is therefore no shortage of rugby union talent in the Pacific Islands. The IRB has recognized the potential of rugby in the region and committed significant funds for the development of the code. In the period 2005–2008, the investment in Pacific Islands Rugby is over 3 million pounds, excluding funding for tournaments such as the Pacific Rugby Cup and Pacific Nations Cup. In addition, Fiji, Samoa and Tonga will receive 150,000 pounds in participation fees and for travel and accommodation for 2007 RWC.

Rugby union in these three nations has also been recognized through the relatively recent addition of two tournaments. The Pacific Rugby Cup, first staged in 2006, is fully sanctioned and supported by the IRB, involves two representative teams from each of Fiji, Samoa and Tonga and is seen as instrumental in preparing players for test match rugby. The Pacific Rugby Cup follows the completion of Fiji's Colonial Cup, Samoa's Vailima National Provincial Championship and Tonga's Datec Cup Provincial Championship and involves around 180 locally based players. Further the establishment of the Pacific Nations Cup comprised of Australia A, Junior All Blacks, Japan, Fiji, Samoa and Tonga has enabled the island sides to have meaningful test matches which, given its' scheduling allows them to call on their European-based players.

However, the financial structure, contractual obligations and competitive nature of professional rugby throws up an interesting conundrum for all international teams. As previously stated the Pacific Islanders are comprised the best players available from Fiji, Samoa and Tonga but their availability for international duty is a similarly major issue. With the majority of players selected in the squad plying their trade in Europe, and hence earning their living from club (as opposed to international) rugby, the challenge is to ensure that the best players are available for designated matches. Inordinate pressure is sometimes placed on players by their club to make themselves unavailable for international duty.

In response to this the IRB has formulated 21 regulations regarding many aspects of the game including broadcasting rights, medical protocols and wagering. Regulation 9 is designed specifically to allow players to represent their country and in this case the combined nations of the Pacific Islanders. In particular Regulation 9.4 (where players not making themselves available are prevented from playing for their clubs for the duration of any designated tour plus 10 days) was used by management to overcome some of the difficulties associated with availability.

With the squad for the Pacific Islanders picked from the best players available, there was also a question of how to 'brand' the side. The general idea in the sporting world that a brand is merely a logo is far from the truth. Although the physical aspects of a sporting organization (including but not limited to the logo) are key, the true definition of a brand is more encompassing. A brand is more widely and adequately defined as a distinctive picture and association positioned in the mind of consumers of an object (product, service) or a subject (person, institution) (Pedersen, 2004; Apostolopoulou and Gladden, 2007). Brands create imaginations and can direct behaviour patterns amongst customers and consumers. When applied to sports, this definition means that a product or a service, such as a type of sport (e.g. rugby union), an event (Pacific Nations Cup) a person (Jonny Wilkinson), and institution (Union) can be perceived as a brand. It also means that sports consumers perceive such objects and subjects in a totally different way.

A clear brand determines all future marketing activities (including public and media relations) and therefore represents an important instrument to influence the market. Brand management as a management task can be practically defined as finding strategies to build and to cultivate a brand in order to achieve competitive advantage. The main objective in brand management is to achieve a strong position within the mindset of customers and to generate public confidence (Pedersen, 2004).

Thus, the establishment of a Pacific Islander 'brand' was seen as vital. However, this is not as easy as it may seem as the Pacific Islanders were only formed in 2004 for three games against Australia, South Africa and New Zealand, respectively. The inaugural tour was an onerous undertaking as Pacific Islanders.co.nz (2007) put it:

The team started with two provincial games against a Queensland XV and NSW and then they were facing the three top teams out of the top 5 in the world, one week it was the great Wallabies from Australia ... twice winners of the World Cup, the next week it was the famous All Blacks of New Zealand ... winners of the first World Cup and the last week was against the uncompromising Springboks of South Africa, winners of the 1995 World Cup.

History records three losses, 29–14 to Australia in Adelaide, 41–26 to New Zealand in Albany and 38–24 to South Africa in Gosford. The on field losses prompted great conjecture as to the usefulness of the short tour for the three island nations however there was just as much off field conjecture due to the commercial performance of the Pacific Islands Rugby Alliance (PIRA). Setup in 2002 as a basis of co-operation between the Fijian, Samoan and Tongan Rugby Unions but also including the Niue and Cook Islands Unions, PIRA was beset by allegations of financial mismanagement with claim and counter claim common place. Between the 2004 and 2006 tours a new management vehicle Pacific Rugby Limited (PRL) was formed to administer Pacific Islander rugby union in general and the 2006 tour in particular. Further information on all aspects of the 2004 tour can be obtained from the Teivovo website (http://www.teivovo.com) and from other websites referred to later in this chapter.

With limited tradition per se there was a requirement to use the long history of rugby in the constituent nations as a basis for branding the Pacific Islanders. According to Teivovo rugby was first played in Fiji by European and Fijian soldiers of the Native Constabulary at Ba, on Viti Levu Island around 1884. However, it was not until 1924 that Fiji played its first test match. The game took place in Apia, Samoa, in August while the team was in transit to Tonga. The match was played at 7 a.m. to allow Samoan opponents time to get to work afterwards and was played on a pitch with a large tree on the halfway line! Fiji played in black and won 6–0. The Official Manu Samoa site (http://www.manusamoa.com.ws/) records this game as Western Samoa's initial test match as well. The Western Samoa Rugby Football Union was formed in 1924, after the Marist Brothers brought the game to Western Samoa in 1920. However, it was not until 1954 that the Western Samoan side visited both Pacific Island neighbours Fiji and Tonga and a further 20 years before a tour of New Zealand took place. According to Planet Rugby (http://www.planetrugby.com) Tonga also played their first test in 1924 when they beat Fiji. Their greatest moment however came in 1973 when they beat the might of Australia at Ballymore in Brisbane 16–11, scoring four tries to two.

One of the major traditions associated with rugby in the Pacific Islands is the 'war dance' that precedes every test match. The best known of these is the 'Haka' performed by New Zealand however Fiji, Samoa and Tonga all possess their own unique brand. Fiji's 'cibi' (pronounced 'thimbi') war dance has been used on the rugby field since 1939, though its origins date back to the war against their Pacific neighbours (http://www.teivovo.com/history/teivovo_info.html). The 2006 Pacific Islander tour was no exception with the performance of the 'Siva Tau' (literally translated Tau is war – Siva is action – three nations go to war) taking place before every test match.

The rugby aspects of the 2006 tour were one thing but there also needed to be a commercial aspect to it. In terms of public relations generally and media, branding and crisis management in particular, PRL commissioned a report in mid-2006 but did not appoint a person to manage this aspect of the tour until a fortnight prior to the squad's departure. Time therefore, was at a premium in planning for the public relations aspects of the tour. With this in mind it was decided to adopt a distinct media relations focus, rather than instigate a broad public relations campaign.

Prior to examining media relations in isolation however, it is important to briefly consider the scope of public relations as a whole. Hopwood (2007, p. 294) lists the following areas as 'typical' in the practice of sport public relations:

- Media relations
- Publicity
- Publications
- Corporate communications
- Public affairs and community relations
- Lobbying
- Sponsorship and donations
- Events management
- Crisis management
- Research and analysis

The remit of public relations is therefore vast – as Hopwood intimates 'public relations has the unique ability to build relationships, establish credibility and create understanding between the organization and its many publics'. Jefkins (1994) proposed a model of public relations planning that was made up of the following six steps (although Hopwood also noted that public relations were far from a linear process):

1 Situation analysis
2 Defining objectives
3 Defining publics
4 Media selection
5 Budget creation
6 Implementation and control

Mullin et al. (2000, p. 318) suggested that in a sporting context PR has two primary components – media relations and community relations or PR=MR+CR. Media relations tend to be short term while community relations tend to be more long term. As such, and given the time constraints alluded to above, media relations became a central tenet of the Pacific Islander plan. Media relations is designed to formulate or shape favourable public opinion via the mass media with some authors suggesting such stories generate seven times the response of advertising. Put simply 'the media are among the most important publics an organization has, for through the media other publics can be reached' (Tymson and Sherman, 1996, p. 150). Care should be taken however as the media has a tendency to focus on the negative aspects of sport.

In terms of media available to communicate a message this is legion and can include:

- Advertising (print, outdoor)
- Advertising (radio, TV, display)
- Advertising (on line, cinema)
- Annual reports
- Multi media presentations
- Audiovisual materials
- Awards
- Broadcast media
- Cable TV
- Company histories
- Competitions
- Conferences
- Corporate identity programs
- Direct mail
- Documentaries
- Donations
- Educational materials
- Email
- Exhibitions and displays
- Face-to-face discussion
- Fact books
- Films
- Lobbying
- Media releases
- Manuals
- News conferences
- Newsletters
- Notice boards and posters
- Open houses and plant visits
- On-line media
- Photographs
- Promotions
- Print media
- Publications
- Seminars
- Special events
- Speeches
- Sponsorships
- Stunts
- World Wide Web

It is also important here to delineate the difference between advertising and publicity. In essence it is simple – advertising is paid for media coverage whilst publicity is free. Competition for publicity is fierce given its cost and the fact that it is considered by many to be more credible than advertising – even more so in sport where the interest levels are high. With funding at a premium for the 2006 Pacific Islander tour it was therefore imperative that media relations be optimal.

In terms of media Nicholson (2007, p. 125) offers a simple media planning and strategy flow chart that encapsulates the essential requirements for effective media planning (see Figure 20.1).

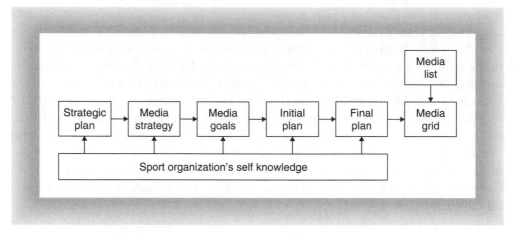

Figure 20.1 Media planning and strategy flow chart
Source: Nicholson (2007, p. 125)

He feels that an organization's media goals should not exist in isolation but should be a consequence of the overall goals and objectives of the organization itself (what he terms 'self knowledge') as well as that organization's strategic plan.

Case Diagnosis

It was well realized that media relations for the Pacific Islanders would not just miraculously happen. To paraphrase the old adage 'those who fail to plan get no media coverage' (Nicholson, 2007, p. 122). Using the aforementioned report into public relations, branding and crisis management as a guide, a media relations strategy was formulated. The plan was designed to promote the Pacific Islanders brand to the various stakeholders and publics and revolved around setting objectives, planning, implementing and evaluating. Essentially, the target publics for the tour included players; coaches; team management; supporters (home and abroad); the media, IRB; Welsh, Scottish and Irish Rugby Unions; sponsors/key stakeholders; and various governments. In formulating and adopting a media plan, the requirements of each of these could be satisfied.

Predominantly due to the short preparation time the media plan was comprised of simple media commitments that were both proactive (sought out by the media manager through contact with agencies and the normal range of activities prior to a test match) and reactive (requests for interview with team members and team management). Thus media events such as team announcements and coach interviews were rigidly scheduled but requests by European and Pacific Island media for player interviews were also granted. The resources of the Welsh, Scottish and Irish Rugby Union's were also utilized and these proved to be very fruitful. In addition the various media organizations in Fiji, Samoa, Tonga and to a lesser extent Australia and New Zealand were also included as vitally important publics.

As an aside, it as decided to direct all media enquiries in the first instance to the media manager. Although many of the players, as professionals competing in Europe, had existing personal relationships with media outlets and individuals such an approach was deemed valid as it would help ensure a total commitment to performance in both training and on match day and allow a sharing of media duties between squad members.

In undertaking the various media commitments that comprised the media plan the basic aim was simply to increase the public's awareness of Pacific Islander rugby and gain the support of the public. It was vital that everybody knew what was going on and what the messages being communicated were. These messages were formulated through rigorous consultation with stakeholders both inside and outside the management group and included:

- An abiding pride in representing the Pacific Islanders on the tour. This was quite apart from each player's representation of their country of birth.
- The tour was an opportunity to show the unique brand of Pacific Islander rugby against some of the world's best sides. The brand was characterized as hard, physical, spontaneous and entertaining.
- Recognition that preparation for the tour was a huge challenge. The squad was literally flown in from around the world to contest the first test (versus Wales) a mere six days later. This is, in contrast to the opposition sides who had been engaged in various sessions for a number of months. Thus, the message communicated was to be content with the 'underdog' status that the squad would naturally be labelled with.
- On no account were players or management allowed to provide messages that could be construed as denigrating the opposition. This is in line with the underdog status above as well as recognizing the challenge that the test matches represented.
- There was also a need to communicate respect for the opposition at all times. These countries had granted the Pacific Islanders the opportunity to tour (often at great financial cost) and Wales in particular were one of the first top tier nations to acknowledge rugby in the Pacific Islands as well as sharing rugby as the national sport.

As well as the messages to be communicated there were a number of major issues that could conceivably arise as part of the media commitments undertaken. It was therefore decided that an 'official' position should be taken on these. Although many issues were distilled through stakeholder consultation, none were declared off limits. The key issues included are as below.

Release of Players

Regulation 9 and in particular 9.4 (players not making themselves available are prevented from playing for the duration of the tour plus 10 days) has proved a boon for Pacific Islander rugby. Without 9.4 the tour would not have happened.

The Future of Pacific Islander Rugby

There are no plans or desire for the Pacific Islanders to compete at the RWC – this remains the domain of the individual countries. The future is very bright with the long-term focus of this tour on 2008 when England and France will be the destination. This year's tour is geared towards giving a legacy for future tours on and off the field.

Relationship with IRB

The relationship with the IRB is very positive – they provided personnel to aid the organization of the tour and have contributed financially to ensure it went ahead.

What about PIRA?

PIRA no longer exists and Fiji, Tonga and Samoa have set up PRL. This has a legal identity with the company registered in Samoa, with the three Chairmen of the home nations as Directors.

The 2004 Tour of Australia and New Zealand

There were some problems off field with the 2004 tour and this is a key reason why PRL was established. In touring again, PRL is laying the foundations for future tours and setting up important future revenue streams for the Fijian, Tongan and Samoan Unions.

Style of Rugby

The way the game is played is important. Although the modern professional game is very structured we aim, within those bounds to express ourselves the Pacific Islander way – entertaining, open, physically hard, instinctive, spontaneous and winning rugby.

Destination for Sport

We are keen to promote the Pacific Islands as a destination for tourism and tourism-related economic benefit for all three islands.

Culture

Culture is vitally important to all Pacific Islanders. On and off the field we are trying to communicate the way we live, our history and our tradition – we are about family values, christian values, giving respect and integrity. This is well illustrated by the Siva Tau (see http://www.youtube.com/watch?v=WbLH8LXlpKM).

In undertaking the 2006 tour to Wales, Scotland and Ireland there were numerous challenges for all personnel to overcome. Whilst definitely not a 'magic bullet' it was felt that the adoption of the media strategy referred to would, at the very least, increase the awareness of Pacific Islander rugby and address some of the issues surrounding competition at the professional level. In addition, it would lay a firm foundation on which future tours could be based.

The lead author toured with the 2006 Pacific Islander squad as media manager. He would like to acknowledge the support of Mr Bob Tuckey, Mr Sakopo Lolohea, Mr Pat Lam, other coaching and management staff as well as all the players involved in undertaking his role.

Case Questions

1 What were the major challenges confronting Pacific Islander management as they embarked on the 2006 tour?
2 The Pacific Islanders have a tour scheduled in 2008 to England, France and Italy. How do you think the challenges will change from the 2006 tour?
3 To what extent do you agree that the needs of international rugby union would be better served if the Pacific Islander concept was abandoned?
4 Develop some objectives for a media relations campaign for the 2008 tour.
5 Mullin et al. (2000, p. 318) felt public relations was a combination of media relations and community relations. In a perfect world which aspects of community relations would you include in a future public relations plan for the Pacific Islanders?

Case Resources

Reading

Anon (2006). Five nations series set to boost Islands rugby http://www. abc.net.au/sport/columns/200606/s1653349.htm?rugbyunion

Apostolopoulou, A. and Gladden, J.M. (2007). Developing and extending sports brands, in Chadwick, S. and Beech, J. (Eds.), *The Marketing of Sport*. Financial Times Prentice Hall, London.

Hopwood, M. (2007). The sports public relations planning process, in Chadwick, S. and Beech, J. (Eds.), *The Marketing of Sport*. Financial Times Prentice Hall, London.

Jefkins, J. (1994). *Public Relations Techniques*, 2nd edition. Butterworth Heinemann, Oxford.

Lam, P. (2006). Coaching the United Nations, International Rugby Board, 15 November, http://www.irb.com/EN/News/Features/061115+SL+PIRA.htm

Mullin, B.J., Hardy, S. and Sutton, W.A. (2000). *Sport Marketing*. Human Kinetics, Champaign, Illinois.

Nicholson, M. (2007). *Sport and the Media: Managing the Nexus*. Butterworth Heinemann, Oxford.

Pedersen, L.H. (2004). Why is branding so important? *FIBA Assist Magazine*, October, pp. 47–48.

Tymson, C. and Sherman, B. (1996). What is public relations anyway? *The Australian and New Zealand Public Relations Manual*. Millenium Books, Sydney.

Websites

Fiji Rugby Union – http://www.fijirugbyunion.com/
International Rugby Board – http://www.irb.com/
Irish Rugby Union – http://www.irishrugby.ie/
Manu Samoa – http://www.manusamoa.net/
Pacific Islanders Worldwide – http://www.pacificislanders.co.nz/
Scottish Rugby Union – http://www.scottishrugby.org/
Teivovo – http://www.teivovo.com/pacific_rugby/Islanders/index_2004.html
Tonga Rugby Union – http://www.planet-tonga.com/ikaletahi/index.php
Welsh Rugby Union – http://www.wru.co.uk/2_6.php

Further Information

Users of the case may want to look at the Wikipedia entries for additional information:

http://en.wikipedia.org/wiki/Fiji_Rugby_Football_Union
http://en.wikipedia.org/wiki/Samoa_Rugby_Football_Union
http://en.wikipedia.org/wiki/Tonga_Rugby_Football_Union
http://en.wikipedia.org/wiki/Pacific_Islanders_rugby_team

21

Integration between broadcasters and transmission companies involved in sports broadcasting

Harry Arne Solberg, Knut Helland and Brita Ytre-Arne

Case Focus

This case examines sports broadcasting as a field where new forms of integration between broadcasters and transmission companies take place. The main case is that of the Norwegian telecom and transmission company Telenor, which is involved in both terrestrial, cable and satellite distribution. The main focus is on football media rights.

Keywords

- Sports rights
- Broadcasting
- Cable and satellite distribution
- Media convergence
- Vertical integration
- Norway

Case Summary

The case is based on recent developments related to TV sports rights in Norway, and shows how the attraction value of popular sports is reconfiguring the traditional broadcasting landscape. The main 'sports focus' is on soccer (football); the Norwegian football deal 2006–2009/2010, the English Premier League (EPL) and the Euro 2008. The main 'media focus' is on the Norwegian telecom and transmission company Telenor, which is involved in both terrestrial, cable and satellite distribution. Recently, the company has also become increasingly involved in media production companies. The activities of Telenor are analysed as strategies of expansion and integration, and a particular focus is put on different forms of vertical integration; merger and acquisitions, alliances and new establishment/internal expansion.

Case Study

Introduction

Strong price increases on popular TV sports rights have been a well-known phenomenon on practically all continents during the first years of the 21st century. Football (soccer) has been the leading TV revenue generator across all European markets, and has even accounted for more than 50 per cent of the total sports rights fees in some nations. The main reason for this development is that fierce competition has enabled owners of popular sports rights to orchestrate bidding wars, resulting in prices that were unimaginable only a few years ago. In recent years, the competition has not only involved broadcasters, but also transmission companies such as satellite and cable operators. This seems to have added extra fuel to the growth in sports rights fees.

This development in sport broadcasting is related to other changes in the distribution of broadcasting. New digital technology has increased the transmission capacity considerably, and created a fierce competition for 'content' among operators. Another consequence of this development has been incidents of *vertical integration* between TV broadcasters and transmission companies. The general definition of vertical integration is that firms participate in more than one successive stage of the production or distribution of goods or services.

This chapter will analyse how sports rights acquisitions have contributed to vertical integration between broadcasters and cable/satellite operators by examining some cases from the Scandinavian markets. Special attention is paid to the role of Telenor, a Norwegian telecommunication and transmission company involved in both terrestrial, cable and satellite transmission. In 2005 and 2006, the company participated in the following three football rights acquisitions in the Scandinavian markets:

1 The domestic Norwegian football rights (club football and national teams).
2 The EPL rights for the entire Scandinavian market.
3 The TV rights for the European football championship for national teams in 2008 (Euro 2008) for Norway, Sweden and Denmark.

In all these three acquisitions, Telenor formed alliances with (different) broadcasters. When bidding on the EPL rights Telenor even backed a broadcaster (Canal Plus) which was a rival in the competition for the Norwegian rights. The prices for the rights increased considerably in all these auctions, particularly in the case of the domestic Norwegian football rights.

The next section provides an overview of Norwegian broadcasters and transmission companies involved in sports broadcasting. This is followed by a presentation of the three cases mentioned above. The final sections discuss the lessons to be learned from these cases by means of economic theory.

Norwegian Sports Broadcasting

Table 21.1 provides an overview of the broadcasters that have been involved in Norwegian sports broadcasting in recent years, while Table 21.2 presents the main transmission companies. The Norwegian Broadcasting Corporation (NRK) started television broadcasts in 1960, while the other channels have emerged since the late 1980s. Both the NRK and TV2 are public service broadcasters (PSB), distributed free-to-air through terrestrial transmission and on cable and satellite platforms. By 2007, the NRK is a non-commercial broadcaster with two channels, financed by license fees and owned by the Norwegian state. TV2 is a commercial PSB financed by advertising and holds an exclusive concession as a nation wide, terrestrially transmitted commercial TV channel. The concession includes public service commitments that oblige TV2's main channel to follow programming guidelines set by the Norwegian authorities. In addition, TV2 has recently established a sports and entertainment channel, TV2 Zebra, which is transmitted through digital platforms.

Table 21.1 The Norwegian TV landscape – sports broadcasters

Parental company	Channels	Type of channel – revenue source	Penetration (2007)
Norwegian Broadcasting Corporation (NRK)	NRK1	PSB – licence	100%
	NRK2	PSB – licence	89%
TV 2	TV 2	PSB – advertising	98%
	TV 2 Zebra	Entertainment – advertising	61%
SBS Broadcasting Group	TV Norge	Entertainment – advertising	92%
	Canal Plus	Entertainment – pay-TV channels	Unknown
Modern Times Group (MTG)	TV 3	Entertainment – advertising	63%
	Viasat/TV-1000	Entertainment – pay-TV channels	Unknown
	SportN	Entertainment – pay-TV channel	Unknown

Source: Kampanje.com. Retrieved 03 January 2007, from http://www.kampanje.com/medier/article52225.ece

Table 21.2 Transmission companies involved in Norwegian broadcasting

Terrestrial operators	Telenor (Norkring)
Satellite operators	Telenor (Canal Digital) Viasat
Cable operators	Telenor (Canal Digital) UPC

Other Norwegian sports broadcasters include TV Norge and TV 3 which are both financed by advertising. TV Norge is transmitted terrestrially because the channel cooperates with local TV stations, while TV 3 is distributed through cable and digital platforms. In addition, SBS Broadcasting Group and Modern Times Group (MTG) both have several pay-TV channels, which are totally or partly decicated to sports programmes. The sports channel SportN is collaboration between MTG and the NRK, but it is owned by MTG.

Telenor has been the dominant transmission company in the Norwegian market. It has been involved in terrestrial transmission through Norkring, and in cable and satellite transmission through the platform Canal Digital. Its main rival has been Viasat, which is owned by MTG. While Telenor has been involved in all the three ways of transmission, Viasat has only been involved in satellite transmission.

Norwegian broadcasting will be dramatically altered by a new digital terrestrial transmission network which will be launched in the period 2007–2009. The Norwegian Parliament has decided that the network will be built and operated by private enterprise, and in 2005 the company Norsk television (Ntv) was given a concession to construct and operate the network. Ntv is owned by the NRK, TV 2 and Telenor, who all have equal shares in the company. The new network will provide several broadcasters with the same household penetration as NRK and TV 2. Hence, TV 2's advantage of having higher penetration than its commercial rivals will come to and end.

Table 21.3 shows the most popular sports products in Norway and the channels that have broadcasted them during the first years of the 21st century. During its period as monopolist, the NRK was obviously the only

Table 21.3 Norwegian sport broadcasting

Products	Right holder
Football	
• The Tippeliga[a]	TV 2/Telenor
• World Cup soccer finals (2006)	TV 2/NRK
• European football championship (EURO) 2004 and 2008	TV 2
• Qualifying matches to WC and Euro (home matches)	TV 2
• Qualifying matches to WC and Euro (away matches)	TV 3
• UEFA's Champions league	TV 3/Viasat
• English Premier League	Canal Plus
• Royal League[b]	TV Norge
Skiing	
• World Cup	
• World Championship	NRK
• National Championship	
Biathlon	
• World Cup	
• World Championship	NRK
• National Championship	
Handball	
• Domestic Premier League	
• International championships including qualifying matches	TV 2
Olympic Games	NRK

[a]The Norwegian Premier League
[b]A league including the teams finishing from 1 to 4 in Norway, Sweden and Denmark

broadcaster of sports programmes. However, similar to many other European non-commercial PSBs, the NRK has been forced to give up many popular (and expensive) sports programmes to commercial rivals. This particularly applies to football. Since the start of the 2006 season, the NRK has been completely without football, except from the World Cup finals which it shares with TV2. In recent years, the NRK has mainly concentrated its efforts on winter sports, such as cross-country skiing, biathlon, ski-jumping and skating. These sports have historically been very popular among Norwegian TV viewers. In addition, the collaboration with MTG has also enabled NRK to air 'new' television sports such as golf, which traditionally have received moderate attention from Norwegian TV viewers.

Football is the sport that has generated the highest television revenues, in Norway as in the rest of Europe. The most valuable assets are the Tippeliga (the Norwegian Premier League) and the EPL, but tournaments such as the World Cup soccer finals, the European Championship for national teams as well as UEFA's Champions League are also important to broadcasters. The three following sections will examine the auction of the following three football deals:

1 Norwegian football deal from the seasons 2006/2007 to 2009/2010.
2 The Scandinavian broadcasting rights for the EPL from 2007 to 2010.
3 The Scandinavian rights for the Euro 2008 tournament.

The Norwegian Football Deal 2006–2009/2010

When the Norwegian football rights were put out for sale in the spring of 2005, all the broadcasters mentioned in Table 21.3 submitted bids, either individually or together with one of the transmission companies Telenor and Viasat. The rights were divided into different packages of three to four years of television, Internet and mobile broadcasting rights for the different leagues and tournaments at the top level of Norwegian football. It covered the two upper domestic football leagues (three years) and the national cup, national team matches and women's league (four years).

The NRK and TV2 held the rights together for the previous period, which ended with the 2005 season. This deal guaranteed them a 'matching offer' clause the next time the rights were to be sold. However, in 2005 the Norwegian Football Association (NFF) and its agent, Rune Hauge, argued that the clause might be invalid. This claim was based on a report by the Norwegian Competition Authority which questioned whether an alliance between the two largest broadcasters would be in violation of Norwegian competition laws. Therefore, the NRK and TV2 decided not to make a joint bid for the upcoming period, allegedly due to fear of being accused of competition law violations, which might harm their brands and reputations (Taalesen, 2006, pp. 70–87).

Neither the NRK nor TV2 could afford to acquire the entire rights package alone. Although they could have submitted bids on separate packages, both preferred to compete for the entire package together with others. The NRK formed an alliance with MTG, and together they submitted a bid on about NOK 800 million (€97 million). This was the first bid in the auction and amounted to more than 200 per cent of the value on the current deal. MTG could have been a strong competitor for the rights alone, but with one major weakness: its main channel, TV3, only had a household penetration of 63 per cent. This, however, would be outbalanced by the NRK's higher penetration. By 2007, the two NRK channels can be taken in by 100 per cent and 88 per cent of the Norwegian TV households.

The NRK/MTG alliance came as a shock to TV2. Given the new competition scenario this alliance represented, TV2 adopted a similar strategy and formed an alliance with Telenor. This alliance resulted in a joint bid on NOK 1 billion (€122 million). In addition, SBS Broadcasting, the parental company of TV Norge and Canal Plus, also submitted a bid on NOK 1.2 billion. However, this offer assumed the Tippeliga deal to be extended from three to four years. Hence, SBS's bid was equivalent to the bid from TV2/Telenor in terms of annual fees. The NFF preferred the TV2/Telenor bid – allegedly due to TV2's advantage of higher penetration than TV Norge.

The deal on NOK 1 billion was the most expensive sports rights deal ever in Norway. Table 21.4 presents the TV right deals from domestic Premier

Table 21.4 Football right fees European domestic Premier Leagues 2006/2007 season

	Fee per capita €	Annual fee (€ million)	Fee change (%)
England + Wales	12.85	608.6	−19
Spain	11.14	450.0	+34
France	10.63	647.0	+61
Italy	9.92	567.6	+20
Norway	5.25	24.2	+384
Germany	5.01	413.0	+41
The Netherlands	4.32	71.3	±67
Scotland	4.16	21.2	+59
Belgium	3.49	36.2	+141
Denmark	2.66	14.5	+20
Greece	2.60	27.8	+11
Turkey	1.58	111.0	+59
Switzerland	1.01	7.6	+81
Austria	1.00	8.2	+71
Poland	0.34	13.0	+30
Czech Republic	0.34	3.5	+40
Hungary	0.08	0.8	−20
Russia	0.03	3.9	−71

Source: World Football Leagues and TV rights, TV Sports Markets; CIA Factbook 2006, Retrieved 02 January 2007, from https://www.cia.gov/cia/publications/factbook/geos/no.html; http://www.statistics.gov.uk/CCI/nugget.asp?ID=6

Leagues across Europe for the 2006/2007 season and reveals that the Norwegian rights are the fifth most expensive in per capita terms, that is more expensive than Germany. The table reveals enormous variations, from bottom €0.03 (Russia) to top of €12.85 (England + Wales) in per capita terms, and from bottom €0.8 million (Hungary) to €647 million (France) in aggregate terms. Fifteen of the eighteen nations experienced a growth in price level compared to the former deal, and Norway had by far the strongest increase (384 per cent). The fact that the Norwegian sale process involved both TV broadcasters and transmission companies seems to be a likely explanation for the enormous increase in fees on this occasion.

There were several reasons why the broadcasters were willing to put so many resources into acquiring the Norwegian football rights. Bjørn Taalesen, sports editor of TV2, outlines some of the advantages TV2 had experienced in an interview with *International Journal of Sport Marketing and Sponsorship* (IJSMS) towards the end of the first season of the period (Helland, 2006):

> *This entire contract has elevated TV2 as an organisation and has accelerated a great deal of internal developments. The way in which we have taken on challenges of web-TV, mobile phone technology and the integration of different platforms, and made all these features function together as a whole, has been surprising. Thanks to football, our developments have been sensational to a degree that is really unheard in the television world. On many platforms – not least TV2 Zebra – football and the contract itself have become the primary selling point … Without this football contract it would have taken TV2 a lot longer to get to where we are today.*

During the 2006 season, all the Tippeliga matches were aired on television. One match each round was aired on TV2's main channel, two on TV2 Zebra and the remaining four matches on pay-per-view channels transmitted through Canal Digital's digital platforms. TV2 produced all the matches, including those being transmitted by Canal Digital. TV2 Zebra was separated from TV2 into a new company, TV2 Zebra AS, in which Telenor acquired a 45 per cent share. This share corresponds with how the fees for the rights were divided between TV2 and Telenor. Hence, the alliance between TV2 and Telenor was extended beyond the field of football broadcasting. The alliance with TV2 gave Telenor influence over the broadcasting part of the value chain in several ways: co-ownership of attractive sports rights, co-ownership of TV2 Zebra and cooperation in the production of football for their pay-per-view channels.

The EPL Rights 2007–2010

In November 2006, one and a half year after the sale of the Norwegian football rights, some of the companies involved in that auction were involved in another football rights auction, namely the sale of the EPL rights for Scandinavia (covering Norway, Sweden, Denmark and Finland). On this occasion the rights were won by a joint bid from Canal Plus (the incumbent holder) and Telenor. The fee amounted to €89 million for a three-year deal and represented a 45 per cent rise from the former deal that was held entirely by Canal Plus.

Note that on this occasion, Telenor collaborated with a broadcaster which parental company, SBS Broadcasting, was a fierce rival for the Norwegian football rights one year earlier. Telenor's partner in the acquisition of the Norwegian football rights, TV 2, was also interested in the EPL rights for Norway. TV 2 attempted a joint bid with commercial broadcasters in Denmark and Sweden, but these broadcasters were unwilling to put up the necessary fees, and thus the bid was never viable.

If Telenor had joined TV 2 or other commercial channels in the auction for the EPL rights, that would have been a 'declaration of war' against Canal Plus at a time when Telenor was trying to renegotiate an exclusive carriage agreement with the Canal Plus channels for the direct-to-home satellite platform Canal Digital (TV Sports Markets, 2006). Canal Plus has been the key subscription driver for Canal Digital. A straining relationship could have lead to Canal Plus forming a carriage deal with Canal Digital's rival platform Viasat, owned by MTG. Instead, Telenor and Canal Digital formed a new exclusive satellite carriage deal for the period 2007–2010 in November 2006.

Canal Plus could possibly have acquired the EPL rights alone, but the alliance with Telenor still provided a number of advantages. The financial muscle of the alliance might have dissuaded others from bidding, and thereby the total price might have been higher for Canal Plus. In addition, the cost of paying for the rights would obviously be higher for Canal Plus if the company had to pay the entire fee alone.

Retaining the EPL rights was a huge relief for Canal Plus, as the Premier League has been the company's main subscriber driver across the region and its only significant property in Norway and Denmark. In Sweden, Canal Plus has also acquired the broadcasting rights for the elite ice hockey league, which is a major asset in the Swedish market.

The European Football Championship for National Teams in 2008 (Euro 2008)

Some weeks after securing the EPL deal, Telenor was involved in a joint purchase of the Scandinavian TV rights for the European Soccer Championship for national teams (Euro 2008) together with (TV 2), Sweden (TV 4) and Denmark (TV 2), which all are commercial PSBs. This deal allows the three broadcasters to air 19 or 20 of the 31 matches, while Telenor's pay-TV platform, Canal Digital will air 11 or 12 matches. In addition, Canal Digital will also air all 31 matches in high definition on its HDTV platform (TV Sports Markets, 2006).

This acquisition split a planned collaboration between all the PSBs of the three respective nations, which also would have included the non-commercial broadcasters such as the NRK, Swedish Television and TV Denmark (Kampanje.com, 2006). Historically, the rights for the World Cup soccer finals, European soccer championships and the Olympic Games have been acquired by PSBs in Scandinavia as a consequence of their membership in the European Broadcasting Union (EBU). This pattern, however, has come to an end for the two football tournaments. EBU has not acquired the World Cup soccer rights since 1998 and the Euro rights since 2000. Some PSBs have nevertheless acquired these rights, either in collaboration with other channels or alone. The Olympic rights are still available for PSBs through the EBU.

These three cases have illustrated how market forces can work when broadcasters and transmission companies form alliances in purchasing sports rights. They also show how unstable such alliances can be. A company which is a partner on one occasion can very well be a rival the next time sports rights are sold. The next section will try to shed some light on different forms of integration and also discuss the advantages and disadvantages related to the alternative categories of integration.

Expansion and Integration

When companies involved in (sports) broadcasting expand their activity, such expansion can take four different directions, as illustrated in Figure 21.1. *Upward expansion* is when a company establishes a closer connection to its

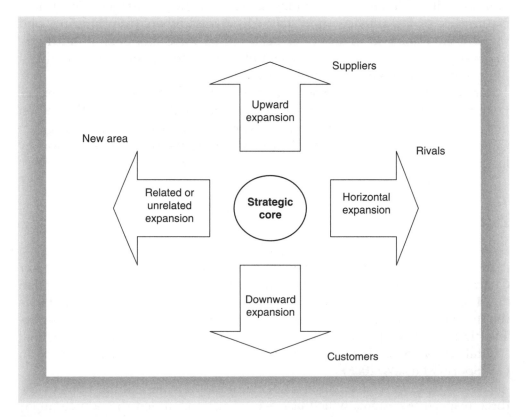

Figure 21.1 Direction of expansion
Adapted from Reve (1990)

supplier(s) of inputs, for example when a transmission company acquires stakes in a TV channel. *Downward expansion* is when a company gets more involved in activities closer to its customers, for instance a TV channel buying stakes in a satellite or cable operator. *Horizontal expansion* is when it establishes closer relationships to its rivals, for instance by merging. *Related* or *unrelated* expansion is when activity is extended into a completely new area.

To understand the consequences of such integration, it can be useful to regard the participants as part of a production process. In this context, TV channels are the producers of sport programming, while clubs, event organizers (and sport governing bodies) are the producers of the contests. Transmission companies, such as terrestrial, satellite and cable operators are the distributors of output (programmes) to viewers. Integration between these actors can create *economies of scale* and *economies of scope* advantages. *Economies of scale advantages* refers to production processes where the costs per unit (average costs) declines with the number of units produced. *Economies of scope advantages* exist when it is cheaper to produce two products together (joint production) than to produce them separately. Average costs decline through the increase in the number of outputs produced using the same input. Integrated firms will have access to complementary resources, for instance the sharing of technical and organizational knowledge.

Why do Broadcasters and Transmission Companies Seek Vertical Integration?

The term *vertical integration* is used about companies that participate in more than one successive stage of the production or distribution of goods or services. The collaborations between Telenor and different broadcasters illustrated in these three cases are examples of vertical integration.

The prospect of *reduced transaction costs* is often regarded to be a major advantage from vertical integration (Williamson, 1979). A firm may choose to perform activities itself rather than rely on the market when transaction costs are likely to be high. Economies of scale advantages can be internalized within the company from combined operations, sharing of activities and maintenance of a stable through put in a long stretch of the value chain. One can also reduce any cost penalties in case the firm is unable to pay in time. Recent history contains many incidents in which broadcasters have had severe problems with paying in time after acquiring TV rights (Solberg, 2006):

- In September 1996, Sport 7 (a pay service channel), acquired a seven-year contract with the Dutch Eresdivisie (the soccer elite division) for a fee of DFL 1.04 billion for nearly all the soccer matches in the Netherlands. Four months later, in December 1996, the channel collapsed, after incurring losses of DFL 100 million.[1]

---

[1]*Source*: Baskerville Communication Corporations (1997). *Global TV-sports rights*, London.

- ITV Digital was unable to fulfil its' £378 million contract with the Nationwide League which was supposed to run from 2001 to 2004, and went bankrupt. The league brought the case to court and demanded the owner of ITV Digital to pay the necessary amount, but lost the case. Later on, BSkyB acquired 'the remaining' part of this deal at a price of £95 million, which represented a large discount, compared to the original price (Solberg, 2006).
- Telepiu and Stream, two Italian pay-TV broadcasters, lost respectively $300 million and $200 million each from broadcasting the Italian Serie A during the 2001/2002 season. Thus, the renewal of the deals before the 2002/2003 Serie A season did not go as smoothly as before. The poorest clubs rejected the new offer from the TV channels and therefore the league was delayed by two weeks. The problems were solved when the six wealthiest clubs paid the difference between the offer from the TV channels and what the poorest clubs demanded. As a consequence of these problems the Italian authorities have later accepted a merger between the two (former) rivals.
- Premiere, Kirch Medias' pay-TV channel, was unable to recruit enough subscribers to make the deal with the German Bundesliga, profitable for the 2001–2004 period. Thus the deal was renegotiated – with the result that its value dropped by 20–25 per cent.

Similar problems have also occurred regularly on the North American markets where TV sport has been a commodity since the 1960s, which is a considerably longer period of time than in Europe. It is well known that CBS (one of the major broadcasting networks) almost went bankrupt in the early 1990s after paying too much for the Major League Baseball (MLB) rights (Fort, 2003). In 2002, News Corporation, a media company partly owned by Rupert Murdoch, took a write-down of $909 million on unprofitable sports rights deals, while National Broadcasting Corporation (NBC) (another broadcasting network) reported losses on their National Basketball Association (NBA) deal estimated at $300 million over two seasons.[2]

Companies which integrate upwards achieve more control of the supply of inputs, while those that integrate downwards will have more control over distribution. Such motives must have been important for Telenor as well as the broadcasters. At the start of the 21st century, all companies involved in broadcasting have invested (or are about to invest) heavily in digital technology. Most of these costs are *sunk costs*, which are independent of whether (and to which degree) any outputs are produced. Making these investments profitable requires popular content, both for the transmission companies and the broadcasters. Transmissions companies with close ties to broadcasters do not only secure deliverance, but can also block rivalling companies from the same suppliers. For instance, Telenor's alliance with

---

[2]*Source*: http://www.gouldmedia.com/tsr.html.

Canal Plus in purchasing the EPL rights may also helped them maintaining an exclusive position as the only distributor of Canal Plus. However, this not only prolonged the deal, but also prevented Canal Plus from forming a deal with Canal Digital's main rival, MTG.

The gain from achieving more upward and downward control depends on the ability to substitute inputs and outputs at the other levels of the value chain. If providers of input have many alternatives, then each and every distributor can benefit from blocking the providers from distributing through the rivals. On the other hand, upward integration may also reduce the ability to tap different suppliers, which can be risky if the commercial values on the input fluctuate. If demand shifts negatively, producers can be left with input that no one wants. Football fans, as anybody else, have limited resources of time and money to spend watching TV. If two rivalling broadcasters offer too much similar content in the same market, the result of such uncoordinated activity can be devastating due to the high degree of sunk costs that characterizes sport broadcasting. In such cases, one cannot reduce the costs by reducing production. Hence, an excess supply of football programmes will reduce revenues per programme and per channel, while costs are unchanged.

The EPL has turned out to be an effective instrument for recruiting subscribers to pay-TV platforms. BSkyB could risk loosing 50 per cent of their subscribers without these rights, according to their own surveys (Solberg, 2002). Surveys among Norwegian TV viewers have uncovered a similar pattern, and documented that those who are interested in football are more willing to pay to watch their favourite sport on TV than fans of other sports (Hammervold and Solberg, 2005). This explains why both Canal Plus and Telenor (Canal Digital) were extremely eager to retain these rights. The consequences could have been dramatic for both companies, had they been acquired by a rivalling platform such as MTG/Viasat. Canal Plus would have lost its most popular content, and hence also risked loosing subscribers to its closest rival. This, in turn, would also affect Canal Digital negatively.

The Tippeliga might be popular enough to replace the EPL as a subscription driver in Norway. It has a total of 182 matches, and a long season (from April to November). However, one of many conditions the Football Association set for selling the rights was that a significant number of matches should be aired on channels with at least 60 per cent penetration. The Football Association also demanded influence in the process of dividing matches between free-to-air channels and pay TV.

TV 2 Zebra's penetration has increased significantly after airing Tippeliga matches. This, in turn, has also increased the rating figures on the channel's other non-sport programmes and hence generated indirect revenues. However, the fee that viewers have to pay to watch TV 2 Zebra is considerably lower than the subscription fee on Canal Plus. Thus, TV 2 Zebra's results are not a precise indicator of the Tippeliga's potential as a subscription driver.

Forms of Vertical Integration

In principle, a firm can expand its activity by any of the following three alternatives:

1 Merger and acquisition
2 Alliances
3 New establishment

Merger and Acquisition

The potential advantages from merger and acquisition will be related to the prospect of achieving synergy effects, for example *economies of scale* and *economies of scope advantages*. Synergy occurs if the interaction between two or more forces results in their combined effect being greater than the sum of their individual effects. In the case of a merger, the synergy effects make the value of a merged company greater than the sum of the value of the two individual companies (Brown, 1995).

The merger/acquisition alternative can also generate *financial synergy* effects by reducing capital costs. Firms of a large size can be offered more favourable terms when applying for funding. Larger firms also have more funding and thus can afford heavier investments. This can turn out as a major advantage due to the extremely expensive fees on the most popular sports rights. In addition, they can also take more risk than smaller firms. Furthermore, a large capital base can also improve the capability of going through a period of deficit. Having this ability may turn out to be important in cases where it is necessary to acquire extremely expensive sports rights. These factors might represent some of the advantages Telenor expected to achieve by acquiring stakes in TV 2 Zebra.

Alliances

Companies involved in sports broadcasting can also enter into alliances, which is a less formal way of integrating than merger/acquisition. Figure 21.2

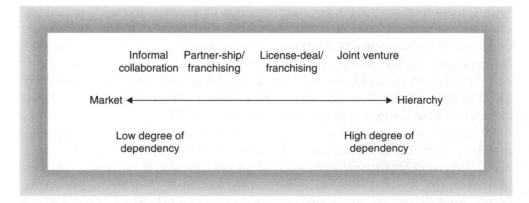

Figure 21.2 Forms of alliances
Source: Haugland (2004)

gives an overview of categories of alliances, and also how the dependency between the actors will vary. In the case of *full vertical integration*, the integrated firm(s) will obtain control over all inputs or the entire supply chain toward the customer. However, there are alternative ways to achieve some of the benefits of integration. In a market situation, the firms are relatively independent of each other. At the same time, the possibilities to control and influence one another are restricted. On the other hand, the dependency will be stronger in a hierarchical situation, where the firms also have better possibilities to control and influence on one another (Meyer, 1998).

Alliances, as presented in the figure, can be an alternative when acquisition is blocked, for example by anti-trust regulations. Competition authorities in general tend to be careful about allowing large companies to merge. Therefore, firms with market power will have to apply to competition authorities before being allowed to merge with one another. The application can be rejected if the competition authority fears that the merged firm will become too powerful. The Telenor/TV2 alliance is powerful in the Norwegian broadcasting market, but since there also are other powerful broadcasters on this market, the competition authorities have accepted the collaboration.

Alliances can provide the companies involved admission to many of the *economies of scale* and *economies of scope advantages*, as well as the other synergy effects. Companies that are part of an alliance can also transfer competence between each other. Furthermore, the integrated firms can also achieve the same tempo advantages as in the case of merger or acquisition. Hence, it is possible to realize the benefits quickly, a fact that was illustrated by the interview with Taalesen, TV2's sport editor above, where he described how TV2 had used football to accelerate the development of web and mobile phone broadcasting, as well as establishing the new sports and entertainment channel TV2 Zebra (Taalesen in Helland, 2006).

Alliances will require lower investment costs than acquisition, and will thus be less risky. Moreover, the firms that form alliances will be more flexible than merged firms, for example if the market conditions change. It will generally be much easier to walk out from an alliance than to resell an acquired firm. This, however, represents a double-edged sword as the allied firms will have less management control over one another. Hence, alliances are less stable than merger and acquisition, as the behaviour of Telenor illustrated on all three occasions.

New Establishment/Internal Expansion

A third way of integrating or expanding is by establishing a new firm (also covering internal expansion). Directly after securing the Norwegian football rights, TV2 and Telenor announced that they would establish a new premium channel distributed through Canal Digital and possibly other platforms. However, after a few months of planning and negotiating between the companies, they decided to cancel the project. The reason for this was the high risk of establishing a premium channel like Canal Plus, which is sold as a separate entity on top of a basic channel package. Many Norwegian football fans were already subscribing to Canal Plus because of the EPL matches. This would make it difficult to recruit enough subscribers to the new premium channel to be economically viable. Instead, TV 2 and Canal Digital decided to broadcast Norwegian football on TV 2's main channel, TV 2 Zebra and on pay-per-view basis through Canal Digital. Indeed, neither of the three sports rights acquisitions investigated in this article initiated any new establishments. All broadcasters preferred to use the football rights to strengthen the market position of their existing channels.

Contrary to the other two alternative forms of expansion, establishing a new broadcaster will increase the competition, which in some cases can lead to excess capacity on the supply side. If TV 2 and Telenor had established a new premium pay-TV broadcaster after acquiring the Norwegian football rights, it is possible that Canal Plus would have lost customers while the new channel would struggle to recruit enough subscribers become economically viable. This could have caused severe financial problems due to the high degree of sunk cost, which is discussed elsewhere in this chapter.

A new broadcaster might have better chances of becoming profitable when the products (which in this case are TV programmes) are in an early stage of their life cycle. The other alternatives, such as merger, acquisition and alliances are more common when the products are mature and have been in the market for some time, and also have their advantages in cases when there are high barriers to entry. As another potential disadvantage, new establishment and internal expansion may also require more funding than an alliance, which is the alternative that requires the least resources.

Companies that expand gradually will have better abilities to prioritize along the way and to influence the situation themselves. Gradual expansion is in itself an advantage in case the market conditions alter or are difficult to predict. Internal expansion also provides an ability to customize products. On the other hand, a disadvantage with gradual development is that it will take more time before the potential advantages can be exploited. One cannot expect to build up a strong market position overnight by a new establishment.

Case Questions

1 What do you understand by horizontal and vertical integration?
2 Give examples of vertical integration from your own nation/market related to:
   (a) Broadcasting
   (b) Non-broadcasting activities
3 Discuss the advantages and disadvantages of vertical integration for companies involved in:
   (a) Broadcasting
   (b) Sport broadcasting
4 Discuss if the cost structure of a company can influence whether it will benefit from vertical integration.
5 Discuss which consequences vertical integration of broadcasters and transmission companies might have for producers of sport competitions (sports clubs, sporting event organizers and sport governing bodies).

Case Resources

Baskerville Communication Corporations (1997). *Global TV-Sports Rights*. Baskerville Communication Ltd, London.

Brown, W.S. (1995). *Principles of Economics*. West Publishing Company, St. Paul, MN.

Collis, D. and Montgomery, C. (1997). *Corporate Strategy: A Resource-Based Approach*. Irwin, Burr Ridge, IL.

Fort, R. (2003). *Sports Economics*. Pearson Education, Prentice Hall, London.

Hammervold, R. and Solberg, H.A. (2006). TV sports programmes – who is willing to pay to watch? *Journal of Media Economics*, Vol. 19, pp. 147–162.

Haugland, S.A. (2004). *Samarbeid, Allianser og nettverk (Cooperation, Alliances and Networks)*, 2nd edition. Norwegian University Press, Oslo.

Helland, K. (2006). Football, sports rights, marketing and journalism. Interview with Bjørn Taalesen, Sports Editor of TV 2, Norway. *International Journal of Sports Marketing and Sponsorship*. Vol. 8, No. 1, pp. 11–15.

Kampanje (2006). NRK og TV 2 i nytt fotballdrama. Retrieved 20 February 2007, from http://www.kampanje.com/medier/article51025.ece

Meyer, C.B. (1998). Strategiske veivalg og motiver for fusjoner og okjøp (strategically choose of direction and motives for mergers and acquisitions), in Boye, K. and Meyer, C.B. (Eds.), *Cappelen, Fusjoner og oppkjøp (Mergers and Acquisitions)*. Akademisk Forlag, Oslo.

Reve, T. (1990). Mimetic behaviour in banking. Working Paper 48, Center for Applied Research, Bergen.

Solberg, H.A. (2002). The economics of television sports rights. Europe and the US – a comparative analysis. *Norsk Medietidskrift (A Norwegian Mediajournal)*, Vol. 10, No. 2, pp. 59–81.

Solberg, H.A. (2006). The auctioning of TV sports rights. *International Journal of Sports Finance*, Vol. 1, pp. 33–45.

Taalesen, Bjørn (2006). *Milliardspillet. Kampen mellom TV 2 og NRK om TV-fotballen – sett fra innsiden*. Damm, Oslo.

TV Sports Markets (2006). *Delicate political game of choosing partners and winning*. Vol. 10, No. 21.

Williamson, O.E. (1979) Transaction-cost economics: The governance of contractual relations. *Journal of Law and Economics*, Vol. 22, No. 2, 233–261.

22

How to use naming rights in the business of sport

Thomas Bezold

Case Focus

The case examines the multifaceted appearance of naming rights with their different functions as a marketing and financing instrument. Additionally it provides an insight into the control of impacts and shows up future risks and chances for this sport marketing tool. Therefore the case study investigates and explains the origin, theoretical marketing framework and the operational area for use of naming rights in sports. It enables the reader to understand the benefits of this marketing – and financing instrument and supplies a substructure for the integration into the corporate communication policy of a company respectively a sports organization.

Keywords
• Naming rights
• Sports sponsoring
• Sport marketing
• Brand management
• Strategic partnership
• Networked communication
• Facility management

Case Summary

This paper explores and describes the applications and benefits of using naming rights at football stadiums and multipurpose indoor arenas. For the namesake naming rights offer a broad range of marketing activities, for the arena operator the selling of the naming right generates an additional source of income. In this context independent research was undertaken to compare the naming right activities and contracted revenues in Germany, Europe and USA on the basis of selected examples of stadiums and indoor arenas. Further it shows the options of naming rights and discusses the main communicative functions to a sponsor and the networking possibilities. Finally some light is shed to the critical point of the advertising effectiveness of this sponsorship tool and the problems that might rise with fan protests and resistance by changing a traditional name of an arena to a commercial one.

Case Elements

Introduction

The allocation of naming rights in the sports sector has experienced a real boom in the last few years. While in the past sports facilities were traditionally named after regions, districts, rivers or merited individuals, today naming by a sponsor represents a business-oriented alternative. Particularly the naming of football stadiums and large multipurpose arenas by sponsor companies against the background of new developments or conversions of German stadiums and declining public sponsorship of sport sites has led to a heightened allocation of naming rights. While an additional source of finance is made available for the proprietor or operating company of a sports facility in the first place with the, mostly temporary, sale of naming rights, the use of the naming rights for the naming sponsor is a promising instrument within their communication and marketing activities. Here the biggest communicative use for a sponsor in a cleverly built-in integration of the naming rights is in a networked, strategically aligned business communication (cf. Bezold, 2005).

This article highlights the legal problem with the sale and transfer of naming rights according to an international scheme on the historical and financial development of naming rights. The various types of naming rights with the different roles as a financial and marketing instrument as well as the designs to control the effect of advertising form the emphasis of the article, which will be rounded off by notes on the risks and prospects of naming rights.

Origins of the Allocation of Naming Rights

Like many other trends in the commercialization of sport the allocation of naming rights has its historic roots in the USA for (cf. Friedmann et al., 1999). Since in America the naming of halls of residences, libraries or charitable establishments, for instance, through privately motivated, magnanimous contributions and financings is basically accepted without question, the commercial allocation of naming rights also began there much earlier than in Germany or Europe. The metaphoric starter's gun fired with the opening of Disneyland on 17 July 1955 in Anaheim, California, by the Walt Disney Company. In the sphere of multipurpose arenas, the Key Arena in Seattle became the first large arena to market the naming right for $0.75 million/year with a validity period of 15 years in 1962. Meanwhile in America the naming of sports facilities by a sponsor company was a part of the standard repertoire of sports facility marketing. It should be pointed out that in North America, contracts are valid for between 15 and 30 years on average and therefore it can be called a 'strategic communication (state) decision', which is connected to long-term financial obligations. Table 22.1 summarizes current, selected naming rights deals in America. First in 2001, the renaming of the time-honoured Volksparkstadion in Hamburg to AOL-Arena stirred up the industry and public interest in Germany. Meanwhile, many arenas and stadiums have changed names, which will be discussed below. Across Europe the recently publicized deal between the airline company Emirates and the Arsenal football club in London has caused a sensation. For €6.9 million/year with a validity period of 15 years, from the start of the 2006/2007 season the Gunners new home, having left Highbury, will be sporting the name of the Arabic airline company (cf. Horizont Sport Business Daily News from 1 December 2004).

According to newest findings of Europe's leading sport marketing research company Sport&Markt there are approximately 120 commercial naming rights in Europe with a total revenue of €75 million per year. Hereby the three top branches using naming rights are the automobile industry, energy providers and financial services (cf. Sport&Markt 2007, pp. 8–12).

Generally spoken football dominates the scene, most of the naming right deals are connected with football arenas. In this sport the average income developed from €11.5 million in season 2004/2005 over €32.6 million in 2005/2006 up to €39.6 million in season 2006/2007. Observing European football season 2006/2007 in the German first league 'Bundesliga' naming right deals are most developed regarding to the number of naming right deals and the generated revenues, as you can see in Figure 22.1.

Table 22.1 Topic naming rights deals in America (independent research)

Stadium name	Sponsor	Home teams	Average $/Year	Expires
Reliant Stadium	Reliant Energy	Houston Texans	$10 million	2032
Phillips Arena	Royal Phillips Electronics	Atlanta Hawks, Thrashers	$9.3 million	2019
Gillette Stadium	Gillette	New England Patriots	$8 million	2017
FedEx Field	Federal Express	Washington Red skins	$ 7.6 million	2025
Bank of America Stadium	Bank of America	Carolina Panthers	$7 million	2024
Linco In Financial Field	Linco In Financial Group	Philadelphia Eagles	$6.7 million	2022
American Airlines Center	American Airlines	Dallas Mavericks, Stars	$6.5 million	2031
Minute Maid Park	Coca-Cola	Houston Astros	$6 million	2030
Invesco Field at Mile High	Invesco Funds	Denver Broncos	$6 million	2021
Staples Center	Staples	Los Angeles Lakers, Kings, Clippers, Sparks	$5.8 million	2019
FedEx Forum	Federal Express	Memphis Grizzlies	$4.5 million	2023
M & T Bank Stadium	M & T Bank	Baltimore Ravens	$5 million	2018

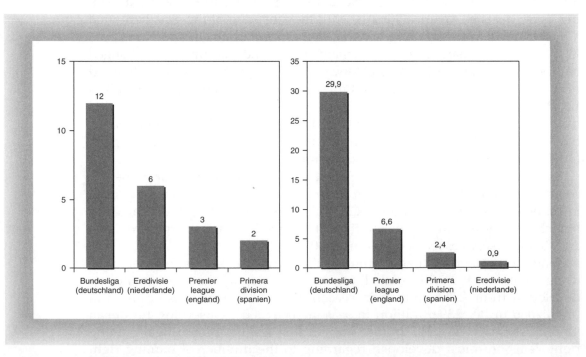

Figure 22.1 Number of naming right deals and generated revenues in million € per year of selected European Football Leagues
Source: Sport & Markt, 2007, pp. 8–12

Options and Roles of Allocating Names

Essentially anyone who holds a right, regardless of whether they are a proprietor, leaseholder, promoter or organizer, is free to allocate a commercial naming right for their stadium, event, tournament or league. In reality however, through frequency of use, the following forms have become accepted, namely the option to market the name of:

- Arenas and stadiums
- Teams (cycling/motor sports)
- Events (golf/tennis)
- Clubs (basketball)
- Series (alpine ski World Cup)
- Leagues (football, basketball)
- Track sections (motor racing).

Below the two main roles of naming rights will be discussed in detail, which are connected to the sale or use of the naming right. The temporary sale of the naming right particularly represents an additional financial instrument for the namesake, while for the naming sponsor it is a tool for their communication and marketing measures.

Naming Rights As a Financial Instrument

For proprietors of arenas and stadiums, for promoters of sporting events in organizational or commercial sponsorship, for clubs or teams, with the mostly temporary sale of the name, the opening up of financial means is top priority (cf. Petry, 2002). However, this does not inevitably have to be the only reason. At best, a long-term naming rights deal also opens up strategic partnerships, which provides desired access to resources on the procurement market or in distribution, if the products or services are important for the naming right sale or to the target groups approached. Examples of this would be financial services or drinks suppliers, which if applicable, involve favourable logistical conditions or purchasing conditions for the arena operator.

To clarify the current naming right situation in Germany, the football stadiums or large multipurpose arenas should ideally be referred back to as a benchmark.

In the first German football league 'Bundesliga' 12 out of 18 of the stadiums are allocated a commercial naming right, as can be seen in the summary in Table 22.2.

Here, the level of income lies between €0.6 million and €6.12 million per annum

In the case of the Allianz Arena, according to information from the Vice President of FC Bayern, Bernd Rauch, about 30–35 per cent of the estimated €330–340 million building costs could be generated through an cumulated income of approximately €92 million. In this context it is interesting to ascertain that only 10 per cent of the financial costs are to be covered by the traditional sales of entry tickets (ticketing) (cf. Kürbs, 2004, p. 14). The majority of

Table 22.2 Naming rights of stadiums in the German Bundesliga, season 2005/2006 (independent research)

Name of stadium	Naming right	Duration/Years	Sum per annum/Total in €	Property	Main user
Allianz-Arena	Allianz AG	2005–2020/15 years	6.12 Mio./92 Mio.	Ownership by 2 clubs	Bayern (1860)
AOL-Arena	AOL	2001–2006/5 years	3 Mio./15 Mio.	HSV Stadium Group	Hamburger SV
AWD-Arena	AWD AG	2002–2010/8 years	2 Mio./16 Mio.	Municipal ownership	Hannover 96
BayArena	Bayer AG	Since 1997–unlimited	3 Mio.	Bayer AG	Bayer 04 Leverkusen
easyCredit-Stadion	Norisbank AG	2006–2011/5 years	1.2 million/6.0 million	Municipal ownership	1. FC Nürnberg
Commerzbank-Arena	Commerzbank AG	2005–2015/10 years	3 Mio./30 Mio.	Municipal ownership	Eintracht Frankfurt
Gottlieb-Daimler Stadion	Daimler Chrysler AG	since 1993–unlimited	one-time 5.5 Mio.	Municipal ownership	VfB Stuttgart
RheinEnergie Stadion	RheinEnergie AG	2002–2009/7 years	2.1 Mio./14.7 Mio.	Municipal ownership	1. FC Köln
Schüco Arena	Schüco	2004–2007/3 years	0.65 Mio./1.95 Mio	Ownership by club	Arminia Bielefeld
SIGNAL-IDUNA-Park	Signal-Iduna	2005–2011/5 years	4 Mio./20 Mio.	Ownership by club	Borussia Dortmund
VELTINS-Arena	Veltins Brauerei	2005–2015/10 years	3 Mio./30 Mio.	FC Schalke 04	Schalke 04
Volkswagen Arena	Volkswagen AG	since 2002–unlimited	2 Mio.	Volkswagen AG	VfL Wolfsburg
Borussia-Park	none			Ownership by club	Mönchengladbach
Fritz-Walter Stadion	none			Ownership by club	1. FC Kaiserslautern
MSV-Arena	none			Ownership by club	MSV Duisburg
Olympiastadion	none			Municipal ownership	Hertha BSC Berlin
Stadion am Bruchweg	none			Ownership by club	FSV Mainz 05
Weserstadion	none			Municipal ownership	Werder Bremen

contracts are valid for approximately five years, which is especially attributed to German companies' lack of experience with this advertising tool and therefore the accompanying cautious treatment. cp.: in the USA, contracts are usually valid for 15–30 years.

In the second Bundesliga, a clear reduction in the amount paid is to be noted on the one hand and on the other hand, only 8 out of 18 stadiums use a naming right for commercial purposes. Here the sum ranges from €0.4 million to €0.9 million per annum.

With multipurpose indoor arenas, which are characterized by a wide range of sports, culture and entertainment, the revenues achieved fall between €20,000 and €2 million per annum, whereby contracts tend to be have a medium-term validity of up to 10 years (cf. Table 22.3).

In this context, it must be pointed out that some stadiums and arenas consciously do not sell the naming right and instead prefer the strategic design of a private brand. In this way, the name, as in the case of the Kölnarena substantially contributes to the brand recognition and brand positioning within the relevant event market.

Independent of whether in a community or private sector sponsorship, most of the arenas named after the city or region (e.g. Westfalenhalle Dortmund or Kölnarena) take on an important role within the city marketing for the respective community. The medial equivalent through the multiplicative name reference here leads to competitive numbers of contacts and positive image values.

Naming Rights As a Marketing Instrument

Various possibilities within the communication and marketing activities for companies, which first of all enquire about purchasing the naming right, open up with the conclusion of a naming right deal. Sponsors benefit from being able to integrate five areas, which are shown in Figure 22.2.

Alongside the traditional advertising objectives such as increasing the level of recognition and image design, a naming right particularly serves as a suitable platform to combine sport with the company-specific associations.

The assumed high costs for the temporary acquisition of the naming right and the additional costs to implement and use the other tools of the communication policies are accordingly seen alongside numbers of contacts through the medial and multiplicative reproduction of the name as well as various options to combine other marketing measures.

Forming Contacts and Coverage
The great advantage of the 'naming right' tool, in comparison to other sponsoring measures such as perimeter advertising or shirt advertising, lies in the various multiplier effects of this form of advertising. Because by

Table 22.3 Selected examples of naming rights of indoor arenas, season 2005/2006 (independent research)

Indoor-Arenas	Naming right	Duration/years	Sum per annum/ Total in €	Sports
Color Line Arena Hamburg	Color Line	2001–2011/10 years	1 Mio./10 Mio.	Hockey, Handball
TUI Arena Hannover	TUI AG	2004–2009/5 years	1 Mio./5 Mio.	Hockey, Handball
AWD Dome Bremen	AWD AG	2005–2010/5 years	650,000/3.25 Mio.	Basketball
AWD-Hall Hannover	AWD AG	2005–2009/5 years	0.2 Mio./1 Mio.	Boxing, Handball
König Pilsener Arena Oberhausen	König-Brauerei	2002–2012/10 years	0.5 Mio./5 Mio.	Handball
KönigPALAST Krefeld	König-Brauerei	2004–2014/10 years	N/A	Hockey
SAP Arena Mannheim	SAP AG	2005–2015/10 years	Investment costs	Hockey, Handball
Volkswagenhalle Braunschweig	VW AG	2000–2020/20 years	Investment costs	Basketball
Scania Arena Duisburg	Scania	2004–2007/3 years	0.5 Mio.	Hockey
Saturn-Arena Ingolstadt	Saturn	2003-N/A	N/A	Hockey
erdgas arena Riesa	erdgas AG	2002–2012/10 years	N/A	Sporting events
GEW EnergyDome Köln	GEW	2001-N/A	2 Mio.	Am. Football
Hacker-Pschorr Arena Bad Tölz	Hacker Pschorr	2003–2013/10 years	N/A	Hockey
KNORR Arena Heilbronn	KNORR	2002–2007/5 years	0.05 Mio./0.25 Mio.	Hockey
s. Oliver Arena Würzburg	s. Oliver	2004–2009/5 years	0.05 Mio./0.25 Mio.	Basketball
Porsche-Arena Stuttgart	Porsche AG	2006–2026/20 years	0.5 Mio./10 Mio.	Tennis, Handball, Basketball, Hockey

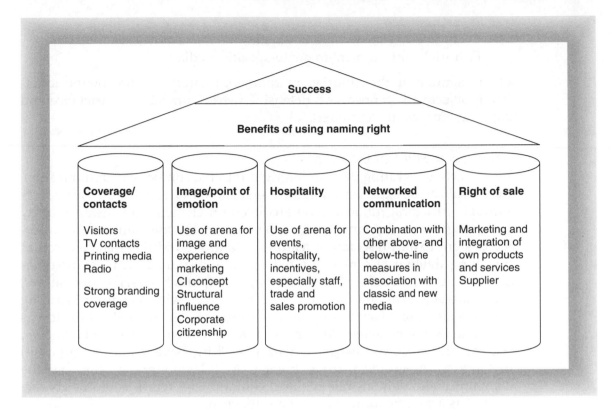

Figure 22.2 Benefits for the namesake

using the naming right, diverse contacts are made through the different media:

- *TV*
  - Mentions the name in editorial reports
  - Visibility/showing the name
- *Print*
  - Printing the name in preliminary and secondary reports in the editorial environment of daily newspapers, trade publications or specialist magazines
- *Radio*
  - Mentions within preliminary, live and secondary reports
- *Internet*
  - Use of the club or sponsor website
  - Use of info services or sports portals
- *Outdoor advertising*
  - Signs, maps, lighting
- *Stadium*
  - Tickets, spectators, signs, flags, CI concept
- *Special forms of advertising*
  - Flyers, event advertising, posters, flags

- *Editorial mentions*
  - Event information in different media
  - Editorial reinforcement in genre-specific media.

Often mentions in the editorial environment is effected, whereby the advertising objective is refined and defensive behaviours such as reactance and zapping are virtually excluded.

Arena As a 'Point of Emotion'

By cleverly integrating the naming right into the company communication, the brand can be experienced in the arena and its surroundings. This occurs through structural influences on architectural elements for instance or by designing the stadium in a colour scheme to match the namesake's corporate design. Extra presentation features in and around the arena as well as matching lighting also reinforce the brand appearance. At most, it comes down to image transfer effects with popular sports between sports shows, arena management and the namesake. Moreover, with the current naming rights deals, sports facilities significantly prefer to list in which of the towns associated with the namesake they want to have their site (AWD-Hannover, Allianz-München, Volkswagen, Arena-Wolfsburg, Bayer Arena-Leverkusen) or have an important overseas branch (AOL-Hamburg). In this way, the companies also demonstrate regional commitment, which could be characterized as a specific form of corporate citizenship.

Hospitality

With the transfer of the name, many sponsors reserve relevant ticket deals, business seats and VIP lounges at the same time. This way further hospitality possibilities open up for customer acquisition and care. Various measures to manage customer relations can be transferred and used here. Ticket quotas and VIP boxes can also be used accordingly for internal marketing and for staff and trade promotions.

Sales Rights

With many stadium projects, it is possible for the named sponsor to assure brand exclusivity within the naming right contract. In addition, a relevant suppliers right for certain products and/or services can also be agreed, whereby the sponsor acquires the option to demonstrate the capability and quality of the product. Furthermore, football sales promotions and incentives would think of affine in-house and external target groups, for whom the experience world of a stadium is particularly well suited.

Networked Communication

A named sponsor provides the greatest use by cleverly networking the naming right into the various other features of the communication policy (cf. Lohrer, 2001). Here not just other sponsoring measures such as perimeter advertising,

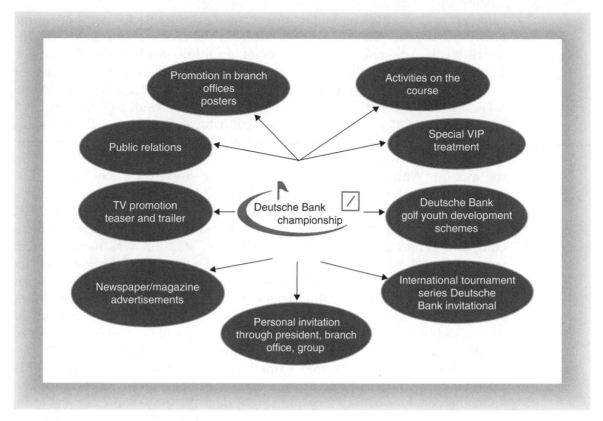

Figure 22.3 Networking possibilities

loudspeaker announcements or hospitality features should be considered, but also networking with the classic media advertising (TV spots, printing, radio) should take place. Using the example of the Deutsche Bank Championship golf tournament, Figure 22.3 outlines with the example of the 'Deutsche Bank Championship'– golf tournament how one such integrated network of the naming right can be implemented.

Internal and external marketing processes or lotteries can also be merged with the naming right. This advertising tool only becomes fully effective by incorporating and integrating the naming right in a textual–conceptual manner into other campaigns.

Advertising Effectiveness of Naming Rights: Some Empirical Findings

Since the metaphoric starter's gun fired in 2001 with the AOL-Arena and also taking into account the few experiences with this advertising tool, the advertising effectiveness study of naming rights in Germany is still in its infancy. Basically the same instruments can draw on the classic advertising effectiveness study and be adapted to the 'naming right' application field. Recording recall values in the supported or unsupported form or calculating thousands of contact prices are also suitable for naming rights. However, the fact that the medial effect on the naming cumulates on different levels is therefore always to be taken into consideration. The classic advertising value analysis appears to be particularly suitable, the use of which makes it possible to include the individual media categories in the total sum the advertising value. Through this, the result can also be used to assess to what extent the costs of acquiring the naming right are justified. On the other hand, this method can also determine a price for new naming rights. Very limited empirical data is published and available on the market. Within an independent telephone study conducted in the UK and USA by Performance research (from http:// www.performanceresearch.com/naming-rights.htm) less than one-fourth (23 per cent) of UK respondents were able to correctly recall sports stadiums named after a company, brand or product. Bolton's Reebok stadium was recalled most frequently (54 per cent), followed by Huddersfield's McAlpine stadium (48 per cent). Another interesting question was, if sponsors benefit from stadium naming? One-fourth (25 per cent) of fans in the UK indicated that stadium sponsorship 'Has, or would increase purchase consideration' of that brand or product. Moreover, roughly one-half of fans reported a 'More positive' opinion of a company sponsoring a sports stadium, and 25 per cent reported a sports stadium named after a sponsoring company holds positive connotations, implying the team must be good. However, before sponsors consider to sign a naming right deal there are some aspects to be cautious. Despite nearly one-half (47 per cent) of UK respondents reporting they were 'Very' or 'Moderately' in favour of a new sports arena named after a corporate sponsor, fewer than one-third of UK fans indicated they would be 'Very' or 'Moderately' in favour of changing the name of an existing stadium. Moreover, one in five UK sports fans reported just because a company was a sponsor did not make it right for them to change the name of the stadium, and unlike fans in the USA the majority (88 per cent) of fans in the UK reported stadium naming would be of no benefit to them, indicating that stadium sponsorship was unlikely to result in lower ticket prices.

According to Mark Knight, Project Manager, Performance Research Europe, a company which undertakes sponsorship naming of a stadium without considering the needs of the club or fans is guilty of 'brandalism' of the worse kind and is only going to harm their brand image. A stadium can be a national icon or community focal point, an unnecessary name change may be seen as little more than a cold-hearted attempt to buy their way into a sport they ultimately don't understand.

Generally fans in Germany have a very pragmatic understanding of accepting new sponsoring tools like naming rights as an additional source of income for the football club. But it could be observed a greater level of resistance in the case of Bundesliga club 1. FC Nuremberg, when fans were against the rename of the beloved 'Frankenstadion', what 'used to be' a local icon and regional identification factor, into 'easy credit-Stadion' of a private bank. At a more ideological level, fan representatives complained that the deal was nothing else than a last step into the 'total commercialisation' and the loss of club and fan identity. The management of the club stated that all relevant supporters club were involved in and agreed with the deal and the opposition was only pushed by the local media, who made a negative story out of it. However, fans aspects should be taken seriously (see Chadwick, 2005). On the other hand people have to see, that fans always want to have and see the best competitive team playing for their club. That pressure forces club management to explore new resources of incomes like naming rights is one. In this greater context the often very emotional and sometimes very polemic discussion of football fans has to be seen as well.

Conclusion

The future market is limited for attractive naming rights in the area of arenas and stadiums because only a limited number of sports sites are suitable in the current types of sport. It is the same with large indoor arenas, because even here there are saturation tendencies on the market for cultural or musical events. However, in the future, it will also be attractive for smaller arenas or sports facilities to use this tool because extra income can be generated through the temporary allocation of naming rights, where – apart from marketing efforts – no important costs are faced. Furthermore, a naming right contract can form the basis of a strategic partnership, which can involve further synergy effects in procurement, logistics and sales distribution for both partners. A high demand for coordination could have a negative effect through a granted industry or product exclusivity and, connected to this, an industry exclusion of potential advertising partners. For enquirers of naming rights, this advertising tool enables highly connected coverage and offers various networking possibilities within the integrated communication. Particular attention is to be placed on the form of contract in order to avoid problematic areas from the first such as advertising freedom for certain events, industry exclusivity, pre-emption rights, supplier rights or aspects of arena management. Particularly in Germany, due to lack of experience with naming rights and cautious treatment, contracts are agreed with rather shorter periods of validity from approximately five years on average. If the contract is not extended, then a new named sponsor must be found. With re-labelling however, serious delaying is necessary, which at worst prevent a new named sponsor from being found and require when concluding the contract a sensitive treatment of the problem. Here renaming should ideally be combined with structural renovations or a re-opening in order to clearly signalize to the public the beginning of a 'new era.' Also PR measures and accompanying information activities should be used in the phase. New names are essentially unproblematic. With re-naming, the 'old' namesake can possibly even benefit from the reverberation effect, known from consumer research. A crucial point for all participants is to secure a successful arena (marketing) management and a more technically oriented professional facility management (cf. Siebold, 2001). So that the named sponsor experiences the desired positive effects, the different main and secondary users must also ensure positive headlines. Yet this cannot be directly guaranteed in the long term in the domain of sport. In this respect, even the communicative success of a naming right is ultimately dependent on the sporting (and financial) success of the main user. Diverse marketing of an arena can lessen this dependency but never quite remove it. Operationally, a professional facility management should at all times guarantee the outer appearance, functionality, hygiene, catering, maintenance and repair as well as visitor safety. Here all necessary regulations, duties and competences should already have been contractually established very early.

Case Diagnosis

How popular is the use of naming rights for stadiums and sports arenas? What are the purposes for companies of purchasing naming rights and where does this trend have its origins? This topic is worth exploring because it is getting more and more important in the world of professional sport marketers. Once introduced in the USA in the 1960s where naming right contracts belong meanwhile to the standard tools of arena marketing and widely accepted by the public, is it spilled over to Europe since a couple of years, starting with the AOL-Arena in Hamburg or the Phillips Arena in Eindhoven at the beginning of the decade. The still existing differences in this case between Europe and USA can be imagined by a quick view of the allocation and contracts of naming rights. There are two main roles discussed in this paper which point out the growing importance of naming rights such as a financial instrument for the arena operators as well as a marketing and sponsoring tool for the namesake.

It can roughly be accounted that there are five pillars that build the success of naming rights: creation of advertising contacts/media coverage, image promotion, hospitality activities, networked communication possibilities and the combined selling of supplier and sales rights. How a naming right deal can be integrated into a corporate communication policy, is illustrated by the use of networking possibilities of the 'Deutsche Bank Championship' golf tournament. But how can advertising effectiveness be measured and how are the rights calculated? This field of study still is in its infancy, but the classic advertising value analysis is to be considered as a suitable method. What can be said about the risks and prospects of naming rights? It is obvious that the market of naming sports stadiums and multipurpose arenas is limited, mostly to the hosts of division one or two team sport clubs with a frequent use supported by a huge media coverage. If one accepts smaller contract sums, there are also minor sports facilities and conference halls which can be used for this kind of advertising tool. All in all naming right deals on the one hand offer a wide range of marketing activities for the namesake and on the other hand an additional source of income for the stadium or indoor arena operator. Special attention must be given to the sensitive subject of contracts and the point of supporters' protests against naming or renaming 'their' arena, which may rise when the public and fan audience are not prepared and professionally informed before about the naming right deal is launched. Such an incident might harm the public and supporters' acceptance of naming right contracts and therefore it should be treated very carefully.

Case Questions

1 Where and when can the origins of naming rights be found?
2 Which fields of sport can be used to the implementation of naming rights?
3 What are the benefits of naming rights as a marketing instrument?
4 Specify how contacts and coverage can be reached with this tool?
5 Which problems can occur by selling the naming right of an arena or stadium?
6 What financial chances arise from using commercial naming rights?
7 Give an example for the use of a naming right in a networked communication of a company!
8 Can commercial naming rights 'destroy' the soul and the identification of supporters?

Case Resources

Bezold, T. (2005). Namingrights als Finanzierungs – und Marketinginstrument, in Horch, H.-D., Hovemann, G., Kaiser, S. and Viebahn, K. (Hrsg.), Perspektiven des Sportmarketing. Besonderheiten, Herausforderungen, Tendenzen. Köln 2005, pp. 17–28.

Bezold, T. (2006a). Naming rights as a sport marketing instrument.*Sport Marketing Europe*, Issue 1, April 2006, pp. 14–19.

Bezold, T. (2006b). What is so special about the marketing of marathon events? *Sport Marketing Europe*, Issue 2, Autumn 2006, pp. 14–19.

Chadwick, S. (2005). Addressing English football's stadium naming rights dilemma: Towards a model of good practice, in Collins, M.F. (Ed.), *Book of Abstracts of the 13th EASM European Sport Management Congress in Partnership with 75th Institute of Sport an Recreation Management Annual Conference The Power of Sport*, September 7–10 2005, Newcastle/Gateshead.

Friedmann, A. (u.a.) (1999). *Naming Right Deals – Professional Sport Facilities*. Independent Publishers Group Chicago, Chicago.

Horizont Sport Business (2004). Daily Online-News from 1 December, 2004.

Klewenhagen, M. and Hohenauer, R. (2006). Schwierige Preisfindung für Namensgebung. *Sponsors*, Vol. 11 No. 1, pp. 38–39.

Kürbs, U. (2004). Allianz Arena – 2800 leuchtende Luftkissen. *Sponsors*, Vol, 13, No. 11, pp. 14–15.

Lohrer, I. (2001). Vernetzung. *Sponsors* Vol. 6, No. 10, pp. 68–69.

Performance Research: Naming rights, Naming wrongs, from http://www.performanceresearch.com/naming-rights.htm

Petry, K. (2002). Arenasponsoring, Trosien, G. and Dinkel, M. (Eds.), *Sport und neue Märkte 2002*, pp. 120–127.

Siebold, M. (2001). Managementverträge. *Sponsors*, Vol. 6, No. 9, pp. 42–43.

Sport&Markt (2007). Naming rights und Stadionplanung. Vortrag von Stephan Schröder auf dem ISPO-Sportsponsoringkongress am 5.2.2007 in München.

Wichert, J. and Leda, L. (2001). Namensrecht an Stadien und Arenen. *Sponsors*, Vol. 6, No. 3, pp. 54–55.

Further Information

For any further information or questions please contact the author:

Prof. Dr Thomas Bezold, Professor of Sport Management, Heilbronn University at the Reinhold Wuerth University in Künzelsau, Germany
Business address: Daimlerstr. 35, GER-74653 Künzelsau, Telephone ++49 7940-1306251 email: bezold@hs-heilbronn.de. Website: http://www.hs-heilbronn.de/Members/bezold

23

If the shoe fits: a marketing analysis of the Starbury One basketball shoe

David Stotlar and Cheri Bradish

Case Focus

The focus of the case in on marketing and distribution of the Starbury One basketball shoe. The case examines the traditional elements of marketing and product launch which, in this case were very controversial. A price one-tenth that of competitors, little traditional media advertising, and the personal involvement of an athlete endorser in all aspects of product design, development and sales.

Keywords
• Stephon Marbury • National Basketball Association • Athletic shoes • Pricing.

Case Summary

The Starbury One basketball shoe was introduced in the US market in late 2006 at a price of $14.95 US to a market where similar products ranged in price from $100 to $200 US. The uniqueness of this case is that all elements of the marketing mix were seen as revolutionary. The product was touted to be of the same quality of its competitors. The price shocked the sportswear industry and distribution was limited to one, semi-national discount sporting goods chain. Finally, promotional activities were grassroots tours and word of mouth in nature, avoiding high profile electronic and print media sources. The case allows to the exploration and analysis of alternative marketing strategies in a global product category.

Case Elements

The National Basketball Association (NBA) with 30 teams in the USA and Canada has established itself as a global sport business. NBA games and related programming are broadcast to 214 countries in 43 languages with more than 12,000 hours of programming. The league has more than 80 international players from 35 different countries and territories and the trend is growing at 30 per cent per year. To further illustrate the power of NBA basketball, 8 out of 10 international teens could recognize the NBA logo.

Based on this international popularity, the sales of basketball shoes have increased in US and international markets such that the market for athletic shoes has reached $8 billion US. The market has been driven primarily by the growth of the basketball culture and the marketing of highly paid star endorsers. The result in the market place has been an array of expensive, high tech shoes priced between $100 and $200 US. Consumers are continually looking at the market to see the latest model endorsed by star players. Typically these models have been introduced by the industry's leading companies. For example, 2006 top releases from the largest manufacturers were as follows: Nike Air Jordan XXI ($175), Adidas T-Mac 6 ($130), Nike Zoom Kobe I ($130), Reebok Answer IX ($125), adidas KG Bounce ($120), and Nike Zoom LeBron III ($110) (Boeck, 2006).

Against this backdrop, in August of 2006, the discount sporting goods apparel company Steve and Barry's University Sportswear introduced a basketball shoe endorsed by NBA New York Knicks star Stephon Marbury retailing at just under $15 US. All reports were that the shoe would be of comparable quality to $100 US dollar shoes offered by the leading shoe companies. In addition, Marbury would actually wear these 'off-the-shelf' shoes in NBA competition.

Marbury grew up in a disadvantaged part of New York City as one of seven children and saw many families struggling financially with children wanting to fit in with the other kids who were wearing expensive basketball shoes from the leading manufacturers. Through this experience Marbury saw families who had to make decision on buying food or basketball shoes. It created a lot of stress between kids and their parents. Marbury said 'I understand how kids feel when they walk into a store and see a pair of shoes and aren't able to get them'. Because of this childhood, Marbury brings an authenticity to the urban market like few other players could bring.

The concept was reportedly born from a meeting between executives from Steve and Barry's University Sportswear, a national discount sports retailer in the USA, and Marbury's off-the-court marketing representatives. Marbury had told his agents that he wanted to have ownership of his brand and 'make shoes and athletic gear that were both cool and affordable' (Abel, 2006, p. 3). After the concept began to develop, the next meeting included all of the management team and Marbury. He said he wanted to 'change the world'. Given the history of Steve and Barry's (see below) it seemed like a good match. From these meetings in late 2005, an aggressive timeline was set to bring the concept into production by mid-2006.

From this point forward the case elements will be presented through traditional marketing framework of product, price, place and promotion. Additional information on marketing strategy will be introduced as well.

Product

According to Marbury, 'the shoe is the exact same shoe that people are paying $200 for. It's the same quality. You cut my shoe down the middle, cut the $200 shoe down the middle; you'll see the exact same thing' (Boeck, 2006).

Many would argue that a comparable product cannot be produced and sold at one-tenth the price of other products. Talalay (2006) questioned the notion that the Starbury One shoe was the identical quality when compared to more expensive shoes. To test the claim, she had the shoes evaluated by an orthopaedic surgeon and a doctor of podiatry. Both of these physicians evaluated the shoe and found that it was too flexible through the arch. However, one noted that 'I'm not saying it's a bad shoe. For the average player, it's probably one of the best; it's stylish and sensibly priced'. The other physician noted that it would be a better shoe for big players, who don't need as much lateral stability as other players.

From the design point, one of the leading shoe design firms, Rocketfish Design Studio, was used to create the product look. Rocketfish had previous shoe design experience with Nike, Reebok and Converse. Co-founders of Rocketfish, TJ Gray and Ashley Brown, said the Starbury One 'is constructed the same way as the other high performance basketball sneakers'. The original introduction of the shoe came in five different colours, but just one style.

Low priced – low tech products in the athletic market are not new. The Converse 'Chuck Taylor All Star' has been around since the 1930s. Taylor played professional basketball in the 1920s and persuaded Converse to produce shoes, especially for basketball in 1931. The shoes were worn by the 1936 US Olympic basketball team and players on various Olympic teams though the next seven decades. Although once a staple of Olympic and NBA players, the canvas and low tech shoe lost its leadership position in the serious performance shoe category in the early 1970s. Although the Converse brand, now Nike-owned, experienced a resurgence in popularity in the 1990s, it still has a cult following today. However, serious athletes would never consider wearing the shoe in competition. Nike has also introduced low priced shoes through its 'Starter Pro Line' brand at Wal-Mart discount stores. Although not sold as signature models, US football player Brett Farvre has appeared in advertising for the line of shoes that typically retail at around $40 US.

NBA icon Shaquille O'Neal also introduced a discount line of Shaq and Dunkman basketball shoes that retail for around the same $40 US price point at several US discount chains. The major drawback has been that these shoes had little of the technology that went into more expensive shoes and were reportedly much heavier than true competition shoes. O'Neal also signed an endorsement deal with Chinese shoe company LI-NING for an endorsed line of shoes (LI-NING-SHAQ) and apparel released in January 2007. Sales of these products in the USA have been only marginally successful and the impact of the LI-NING arrangement was yet to emerge. Thus, previously introduced low price models were never intended to worn in real competition. The Starbury One was actually worn by Stephon Marbury during the NBA season.

Price

Setting the sports footwear industry in a spin, Steve and Barry's introduced the Starbury One basketball shoe at $14.98 US. As noted above, other models from leading manufacturers were priced at between $100 and $175 US. A key element in the pricing structure for these models is compensation for the product endorser. Endorsement earnings for NBA players reach multi-million dollar levels. LeBron James' contract with Nike pays him a reported $90 million over seven years and Kobe Bryant's contract pays him $45 million over five years (Boeck, 2006). Clearly these costs must be recovered by the manufacturer, adding significantly to the price for the consumer.

Industry experts have estimated that market channel mark-ups often add 200 per cent to the cost of production at each level (White, 2006).

Unlike other NBA stars, Marbury did not sign an endorsement deal based on upfront royalties and licensing fees, but instead opted to make his profits exclusively from sales. With the endorsement structure established by Marbury and their direct-from-manufacturer supply, Steve and Barry's was able to offer the Starbury One at their market-shocking price of $14.98 US. Co-owner of Steve and Barry's Barry Prevor noted 'We seemed to have struck a nerve. People were angry about the price they had to pay for basketball shoes' (Weilheimer, 2006). In fact, Marbury noted at one promotional event, that a parent came up to him with tears in her eyes thanking him for introducing the product line.

Place

Steve and Barry's University Sportswear was conceived by childhood friends and college classmates, Steve Shore and Barry Prevor. As college students, they had limited funds but still desired college-logoed merchandise. Because, in part of the licensing and sports apparel boom that hit the USA in the 1980s, the cost of the licenced logo goods sold at retailers was out of the reach. So they sourced private label clothing and opened a store near the University of Pennsylvania campus in 1985. News of their idea quickly spread around campus and their store soon became a very popular destination for University of Pennsylvania students and friends (Birchall, 2006).

Based on their success at the University of Pennsylvania, Steve and Barry's expanded with retail outlets across the USA including major University cities and other large metropolitan centres (www.steveandbarrys.com). The concept of quality sports apparel at a discounted price resulted in customers driving great distances, to 'load-up' on high value items that could not be purchased in their home town. Steve and Barry's quickly gained a reputation as a discount sports retailer with good quality products at a great price. Thus, was launched the discount sportswear chain that now numbers over 200 stores across the USA.

Their success in sportswear also led to an expansion of their product lines, extending to casual clothes for the entire family. Steve and Barry's was named the 2005 'Hot Retailer of the Year' by the International Association of Shopping Centers. As a privately held company, sales volume figures are not available. According to co-founder Barry Prevor their mission was to 'bring people the most unbelievable values on clothes they've ever seen'. Prevor continued by saying 'we run our business very tightly and efficiently, there are no extra costs anywhere' (Birchall, 2006).

Promotion

The leading marketing agency for the product chosen by Steve and Barry's was the Mastermind Group under the direction of Erin Patton. Mastermind handled advertising, public relations (PR) and other marketing services. Patton came with experience as the former director of the Jordan brand at Nike for five years. He brought the same philosophy to the Starbury line and interacted with the entire Starbury team. Marbury's personal agency also worked as a part of the overall team as did the urban marketing agency, The Run Group.

The launch process took an atypical twist as well. Marbury himself would accompany his promotion team on a 21 day, 41 city tour to promote the shoe in August. Interestingly, the tour concept was originated by Marbury, not his agency or the retailers. Marbury said 'when I saw how people were reacting, I just wanted to go grassroots and let the people see the product and touch the product' (Abel, 2006, p. 35). This tactic seems truly revolutionary where the typical NBA player spends considerable time and effort trying to avoid fans or signing autographs. One NBA executive even had a player approach him and say, 'Just tell me which PR events that you will require me to go to, the fine for not going, and I'll write you a check'.

Little traditional advertising was used as part of the overall marketing strategy. Rather, strategists placed small advertisement in basketball and urban magazines, without mentioning a price, only noting the release date and the product name. Other tactics employed were the use of 'street teams' mobilized to hand out samples on urban playgrounds and at inner city basketball camps. Reportedly the promotions budget was $500,000 less than 10 per cent of the budget for marketing activities for a typical shoe release (Weilheimer, 2006).

During the promotional tour, the buzz started to develop. Marbury was interviewed on local news and talk shows. Parents were bringing their kids to see Marbury, get an autograph and take a look at the product. One father commented that 'most of the shoes my son likes are $100 US, so I love this idea. I think all of the star athletes should drop the prices on products they endorse. Everyone can't pay $80–100 US for a pair of shoes. That's a real good thing he's doing'. The father left the store with four shopping bags full of shoes and clothing from the Starbury product line.

Another tactic implemented based on Marbury's inner city roots came when Steve and Barry's together with Marbury donated 3000 pairs of the shoes and a special DVD message from Marbury to all high school basketball players in New York City. Marbury said he hopes 'that it inspires these kids to be better players and more importantly better men'. Again, the media attention connected to this donation was immediate and extremely positive. Because of Marbury's inner city credentials, it was perceived as authentic, not manipulative.

Collectively, the marketing strategies and tactics created a real buzz in the media, on the web and at the water cooler at offices around the globe. In place of traditional print advertising and television, the word of the innovative price and product appeared in newspapers stories, TV news programming and Internet blogs. All third-party sources. Mortimer (2006) noted that 70 per cent of consumers place more trust in recommendations from friends or family compared to advertisements.

Case Diagnosis

The marketing team projected that their first production run would last through the holiday shopping season. Unfortunately, they were wrong. The first six-week supply of shoes sold out in three days. Lines formed outside of nearly every store. During the first week of its introduction, the New York City store had lines of about 100 people waiting for the store to open. Several stores also reported that lines would begin to form outside the store several hours before the scheduled opening. One store manager said that the shoes were being sold directly out of the shipping cartons, never making it to the shelf.

Within six months, over 3 million pairs had been sold. This, in a market where basketball shoes sales overall had dropped 16 per cent during the year. The primary issues surround pricing and demand. Did demand for the product exist in the market, but was restricted by price? One could propose that the price stimulated demand. As has been seen with other shoe company tactics, an issue could arise where the limited supply and restricted distribution accelerated demand (i.e. a feeding frenzy).

The $14.98 US pricing brings forth the question 'Is premium pricing dead?' Is the perception of the customer inexorably tied with price? It seems that in this market, there are many consumers that will place a value on products of high quality that are available at a low price. On the other hand, the low price may cause consumers who are brand and label conscious, to shun the brand simply because it is 'cheap'. The struggle is interesting, especially in the US market where 'brand is everything'.

The sporting goods business has been around for over 100 years and the sports shoe segment for about the same. However, in the new age of communication one must ask if word-of-mouth marketing and in-the-market marketing are more effective than traditional media buys? The relationship that seems to be developing between Marbury and the parents of urban kids has created a buzz that all the marketing dollars in the world cannot buy. During the explosion of the sports shoe industry in the 1980s, expensive advertising and marketing campaigns were commonplace. Nike, adidas, Reebok and the others spent millions of dollars promoting and selling shoes across the demographic continuum. In the US economy the Generation Y group (those aged 10–24 years) represents 86 million people (up 18 per cent in the last 5 years) and accounts for spending of $150 billion US per year. In addition, they influence an additional $300 billion in spending through their parents. In addition, as can be seen in the music industry, urban influences are strong. In fact, some athletic shoe companies like Reebok have secured endorsements from Rap artists in the past few years. Therefore, Marbury's dependence on and success in the urban environment seems to be a key to success.

Key marketing issues are also embedded in the distribution channel. Does reliance on a limited access, discount retailer make a good business model? According to industry data, only 7.5 per cent of all athletic footwear is sold through discount stores. Another 18.5 per cent is sold by general sporting goods stores while the highest percentage (33.2 per cent) is sold through stores specializing only in athletic footwear. The existent Starbury One model relies on the manufacturer-to-retailer link to keep the mark-ups low and thus reduce the end price. Yet, supply and distribution are negatively affected. Ultimately, the product is sold only in limited markets. The traditional theory in low price offerings is to make profits through large sales volume as opposed to high margins on small volume. Is the low price, small volume theory viable?

In the end, the long-term success of the marketing strategies and tactics will either be supported or discounted based on overall sales figures. The launch of the Starbury One basketball shoe has provided an interesting case from which to discuss a variety of marketing concepts. Future marketers can continue to examine the scenario to determine which of the marketing elements worked and which did not. As with any industry, the dynamics of the market combined with volatility of an athlete endorser will validate the marketing strategy and tactics employed.

Case Questions and Teaching Notes

1 Can an inexpensive shoe attain a status of being 'cool?' For example, is more consumer value placed on limited edition, expensive items that only a few can afford? Is there an argument in that the caché of wearing brands that most people cannot afford enhances the ego of some consumers and creates desire in the psyche of those who can't buy them. Conversely, can consumer value accrue to items that are seen as a 'bargain' with good quality for a reasonable price? At what point and in which cultures is the person who buys at higher value more admired?

2 Is it viable to restrict distribution of a new product to a limited number of outlets? The leading sports shoe companies have global distribution networks that can quickly roll out new models into the marketplace. Steve and Barry's, although expanding in the USA is still extremely limited in its retail outlets, thus restricting sales volume.

3 What impact will this strategy have on other shoe manufacturers? How does the introduction of a low price item in a category affect other sellers? Does it force them to offer competitively priced items? What other strategies might they pursue?

4 Compare and contrast this case to marketing activities associated with other NBA-endorsed shoes. Nike, adidas and Reebok have employed fairly traditional marketing strategies when launching new shoe lines. They create advertising campaigns with significant media presence in print and electronic media. Nike is known for creating a great deal of

publicity abound its new releases, artificially constraining supply and then, once consumer demand is high, it releases more supply into the distribution chain. The Starbury line was promoted predominately through press conferences and a geographically diverse product tour featuring Marbury himself.

5 Analyse the timing of the product release. In the USA, August is the traditional 'back-to-school' shopping season. It is also a few months prior to the beginning of the NBA season. The start of the NBA season is also only a few weeks prior to the beginning of the Christmas holiday shopping season.

6 What is the power of 'Brand?' What would happen if the same shoes were artificially adorned with a Nike Swoosh and introduced to consumers? Would the discussion about quality still ensue? Would consumer-based tests of quality yield the same results?

7 How important is quality as it relates to performance? Industry experts estimate that 85 per cent of sports shoes are never used in serious sport competition. Therefore, if the shoe is comfortable and stylish, it may not matter if it can withstand the rigors of NBA competition.

Case Resources

Reading

Abel, G. (2006, December 25–31). Marbury's new shoe rewrites the rules. *Sport Business Journal*, Vol. 9, No. 34, pp. 3–35.

Birchall, J. (2006, September 26). Basketball dreams on a budget. *Financial Times, Business Life*. London, 13 pp.

Boeck, S (2006, November 6) Sneaker attack: Stephon Marbury has a deal for you. *USA Today*, 8C.

Mortimer, R. (2006, October 10). Recipe for disaster. *Brand Strategy*, 3

Talalay, S. (2006, November 18). Is it in the shoes? *South Florida Sentinel*.

Weilheimer, N. (2006, December 4). Full Court Press. *Footwear News*, 32.

White, T. (2006, September 17). Name-brand, cool, low cost. *Baltimore Sun*, 1A.

Website

www.steveandbarrys.com

24

On tour with the Barmy Army: a case study in sports tourism

John Beech

Case Focus

This case study explores sports tourism in the context of the 2007 Cricket World Cup, with particular reference to the Barmy Army organization and its competitor sports tour operators.

Keywords
• Sports tourism • Cricket • Barmy Army • Fan segmentation • Marketing strategy

Case Summary

In cricket, the four-yearly World Cup is the zenith of international competition. In 2007 it was held for the first time in the West Indies. This posed particular challenges for the range of tour operators officially appointed. These included the multi-country venues, a challenge unique to this competition and the extended nature (48 days) of the competition. Among the 11 official travel agents appointed to produce tour packages for fans was the Barmy Army organization, an organization driven by cricket fans which had moved into the tour operator business from merchandising, rather than a specialist tour operator. This case study explores the competition it faced and the competitive environment in which it operated.

Case Elements

A Background

For those unfamiliar with the game of cricket, a good starting point for a quick introduction to the game can be found at the following websites: A Virtual Dominica – http://www.avirtualdominica.com/cricket.htm Ask AboutSports–http://www.askaboutsports.com/cricket.htmRealbuzz.com–http://www.askaboutsports.com/cricket.htm

The notion of loyal sports fans as an 'army' has a number of possible origins, and perhaps one of the clearest of these is the emergence of Ally's Tartan Army, a soubriquet for the faithful few who travelled to Argentina to support Scotland in the 1978 World Cup. The Scotland manager at that time was Ally (short for Alistair) MacLeod, a charismatic figure who proved to be manna from heaven for the Scottish media.

The Scottish team was arguably no different from any previous or subsequent team in terms of form, but MacLeod, with characteristic overconfidence, announced that he expected to return with at least a medal. Fans promptly adopted an unrealistic optimism and the chant 'We're on the march with Ally's Army' was taken up across much of the nation. A popular comedian (no intended irony!) called Andy Cameron turned the chant, together with a name associated with Scotland's rugby fans, into a song, 'Ally's Tartan Army' which he recorded. This song achieved a surprising popularity not just in Scotland but across the whole UK, reaching number six in the charts.

Notwithstanding the poor performance of the team in the World Cup – they were out after their second match and were dogged by the drugs accusation against one of the players – the song and soubriquet survived. It should be borne in mind that the period was one of resurgent Scottish nationalism, with an increasing support for political policies pursuing some form of separation from the rest of the UK. The notion of a Tartan Army thus captured a zeitgeist and became established in folk culture.

The Tartan Army today is a term applied at two levels – to the general and amorphous body of fans who travel to Scotland's away football matches, and to a non-profit organization which reinforces the sense of identity of those who associate themselves with it.[1] It produces merchandising to make itself sustainable, co-ordinates local groups of supporters and latterly has provided information on tour operators who will put together travel packages for Scottish fans travelling internationally.

The Birth of England Cricket's 'Barmy Army'

The Barmy Army organization's website describes its birth thus:

> *The Barmy Army is synonymous with English cricket fans travelling overseas to support their team. It was in effect created by the Australian media's description during the Ashes series in 1994/95. 'Barmy' because we were spending lots of money supporting a side that couldn't win a game of cricket; England not only lost to Australia and their second team, Australia A, but also suffered the indignity of losing to Zimbabwe and, to cap it all, the Australian Academy Side (youth team) and 'Army' because there were hundreds grouped together at each match singing and partying in concert. 'Atherton's Barmy Army' soon became established as our theme song and we were proud of our image.*

The Barmy Army is described thus by the editor of *All Out Cricket*, the contemporary lifestyle magazine of the Professional Cricketers Association:

> *The Barmy Army is truly a phenomenon. They are that very rare thing, a group of like-minded individuals well-loved wherever they go. They spur the England team on through hard, energy-sapping days, they help keep the economies of any country they visit afloat. And they have the best interests of cricket at heart. Yes, their chanting can be tedious to some, yes, they drink too much and yes, they flout the safe sunbathing regulations. But they are a good thing. A very good thing. Just ask any of the England boys.*
>
> Thacker (2006)

---

[1] Throughout this case study, where reference is made to a general and amorphous body of fans the term 'Army' is used; where a formal non-profit organization is referred to, the term 'Army organization' is used.

There are two obvious parallels between this origin and the origin of the Tartan Army:

- Both soubriquets were to a large extent media driven.
- Both soubriquets carry a sense of irony.

A third parallel can be rapidly deduced:

- Neither organization carries any official sanction from the appropriate governing body of the sport.

This lack of official sanction means, of course, that neither body enjoys any official funding, and must raise revenue from its members/customers.

The Barmy Army organization emerged during the series of international Test matches[2] in Australia referred to above. Shortly after the fourth of the five five-day tests, they produced and sold over 8000 items of merchandising. A key item of merchandising was a T-shirt with 'We came here with backpacks' on the front and 'You with Ball and Chain' on the back. This reference to Australia's early years as a penal colony was designed to be both provocative and yet to be with a sense of good-hearted banter.

Whether this was an act of great entrepreneurial foresight or a means for those involved to finance the next leg of their holiday (or possibly a mix of both) depends on whom you ask. One way or the other, this provided a financial base for the organization to develop from, and one of its first actions was to trademark the term 'Barmy Army'. There is clearly an altruistic vein to the Barmy Army organization, it should be pointed out. It makes regular donations to charity, and was very swift to arrange a charity cricket match during England's tour of South Africa in order to raise money for the victims of the Boxing Day tsunami in 2004.

The registration of 'Tartan Army' was not made so promptly and remains a contentious issue as it is not owned by the Tartan Army organization, but rather by two people active within the Tartan Army organization – Bob Shields and Don Lawson (Grant, 2006). They now exploit the trademark commercially, but have made it clear that they do not see themselves as owning 'The Tartan Army'.

The Barmy Army organization, on the other hand, by owning the trademark, has been able to build up a business focusing on merchandising and, more recently, on travel packages. A heavy emphasis is placed on direct marketing as the organization has a database of over 25,000 England fans developed in 13 years since the organization was founded.

---

[2] Cricket at an international level has been played for well over a century. The traditional format is a series of matches played 'on tour'. These include a number of friendly matches against teams at the 'second tier' level – for example, against English Counties or Australian States – but centred on five inter-country games, lasting up to five days. More recently, in an attempt to make the game more attractive, one-day matches have become a regular feature of the tour calendar.

Today's Barmy Army organization offers a wide range of services:

- Cricket news and fixtures services, through its website and a newsletter.
- Travel packages for travelling supporters (provided by Travel & Tours Anywhere Ltd., a separate company licensed to use the 'Barmy Army' name; this company also trades as 'Bharat Army', an equivalent organization for Indian cricket fans).
- Bespoke travelling packages for cricket teams wishing to undertake a playing tour.
- A twice-yearly magazine which carries news, song sheets and advertisements.
- Fund-raising advice.
- Its own cricket team, and also a Colts (Juniors) team.

Operating in the post-commercialized world of cricket, it is not surprising that the organization has a major sponsor – Cockspur rum.

The International Cricket Council World Cup 2007

Cricket at an international level is governed by the International Cricket Council (ICC). The ICC has 10 full members (Australia, Bangladesh, England, India, New Zealand, Pakistan, South Africa, Sri Lanka, West Indies and Zimbabwe), 32 associate members (which include smaller former British possessions, other countries with an Anglophonic presence and sundry non-Anglophonic countries) and 55 affiliate members (broadly similar to the associate members but with a lower cricket presence, ranging from, for example, St Helena to China).

The ICC organizes a range of international competitions, ranging from its World Cup, featuring One-Day Internationals (ODIs) in a format very similar to football's more famous World Cup, through the ICC Intercontinental Cup (for its associate members) to bilateral international tours (the traditional five-day Test matches). As it only happens every four years, the ICC World Cup is seen as the zenith of international cricket. The format of the World Cup has changed over the years and in 2007 it adopted for the first time broadly the format of its football equivalent. This was held in the West Indies.

While the ICC World Cup cannot compete with the football World Cup in profile, it is beginning to achieve a high enough profile to command serious money for its broadcasting rights. News Corp paid $550 million for a package of all ICC rights that included the 2007 World Cup.

Although the World Cup dates back to an origin in 1975, 2007 marked the first occasion that it had been hosted by the West Indies, giving it a special significance to the host nations. From the perspective of the destinations, conversations with senior representatives of the various national tourist boards immediately before the start of the ICC World Cup revealed one common concern, one that arises all too frequently with similar sports mega-events – would it be worth it? Frequently mentioned were the opportunity costs associated with major refurbishments and build of the various stadia. In order to minimize the costs of this building work, significant

Table 24.1 ICC World Cup 2007 venues

Country	Stadium	Build	Capacity	Population
Antigua	Sir Vivian Richards Stadium	New stadium constructed in partnership with China	20,000	69,000 (includes Barbuda)
Barbados	Kensington Oval 3Ws Oval	– New venue	28,000 3000	280,000
Grenada	Queens Park	Stadium rebuilt following damage by Hurricane Ivan in 2004	20,000	90,000
Guyana	Providence Stadium	New stadium	20,000	770,000
Jamaica	Sabina Park Trelawny Stadium	Major upgrade New stadium constructed in partnership with China	21,000 25,000	2,760,000
St Kitts	Warner Park Stadium	New stadium	10,000	39,000 (includes Nevis)
St Lucia	Beausejour Stadium	Temporary stands added to increase capacity	20,000	168,000
St Vincent	Arnos Vale*	Major renovation	12,000	118,000 (includes Grenadines)
Trinidad	Queens Park Oval	Minor upgrade	25,000	1,066,000 (includes Tobago)

*This venue was one of four venues used for a series of pre-Cup warm-up matches but not during the actual World Cup.

Sources: iccworldcup07.com and populations from CIA World Factbook.

levels of support had been accepted. The extent of build and the assistance used is shown in Table 24.1.

The Fan's Tour Package

Post-commercialized or not, the primary purpose of the Barmy Army organization is to facilitate support of the England cricket team at internationals, and, although not one of the first services to be offered, the travel service in many ways is at the core of the spirit of the Barmy Army organization. For the 2007 the ICC World Cup in the West Indies, the Barmy Army organization was one of a number of official travel agents (OTCs) appointed by the ICC.

The structure of the matches in this World Cup illustrates the problems that any organizer of tours would face and the peculiarity of cricket as an object of sports tourism:

- Although an international game, cricket is clearly not a global game. In the countries where it is played, it often is a very popular sport. In the UK, for example, Mintel (2006) assesses cricket as the fifth most popular sport in terms of revenues from paying spectators. Given that cricket is much less popular in Scotland, Wales and Northern Ireland, it is likely that within England cricket overtakes the fourth-placed sport, Rugby Union. The participants in the 2007 World Cup were:

Australia	Ireland	South Africa
Bangladesh	Kenya	Sri Lanka
Bermuda	The Netherlands	West Indies
Canada	New Zealand	Zimbabwe
England	Pakistan	
India	Scotland	

These 16 nations constitute the 10 full members plus 6 nations who have been successful in the supporting ICC Trophy competition.

With the exception of the Netherlands, all countries are Anglophonic. The only major Anglophonic country not participating is the USA. Participants are from every continent except South America (although Guyana is included in the West Indies representation).

- The Cup is played in two stages. The first consists of four groups of four teams playing each other once – the Group stage. The top two in each Group go forward to the 'Super 8s', a stage played as a single league of eight qualifying teams. Each team in the Super 8s brings forward the points from the match it played against the other qualifier from the same Group. Each of the eight teams therefore plays six matches rather than seven. This format reflects the fact that, with relatively few countries competing, there is still a sense of 'mainstream' countries and 'minnows'.[3]
- The Group stage, which comprises 24 matches, is played at four venues – Jamaica, St Kitts and Nevis, St Lucia and Trinidad. The first set of matches in the Super 8s is played in Antigua and Guyana (six matches each), while the teams then move to Barbados and Grenada for the second set.
- The four highest teams in the Super 8s table proceed to two semi-finals, and the two winners of the semi-finals play for the Cup in the Final. Venues for the two semi-finals are in Jamaica and St Lucia, and the Final is played in Barbados. This format of multiple venues is thus similar in some

---

[3] This analysis is not entirely justified as upsets can still occur (e.g. the departure of Pakistan at the Group stage, with Ireland going forward to the Super 8s).

respects to that of the football World Cup, but with the obvious differences that the structure of the tournament requires more movement between venues and any travel between two venues is between two republics with no land connection. The furthest distance between two venues is that between Jamaica and Guyana, approximately 1500 miles or 2400 km. Jamaica, the most westerly of the venues is one hour behind the others. Because the Super 8s are scheduled on the familiar basis of 'Winner Group A plays Runner-up Group B', etc., following one's team to the Final involves considerable uncertainty in terms of pre-booking flights and accommodation.

- The time scale of the Cup – the event opened with a spectacular ceremony in Jamaica on 11th March and concluded with the Final in Barbados on 28th April – presented particular challenges as to attend the whole series would require someone taking a holiday of at least 48 days. (If a Barmy Army fan also wanted to watch England's two pre-competition warm-up matches in St Vincent, this holiday period would have to extend to 54 days.)

The basic elements that the Barmy Army organization, or a competitor, needs to include in a package are as follows:

1 *The flight and destination transfers*: In the case of the ICC World Cup 2007 there are severe limitations. Few carriers fly direct from England to the West Indies. To fly, for example, to Kingston, Jamaica, one is restricted to British Airways or Air Jamaica. If the fan is prepared to make one change of flight, the possibilities extend to include American Airlines or Virgin Atlantic via JFK. A similar situation exists if wanting to fly to Trinidad, with Caribbean Airlines (the successor to British West Indies) replacing Air Jamaica.

   There are some better opportunities to some destinations because of their appeal as conventional sunlust destinations. To fly to St Lucia from London, it is possible to fly direct with Virgin Atlantic. Flights within the Caribbean area can be problematic, involving changes at intermediate airports.

2 *Accommodation*: Although the ICC World Cup is in March, there is no period in the Caribbean which can be described as entirely off-season. Indeed, one of the strengths of Caribbean destinations for general tourists is the warmth they offer all year round. In other words, cricket fans offer a 'top up' possibility to Caribbean hotels – room occupancy is already at reasonable levels. The only arguable exception to this is Guyana, which is still young in terms of tourism development.

   A particular problem for tour operators with this World Cup is the range of currencies used by the host nations (see Table 24.2).

3 *Match tickets*: The ICC releases match tickets to tour operators to be sold as part of a package through a single company – Cricket Logistics 2007. This company is a division of Gullivers Sports Travel. (Hospitality packages are similarly handled by a single company, Hospitality in Partnership, a division of Cavendish Hospitality.)

   Cricket Logistics does not sell directly to the public, but rather to the appointed Official Tour Agents (OTAs) (see Table 24.3).

Table 24.2 Currencies of ICC World Cup 2007 host nations

Antigua	Eastern Caribbean Dollar
Barbados	Barbados Dollar
Grenada	Eastern Caribbean Dollar
Guyana	Guyana Dollar
Jamaica	Jamaica Dollar
St Kitts	Eastern Caribbean Dollar
St Lucia	Eastern Caribbean Dollar
Trinidad and Tobago	Trinidad and Tobago Dollar

Table 24.3 ICC World Cup 2007 OTAs in the UK

Best At Travel Plc T/A Sporting Journeys	Small independent specializing in sport tourism, with emphasis on cricket
Grand Cru Travel	Small independent specializing in cricket tourism. Official Tour Operator England & Wales Cricket Board
Gullivers Sports Travel	Small independent specializing in cricket and rugby tourism
ITC Sports	Small independent covering a wide range of sports tourism
Kuoni Sport Abroad	Specialist sports division of Kuoni Travel; part of the Kuoni Group, a Swiss-based multinational
Rumsey Travel Limited	Small independent
Taj Tours and Travel	Medium independent, with overseas offices
The Cricket Tour Company	Small independent offering only cricket tours (escorted and unescorted)
The Sporting Traveller	Small independent covering a range of sports
Thomas Cook Sport	Specialist sports division of Thomas Cook AG, a German-based multinational
Travel & Tours Anywhere Ltd	Tour operator licensed by the Barmy Army organization to use the 'Barmy Army' name. Described on the Barmy Army organization website as 'Barmy Army Travel'

Examples of the packages offered are shown in Table 24.4.

To give these packages a context, major UK tour operators were simultaneously offering packages in the Mediterranean from around £100 for seven nights.

Table 24.4 Examples of cricket package tours for ICC World Cup 2007

Tour operator	Package	Price (per person)
Gullivers Sports Travel	12 days; 1 Super 8s match, 1 semi-final, the Final. Accommodation on cruise liner. Accompanied by Dickie Bird, formerly a leading cricket umpire	£4770
Thomas Cook Sport	10 nights; 1 semi-final, the Final. Hotel based	£3399 (assuming sharing a twin)
Travel & Tours Anywhere Ltd	14 nights economy package (excludes match tickets). Hotel based	£1436.50

The OTAs thus consist of two organizations that are divisions of global tour operators (Kuoni and Thomas Cook) and nine considerably smaller independent operators (including the Barmy Army organization), all specializing in sports tourism, but with a varying focus on cricket. Travel & Tours Anywhere Ltd offers a range of packages from 'economy' through 'economy +' and 'superior' to 'luxury' but is distinguishable from its competitors in offering such a package as 'economy' at what is a very low price in comparison to its competitors' prices.

OTAs may also want to package visa applications as a fourth element. As each host nation normally has different visa requirements, the Caribbean Community (CARICOM) instituted special arrangements for the period of the World Cup. During the period 1 February to 15 May 2007, no visa is required for nationals from the following countries:

Canada	Italy
France & overseas countries and Territories	South Africa
	Spain
Germany	The Netherlands & Overseas Countries and
Japan	Territories
Ireland	United Kingdom and Dependent Territories
Nationals and Residents of CARICOM	United States and Dependent Territories
Member States (except Haiti)	

Fans from other countries – this includes Australia, Bangladesh, India, Kenya, New Zealand, Pakistan, Sri Lanka and Zimbabwe – needed only to acquire a single special CARICOM visa, facilitating travel between venues.

This arrangement certainly made life easier for travel agents and tour operators as well as for fans.

It should be noted that an important difference between the case of English cricket and the case of Scottish football is that the Scottish Football Association runs its own travel agency, the Scotball Travel Agency, which the Tartan Army organization might well feel reluctant to undermine by setting up in opposition. The England and Wales Cricket Board has no such commercial operation, and this provides the Barmy Army organization, and its competitors, with a business opportunity.

Case Diagnosis

When the Barmy Army organization was founded, the specialist cricket tourism market had not been tapped to a great extent. The two key players were both small independents – Mike Burton Sports Travel (still operating in the sports tourism sector, but not one of the OTAs for the 2007 World Cup) and Gullivers Sports Travel. Both tour operators covered a range of sports tourism niches, usually associated with specific tournaments or cups.

In many ways, these two old-established operators are typical of the niche tour operators who have chosen to become ICC World Cup OTAs. They may be characterized as:

- Small and independent.
- Catering for higher socio-economic segments.
- Offering accompanied tours with a known cricket 'name' as guide.
- Adding value through the expertise, particularly with respect to cricket, of the guide.
- Drawing on experience from other sports tourism sectors.
- Outwith mainstream tourism.

The two OTAs who are not, in terms of their parent organizations, niche tour operators are Kuoni Sport Abroad and Thomas Cook Sport. They may be characterized as:

- Small specialist travel divisions of very large global tour operators.
- Catering for higher socio-economic segments.
- Offering support through local representatives.
- Potentially adding value through (a) experience at the destination and (b) non-sport add-ons.
- Drawing on experience from other non-sports tourism sectors.
- Within mainstream tourism.

The Barmy Army organization does not fit exactly with either characterization, although it overlaps more with the small independent OTAs as might be expected:

- Small and independent.
- Catering for lower socio-economic segments.

- Offering semi-accompanied tours with a cricket expert as guide.
- Adding value through the expertise, particularly with respect to cricket, of the guide and through a sense of identity with the Barmy Army.
- Outwith mainstream tourism.

The Barmy Army organization tours are thus operating in a key segment largely ignored by the other tour operators: the lower socio-economic segments. This provides it with both a strength:

- Lack of competition from other tour operators

and weaknesses:

- Vulnerability to the 'organize-it-ourselves' segment of cricket travellers.

    This vulnerability to what is termed disintermediation – the removal of the 'middle-man' in a purchase chain – is especially a problem in a price-sensitive market, exactly the market in which the Barmy Army organization has placed itself. Sports tourists are more likely to be (a) travelling as a large group; (b) in the younger market segments and (c) hence 'net-wise'. The hunt for cheaper alternatives is facilitated by meta-search engines such as lastminute.com.

    The adoption of a differential pricing strategy for match tickets for the ICC World Cup 2007 – essentially, higher prices for tickets sold in England through the OCAs, and lower prices for tickets sold in the West Indies – meant that Barmy Army fans might be tempted to take a risk by not pre-booking at home before travelling, predicting that they would be able to buy cheaper tickets once they had arrived in the West Indies. This decision might well be influenced from previous experiences at international matches, when even tickets bought from touts were available cheaper than tickets pre-booked in England (anecdotal evidence from interviewees).
- Promoting an identity that some potential customers may wish to avoid

    A cynical view might be that the Barmy Army organization is the Club 18–30 of cricket tourism. Certainly their add-on options focus on parties, barbecues and booze cruises. One respect in which they score well is that, by providing this kind of add-on, they are catering for the many female travelling partners who go with their male cricket-fan partner. Their competitors focus strongly on just the male cricket fan, thereby failing to maximize revenues and hence profit.

This view would indeed be cynical. Even a short conversation with Paul Burnham, the head of the Barmy Army organisation, reveals that his organisation is not commercial in the conventional 'for profit' business sense. As he puts it, "[The Barmy Army organisation] is a supporters' club, but, yes, it is also a business". The operation has grown organically, but has resisted, for example, imposing a membership fee as a revenue stream.

The tours operation began only in 2003 and was outsourced to Travel & Tours Anywhere Ltd, who use the name 'Barmy Army' under licence.

In 2003, for the first time, Paul drew a salary, and, in 2007 the Barmy Army organisation employs only two other members of staff full-time.

Paul sees the key business dimensions of the organisation as:

- Travel
- The website
- Merchandising
- The Colts team
- The Cricket Club
- and sponsors

From his personal perspective, Paul says "I love it! It's a challenge!". His engagement with the organisation extends to him living in a flat above his office.

The travel operation has not been as commercially successful as he had hoped, and the future of how the Barmy organisation operates as a tour operator may come under review.

It should be pointed out in the context of meeting the needs of travelling cricket fans that the nature of watching cricket can be quite different from watching other team sports. The action on the pitch is much less continuous, the duration of play is considerably longer, cricket grounds are less enclosing than, for example, football stadia, the size of a cricket pitch is considerably larger than pitches in other team sports and spectating areas are not exclusively all-seat domains. As a result, the spectator is less engaged, and less continuously engaged, than in other sports. The opportunity for 'disengaged spectating' is thus considerably greater, and those who by preference are less engaged can still enjoy the social milieu of a cricket audience in a way that it is not possible at, for example, a football match.

Another example of this segmentation differential among the niche sports tour operators can be seen with the area of merchandising. Gullivers, for example, provides each of their clientele with one discreetly branded polo shirt at no additional charge, whereas the Barmy Army organization sell their clients, and of course other fans, T-shirts at each venue, often generating match-specific merchandising to encourage repeat purchasing.

It must be pointed out, however, that the Barmy Army organization, in keeping with its fan-based origin, donates significantly to appropriate charities and encourages others to do so.

In addition to the well-known typologies of market segmentation, it is useful to apply typologies from sport-fandom and tourism to the cricket tourism niche:

- Tapp and Clowes (2002) offer a typology that segments fans into groups such as 'committed casuals', 'carefree casuals', 'repertoire supporters' and 'professional wanderers', with major dimensions of fandom being commitment to the sport versus seeking alternatives and entertainment versus winning. While one might expect the majority of those in the Barmy Army to be seen as strong in 'commitment to the sport' and in 'winning', because of the extended nature of the ICC World Cup and the fact that in 2007 it is taking place in a major sunlust destination, there are strong opportunities to sell to those who are not strongly fanatical in their support, but who rather want a holiday with a cricket leitmotif. The two global OTAs are strongly placed to offer such holidays, the small independent OTAs less so.

- Plog (1974) classifies tourists along a spectrum from allocentrics (those who like their chosen destination to be extremely different from their home) to psychocentrics (those who prefer their chosen destination to be like home as much as possible). With its overwhelmingly anglophonic locations, cricket provides a rare opportunity to market long-haul destinations to psychocentrics.

Research specifically on cricket fans is sparse. One notable exception is Kuenzel and Yassim (2007), who investigated cricket fans at English County games (the top flight of English league cricket). Findings of particular relevance here are as follows:

- Fans interviewed were in the proportion roughly of five male to one female.
- Social facilitation was a more significant game experience variable than quality of the game, and was second only to the presence of star players.

At the international level, whether at a World Cup or one of the international Test matches, the presence of stars players is a sine qua non, making social facilitation the most important factor that actually varies.

Anecdotal evidence would suggest that cricket fans touring with the Barmy Army organization are different in some particular respects from those travelling with, for example, Gullivers. Barmy Army fans tend to be football supporters seeking an alternative platform to supporting their national team, thus transferring, in the football 'off season', to supporting the English cricket team, while for the rest of the year they support their football club and nation. Barmy Army fans tend to play both football and cricket. Gullivers' tourists, however, are more committed with their cricket support, supporting their local cricket team and, at a senior level, their County team. Most do not play cricket, although they have done when younger, and would not be football players.

The author greatly acknowledges the help provided through interviews, especially that with Paul Burnham and those with his colleagues and Barmy Army tourists, Nigel Berkeley and Ian Webster.

Since this case study was submitted, it has been announced that that Travel & Tours Anywhere Ltd., the tour operator licensed by the Barmy Army to use the latter's name, has ceased trading. An account of the problems generated, from the customers' perspective, can be found at "http://www.bbc.co.uk/consumer/tv_and_radio/watchdog/reports/holidays_and_travel/holiday_20070411.shtml" and a more detailed account of the circumstances leading to the liquidation at "http://www.nationnews.com/story/288966773809153.php."

At the time of writing this update (June 2007) no replacement organization had been licensed to operate the travel arm of the Barmy Army. If a replacement has been licensed by the time you buy this book, it should be assumed that it has no connection with Travel & Tours Anywhere Ltd.

Case Questions

1 How is cricket tourism different from other forms of sports tourism?
2 Draw up a SWOT analysis for the Barmy Army organization's travel arm.
3 What strategy would you recommend to Paul Burnham that he pursues in future? why?
4 If another of the global tour operators, TUI for example, decided to open a specialist sports tourism division, what strategic advice would you give them?
5 In spite of the presence of global tour operators in the marketplace, their sport travel divisions remain rather isolated from their mainstream operations. What would be the advantages and disadvantages of making them more integrated with that mainstream? Would you recommend such a move to them? Why or why not?
6 Is copyrighting and/or trademarking a generic name for a group of fans necessarily a clever move?
7 With an increasing interest in mega-events such as World Cups and the Olympic Games, is there scope for more players in the marketplace, or is a series of mergers and acquisitions a more likely scenario?
8 How might cricket tour operators cater better for the needs of 'tag-along partners' who are less committed to the cricket features of a holiday?

Case Resources

Reading

Beech, J. and Chadwick, S. (Eds.) (2004). *The Business of Sport Management*. Pearson Education, Harlow. (See in particular the chapter on *Marketing* by Sullivan, M.)

Beech, J. and Chadwick, S. (Eds.) (2006). *The Business of Tourism Management*. Pearson Education, Harlow. (See in particular the chapters on *Marketing* by Cope, B. and *Sports Tourism* by Weed, M.)

Beech, J. and Chadwick, S. (Eds.) (2007). *The Marketing of Sport*. Pearson Education, Harlow.

Bull, C. and Weed, M. (2003). *Sports Tourism: Participants, Policy and Providers*. Butterworth-Heinemann, Oxford.

Grant, M. (2006). Tartan Army Truce. *Sunday Herald*, 27 August, Glasgow.

Kuenzel, S. and Yassim, M. (2007). The effect of joy on the behaviour of cricket spectators: The mediating role of satisfaction. *Managing Leisure: An International Journal*, Vol. 12, No. 1.

Mintel (2006). *Cricket and Rugby*. Mintel International Group Limited, London. Available online (with subscription) through http://academic.mintel.com/sinatra/academic/

Parry, M. and Malcolm, D. (2004). England's Barmy Army: Commercialisation, masculinity and nationalism. *International Review for the Sociology of Sport*, Vol. 39, No. 1.

Plog, S.C. (1974). Why destination areas rise and fall in popularity. *Cornel Hotel and Restaurant Quarterly*, Vol. 14, No. 4.

Tapp, A. and Clowes, J. (2002). From carefree casuals to football anoraks: Segmentation possibilities for football supporters. *European Journal of Marketing*, Vol. 36, No. 11.

Thacker, M. (2006). *Barmy Cricket – The Official Barmy Army Book of Cricket*. Barmy Army Productions, Sutton.

Websites

Barmy Army organization – http://www.barmyarmy.com/index.cfm

Bharat Army http://www.bharatarmy.com

Gullivers Sports travel – http://www.gulliversports.co.uk/

ICC Cricket World Cup 2007 (unofficial) – http://iccworldcup07.wordpress.com/ and http://cricketworldcup.indya.com/

International Cricket Council – http://www.icc-cricket.com

Kuoni Sport Abroad – http://www.sportabroad.co.uk/cricket/index.shtml

Mike Burton Group – http://www.mikeburton.com/home.htm

Tartan Army – http://www.t-army.com/

Thomas Cook Sport – http://www.thomascooksport.com/cricket.php

Travel & Tours Anywhere Ltd – http://www.ttal.co.uk/

25

The future of the Tour de France: from an independent style of organization to 'A Formula One Model'?

Michel Desbordes

Case Focus

The case examines the move by the UCI (*Union Cycliste Internationale* – International Cycling Union) Committee to try to regulate the organization of the competitions in professional cycling. The case will particularly focus on the Tour de France.

Keywords
• Regulation and control of sport events • Internationalization • Development of a closed league • US model • Sponsorship • Marketing and merchandised products

Case Summary

Race of legend in world cycling, Le Tour de France is one of the premier events attracting the widest worldwide media coverage. It is also a great popular festival where almost 15 million fans hug the roadside each year to see riders and the publicity caravan go by. But it has always been an independent event in its organization, as for the Giro d'Italia and The Spanish Vuelta.

In 2005, the UCI created the UCI Pro Tour to try to take control to the races and the teams.

The UCI Pro Tour groups together the best races, the biggest teams and the best riders in the world. It is an international calendar with an individual ranking, a team ranking and a country ranking. Of course, the local organizers did not agree with this loss of control on their events: this case study therefore sets out to examine the conflicted relationships that occurred and tries to find out some solutions for the future.

Case Elements

History

Cycling can be considered as one of the oldest professional sports and its situation has not changed as much as rugby in the last 10 years for example.[1] Sponsorship and media coverage are historically linked to cycling. In the 1930s the Tour de France started appealing to private companies to finance the race and the teams: the Publicity Caravan was born. This tendency to look for a private fund was increased by the fact cycling is the only free professional sport: the audience does not pay tickets to watch the race. The organization depends on TV rights, marketing rights and local communities fees (mostly for the Tour de France) to balance the race's budget. But since the 1980s financial stakes have become more prominent, hence the sport economists' growing interest in cycling. In 2003, to top it all, Le Tour is a centenary

---

[1] The changes in rugby can be compared to a 'cultural revolution' in mentalities.

event, part of sporting heritage, present in the heart of every Frenchman, every Frenchwoman. It continues to move with the times: 73 per cent of those interviewed were convinced that it will still be around in 100 years.[2]

Some Facts about Cycling

Cycling is a leading leisure sport in Europe. Here are some data among different countries:[3]

- *France*: 1st most practised sport – 29 per cent of the population.
- *UK*: 5th most practised sport – 5 per cent of the population.
- *Belgium*: 1st most practised sport – 29 per cent of the population.
- *Germany*: 1st most practised sport – 22 per cent of the population.
- *Poland*: 2nd most practised sport – 25 per cent of the population.
- *Italy*: 5th most practised sport – 7 per cent of the population.
- *Spain*: 4th most practised sport – 10 per cent of the population.
- *USA*: 3rd most practised sport – 27 per cent of the population.

Concerning the interest of the public, cycling is very popular:

- 50 per cent of the French population (men and women) is interested in cycling.[4]
- In Germany it is the third favourite sport (19 per cent of the population is interested in cycling), in Italy it is the third favourite sport (23 per cent) and in Spain the fourth favourite sport (20 per cent).[5]

The values of cycling, according to the date, are highly positive, except for doping.[6]

- Cycling has strong closeness with the fans (historical races with strong national, regional and familial roots; a popular sport which meets the public; a sport for everyone; a sport synonymous of conviviality and sharing).
- Cycling is a generous sport (a team sport which highlights solidarity and generosity, a free show along the roads, with fun and animation, a sport synonymous of gift through the advertising caravan).
- Cycling is a heroic sport (achievements done by champions considered as popular heroes, heroes admired for their exceptional qualities and for their human sense, heroin the victory and in the defeat).

---

[2] *Source*: http://www.aso.fr/2005/cyclisme/us/tdf01.html
[3] *Sources*: McCann Governance/TNS Sport, COIB (Belgium), INSEE (France), Outdoor Industry Association (USA).
[4] *Source*: Sportlab/Sportimat, 2004 (percentage of the individuals who declare to follow a sport with great, fairly or little interest).
[5] *Source*: BMRB, May 2004 (percentage of the persons who declare to be interested or very interested in a sport).
[6] *Source*: Qualitative studies led in 2000 and 2002 and based on focus groups and semi-directive interviews (BVA/Research International).

The Tour de France

The Tour de France is considered as the sport event in the world.[7] It is a legendary race with a 104-year history and the absolute reference of the worldwide cycling. The organizer calls it 'a shared event' with 12–15 million spectators along the roads, around 600 cities crossed every year and a publicity caravan with 220 vehicles and 16 million goodies offered to the public. Its media resonance is exceptional (Figures 25.1 and 25.2):

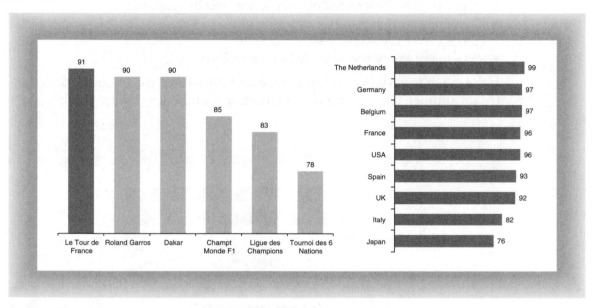

Figure 25.1 Prompted awareness of major events in France

Figure 25.2 Prompted awareness of the Tour de France (%)
Source: TNS Sofres/Ipsos

- 3200 hours of TV broadcast in 185 countries.
- 4–5 billion TV contacts all over the world.
- 617 media and 1700 journalists on-field.
- Notoriety higher than 90 per cent in main markets.

---

[7] *Source*: TNS Sofres/Ipsos.

The event concerns the whole French population (*Sources*: Louis Harris 2003; TNS Sofres, 2006) because France is a country with a deep cycling tradition:

- It is the first sport in France with 18 million amateur cyclists.
- It is the first country in terms of competition days per year.
- France has nine professional cycling teams in 2007.

The Tour de France is considered as 'a shared event' for the French population:

- 35 per cent are interested or very interested by the Tour.
- 73 per cent watch it on TV every year.
- 76 per cent have already seen it on-site.
- 96 per cent know the Tour de France in 2006.

If the event is very popular in France and represents the image of the country in summer, it has also a real international audience (Figure 25.3):[8]

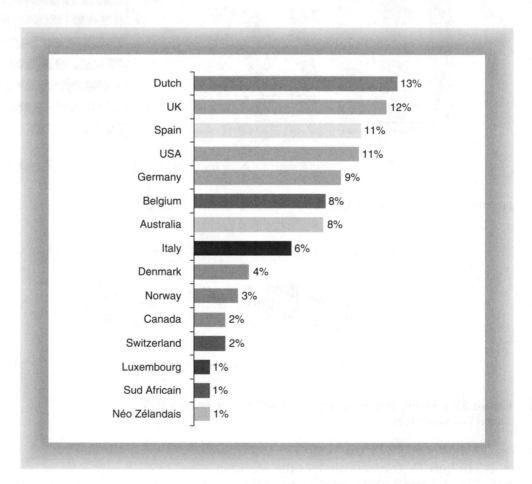

Figure 25.3 Top 15 countries (percentage of the foreign spectators)

---

[8] *Source*: TNS Sofres, August 2006.

- There are 20 per cent of foreign spectators on the Tour de France (30 per cent on the mountain stages and 74 per cent in Paris for the final stage on the Champs-Elysées).
- More than 40 countries are represented among spectators (55 per cent of the foreign spectators come especially for the Tour).
- Around 27 million foreigners have seen the Tour on-site, that is to say 1 inhabitant out of 10 in the bordering countries.

The TV coverage is excellent in France[9] in 2006:

- There are 132 hours broadcasted on France TV (79 hours live on France TV, 44 hours of magazines related to the Tour, 9 hours of TV news and sports documentaries).
- There are 3.6 million TV viewers on average for each live broadcast (40 per cent audience) and 4.7 million TV viewers for each finish (54 per cent audience share).
- 93 per cent of the French population saw TV images of the Tour in 2006 through 24 different programmes (free-to-air broadcasters only).
- It is the most powerful annual sports event in France: with 5h50 per TV viewer (including 4h40 in live), the Tour de France is the most watched sports event.

But this TV coverage is not only national. The audience is really international and concerns the five continents:

- There were 3200 hours of TV broadcast all over the world (+8 per cent versus 2005), that includes 1781 hours in Europe, 544 hours in America, 575 hours in Asia, 123 hours in Africa, 102 hours in the Middle East and 79 hours worldwide (Figure 25.4).
- 185 countries covered the event through 81 TV channels (excluding news).
- Two channels out of three have broadcast the Tour 2006 live.

Historically, the coverage was strong in Europe: the broadcasting of the Tour de France in Europe still stands for more than half of the worldwide coverage (56 per cent in 2006, 67 per cent in 2000), but we can observe a very strong dynamics in Asia, in Middle East and in America (above 300 per cent growth in six years). Thirty-five new markets were reached since 2000 (Norway, Eastern Europe, USA (live), Colombia, China and India).

Considering these facts, no wonder the Tour de France has many sponsors, in spite of the doping scandals that occurred since 1998 and the famous 'Festina case'. The Tour de France is popular, and gives the opportunity to reach millions of people directly.

Besides this marketing structure, there is also an original and powerful communication tool which is the Publicity Caravan. It is a great promotion

---

[9] *Sources*: Sports Marketing Surveys, Carat Sport.

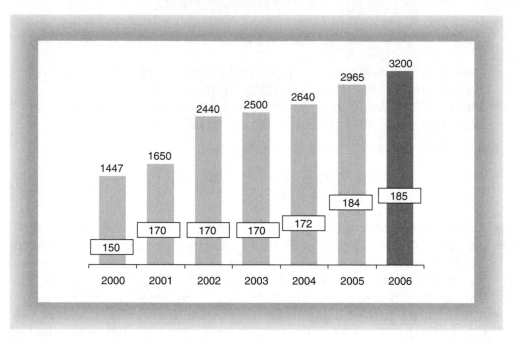

Figure 25.4 Evolution of the worldwide TV broadcast (total hours of broadcast and number of countries)

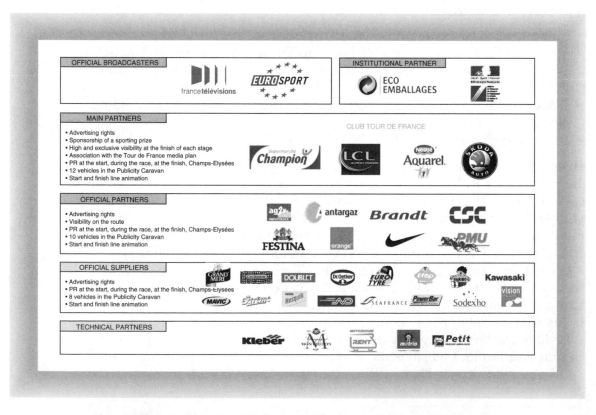

Figure 25.5 Marketing structure of the Tour de France 2007
Source: ASO

support created in 1930, now indissociable from the Tour de France and the summer (Figure 25.5):

- It consists in a procession stretching out over 20 km on the official road.
- 47 brands are represented through 220 decorated/animated vehicles.
- 16 million goodies are distributed to the public.

It is an original media that carries the great values of the Tour (proximity, generosity, festivity) and an unique direct marketing tool expected by its target: the Publicity Caravan is the second reason for motivation of the public. The ROI (Return on Investment) is exceptional for the partners, for example (*Source*: ASO, 2007):

- Nestlé Aquarel (Mineral water) has increased its prompted awareness between June and August (+25 points).
- Café Grand'Mère has observed a +20 per cent market share in July 2006 versus June 2006.
- Cochonou (sausage maker) increased its sales in July 2006 versus June 2006 (+30 per cent).

The Organizers of the Big Races (Tour de France, Giro, Vuelta)

Together with the Giro d'Italia (Tour of Italy) and Vuelta a España (Tour of Spain), the Tour de France is one of the three major stage races and the longest of the UCI calendar at three weeks each. While the other two European Grand Tours are well known in Europe, they are relatively unknown outside the continent, and even the UCI World Cycling Championship is familiar only to cycling enthusiasts. The Tour de France, in contrast, has long been a household sporting name around the globe, known even to those not generally interested in cycling.

But this three Tours have a common point: historically, they are all organized by private and independent companies.

The Giro was inspired by the Tour de France and, just as the French race was intended to boost circulation of L'Auto, so Emilio Camillo Costamagna, the editor of *La Gazzetta dello Sport* newspaper, aimed to increase his circulation. The organizing ability of the *Gazzetta dello Sport* appears from the beginning of the existence of the newspaper which first came out on 2 April 1896 from the merger of 'Il Ciclista' and 'La Tripletta'. Issue number one showed a framed announcement of the Milan-Monza-Lecco-Erba race organized by the same. At first coming out twice weekly the Gazzetta got a three times a week edition on the occasion of the first Giro d'Italia, that is 1909 and became then a daily paper for the 1913 edition. The paper got its pink colour from the first issue of year 1899. On 7 August 1908 the *Gazzetta dello Sport* announced in its first page the first Giro d'Italia to take place in 1909, beating the Corriere della Sera which had in mind to promote a cycling race after the success encountered with its automobile race. With great class and elegance the Corriere acknowledged the Gazzetta victory by offering the winner a price amounting 3000 Lire. The first Giro d'Italia starts on 13 May 1909 at 2.53 a.m. from the Loreto place in Milan. Laps are 8 for a total of 2448 km and the competitors are 127, only 49 of which were able to reach Milan. Information about the race, winner of which is Luigi Ganna, are transmitted by telegraphic dispatches attached to the windows of the Lancia-Lyon Peugeot shop in Piazza Castello, while the happy few who have a telephone can get news by calling the 33.68 number. Luigi Ganna, first winner of the Giro got a prize of 5.325 Lire and the last classified got 300 Lire. To make a useful comparison, Armand Cougnet, the Giro's Director (and also member of the paper board as well as chief editor for cycling) got at that time a monthly salary of 150 Lire.

Today the Giro is organized by *La Gazzetta dello Sport* (press group RCS).

First held in 1935 and annually since 1955, the Vuelta runs for three weeks in a changing route across Spain. The inaugural event (1935) saw 50 entrants face a 3411 km (2119 mile) course over only 14 stages, averaging over 240 km (149 mile) per stage. It was inspired by the success of the Tours in France and Italy, and the boost they brought to the circulations of their sponsoring newspapers (*L'Auto* and *La Gazzetta dello Sport*, respectively); Juan Pujol of the daily Informaciones instigated the race to increase his circulation.

It was formerly held in the spring, but since 1995 the race has been run in September. The course includes two individual time trials. The finish of the Vuelta is traditionally the Spanish capital, Madrid. Today the Vuelta is organized by the sport events company Unipublic.

The Tour de France is organized by the company ASO (Amaury Sport Organization).

ASO belongs to the French press group, EPA (Philippe Amaury Publications), which owns the newspapers and magazine publications *l'Equipe*, *France Football*, *l'Equipe Magazine*, *Vélo Magazine*, *Le Parisien* and *Aujourd'hui* in France. The group has also developed an audio-visual branch, with the creation of *l'Equipe TV*, and new technologies with the websites www.lequipe.fr and www.leparisien.fr, to such an extent that it is today one of the key figures in the French media world.

ASO, created in September 1992, is specialized in the organization of renowned sports events, such as the Tour de France, the Dakar and the Paris Marathon. Over the last few years, the company has expanded, ASO having intensified its activities in the domain of cycling (Paris-Nice, Tour of Qatar, Tour du Faso) and taken up new disciplines, such as golf (the Open de France, the oldest tournament on the European continent) and equestrian sports (creating for the occasion a yearly event christened RIDE: Rencontres Internationales des Disciplines Equestres).

Behind the range of internationally renowned and recognized events, ASO is focused on a precise goal: the design and management of spectacular top flight competitions respecting the sporting code of values and ethics, with long-term dedication.

Case Diagnosis

The Launching of the UCI Pro Tour

Season-long competitions for professional road racing were first instituted in 1948, and continued until the late 1980s when the UCI instituted the UCI Road World Cup series which ran until 2004.

In replacing the World Cup, the Pro Tour was designed to follow the format of the Formula One motor-racing series, and was intended to address several concerns:

- The Grand Tours were not part of the UCI Road World Cup series.
- Different riders and different teams targeted different types of races, making direct comparisons during competition difficult.
- Team sponsorships tended to last only a very few years.
- Many teams had financial difficulty in paying their riders and staff members.
- Several teams had been plagued by doping issues.

The UCI lobbied the organizers of the Grand Tours to participate in the Pro Tour, and was successful in obtaining their agreement despite prior disagreements and threats to completely pull out of the Pro Tour.

The Pro Tour has been criticized for not having a system in place for a timely upgrade and downgrade of teams from/to the lower-tier UCI Continental Circuits.

Originally, UCI and the organizers of the Grand Tour had been unable to come to terms on the 2006 UCI Pro Tour, with the result that the status of both the Grand Tours and some of the other races organized by the organizations behind the Grand Tours are unclear. A deal was finally reached on April 7.

For the 2007 UCI Pro Tour season, the ASO, RCS and Unipublic, organizers of the Tour de France, Giro d'Italia and Vuelta a España, respectively, remain at odds with each other. The primary reason is that grand tour organizers would like to have more freedom to invite popular national teams (e.g. UCI Professional Continental teams) and are attempting to exclude some UCI Pro Tour teams such as Unibet.com. The riders' organization, the International Association of Pro Tour Cycling Teams (IPCT), has demanded a meeting between the UCI and the Grand Tour organizers to settle the dispute.

The Point of View of the UCI

Source: UCI Pro Tour website http://www.uciprotour.com/templates/UCI/ UCI1/layout.asp?MenuId=MTcxNw – accessed on 26 March 2007.

The UCI Pro Tour groups together the best races, the biggest teams and the best riders in the world. It is an international calendar with an individual ranking, a team ranking and a country ranking. UCI Pro Teams have all obtained a UCI Pro Tour licence, giving them the assurance and obligation of taking part in all the races of the UCI Pro Tour calendar. Only teams who respect a series of very strict criteria – sporting quality of their team, respect of ethics, legal and financial compliance – can benefit from this right. By ensuring the professionalism of all those involved, the UCI Pro Tour gives top level cycling greater stability and helps to improve the quality of the racing. Currently, 16 teams have a sponsor until at least 2008, or even longer, six of which until 2010 or beyond. New sponsors have signed up this year and others have expressed an interest for the future.

Participation

The races of the UCI Pro Tour calendar are open first and foremost to UCI Pro Teams. UCI Professional Continental Teams, ranked second in the hierarchy and structures taking part primarily in all races on their continental circuit, are able to ride in the races of the UCI Pro Tour calendar, but only if they are invited.

Riders belonging to a UCI Pro Team are not obliged to take part in all the competitions. This would be impossible and the consequences would be damaging. However, each team must take part in all races, which ensures that the greatest champions will be competing throughout the entire season. As a result, we have noted that between 2004 and 2005 (the first year of the UCI Pro Tour), the participation of the world's best 20 riders had increased by an average of 17 per cent in races in the series. This increase has continued at the same level as 2006 (+17 per cent compared to 2005).

Individual Ranking

Riders belonging to a UCI Pro Team score points in the races of the UCI Pro Tour calendar based on the scale featured in the UCI Regulations. The leader of the individual ranking wears a distinctive jersey.

Riders who are part of a UCI Professional Continental Team do not score any points. The points corresponding to the place obtained are not awarded.

Points awarded for stages are calculated on the last day of the race.

From 2007, the team time-trial awards points to riders from the 10 best teams.

Team Ranking

At the end of one-day races, points are awarded to the first three riders from each team. These points determine the team's ranking in the race, which consequently determines the final number of points obtained by the team (see articles 2.10.2004–2.10.2007 of the UCI Regulations).

Teams may also earn points according to their position in the final classification of stage races.

Country Ranking

The country ranking is worked out on the basis of points obtained by the five first riders of each nationality in the individual ranking (see article 2.10.2008 of the UCI Regulations).

UCI Pro Tour rankings are updated and published on www.uciprotour. com at the end of each UCI Pro Tour race.

The Conflict

After two years, it is obvious that a conflict occurred: its major stake is the control of the professional cycling events. The international federation wants to create kind of a 'closed league', on the model of the National Basketball Association (NBA), the National Football League (NFL) or the Formula 1 championship. These so-called leagues give sponsors security in their investment. Whatever happens in the NBA, a major team sponsor knows it will be present in five years for example, which was not the case in the cycling system before the UCI Pro Tour. Teams were selected by the local organizers and their ROI was very unpredictable. The UCI wants to give these teams a better predictability in their investment. The second point is also to give cycling a more international audience by developing races on five continents: the Tour of California (USA) or the Down Under Tour (Australia) are the major objectives for the UCI because their popular success leads sponsors to reach new emergent markets.

But, on the other hand, the three 'Big Tours' do not want to give up for several reasons: the main one is of course economical, when you realize that the estimated turnover of the Tour de France is about €120 million (in only three weeks of competition).

Case Questions

1 In which sense the marketing model of the Tour de France is original among the world of sport events? Think particularly of ticketing.
2 In which sense can the history of the Tours explain their current marketing structure?
3 What do brands look for in sponsoring cycling? Do doping scandals threaten the system?
4 The UCI wants to develop an organization model which is similar to the NBA, Formula 1 or NFL. Do you think this system is transferable to cycling or there are major cultural constraints (e.g. consumers) that will prevent this shift?
5 Considering the conflict that occurred between the UCI and the three 'Big Tours', what is the future of this system, according to you?
6 As a personal investor, would you take the risk of investing in cycling? Why? What are the strengths and weaknesses of such an investment?

Case Resources

Reading

Andreff, W., Szymanski, S. and Borland, J. (Eds.). (2006). *The Handbook on the Economics of Sport*. Edward Elgar, Cheltenham, UK, 800 pp.

Barros, C., Ibrahimo, M. and Szymanski, S. (2002). *Transatlantic Sport: The Comparative Economics of North American and European Sports*. Cheltenham, E. Elgar, UK.

Desbordes, M. (2006). The economics of cycling, in Andreff, W., Szymanski, S. and Borland, J. (Eds.), *The Edward Elgar Companion to the Economics of Sports*. Edward Elgar Publishing, pp. 645–662.

Desbordes, M. (2007). The economic impact of a major sport event: The case of the Tour de France among different regions. *International Journal of Sport Management and Marketing* (in press).

Hoehn, T. and Szymanski, S. (2001). The Americanization of European football, in Zimbalist, A. (Ed.), *The Economics of Sport*. Cheltenham, Edward Elgar, UK, pp. 605–634.

Szymanski, S. (2004). Is there a European model of sport? in Fort, R.D. and Fizel, J. (Eds.), *International Sports Economics Comparisons*, Conn., Praeger, pp. 19–38.

Szymanski, S. and Kesenne, S. (2004). Competitive balance and gate revenue sharing in team sports. *Journal of Industrial Economics*, Vol. 52, pp. 165–177.

Websites

ASO (Amaury Sport Organization – Organizer of the Tour de France) – http://www.aso.fr/2005/events_us.html

Cycling News – http://www.cyclingnews.com

Formula 1 – http://www.formula1.com/

Giro d'Italia – http://www.gazzetta.it/Speciali/Giroditalia/2006/en/storia.shtml

La Gazzetta dello Sport (Organizer of the Giro) – http://www.gazzetta.it/

La Vuelta – http://www.lavuelta.com/07/ingles/recorrido/index.asp

NBA – http://www.nba.com/

NFL – http://www.nfl.com/

Tour de France – http://www.letour.fr/indexus.html

Tour Down Under – http://www.tourdownunder.com.au/node

Tour of California – http://www.amgentourofcalifornia.com/

UCI Pro Tour – http://www.uciprotour.com/Templates/UCI/UCI5/layout.asp?MenuID=MTY5Mw

Unipublic (Spanish organizer of the Vuelta) – http://www.unipublic.es/

Further Information

Users of the case may want to take a look at the Wikipedia entries for the following:

Formula 1 – http://en.wikipedia.org/wiki/F1
Giro d'Italia – http://en.wikipedia.org/wiki/Giro_d'Italia
La Vuelta – http://en.wikipedia.org/wiki/Vuelta_a_Espa%C3%B1a
NBA – http://en.wikipedia.org/wiki/NBA
NFL – http://en.wikipedia.org/wiki/NFL
Tour de France – http://en.wikipedia.org/wiki/Tour_de_France
Tour of California – http://en.wikipedia.org/wiki/Tour_of_California
UCI Pro Tour – http://en.wikipedia.org/wiki/UCI_ProTour

26

Sports development meets sports marketing in Africa: Basketball without Borders and the NBA in Africa

Jason Means and John Nauright

Case Focus

This case examines the development of the National Basketball Association's (NBA's) 'Basketball without Borders' (BWOB) programme generally and in particular in South Africa. It addresses some of the factors that led to its establishment in the region as well as the factors that contribute to its ongoing success.

Keywords

- National Basketball Association (NBA)
- Basketball without Borders (BWOB)
- South Africa
- Basketball
- Globalization
- Marketing

Case Summary

Over the past several years, professional sports leagues in North America have sought to expand their fan base and marketability outside of the North American continent as the marketplace in North America becomes ever more saturated. While much of the thrust has centered on Europe and Asia, the National Basketball Association (NBA) at least has not ignored other areas such as South America and Africa. In particular its Basketball without Borders (BWOB) camps have been held in many locations including South Africa on the African continent. This chapter examines why South Africa was chosen as the primary location for BWOB, and how the NBA is establishing a programme there with the long-term position of basketball in Africa in mind. Then, what actually occurs at the camp in terms of basketball and community outreach activities is explored. Finally, an analysis will be presented as to whether the NBA is meeting the goals it has set for itself, the community, and for basketball development, and a view of what the future has in store for the NBA, Africa, and its up-and-coming basketball players, will be offered. It is clear that BWOB can serve as a model programme for a synergistic approach to development through sports and to the expansion of sports markets.

Case Elements

BWOB inaugural event took place in Europe in the summer of 2001. Led by seven prominent NBA players of the time, 50 children received basketball instruction in Treviso, Italy. Since this time, BWOB has grown to encompass four continents and is currently held in Beijing, China; Buenos Aires, Argentina; and Johannesburg, South Africa (NBA basketball stars, 2005). Beginning with the Africa 100 camp in 2003, the NBA began to expand the interest in basketball across the continent, utilizing formal education and community outreach initiatives. This programme morphed into BWOB Africa in 2004 and is now a yearly event for the NBA (NBA players unite, 2003).

The NBA's goals are simple. According to Commissioner David Stern, 'BWOB is a global programme that brings people together to discuss important social issues such as HIV/AIDS prevention while emphasizing the importance of education and healthy living.' In addition, he stated that a major goal of the programme is to 'help young people from diverse national and economic backgrounds come together and learn through the sport of basketball.' (NBA basketball stars, 2005). This grassroots basketball development will allow for the exploration, development, and nurturing of the top youth basketball talent on a continent that has just begun to develop a basketball infrastructure. The camp will promote education, sportsmanship, leadership, and healthy living through basketball instruction, educational seminars, and community outreach activities in partnership with local organizations who share goals with the NBA (Basketball without Borders fact sheet, 2005). Of course there are spin-off benefits for the NBA and these will be discussed later.

Why South Africa? Why Now?

In the post-apartheid era, the majority of people in South Africa are still living in poverty. Thirty per cent of adults above age 15 years are not functionally literate (Garson, 2005). HIV-positive estimates range from 2.5 million to 4.2 million people infected. This is nearly 10 per cent of the population. In addition, housing and medical care are lacking. In Kliptown, a township located just outside of Johannesburg, there is no plumbing or electricity. Forty thousand people have to take buckets to get water from one of only 49 public fountains and bring it back to their homes for use. The only places to use the bathroom are port-a-potties, which are shared by as many as five families of seven or more members (NBA players see, 2005). The housing that is available is made with tin roofs, and connected by dirt roads. Scavenging is common as people go to landfill-like mounds to search for discarded food from restaurants, furniture, or anything else that may be of use (West, 2005). It is possible every day to witness horse drawn carts carrying waste products to use for building of some form of shelter for families heading to the many townships that surround South Africa's major cities.

Low cost housing is being built with the help of government subsidies, but the majority of the people won't be able to afford it because they don't have jobs to pay the rent. The first Reading and Learning Center built by the NBA is 'the best-looking building in the community' according to Phoenix Suns assistant general manager Mark West. It has been over a decade since the fall of apartheid, and players who have been to the area in recent years have noted that equal rights are just now becoming equal, that voting is now available to all, and that opportunities for work have finally started to increase. However, it is widely recognized that more time is needed to progress and adapt to the new way of life especially in a country where unemployment ranges somewhere between 30 and 50 per cent (West, 2005).

Even with all of these problems, there are high hopes for South Africa to lead the way for the rest of the continent. Right now, it is the most advanced African country in economic terms. Between 1994 and 2004, GDP increased by an average of 3 per cent per year (South Africa economy, 2005). South Africa has set goals to capitalize on its natural resources, as well as financial, legal, energy, and transportation sectors to grow the already modern infrastructure into the future. The government's economic policy is to promote employment and growth while ensuring equal distribution of income to the population. As a member of the World Trade Organization, South Africa has hopes of increasing the overall levels of exports and direct investment through investors into the country in the coming years (Summary of, 2005).

South Africa is the gateway to Africa, 'providing access to an extended market of more than 180 million people south of the Equator' (South Africa: economy overview, 2005). The Johannesburg International Airport is the primary airport in sub-Saharan Africa, serving as a central hub with spokes to many African countries. There are abundant cellular and Internet services available, along with increasing transportation links, such as the new Gautrain, which is a high speed rail linking the airport to Johannesburg and Pretoria (Gautang's bullet, 2005). Although this train is being built with the 2010 World Cup in mind, this and the above factors all point to why the NBA chose Johannesburg as its primary location to hold BWOB Africa. It is a viable market for the NBA product in the long-term future. The people living there genuinely need and want the help the NBA can provide as it uses basketball as its medium. In addition, basketball was not a major South African sport during the apartheid era and is not tainted with aspects of racism that major sports such as rugby and cricket have had to overcome (Nauright, 1996). Basketball has tremendous room for growth in the post-apartheid era and can look to the future in South Africa at least with confidence.

The NBA is an American corporation, and it ultimately wants positive returns on the bottom line. As revenue from the product the NBA puts on the court in North America has become scarcer because of market saturation and increasing competition from other sports and entertainment outlets, there has become an increasing need for the professional sports leagues in North America to look outside of the continent to newly emerging markets for long-term financial returns (Burton, 1999).

Additionally, the look to the international market comes at a time when there is a renewed focus on the role of sport in development of poorer societies. As a result there has been a push for humanitarianism and social responsibility in all sports particularly when they venture from developed to developing markets. There has been an emerging need for USA and other 'first world' companies to help developing countries and regions. 'By laying a foundation for participation and exposure, these entities are allowing millions of people, especially youngsters, to develop into the future athletes and consumers they will need to maintain and meet their own growth goals' (Singh, 2005). The most important point is that the NBA must 'develop the non-financial as well as financial benefit/impact of sports in the newer markets they are trying to conquer' (Singh, 2005).

Jeffrey Rosensweig of Emory University makes it clear: 'Increased investment into previously ignored/untapped nations has helped them develop infrastructure, educational systems, and professional training programmes, all keys to economic development, continuing investment, and subsequent growth and prosperity.' By involving their players and coaches, the NBA is establishing its brand in Africa. Reebok and Sprite, two of the NBA's official partners, are providing the apparel and drinks to all of the invited African players and coaches. Together, these companies are establishing a first-movers advantage whereby the future generations of basketball talent will grow up knowing and using these particular brands, which will equate to future talent and dollars in the long term, for the NBA and its partners (Singh, 2005). Finally, the NBA has utilized African players who have made the NBA and African-American stars in their BWOB programme in South Africa as a way of providing inspiration to aspiring African basketball talent.

Dikembe Mutombo Leads a Contingent of NBA Players and Coaches

Hakeem Olajuwon may have been the first African NBA basketball player to cross the cultural divide into the NBA, but Congo-native Dikembe Mutombo is the catalyst that will increase the basketball talent flow between the USA and Africa thanks to his ongoing efforts. Mutombo first took the NBA to Africa in 1993 with a number of officials and coaches including now Toronto Raptors assistant coach Alex English and current Miami Heat assistant coach Bob McAdoo, both former NBA standouts. In 1994 Mutombo returned to Africa with League Commissioner David Stern and NBA stars Alonzo Mourning and Patrick Ewing, among others, to present youth basketball clinics. While there, they were able to meet Nelson Mandela, then President of the African National Congress and of South Africa. On a third trip to South Africa, Mutombo was accompanied by Mwadi Mabika of the WNBA on a special tour conducting clinics in Cape Town, Durban, and Johannesburg (NBA basketball stars, 2005a).

On arriving in the NBA in 1991, Mutombo established himself as one of the league's most charitable players. During the off-seasons, he traverses Africa on behalf of the NBA, conducting free basketball clinics for up to 2000 children at a time and helping immunize many African children with the polio vaccination. Mutombo has visited Somali refugee camps in Northern Kenya and paid for the Zairian women's basketball team to travel to the Atlanta Olympics in 1996, while also supplying them with new uniforms. At the first BWOB Africa in 2004, the Dikembe Mutombo Foundation (DMF), which was created in 1997 with the goal of 'improving the health, education, and quality of life for the people of the Democratic Republic of Congo (Dikembe Mutombo Foundation, 2005),' dedicated refurbished dormitories to the Ithuteng Trust (a local youth empowerment movement that provides for needy children) and their children, who previously had been sleeping on the floor of a building without bathrooms (Dikembe, 2005). Recently, Mutombo made another donation, pledging $100,000 to the Ithuteng Trust, which is the single largest donation the Trust has received to date (Wurst, 2005).

Mutombo has been honoured with USA Weekend's 'Most Caring Athlete Award', the President's Service Award (2000), and the Henry Iba Citizen Athlete Award among a multitude of others. Mutombo's list of basketball accomplishments is equally as impressive and integral in what he's been able to do for his home continent. After coming to the USA to attend Georgetown University as a pre-med major, the 7'2" Mutombo was invited by coach John Thompson to try out for the basketball team during his second year. After making the team, Mutombo began to concentrate on basketball, and changed his studies to Linguistics and Diplomacy, which is a perfect fit because of his ability to speak nine languages, five of which are African. His skills are just as diverse on the basketball court, where he has consistently rebounded, defended, and blocked shots at the highest level throughout his career. He is a four-time defensive player of the year, an eight-time all-star, and made it to the NBA finals in 2001 with the Philadelphia 76ers. Because of all of the positive media attention he receives on and off of the court, he is the perfect headliner for the NBA as it takes on Africa, and Mutombo knows, with the NBA backing him, that he can continue to touch the lives of millions in need (Dikembe, 2005). Clearly, Mutombo's goals are in line with the camp's stated goals: 'It is an honour to be able to represent your homeland while directly contributing to the communities that need it most; the BWOB programme encapsulates both' (NBA basketball stars, 2005a).

Mutombo recently led a group of players that included Darvin Ham, Maciej Lampe, Manadoi N'diaye (from Senegal), Marcus Camby, Jim Jackson, and the recently retired Jerome Williams. There were 10 coaches attending from the NBA including Alex English, Mark West, and NBA Senior Vice President of Basketball Operations Stu Jackson. Six NBA personnel acted as Camp Directors, including Amadou Gallo Fall, a native of Senegal, who was the Director of Scouting for the Dallas Mavericks, Masai Ujiri, a native of Nigeria, coaching for the Denver Nuggets, and Joe Touomou, a native of Cameroon, an NBA scout also joined the group. With the exception of Lampe (Poland), all other players, coaches, and directors are from the USA (Basketball without Borders Africa, 2005).

Camp Structure and Timeline

Invitees to the camp (ages 19 years and below) are selected by the International Basketball Federation (FIBA), the NBA, and Basketball South Africa (BSA) based on basketball skills, leadership abilities, and dedication to the sport of basketball. Teams are formed by dividing the attending players, giving no consideration to nationality or race, in hopes of promoting diversity between the teams in the camp (Basketball without Borders fact sheet, 2005). This creates language barriers from player-to-coach and player-to-player, but it's all part of a learning process that focuses on teaching acceptance in a continent that has 53 countries, some with very intense rivalries (Blinebury, 2005a).

In all, 106 participants were selected from 28 different countries to participate in the programme at the American International School of Johannesburg, which took place on 7–12 September 2005. Of the 28 countries, Angola, Cameroon, Nigeria, Senegal, and South Africa had the highest player representation, with each contributing nine or more players to the field. Players were flown into the camp from their home countries with the help of South African Airways, one of the event sponsors. Molten, Reebok, Spalding, and Sprite were the other major sponsors. Nineteen of the attending athletes have taken part in the recently formed Sprite tournaments across the continent, earning votes as 'Most Valuable Players' for their respective tournaments, which directly resulted in their invitations (Participants selected, 2005).

The format of the camp is set up so that the players are divided into ten teams of ten players each. Each team is coached by FIBA and NBA players and coaches. The mornings begin with daily clinics teaching basketball fundamentals. Games are played during the afternoons and evenings, with individual and team shooting games taking place throughout the day. To make sure all players are on a level playing field, they are all given a Reebok gym bag containing shoes, socks, and mesh practice gear (Basketball without Borders – Africa, 2005).

At the beginning of the five-day basketball camp, day one included scrimmages that mixed and matched players on different teams so the NBA coaches and players could evaluate the talent level present and determine balanced teams for the coming days (Day 1, 2005). After this was done, the NBA players, accompanied by some of their families, visited the Apartheid Museum for a much-needed culture shock. The mission of the players clearly takes into account both basketball and education, as Jerome Williams illustrates here: 'By coming here to Africa and working with the basketball players, we can give the BWOB campers knowledge of the NBA and balance that with educational themes – not only in regard to their school work but also AIDS and HIV' (Williams, 2005). Williams also commented on the importance of NBA players using their celebrity status to become 'ambassadors of the game,' as well as serve as role models both on and off the court for kids not only in the United States, but also in Africa (Williams, 2005). To this extent, the NBA player involvement and the accompanying media attention have struck a chord with celebrities Brad Pitt, Oprah Winfrey, and the man who first started the HIV/AIDS awareness campaign for the NBA, Magic Johnson, all of whom have volunteered or donated for the cause the NBA began in Africa (Kwenda, 2005). The 2005 BWOB included special guest speaker Chris Tucker, who earlier in the year visited the Ithuteng

Trust in South Africa, and was so touched by the experience that he flew 21 children from Africa to Los Angeles to watch the NAACP Image Awards, which he hosted. He is also currently raising money for two new buses, a classroom, and a dormitory for the kids whom he has returned to see on this visit (Wurst, 2005).

Day two opened with a camp overview to prepare the invitees for what they were to expect, as well as a life-skills seminar. After an extensive stretching session, the players were led through 10 stations covering fundamentals of the game. The players were then informed of their teams and given time to practice their newly learned offensive and defensive skills together before beginning games (Africa – day two, 2005). As the day went on, the players got the chance to interact with the 500 students at Soweto Kliptown Youth Trust (SKY), led by Bob Nemenga, the founder and head of SKY Trust, which, in partnership with 'Feed the Children', provides needy kids with daily meals. The kids of this youth empowerment movement acted out personal and emotional stories of rape, child abuse, and HIV/AIDS for their NBA visitors, leaving the gentle giants teary-eyed, before bringing their spirits back up with displays of traditional dancing, showcasing their uniquely positive attitudes. After the youths presented their stories and experiences to the players, who were deeply touched, the players reciprocated to these kids, who basically have nothing but hope (NBA players see, 2005). It is widely known that many NBA players have grown up in ghettos raised by a single parent, but many players commented on how their personal situations were nothing compared to the poverty level of these young people. They also noted the incredibly positive attitudes the youngsters displayed while living in such desperate situations. Despite the living conditions, the players brought smiles to the faces of the children and described the hope they saw in the kids as 'mind-blowing,' 'amazing,' and 'wonderful to see' (Williams, 2005).

Day three started with basic practices on skills and drills, before the HIV/AIDS awareness events took place. The Moletsane Sports Complex, in poverty-stricken Soweto, hosted drama presentations, music, dance, personal testimonials, and a health fair titled 'Get Informed: Outsmart AIDS.' Jerome Williams and his brother Johnny provided a dramatic presentation to the kids, illustrating to them the countless number of people infected with HIV/AIDS worldwide with a visual demonstration before performing a rap called 'mission possible' (NBA basketball event, 2005). After discussing prevention methods and how to prevail through adversity in life, the kids and players both were left with an emotional day to reflect upon (Africa – day three, 2005).

The fourth day of the event began on a very bright note, with the opening of two much-needed new buildings at the Ithuteng Trust: a laundry room and a guesthouse. Last year before the camp was held, the people living there did their laundry in buckets of dirty water (Williams, 2005). The Ithuteng Trust is a youth empowerment movement created by Jackey 'Mama Jackey' Maarohanye in 1990. It seeks to give at-risk youth the education and life skills they desperately lack. During BWOB Africa 2004, the NBA teamed up with Mama Jackey, who works with thousands of teenagers who were once the victims of violent crimes or on the path to becoming criminals. Her achievements in education have been praised by Nelson Mandela, as 100 per cent of her students passed the school examinations since 2003, dwarfing the pass-rate in governmental schools. The pupils also learn awareness of their culture and perform volunteer work in orphanages and hospitals as part of their educational experience (Ithuteng, 2005). Most of these kids had never experienced love until meeting Mama Jackey. The number one lesson she preaches to the kids is to 'love themselves.' Because Mama Jackey is so committed to the children and the betterment of South Africa, the NBA has created a partnership with her based on these mutual goals. Through this partnership, two Reading and Learning Centers have been built, with dormitory-style living quarters, books, and computers provided by Dell. In addition, a new basketball court available for daily use has been built nearby (Africa – day four, 2005).

As the camp came to a close, what better way to end it than in the style of a true NBA spectacle. A championship game, a slam-dunk contest, and two all-star games capped the final day along with giveaways, music, and a barbeque. A TV production set was also on hand for the filming of public service announcements including the NBA players and stars of a South African TV show called 'Tsha Tsha.' The show focuses on the impact of HIV/AIDS and other social issues on its young actors, and is targeted at 15–25-year olds (Zurba, 2005). The campers watched the filming before exchanging contact information with one another. At the end of the day, NBA players and participants expressed the same view of the trip: 'This was the best trip of my life' (Africa – day five, 2005).

Case Diagnosis

In an event such as this, where young players are chosen to participate based on talent, among other factors, it is easy to spot the players with potential, especially by watching the championship and all-star games. Based on the observations of Jerome Williams, every one of the all-stars has what it takes to play Division I college basketball in the USA. He goes so far as to say that 'there's [sic] at least three or four that could make it (to the NBA) if they continue working' based on their raw skills (Williams, 2005).

Overall impressions suggested that the talent present at this camp was better than in the past. Progress was clearly being made, with five or six very promising players. It's hard for Africa to develop players as a developed country does because of the lack of resources within the domestic basketball federations. The cost of equipment is too high, and most courts in African countries are in poor condition. There is no access to affordable shoes, which can cost a third of the yearly income of an average family. The local governments can be highly volatile, which affects the parents and has a trickle-down effect on the young men, making basketball a relatively low priority when families are struggling to survive (Q & A, 2005).

Anicet Lavodrama, an African basketball legend, former NBA player, and now Manager of International Relations and Development for FIBA, believes the physical ability of players from Senegal, Nigeria, Mali, and Egypt is more promising than that of those from other countries. The BWOB environment allows the participants to play within a structure, with which they have no experience. The drills and the stations are perfect to give them what they need, which is direction and coaching to better their on-court performance. By giving these young men the resources and structure they need, the talent can be nurtured and developed with the NBA's help. 'The interaction between the NBA players and coaches from the African continent and the young players; it's very significant. It may not always be linked directly to basketball, but basketball exists within an environment; it's a social, political, and economical environment so as to give a chance to the people from the African continent' (Q & A, 2005).

Lavodrama also believes that African players will soon be competing with those from countries like Spain, France, and Argentina. He believes there are a couple of players ready from the first BWOB who will have a good shot at making it to the NBA in a year or two. In addition, he thinks there are two particular players from the 2005 camp who have the potential to make it to the NBA sooner rather than later (Q & A, 2005). Although BWOB Africa has yet to have a past participant play a game in the NBA, as of opening night, eight players represented Africa on active NBA rosters. By the 2005–2006 Season, there were 82 international players representing 36 countries in the league out of a total of 450 players on 30 teams (NBA players from, 2005). There is no doubt that NBA-calibre basketball is becoming a global as opposed to an American phenomenon and it's only a matter of time before BWOB Africa starts producing talent for the NBA.

Vusi Mgobhozi, Executive President of BSA, knows it's not just about basketball for these youngsters: 'This assembly of African players is an opportunity for advancement in their sporting and academic careers' (NBA basketball stars, 2005a). Although there has been some trouble with kids getting student visas since 9/11, 14 of the players who attended BWOB Africa 2004 enroled in American colleges. In Africa, an education is valued much more than a career in sports, which is quite the opposite of how most young people feel in the USA. Paulo Muquixe, an 18-yearold Angolan forward, doesn't 'believe he is the next LeBron James.' He just wants the chance to go to school in America, and if basketball is the means to this end, then he will go for it. DeSagana Diop, a native of Senegal, was the eighth overall pick in the 2001 draft by the Cleveland Cavaliers, which made him a millionaire, but his parents were upset that he went straight from high school to the NBA without completing his educational plans. So far, the NBA is embracing the education-first approach as well. 'The message we are trying to spread is that the game can give you an opportunity to do so many other things,' said Bob Lanier, NBA spokesman for international programmes around the world. Because these players have only been playing for four years, and in many cases, much less, the focus is on giving them the opportunity to get proper coaching, play in well-maintained facilities, and hone their games against proper competition, whether it be in Africa or abroad (Blinebury, 2005b).

Make no mistake about it; the NBA is looking to mine the talent out of Africa sooner rather than later. 'For now, though, it's about getting the developmental programmes established and getting these young men to the USA and into American schools. The more we can get them focused on an opportunity to go to an American college, the easier it will be to open the pipeline in years to come' said Amadou Gallo Fall (Blinebury, 2005b). Africa was supposed to be the next basketball Mecca after it produced Olajuwon, Mutombo, and Manute Bol of Sudan, but the NBA has been more shaped by the imports from Europe and South America. The pipeline was supposed to be flowing steadily by now, but instead has produced only drips, causing the NBA to reengineer the system as it looks for speedier results (Blinebury, 2005a).

What Does the Future Hold for the Ever-Globalizing NBA?

As the NBA looks toward future expansion and social responsibility efforts, a cause-related marketing programme called NBA Cares has emerged, with lofty goals of generating $100 million in charitable dollars by 2010. The focus will be on helping improve the lives of individual children as well as entire communities (League launches, 2005). As the BWOB and Read to Achieve (which is a year-round educational outreach campaign to help young people develop a lifelong love for reading and encourage adults to read regularly to children) programmes continue, there will be a plethora of charitable events, including volunteering at soup kitchens, Thanksgiving turkey giveaways, and coat drives with the players and the league at the forefront, receiving much-needed positive media exposure. David Stern understands how to use his players' celebrity to market the league in a positive light, stating: 'Image enhancement will be a byproduct of this, but … We want people to understand that corporate social responsibility is embedded in the NBA's DNA' (Lefton, 2005a).

Kathy Behrens, NBA senior vice president of community and player programmes, is in charge of player involvement in charitable efforts for NBA Cares programmes. In addition to running future BWOB programmes, she will ensure a global 'presence that doesn't just promote the game of basketball.' On the very day that the league announced that it raised $2.5 million for Hurricane Katrina victims, a new Feed the Children campaign began in South Africa, which shows the NBA is planting its roots in South Africa and its community for the long-term future (Lombardo, 2005) though there are certainly other places in Africa worse off than most of South Africa.

As the NBA continues to delve deeper into Africa, the American public will get the chance to see more of Africa as well. The Africa Channel, which is run by co-founder and CEO James Makawa, and also has been invested in by NBA players Theo Ratliff and Dikembe Mutombo, was put on air in Louisiana on Cox Communications on 1 September 2005. The Johannesburg-based channel shows lifestyle and information programming, soap operas, and even reality TV, in what will look like a hybrid of the Discovery Channel, the National Geographic Channel, and a fusion of many entertainment channels. Although the all-English channel shows some of the hardships in Africa, such as HIV/AIDS, the channel focuses on the positive aspects of Africa in an attempt to show America what South Africa has to offer. The channel utilizes high definition where available and video-on-demand as it tries to market itself to DirecTV, EchoStar's DISH Network, and other major cable operators in hopes of reaching a more globalized viewer base (Crupi, 2005).

The channel is based in Los Angeles to take advantage of the media and celebrity base that already thrives there. A major goal of the channel is to rid itself of the third-world 'Tarzan' stereotype and show America that South Africa has a lot of buying power. By informing Americans about opportunities in Africa, there will be a greater flow of information and business to and from the continents (Alexander, 2005). The channel also serves the community of South Africa, with a highly visible agenda rooted in education and the betterment of its local market (Cox to debut, 2005).

Another benefit of the NBA's expanding global involvement is generating partnerships with new sponsors and re-signing current sponsors to long-term deals. FedEx, a global delivery and logistics specialist, has decided to sign a deal that increases its sponsorship involvement to a 'partner level' using the NBA's increasing international player base to represent its increasing global capabilities (Lefton, 2005b). Southwest Airlines, a long-time league sponsor, has created a league-themed aeroplane called the 'Slam Dunk One.' The plane has a customized paint job and will be used as part of the league's NBA Cares programme before it goes into the regular rotation of Southwest's jets (McCarthy, 2005). TNT, a TV channel that carries a large portion of televised NBA games, will begin running a series of 12 feature segments called 'TNT NBA Planet,' showing behind-the-scenes information on how the game is 'passed and received' around the world (Global, 2005).

The US Department of State has recently made two moves that will have an immediate impact on the promotion and development of youth basketball in Africa. Through a public–private partnership between the NBA and Reebok in conjunction with the US embassies in Algeria, Nigeria, and Senegal, basketball clinics will be held for 12,000 youth, all of whom will receive new basketball shoes. The clinics are run by players and coaches from the WNBA and NBA, including previous BWOB Africa attendee Jim Jackson, and will emphasize the values of teamwork, life skills, achievements in the classroom, respect, and leadership through basketball (A slam-dunk! 2005).

The second major announcement is that the US Department of State is providing a $326,000 grant to the University of Delaware (UD), which will work with the NBA to conduct an educational sports exchange programme with Senegal. UD will work with BWOB Africa, non-profit organization Sports for Education and Economic Development (SEED), and the Senegalese Basketball Federation to execute the grant. Six coaches will be brought from Senegal to UD for three weeks. They will work with the basketball staff, visit the NBA league office, attend NBA games and practices, and attend a coaching clinic at the University of North Carolina. Two Senegalese graduate students began classes fall 2006 before working with the basketball staff at UD and interning with the Dallas Mavericks in the summer of 2007. Once their studies are finished, they will return to Senegal to take on leadership roles in the Senegalese Basketball Federation, with the goal of expanding youth basketball participation. For BWOB Africa 2006 coaches from UD travelled with the NBA for coaching clinics, raising HIV/AIDS awareness, and conducting community outreach initiatives. A programme like this was successful in Turkey in 2003, and the hope is that more African nations will obtain grants of this nature in the near future (University of Delaware, 2005).

NBA players, coaches, and personnel need to be at the forefront of the global movement. They will play an integral role in creating awareness in local, regional, and national markets by using their celebrity status to attract media and to market the NBA global campaign. The continued and cyclical involvement of key players and coaches will allow the NBA to continue aligning itself with partners in Africa, such as SKY and the Ithuteng Trust, as it continues to develop basketball and educational infrastructure in South Africa and Africa in the long-term future. By establishing itself in South Africa, and moving into the rest of Africa slowly, the NBA can assist in the creation of a pipeline to help the people of Africa to obtain the resources they need, such as education, literacy, and HIV/AIDS awareness. Basketball is the medium, and the grassroots development the NBA is generating should lead to positive returns for Africa and North America in the future, both on and off the court.

Case Questions

1 What is the relationship between 'marketing' and 'development' when sports organizations from developed countries operate in developing ones?
2 Rate the arguments used by the NBA to justify its involvement in Africa. Does the evidence support the claims made by the league? If not, what can be done to improve the operation of its programmes in Africa?
3 Why did the NBA locate its main African programme in the most developed sub-Saharan African country? Can you think of more deserving locations? What problems might exist elsewhere?

4 Devise an argument for or against South Africa as the location of BWOB.

5 Compare the involvement of the NBA in Africa with other sports organizations such as FIFA or the IOC or particular clubs such as Ajax FC from Amsterdam who are involved in the operation of Ajax Cape Town in South Africa.

6 What do leagues, sports brands, and teams hope to achieve from their involvement with Africa? What can or should be done to improve any of these programmes? Do leagues or teams on balance benefit in a marketing sense from their involvement in Africa?

Case Resources

Reading

A slam-dunk! US Department of State partners with the NBA and Reebok to promote youth basketball in Africa (2005). National Basketball Association. Retrieved October 10, 2005 from http://www.nba.com/global/state_youth_basketball.html

Africa – day five recap (2005). National Basketball Association. Retrieved September 16, 2005 from http://www.nba.com/bwb/africa_recap_050911.html

Africa – day four recap (2005). National Basketball Association. Retrieved September 16, 2005 from http://www.nba.com/bwb/africa_recap_050910.html

Africa – day three recap (2005). National Basketball Association. Retrieved September 16, 2005 from http://www.nba.com/bwb/africa_recap_050909.html

Africa – day two recap (2005). National Basketball Association. Retrieved September 16, 2005 from http://www.nba.com/bwb/africa_recap_050908.html

Alexander, V. (2005, July 24). All Africa, all the time. The Africa Channel. Retrieved October 16, 2005 from http://www.theafricachannel.com/pressroom.php?news=4

Basketball without Borders – Africa (2005). National Basketball Association. Retrieved September 16, 2005 from http://www.nba.com/bwb/africa_report2005.html

Basketball without Borders Africa: fact sheet (2005). National Basketball Association. Retrieved September 16, 2005 from http://www.nba.com/bwb/africa_2005.html

Basketball without Borders fact sheet (2005). National Basketball Association. Retrieved August 25, 2005 from http://www.nba.com/bwb/bwb2005facts.html

Blinebury, F. (2005a, June 21). The next African dream. Houston Chronicle. Retrieved August 27, 2005 from http://www.chron.com/cs/CDA/printstory.mpl/sports/2790141

Blinebury, F. (2005b, June 21). Young Africans see sport as ticket to US education. Houston Chronicle. Retrieved September 16, 2005 from http://www.chron.com/cs/CDA/printstory.mpl/sports/2794256

Burton, R. (1999). Does the National Football League's Current economic model threaten the long term growth of professional football globally? *Football Studies*, Vol. 2, No. 2, pp. 5–17.

Cox to debut channel devoted to Africa (2005). BizNewOrleans.com. Retrieved October 16, 2005 from http://bizneworleans.com/109+M505feda7d8a.html

Crupi, A. (2005, July 18). Africa Channel bows September 1. MediaWeek.com. Retrieved October 16, 2005 from http://www.mediaweek.com/mw/news/cabletv/article_display.jsp?vnu_content_id=1000980416

Day 1: Campers Gather (2005, September 7). National Basketball Association. Retrieved September 16, 2005 from http://www.nba.com/bwb/BWBAfrica_Day_1_Recap.html

Dikembe Mutombo (2005). Dikembe Mutombo Foundation. Retrieved October 30, 2005 from http://dmf.org/About.html

Dikembe Mutombo Foundation, Inc. brochure (2005). Dikembe Mutombo Foundation. Retrieved October 30, 2005 from http://dmf.org/PDF/brochure.html

Garson, P. (2005). Education in South Africa. South Africa.info The Official Gateway. Retrieved October 21, 2005 from http://www.southafrica.info/ess_info/sa_glance/education/education.htm

Gautang's bullet train on track (2005, August 8). South Africa.info The Official Gateway. Retrieved October 21, 2005 from http://www.southafrica.info/doing_business/economy/infrastructure/gautrain.htm

Global experience (2005). National Basketball Association. Retrieved November 11, 2005 from http://www.nba.com/nbabuzz/Global_Experience.html

Ithuteng Trust (2005). Smiling Children e.V. Retrieved October 30, 2005 from http://www.smiling-children.de/en/ithuteng.php?nav=6&sub=14

Kwenda, S. (2005, August 18). Dikembe in the hood. *Financial Gazette (Harare)*. Retrieved September 16, 2005 from http://www.allafrica.com/stories/printable/200508180534.html

League launches 'NBA Cares' global outreach initiative. (2005, October 18). National Basketball Association. Retrieved October 20, 2005 from http://www.nba.com/community/NBACARES_051018.html

Lefton, T. (2005a). 'NBA Cares' sets $100M charitable goal. *Sports Business Journal*, Vol. 8, No. 24, pp. 1 and 32.

Lefton, T. (2005b). Package deal. *Sports Business Journal*, Vol. 8, No. 26, p. 10.

Lombardo, J. (2005). Behrens gets players involved in community. *Sports Business Journal*, Vol. 8, No. 25, p. 23.

McCarthy, M. (2005, November 3). NBA hopes unique publicity idea will fly. USA Today, p. C1.

Nauright, J. (1996). Sport, cultures, and identities in South Africa. Leicester University Press, London and David Phillip, Cape Town.

NBA basketball event – 'Get Informed: Outsmart AIDS' HIV/AIDS awareness sports event (2005, September 9). United States Embassy in South Africa. Retrieved October 30, 2005 from http://pepfar.pretoria. usembassy.gov/wwwh2005nbaevent.html

NBA basketball stars reunite for Basketball without Borders Africa. (2005, April 12). National Basketball Association. Retrieved August 25, 2005 from http://www.nba.com/bwb/starsreuniteafrica.html

NBA basketball stars reunite for Basketball without Borders Africa (2005, August 22). National Basketball Association. Retrieved September 16, 2005 from http://www.nba.com/bwb/starsreuniteafrica.html

NBA players from around the world: 2005–2006 season. (2005, October 31). National Basketball Association. Retrieved November 7, 2005 from http://www.nba.com/news/international_players.html

NBA players see a new world (2005, September 7). National Basketball Association. Retrieved September 16, 2005 from http://www.nba. com/bwb/NBA_Players_See_a_New_World.html

NBA players unite for Africa 100 Camp (2003, August 14). National Basketball Association. Retrieved September 16, 2005 from http:// www.nba.com/global/africa100_030813.html

Participants selected for Basketball without Borders Africa 2005 (2005, August 26). National Basketball Association. Retrieved September 16, 2005 from http://www.nba.com/bwb/africa2005_participants.html

Q&A with Anicet Lavodrama, FIBA's International Relations and Development Manager (2005). National Basketball Association. Retrieved September 16, 2005 from http://www.nba.com/bwb/lavodrama_050911.html

Singh, S. (2005). Sports has world of opportunity to help others, help itself. *Sports Business Journal*, Vol. 8, No. 24, p. 25.

South Africa economy (2005). Travel Document Systems. Retrieved October 5, 2005 from http://www.traveldocs.com/za/economy.htm

South Africa: economy overview (2005). South Africa.info The Official Gateway. Retrieved October 5, 2005 from http://www.southafrica. info/doing_business/economy/econoverview.htm

Summary of South Africa – Yahoo! Finance (2005). Yahoo Finance. Retrieved October 5, 2005 from http://biz.yahoo.com/ifc/za.html

University of Delaware received grant for an educational sports exchange program (2005, August 16). National Basketball Association. Retrieved October 10, 2005 from http://www.nba.com/global/univ_del_grant. html

West, M. (2005, September 8). Mark West' South African journal. National Basketball Association. Retrieved September 16, 2005 from http:// www.nba.com/suns/news/west_africa.html

Williams, J. (2005, September 12). The Junk Yard Dog blog. National Basketball Association. Retrieved September 16, 2005 from http://www.nba.com/bwb/jyd_blog.html

Wurst, M. (2005). Generosity and inspirations across borders. Women's National Basketball Association. Retrieved September 16, 2005 from http://www.wnba.com/features/mccray_africatrip_050329.html

Zurba, R. (2005, September 12). NBA stars make TV public service announcements with South African TV stars. USAID South Africa. Retrieved October 30, 2005 from http://www.sn.apc.org/usaidsa/nba%20in%20South%20Africa.html

Websites

National Basketball Association – www.nba.com
South Africa 'Alive with Possibility' – www.southafrica.info
Reebok www.rbk.com

27

New marketing challenge of the South Korean Professional Baseball League and the Lotte Giants

Jaemin Hong and Chanil Lee

Case Focus

This case study explores the market changes and subsequent reaction of the South Korean Professional Baseball League using the case of the Lotte Giants.

Keywords

- The Korea Professional Baseball League
- The Lotte Giants
- Market environment change
- Contingencies
- Organizational objectives
- Baseball

Case Summary

The Korean Baseball League (KBL) is the oldest, and still the leading, professional sports league in South Korea after 25 years. Despite its beginnings being motivated by the then militant government of the 1980s, the KBL has enjoyed duopolistic status in the sports market, alongside the soccer K-League which was founded in the following year. However, in the mid-1990s, the KBL was affected by a boom in interest due to the success of Korean baseball players in foreign leagues, in growing interest in US Major League Baseball (MLB) and the promotion of football by the South Korean government prior to the 2002 FIFA World Cup.

All KBL teams were owned by conglomerates, who appeared reluctant to address the new market challenges; the Lotte Giants, regarded by many as the most popular team in the League, were no different. This case study examines changing conditions in the marketing environment, specifically with reference to the Lotte Giants. In particular, the case highlights the influence and commercial effort required to regain the competitive league advantage in the domestic marketplace.

Case Elements

League Overview

The KBL is the oldest professional sports league in South Korea, and attracts the largest number of spectators amongst all professional sports including soccer (football). In the 2006 World Baseball Classic (WBC) competition, the equivalent of the FIFA World Cup in football, 3.3 million Internet users accessed a streaming video service of the game against Japan (Ohmy news.com, 18 March 2006).

The KBL was founded in 1982 by the militant predictor Doo-Hwan Cheon, as part of his popularist policies that utilized sport as a social marketing instrument (Kotler and Zaltman, 1971). It was a natural decision to choose baseball as the first professional league, rather than football, due to the

Table 27.1 KBL teams

Team	Home city (population in million)	Owning company	Championship winning[a]
KIA Tigers	Kwang-Ju (1.4)	KIA Motors	9
Samsung Lions	Dae-Gu (2.4)	Samsung	4
Hyundai Unicorns	Seoul[2] (9.8)[b]	Hyundai	4
Doosan Bears	Seoul (9.8)	Doosan	3
LG Twins	Seoul (9.8)	LG	2
Lotte Giants	Busan (3.5)	Lotte	2
Hanhwa Eagles	Dae-jeon (1.4)	Hanhwa	1
SK Wiberns	In-Cheon (2.5)	SK	–

[a]1982–2006 Seasons' results
[b]Home ground is located in Su-Won city due to not having proper baseball stadium in Seoul

dominant influence of the USA in social, cultural, and even political areas. Six teams participated in the inaugural season (1982) and there are currently eight teams in the league following two additions in 1986 and 2000, respectively (see Table 27.1).

The league has been run on the MLB franchise-based model since its inaugural season. The existing constituent franchises have been guaranteed exclusive business rights in their particular location. The national capital region (Seoul also a regional capital) comprises almost half of the South Korean population. Therefore, four teams are allocated in this region (three teams exclusively in Seoul). The league promotes competitive balance by using draft regulation. Each team can pick and sign two home-grown players at the first stage, and unpicked players are selected by all teams in reverse order based on the previous season's league position at the second stage. However, there is an issue with the current draft regulation as some franchises are blessed with many numbers of high school and university baseball teams who produce a high volume of talent each year. Other areas do not have the same volume and do not produce enough local talent from schools.

The most successful team in the KBL's history, the KIA Tigers, is owned by the KIA Corporation. They have won the championship nine times in 25 years. The current champions are the Samsung Lions. The season runs from April to September each year. Each team plays 126 games, with 18 games played against the same opposition in a single season. A total number of 504 games are played each season. After the regular season, the playoff season takes place from September to October, with the semi-final playoff taking place between the third and fourth placed teams, followed by the playoff between second placed team and winner of the semi-playoff. This is finally followed by the Korean Series Championship between the top placed team of the regular season and winner of the playoff in order to decide season's champion.

Market Size and Game Attendance

The market size of the league was estimated at £42.9 million in 2003, with a total attendance of 2.9 million (KSSI, 2006) – the largest figures amongst any professional sports league in South Korea. The inaugural season of 1982 recorded 1.4 million total attendances in 240 games played by six teams. This figure rose steeply after the Seoul Olympics in 1988 and peaked at 5.4 million in the 1995 season. The most supported team in the league is the LG Twins with 16 million of the accumulated attendance from 1982 to 2005. Following the Twins, the Lotte Giants and Doosan Bears recorded 13.8 and 11 million, respectively. Given that the LG Twins and Doosan Bears are ground sharing in Seoul, the capital city with a 9.8 million population, the Lotte Giants' attendance record requires more analysis.

The rising trends of league attendance ended after the 1995 season. The 5.4 million attendance of 1995 dropped down to 4.4 million in following season and it continued to fall down to 2.6 million until the 1998 season. Changes in the marketing environment from the 1996 season will be analysed later in this section.

Team Identity

All eight teams are 100 per cent owned by parent companies (with their names being contained in the name of each team) which subsidize approximately 70–80 per cent of total team income , despite all teams supposedly acting as legally independent companies. The biggest spender, the Samsung Lions, recorded a £17 million[1] turnover in 2003 (Bizpark website, viewed 19 March 2007) but reportedly over 80 per cent of income was subsidised by Samsung Group. In the same season, the Lotte Giants generated only 6.3 per cent of total income from their own business (e.g. gate receipts, merchandising), the rest coming from the parent company. The KBL teams act more like corporate advertising units than financially independent organizations. The most important mission of KBL teams therefore is conducting public relations (PR) activity, maximizing brand awareness, and improving the image of parent companies rather than generating sufficient income to run their organizations. In order to articulate those organizational missions, every team pursues winning games, maximizing brand awareness in media as much as corporate commercials.

Market Changes since the 1990s

The KBL (baseball) and K-League (soccer) were the only two professional sports leagues in South Korea by the mid-1990s. As Seoul hosted mega sports events such as the Summer Olympics and Asian Games in the second half of the 1980s, people's interest in attending sports events naturally grew. Investing heavily on training individual sport talent, domestic players

---

[1] £1 = 1,846 Korean Won

improved enough to compete in foreign leagues, such as those in Japan and USA. As some of the individual star players began to play in the USA and Japanese leagues, those foreign leagues, through television exposure, quickly emerged as direct competitors to the KBL. A similar phenomenon can be found in the football market because of the success of domestic football players in European leagues after the 2002 FIFA World Cup.

Since Chan-Ho Park made his debut for the MLB's Los Angeles Dodgers, and Dong-Yeol Sun, the best pitcher in history, transferred to the Junichi Dragons in the Japanese league in 1995, attendances at domestic baseball league games have dropped rapidly year on year. According to the 2006 KBL yearbook, attendances dropped from 5.4 million in 1995 to 2.6 million by 1998 (see Figure 27.1). Despite rule changes in the KBL, allowing teams to play foreigners from 1997, attendance trends continued to decline until the 2004 season.

Another variable negatively affecting the market was the 2002 FIFA World Cup. In 1997, South Korea and Japan were selected as co-host countries of the 2002 FIFA World Cup and it spread 'football fever' across both countries. Korean people, nurtured towards nationalistic sporting attitudes, quickly became passionate supporters of football once their country was

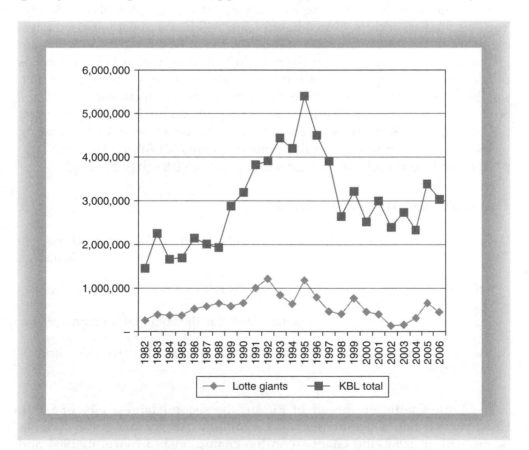

Figure 27.1 Attendance of the KBL and Lotte Giants

selected as one of the hosts. This had a negative effect on baseball with only 2.4 million people attending baseball games in 2002, and only 2.3 million in the 2004 season.

Foreign sports leagues have attracted high interest in South Korea; the professional basketball league started in 1996, and the K-League of soccer expanded the number of teams before and after the 2002 FIFA World Cup, even e-sports and online gaming leagues have begun to dominate the younger generation's consumption behaviour. The KBL attempted to react to these market changes in various ways, but the fact that all the teams are not financially driven organizations has meant that they have been adversely affected by market competition.

The globalization of sport is a growing business phenomenon due to rapid commercialization of sports events and communication innovations that have taken place since the end of the 20th century. This Worldwide business phenomenon has adversely affected the South Korean baseball market mainly due to the export of Korean star players to bigger leagues. The market for the KBL has already been superseded by the globally influential big leagues. The Seoul Broadcasting System (SBS) announced that it will show all the 72 home games of the Japanese Yomiuri Giants on live TV in the 2007 season. The Yomiuri Giants signed the biggest Korean star player, Seung-Yup Lee, in 2006 and the Tokyo-based team will be the most televised baseball team in South Korea in 2007. Similarly, the most televised football team in South Korea is Manchester United (England) for which Ji-Sung Park is playing, not a K-league club. Communication developments (e.g. Internet, satellite television) accelerated the invasion of foreign sports leagues into the South Korean market. Websites of foreign sports teams increasingly attract the attention of Korean fans, emphasising the effectiveness of operating websites for sports teams as sales points, a source of information for supporters, and a promotional tool for wider activities (Beech et al., 2000).

The Lotte Giants and its Fans

Korean people love the national football team and Busan people love the Lotte Giants.

Giants' fan

In the home game against the Giants, I always feel better because more fans are attending the games.

Seung-Rak Sohn, the Hyundai Unicorns' pitcher

I asked the taxi driver. What is the most famous site in Busan? The taxi driver answered the Lotte Giants

Foreign tourist

The Lotte Giants are based in Busan, the second largest city of South Korea which has a population of 3.5 million. As an inaugural member of the KBL in 1982, the Giants won the championship twice, in 1984 and 1992, respectively. Winning two championships in 25 years is not regarded as satisfactory because there are only less successful two teams than the Giants in the league. Despite their underachievement, the Giants are always competing for the top position in terms of the team value, thanks largely to their impressive fan base. In 1991, accumulated attendance over the previous 10 years reached 5 million and home attendance reached 1 million in a single season for the first time in the KBL history. Four years after their second championship victory in 1992, accumulated attendance exceeded 10 million, a league record.

The Lotte Group, parent company of the team, runs a successful business in various fields including consumer retailing, petrochemicals, confectionery, and beverages. In 2005, the Lotte Group recorded a turnover of £6.6 billion, excluding financial results from the Japanese business unit of the group (Lotte Group website, 2007). Major shareholders of the Giants are Lotte Shopping (30 per cent), Lotte Confectionery (30 per cent), and Lotte Beverage (20 per cent). The Lotte group also operates another professional baseball team, the Chiba Lotte Marines, in the Japanese baseball league.

The atmosphere at the Sajik Stadium, home ground of the Giants, is famous for the uniqueness and the passion of its supporters, and for 'Shinmoonji[2] Cheering' and the 'Busan Galmaegi Song'[3]. Both are simple forms of cheering. 'Shinmoonji Cheering' is, as the name suggests, cheering with a newspaper. Every Giants fan brings a newspaper to the game and makes their own show pom-poms with it, waving them in unison. This could be deemed old fashioned, but a 30,000 strong crowd of people waving their own rolled-up newspapers adds atmosphere. In addition their main chant, the Busan Galmaegi song, is the best-known baseball-cheering theme in South Korea. As a port city, the Busan Galmaegi song is representative of the city itself and the seagull is part of the team's emblem as well as its' mascot.

The loyalty of the Giants' supporters is often targeted by other teams that are seeking to promote their ticket sales. The LG Twins and Doosan Bears, both based in Seoul, provided special discount tickets only for the Giants' members when they held league games against the Giants at their home ground (Osen News site, 29 August 2006). It is an unusual marketing promotion to provide discounted tickets for away supporters; however, marketers of both the Seoul-based teams are aware of the fact that thousands of the Giants' fans living in Seoul are potential consumers, thus enabling them to increase their ticket sales.

Lotte Giants attendances since the mid-1990s compare poorly with those of the KBL as a whole. Since the mid-1990s, when the Giants recorded a 1.1 million cumulative attendance (18,739 per game), its attendances fell dramatically until the beginning of new millennium. At the same time, team performance also dropped finishing in the bottom half of the table over the last 10 seasons (1996–2005). In 2002, only 127,995 fans visited the stadium for 126 home games, the worst annual attendance record for the club ever.

---

[2]Shinmoonji is a South Korean newspaper.
[3]Galmaegi is a seagull.

Star players retired or moved to rival teams and inexperienced young players took time to reach the necessary standard. Poor performance (8th place for four consecutive seasons) led to a decline in their loyal fan base. On 27 September 2003, only 395 spectators attended a game at the 30,133 capacity Sajik Stadium.

Marketing Efforts of the KBL and Lotte Giants

As mentioned previously game attendance in the last 10 seasons dropped to half of its peak in 1995. The first reaction of the KBL to promote game attendance was to allow foreign players into the league from the 1997 season onwards. The policy of opening up the sports labour market should have been more effective for game promotion but the KBL established the maximum salary limitation on signing foreign players. Top quality foreign players were proven to be a major drawcard for Korean fans who showed a strong preference for individual players rather than teams. But it was difficult to sign top class foreign with limited maximum salaries.

Ten years after the decline in attendances began, they started to increase modestly in 2005 due to the successful on-field performance of popular teams. In the 2005 and 2006 seasons, over 3 million fans visited KBL stadiums each season for the first time since 1999. Furthermore, the 2006 season began well due to the pre-season WBC competition. The WBC, the equivalent of the FIFA World Cup of soccer, took place before the season's kick-off in Japan and USA, and the South Korean national team performed well beyond fans' expectation. Despite failing to reach the final, the team, with their full range of top quality domestic players, recorded six wins and one defeat including memorable victories against the Japanese and US teams. Thanks to these results, game attendance in the KBL reached 1 million in just 137 games out of 504 total games however weather and the 2006 World Cup prevented the KBL from fully exploiting the success of the national team.

Positive signs of change within the KBL are now emerging. The KBL acceded to TV broadcasters requests to move first pitch time from 5 PM to 2 PM on Sundays. This was because 6 PM to 9 PM on Sundays is prime time and consequently the most competitive entertainment hours in Korea. By shifting the game to 2 PM, it prevented the live games from competing with popular TV shows and dramas. Frequent exposure on TV is one of the key methods to promote the League as a whole. The Lotte Giants published their fan books in English and Japanese and distributed them to hotels and major tourists' attractions in Busan city, believing the appeal of baseball games would attract American and Japanese tourists to their games. The KBL encouraged the attacking parts of the game using rule changes including: the reduction of strike zone, time limits of a single game, and dropping the exclusive rights to recruit local talent in order to promote the competitive balance amongst the league.

Within the venue itself (the Busan City owned, Sajik Stadium) announcements were made that the venue would consider selling the naming rights for the 2007 season. To date, a sponsor has not been found, but it is never-theless regarded as a positive step forward for baseball and for the sport industry. At the same time, the Lotte Giants signed a contract with Busan City to take over the management rights of the 16 snack bars inside of the stadium from the 2007 season. By taking these rights, the previously poor service in these snack bars is expected to improve and greater customer sat-isfaction will ensue due largely to the professional know-how of the Lotte Group, industry leaders in the food retailing industry in Korea.

To improve the fan base, the Lotte Giants invested in supporting young talent in local areas by establishing 'The Lotte Little Baseball Tournament' in 1989. The 19th tournament took place in May 2007 with 26 local school teams participating. The final game was held as a pre-game event before the Lotte Giants game at the Sajik Stadium. As the main prize, the player of the tournament was allowed the honour of throwing the opening ball for the Lotte Giants.

Case Diagnosis

Loyal Fan Base Regardless of Poor Marketing

The biggest reason for the KBL's success in its early years is explained by the duopolistic market status it enjoyed. Territorial exclusivity of sales rights is also a pre-requisite to the franchise sport league system, being only one of two professional sports leagues in country for over 15 years along-side with the K-League of football. Although the business performance of the KBL cannot be evaluated as 'successful', clearly there is an established baseball fan base. A team sports league can run as a season of many games (Whitney, 1988), especially with baseball where matches can take place on a daily basis. This means that each team has plenty of opportunities to enter-tain the fans and generate ticket income throughout the whole season. For the KBL, the peculiarities of a team sports' league, local exclusivity of their business, and a monopolistic status in the sport market could establish a relatively loyal fan base of its own.

The Lotte Giants, based in Busan City, have the most loyal fan base of any baseball team due to their unique location. The annual team evalua-tion, published by the Sports Business Korea Magazine (2005), showed the Giants 'box office index' to be much higher than 'the average competition index', indicating the Giants are well-supported relative to team perform-ances. According to the same magazine's team evaluation, modelled on the Forbes Korea's method in 2006, the Giants ranked as the second high-est in the brand value category. As has already been alluded to, this results largely due to the team's location. As the largest harbour city in the nation, the major characteristic of Busan City is depicted in terms of a *macho cul-ture*. Even the dialect in this area sounds very strong and is famous for simplistic form of daily conversation. The strong sense of locality which the people based in Kyungnam province feel often emerges during sporting events, particularly against the opposition from the capital city, Seoul, or the traditional Honam[4] province. The Lotte Giants is the only KBL team that places the home city's title on the team's emblem. Lee (1998) found that the usual game attendees of the Lotte Giants show a stronger locality bias than non-sports fans when they vote for a member of the National Assembly. In another study by Lim (2003), 83 per cent of respondents from Busan City supported the Giants because it is the local team. Rivalries between the capital city and the second largest city often arise on the sports field, for instance, the rivalry between the Yomiuri Giants of Tokyo and the Hanshin Tigers of Osaka in Japan, Real Madrid of Madrid and FC Barcelona of Barcelona in Spain, Arsenal of London, and Manchester United of Manchester in England.

Economic power as the second largest city was thought to be another major influence on the Giants loyal fan base. Cheon and Nam (2002) verified the relationship between the size of stadium and game attendance. The top three teams in terms of accumulated game attendance (the Lotte Giants, LG Twins, and Doosan Bears) play their home games in the stadiums with 30,000+ capacities (Cheon and Nam, 2002). Their season results also have a large impact on the whole league attendance. For instance, the game attendance increased by 1 million in 2005 compared to 2004 due to that the Lotte Giants, LG Twins and Doosan Bears performing better than in previous seasons.

Organizational Limitations

The abnormal situation of South Korean sports organizations, preventing them from operating their organizations according to business criteria, allowed them to focus on the PR activity of their parent company. If this area is addressed by analysing the KBL case, it might be a somewhat meaningless task. In organizational studies, all sport organizations exist for a certain purpose and organizational goals are a detailed statement to articulate the purpose of a sport organization (Slack, 1997). The organizational mission is not solely based on financial considerations in the case of the eight teams of the KBL and any type of external marketing environment change does not result in a huge impact on their business operation, strategy or mission. Nevertheless, the KBL and its constituent teams, still require professional and market-oriented strategies in order to achieve their organizational goals largely due to the importance of the public relation function. Watt (2003, p. 177) emphasised the importance of PR activity:

> *Public relations (PR) is ... to do with image, with comparing yourself to competitors, it is to do with public perception and is process that should pervade the whole organisation. It*

---

[4]South-west part of Korea peninsular. There has been serious local antagonism between Honam (south-west) and Kyungnam (south-east; where Busan located in) in history.

should start with an assessment of the current situation … to improve image (and thinking) and the detailed consideration of how to implement this plan … Such a plan would have the clear goal of ensuring that a positive image for the sporting organisation was established and maintained through many items of promotion and a full ongoing marketing overview.

Therefore, all eight teams in the KBL need to achieve as much success as possible on and off the field to meet their business mission. Importantly, maintaining a positive and healthy relationship between the teams and fans is desirable off the field. Even if all the teams are heavily subsidised by their parent companies, the marketing effort should be undertaken more strategically, commercially and with an external orientation.

In theory, the biggest customers for the KBL teams are their parent companies, with 70–80 per cent of the total income coming from them and not from fans. Few, if any, teams are ready yet to respond effectively to market changes, monitor environmental changes or evaluate the market in which they operating. Many direct and indirect competitors arose in the marketplace by the 1990s, including a professional basketball league, various outdoor leisure activities as well as foreign sports leagues as domestic players moved to those leagues. External contingencies must be monitored by sport marketers to keep up with the changing dynamic sport industry (Shank, 2005). Moreover, technological developments in communication, for a major influence on market environments, has reduced the visible gap between the domestic consumers and foreign leagues. Nevertheless, the KBL teams has appeared unwilling to react to these kinds of market changes because of their overall organizational mission.

Promotion for Increasing Game Attendance

Income from gate receipts is an essential element of any sporting organization's income stream, despite the growth of television income, sponsorships, and the development of technology. Atmosphere (e.g. screaming, excitements of fans) created by full attendance is one of several important factors to improve the quality of the televised game. Specifically, if one talks of baseball, gate receipts need to be considered as the most decisive factor for operating the team because the league games take place every day throughout the season. There is extensive research identifying the factors that promote game attendance in MLB (e.g. Domazlicky and Kerr, 1990; Boyd and Krehbiel, 2006). Boyd and Krehbiel (2006) identified 17 controllable (by management) variables that have significant correlation for promoting game attendance in MLB.

1 Team	6 Inter-League game
2 Winning percentage	7 Divisional game
3 Opponent's winning percentage	8 Temperature
4 Weekend game	9 Inclement weather
5 Day game	10 Promotion

11 Bobblehead giveaway	15 Two or more special events
12 Giveaway less than $5	16 Giveaway and special events
13 Giveaway more than $5	17 Price discount
14 Special events	

Source: Boyd and Krehbiel (2006)

The largest positively correlated variable in terms of passive marketing effort was found to be the 'Bobblehead Giveaway' promotion, excluding simple factors such as weather or weekend games. The same simple factors have been found significant in the study of the KBL conducted by Cheon and Nam (2002) which showed the highest attendance on Sunday over Saturday. The giveaway of attractive (but not expensive) memorabilia has not been attempted in the KBL due to the comparative absence of baseball tradition. The most common type of promotion in KBL has been a simple price discount for the team's membership but it was proven to have a little impact on promoting game attendance because the initial ticket prices are already affordable to most baseball fans, ranging from £3 to £6 per game in case of the Lotte Giants in the 2007 season.

As Meenaghan and O'Sullivan (1999) noted sport marketers have employed end-user (consumer) business techniques in their marketing strategies as the sport industry became more mainstream with market oriented, customer concerned, and differentiation requirements all required. However, the marketing strategies of sport organizations should be more complicated than those of other consumer businesses due to the peculiar relationship between buyers and sellers. The special relationship between the sporting organization and consumers is the essential part of sport marketing because fans seldom look for alternative objects and loyalty towards 'my team' lasts over a longer period compared with normal consumer activity. This special relationship can never be achieved by short-term marketing tactics. Fluctuation of game attendances in accordance with winning percentages and the existence of star players shows that the KBL teams need to appeal to fan loyalty more than daily income generation. The marketing promotion options that are being conducted in the MLB locate its essence on its history and tradition. What the KBL teams need to do is not a new marketing idea but a long-term brand strategy plan to cement the fan base which should remain largely unaffected by winning percentage.

Therefore, the Lotte Giants need to retrace where their unique loyal fan base was formed. Consistency of brand strategy should be maintained with the highest priority for preventing their business from being affected by team performance. Once the special relationship is established, the Lotte Giants will have more marketing options and tactics at their disposal. The Lotte Giants case would seem to be a very positive one because they have previously experienced special relationships with their fans. The high level of the fan identification can decrease team performance sensitivity in the long term and marketing promotions which can stimulate based on locality and tradition may be the best way to revitalize the Korean baseball industry.

Aside from the peculiar ownership structure of the team, the identity of the company-owned professional baseball team has started to be regarded as an organization which should be competitive on and off the ground in accordance with the marketing environment. Even though there are no changes on the managerial system of KBL teams, market changes keep impacting on many aspects such as planning of naming right sales, efforts to improve the service quality at the venues, and the diversification of marketing promotions. Change may be slow but at least it is occurring in the management and marketing of many KBL teams.

Case Questions

1 What kind of marketing environment changes have recently affected sport organizations?
2 To what extent do the objectives of an organization objectives influence its business goals?
3 To what extent do changes in the marketing environment affect the business strategy of sport organizations?
4 What would your recommendations be for the Lotte Giants in seeking to promote attendances at their games?
5 What type of consumer targeting and segmentation techniques could be employed to the KBL teams?
6 How do you think do the KBL teams could or should reposition themselves in the current market?

Case Resources

Reading

Beech, J., Chadwick, S. and Tapp, A. (2000). Surfing in the Premier League: Key issues for football club marketers using the Internet. *Managing Leisure*. Vol. 5, pp. 51–64.

Boyd, T. and Krehbiel, T. (2006). An analysis of the effects of specific promotion types on attendance at Major League Baseball games. *Mid-American Journal of Business*, Vol. 21, No. 2, pp. 21–32.

Cheon, Y.B. and Nam, J.Y. (2002). Analysis on the attendance of the Korean Professional Baseball (한국 프로야구 관중추이 분석). *Journal of Sport and Leisure Studies*, Vol. 18, pp. 292–407.

Domazlicky, B.R., and Kerr, P.M. (1990). Baseball Attendance and the Designated Hitter. *American Economist*. Vol. 34(1), pp. 62-68.

Jeong, H.Y. (2005). Performance evaluation of the KBL teams in the 2000s (2000 년대프로야구단 실적 평가). *The Sport Business Korea Magazine*, Vol. 35, December 2005.

Korea Institute of Sport Science (2006). *The Sport White Paper 2005* (2005 년 체육백서), Ministry of Culture and Tourism.

Kotler, P. and Zaltman, G. (1971). Social marketing: An approach to planned social change. *Journal of Marketing*, Vol. 35, pp. 3–12.

Lee, J.G. (1998{AQ5}). Relationship between local franchises of the Korean Professional baseball and political localism (한국 프로야구의 지역연고제와 정치적 지역주의의 관계). *The Korean Journal of Physical Education*, Vol. 37, No. 2, pp. 84–95.

Lim, S.W. and Lee, G.M. (2003). Effect of the baseball games between Kyungnam and Honam provinces on the locality (영/호남팀 프로야구 경기가 지역감정에 미치는 영향). *Journal of Korean Sociology of Sport*, Vol. 16, No. 1, pp. 73–92.

Marber, A., Wellen, P. and Posluszny, S. (2005). The merging of marketing and sports: A case study. *The Marketing Management Journal*, Vol. 15, No. 1, pp. 162–171.

Mawson, M. and Coan, E. (1994). Marketing techniques used by NBA franchises to promote home game attendance. *Sport Marketing Quarterly*, Vol. 3, No. 1, pp. 37–45.

Meenaghan, T. and O'Sullivan, P. (1999). Playpower – sports meets marketing. *European Journal of Marketing*, Vol. 33, No. 3/4, pp. 241–249.

Porter, M.E. (1985). *Competitive Advantage: Creating and Sustaining Superior Performance*. Free Press, New York.

Shank, M.D. (2005). *Sports Marketing: International Edition*, 3rd edition. Pearson Education, Inc., New Jersey.

Slack, T. (1997). *Understanding Sport Organisations: The Application of Organisation Theory*, Human Kinetics. New Jersey.

Watt, D.C. (2003). *Sports Management and Administration*, 2nd edition. Routledge, London and New York.

Whitney, J.D. (1988). Winning games versus winning championships: The economics of fan interest and team performance. *Economic Inquiry*, Vol. 26, pp. 703–724.

News Articles from Internet

Author Unknown (2006). Busan selling the naming right of the Sajik stadium. *The Chosun Newspaper*, 29 June, available from http://www.chosun.com/national/news/200606/200606290037.html

CBS Sports Department (2007). Giants host the Lotte Little Baseball Tournament. *The Nocut News*, 2 March, available from http://www.cbs.co.kr/nocut/show.asp?idx=450153

Choi, M.K. (2007). End to the multi-step draft. *The Sports 2.0*, 13 February, available from http://www.sports2.co.kr/feature/feature_view.asp?LCT=2&AID=170390&PG=5

Jang, H.G. (2007). SBS sports get exclusive broadcast right of Lee. *The Younhap News*, 3 April, available from http://app.yonhapnews. co.kr/YNA/Basic/article/search/YIBW_showSearchArticle. aspx?searchpart=article&searchtext=%ea%b3%b5%ea%b2%a9% ec%a0%81%20%eb%a7%88%ec%bc%80%ed%8c%85%20%eb%8 8%88%ea%b8%b8&contents_id=AKR20070403068800007

Lee, S.H. (2006). Yahoo and satellite DMB boosted by WBC. *The Ohmynews*, 18 March, available from http://economy.ohmynews.com/ articleview/article_view.asp?at_code=317483&ar_seq

Park, S.Y. (2006). Promotion to get giants fans of Doosan and LG. *The Osen News*, 29 August, viewed 20 March 2007, available from http://kr.news.yahoo.com/service/news/shellview.htm?linkid= 17&articleid=20060829090058650a4&newssetid=84

Park, T.W. (2007). Giants took over the snack bar management. *The Nocut News*, 28 March, available from http://www.cbs.co.kr/nocut/show. asp?idx=472856

Shin, B.S. (2007). Might change the all-nighters plan of KBL. *The Sports Chosun*, 26 March, available from http://spn.chosun.com/site/data/ html_dir/2007/03/26/2007032600637.html

Websites

The Bizpark.co.kr (Business information site) – http://www.bizpark. co.kr/

The Korea Baseball Organization – http://www.koreabaseball.com/

The Korchambiz.net (Business information site) – http://www.korcham-biz.net/

The Lotte Group – http://www.lotte.co.kr/english/

The Lotte Giants – http://www.lotte-giants.co.kr/

The Sport Business Korea – http://www.sportbusiness.co.kr/main.asp

28

Professional rugby, community rugby clubs and volunteers: creating advantage through better volunteer management

Simon Darcy, Tracy Taylor, Graham Cuskelly and Russell Hoye

Case Focus

The case examines the volunteer management practices within the Australian Rugby Union and its community clubs.

Keywords

- Volunteers
- Human Resource Management
- Community Sports Organizations

Case Summary

The Australian Rugby Union (ARU) has undergone significant change since the professionalism of the code during the 1990s. The game has moved from its amateur origins to participation in a Tri-Nation Super 14 Competition and an expanded international calendar where approximately 150 professional rugby players are contracted to the ARU. In 2003, Australia hosted the International Rugby Board Rugby World Cup, which was a resounding success resulting in a surplus of approximately AU$43 million of which AU$18 million was dedicated to developing the game at the grass roots level. The remainder was committed to the ARU's member unions, and a substantial amount was kept as capital reserves. In conjunction with the 'big' money side of the game, the ARU is a not-for-profit organization that governs approximately 800 community rugby clubs across eight state (provincial) based rugby organizations. The organizational structure of rugby union in Australia brings with it a series of challenging management issues as it grapples with how to manage a sport that encompasses the professional to grass roots delivery of rugby. Within this context, volunteers contribute significantly to running the majority of the community rugby clubs. This case examines the use of a human resource management (HRM) framework and an understanding of motivations of sport volunteers (MSV) in volunteer management.

Case Elements

Introduction

In 1995, the International Rugby Board (IRB) took a decision to professionalize the game. Whether this change to the game was evolutionary or revolutionary is arguable but there is no doubt that rugby fans witnessed a significant change to the organization of the sport that historically prided itself on its amateur status. Amateur traditions were challenged by corporatization and an emphasis on developing accountable and transparent organizational governance structures. In this context, hosting the 2003 IRB World Cup provided the ARU with a unique opportunity to secure a foundation in the competitive professional Australian football marketplace and to address their strategy to grow participation and spectator interest in the game.

The pressures and tensions of the move to professionalism had ramifications right down to the grass roots community level of rugby. While the national and state organizations rapidly adopted corporate business models, the community rugby clubs (CRCs) largely reflected the days of amateur rugby union. At the community level, volunteers still provide the main source of human capital and clubs are faced with many pressures to remain viable. CRCs operate largely on a membership fee and fundraising basis, and there is a limited budget and resources for the delivery of the game at this level. In most CRCs, volunteers manage all aspects of the club from getting teams on the field to play, to providing the coaching, finance and administration. They also provide the foundation for the development of players from juniors to the next generation of elite representatives. The question is how are these volunteers being managed and supported to meet strategic growth objectives of the ARU?

Historical Background

Rugby union is a team sport played in over 100 countries predominantly by males but with a growing female participation rate (IRB, 2007). The inherent characteristics that appear to have provided rugby union with its longevity and relevance to sport today include 'its rich history, traditions, camaraderie and community involvement with the sport' (ARU, 2007a). Australia boasts more than a century of rugby union tradition – with the first formal club established in 1864, the Sydney University Club (ARU, 2007b). The Sydney University Club, and others like it were founded, built and sustained by volunteers whose passion for rugby union was the prime motivator for their involvement (Skinner et al., 2003). For many years rugby union was a proudly amateur sport and a long debate ensued over the relative temptations, benefits and impacts of moving to professionalize (Skinner et al., 2003).

Tensions over its amateur status first surfaced with the 1908 founding of the rival rugby code, rugby league, as a professional version of rugby, over what today would be described as a industrial relations issue involving the payment of injured players. In this sense, the two rugby codes represented the class differences of the day. Rugby league was created to provide payment to players from the working class where injuries sustained on the playing field meant the inability to make a living and provide food for their family. Rugby union was seen as the sport of the upper and middle class where payment was not necessary due to the relative wealth of those involved and the different nature of the work in which they were engaged. At different times through the 20th century and in the new millennium, each code had significant victories over the other code in the battle for players at the elite level. One of the most famous rugby league coups over rugby union was in 1908 when the rugby league signed the whole of the Olympic-medal winning rugby union team including the legendary Dally Messenger. In converse, the Australian Rugby League lamented the recent poaching of marquee players to the ranks of the ARU with the most famous triumvirate of Matt Rogers, Wendell Sailor and Lote Tuqiri. Matt Rogers has since moved back to professional rugby league.

For many years, the IRB placed a blanket ban on professionalism, and if the amateur guidelines were breached, the persons involved would be expelled from their club and the game for life. The IRB and its constituent unions believed that the pride associated with involvement in the game would be enough for participants to remain true to the spirit of the game. During the 1980s and early 1990s, a heightened challenge to the amateur ideals of rugby union became evident. During this time, other football codes had positioned themselves to be able to attract lucrative corporate backing and multimillion-dollar media deals, and they offered players contracts that were previously unimaginable (Skinner et al., 2003). At the same time, the traditional 'touring' of national rugby teams had become far more problematic because of the rising costs involved, the players becoming far more vocal about the profits being accrued by the National union's and an increasing business sports nexus with substantial media interests.

In the 1980s, a number of 'rebel tours' and proposed professional tournaments were mooted. The 'rebel tours' were largely facilitated by the political exclusion of South Africa from international rugby competition because of the apartheid regime. A number of 'rebel tours' proceeded with mixed nation teams and most notably rebel players from the New Zealand Rugby Union (NZRU). Rugby administrators were put on notice that the professionalism of the game may occur without their involvement. The southern hemisphere unions placed growing pressure on the IRB, which brought about the organization of the first IRB Rugby World Cup in 1987. The first Rugby World Cup was jointly hosted by the ARU and the NZRU and was a resounding success for the game in terms of international media coverage, ticket sales and the subsequent profile of the sport. Between 1987 and 1991, pressure intensified on the IRB to make changes to the way that rugby was governed and to professionalize the game. These pressures were initially resisted by the dominant northern hemisphere unions.

Senior rugby union officials were increasingly worried about the sustainability of their elite teams, with players being attracted to the professional rugby league. In June 1995, South Africa, New Zealand and ARUs announced the establishment of SANZAR Incorporated, which offered a commodified Tri-Nations Series, attracting a lucrative 10-year contract with Rupert Murdoch's News Corporation for US$10 million (Dabscheck, 2003). Pressures had reached crisis point whereby a rival proposal was formulated and many of the top rugby stars were courted by the World Rugby Corporation. In reply the ARU's constituent unions negotiated a deal in the 'Ferrier letter' for 95 per cent of the media contract payments to be distributed to the players through the yet unformed Rugby Union Player's Association (Dabscheck, 1998).

In September 1995, the IRB announced a sanction for the professionalism of rugby union around the world. This decision formally brought rugby union into a new era, and closer to its professional football contemporaries. The professional revolution of an institution based upon amateurism and tradition had begun (O'Brien and Slack, 2003). The ARU sought to obtain 'additional financing, new marketing techniques, attract new spectators, and effectively re-invent itself' (Skinner et al., 2003, p. 56). These goals reflected a shift in organizational needs, strategy and managerial approaches. Although the ARU had experienced commercial and corporate environments long before the 1995 IRB decision, the acceptance of professionalism in rugby union presented many opportunities for the ARU and the rugby union community. At both the upper echelons of Australian rugby and the community level, the period of 1996–2003 was 'a period of dramatic growth' (ARU, 2004, p. 12). The ARU recognized that it was competing 'internationally with increasingly better-resourced National Rugby Unions and domestically with well-resourced and well-managed other sports, as well as countless leisure options available to young Australians' (ARU, 2004, p. 13).

The Modern Era: Professionalism and the ARU

It is with this background that the ARU entered the 2003 Rugby World Cup and a new 'professional era'. Up until this time, the ARU as an organization had not strategically reviewed its operations in the light of these environmental changes. Effectively, the ARU remained the peak body for rugby union in Australia, with its constituent unions and hundreds of CRCs. ARU governance and the relationships with its elite players had changed from that of a paternal governing body to that of an employer and contracted employees. At the same time, its relationship with the CRCs remained largely unchanged.

One of the first changes that the professionalized ARU undertook was to launch a marketing campaign to promote the game both nationally and internationally (Hutchins and Phillips, 1999). Recognizing the changed environment and its obligations as a professional sport the ARU had to compete with the other professional Australian sporting codes. Other football codes had been professional (including the Australian Football League and Australian Rugby League) and semi-professional (National Soccer League) for much longer and had varying degrees of sophistication in their organization and marketing. What could not be questioned were the higher participation and spectator rates of some competing codes, which posed difficult questions as to the relative growth of rugby union in relation to these sports. Growing player and supporter numbers was seen as important for the future sustainability of the game, the corporate structures and ability to attract media coverage and sponsorship deals. The Australian football market place has been suggested as the 'the most competitive in the world' (Gary Flowers cited in Toohey, 2007, p. 56), with four football codes striving to attract players, sponsors, staff and volunteers. Organizational change undertaken by the new professional entity posed further threats to rugby union, which was still relying on the enthusiasm of volunteers to administer the sport at senior and elite levels (Skinner et al., 2003). Organizationally, the ARU had a general aim to recruit 'specialists from domains such as management, finance, accounting, marketing, law, sport science, and health and safety' (O'Brien and Slack, 2003, p. 434).

John O'Neill: Strategic Change and Embracing the Grass Roots

The professionalism of the game brought recognition within the ARU that a senior and experienced corporate executive was needed to guide the institution through a period of rapid and unprecedented change. A good leader could instil change within the organization that reflected the demands of the environment (Slack, 1997), as the ARU faced challenges in the competitive global sports market (ABC, 2003). The push into the competitive market place required strategy and direction *immediately*, in contrast to an approach of allowing the organization to gradually evolve (Thomas, 1997). The CEO needed to be a leader with business acumen and financial credibility to attract significant corporate sponsorship. John O'Neill emerged as the likely candidate having successfully directed the State Bank of NSW from its position as a government statutory authority to a listed financial institution on the Australian stock exchange. With a background as a lawyer and a unquestioned corporate pedigree, one commentator noted, John O'Neill was, 'brought in for his business brain and his commercial contacts ... both [proving] useful' (Cubby, 2006). He was appointed as the ARU's first Chief Executive in 1995. His tenure lasted until 2003, and included the role of Managing Director (Masters, 2003). O'Neill commented on his role as an outsider to the organization, 'I couldn't allow myself to become passionate and in love with it, because basically I saw too many examples of where love and emotion got in the way of good decision-making' (ABC, 2003). O'Neill's tenure included securing the rights to host the 2003 IRB Rugby World Cup. Ultimately, the staging of this event offered the ARU an outstanding legacy of a $43 million surplus, a once in a lifetime windfall for a non-profit organization (Masters, 2003).

In the same year as the RWC, O'Neill was recognized as the Sport Executive of the Year at the Australian Sports Awards (ARU, 2003). The ARU press release alluded to the success of O'Neill's management approaches, offering that 'in 1996 the revenue of the ARU was less than $10 million, while [in 2003] it is close to $70 million and during the same period participation [had] grown from fewer than 100,000 players to 148,750' (ARU, 2003). Although the success of the Rugby World Cup and associated developments at the ARU, were largely demonstrative of the O'Neill's hard-headed business acumen, O'Neill accepted the award on behalf of all levels of rugby union contributors, which, he stated, came 'together to make the sport what it is today' (ARU, 2003). O'Neill's management approach offered an emancipatory platform for in the ARU's current strategic status and success. At the time of the 2003 RWC, O'Neill had no hesitations of 'viewing the game as a "product" and fans as "consumers"' (ABC, 2003).

Strategically, O'Neill sought to change the organization from that of an amateur organization to one demonstrating superior corporate strategy and governance. O'Neill recognized that the executive of the member unions would represent a transient group over a period due to elections and other political matters (O'Neill, 2007). Together with the senior management group of the ARU, O'Neill sought to establish comparable operations staff within the ARU and the member unions. By doing so, a comparable culture was built across the operational units of the union where operational practice was understood from head office through to the front line staff (O'Neill, 2007). He proceeded at the executive level of the union to develop organizational objectives that could be agreed to and worked towards over a period. This was achieved in early 1998 after a period of turmoil following the relatively early exit of the Wallabies from the World Cup in 1995 and indifferent Super 10 and Super 12 performances. The ARU and the unions were able to agree on five objectives that were designed with the ultimate aim of winning the 1999 Rugby World Cup. When this was achieved, the focus moved to securing the hosting of the 2003 Rugby World Cup. These successes generated a tremendous momentum, which saw rugby capitalize on the 1999 Rugby World Cup success, leverage this further with the organizational success of the 2003 Rugby World Cup and a strategy for the four years post 2003. Importantly, it had been suggested to O'Neill that there was a need to create separate organizational responses to the elite level and to the CRCs. However, O'Neill asserted that the CRCs are the customers of the elite level and to create a separate organization would be a poor strategic response (O'Neill, 2007). He regarded volunteers as not only the foundation of CRCs but as important culturally and financially for corporate support and sponsorship. The ARU had to embrace both the elite professional level and the CRCs equally for the sport to move forward (O'Neill, 2007).

Strategic Planning: Facilitating the Growth of Rugby Union

The professionalism and inherent cultural change of the ARU are linked with the need for develop a strategic approach to achieve sustainable growth at all levels of the sport. Following the 2003 Rugby World Cup, the ARU aimed 'to take full advantage of ongoing growth and profile of [the] game which reached an all-time high during [the 2003] … Rugby World Cup' (ARU, 2004, p. 2). The ARU's strategic plan, *True Vision* outlined the objectives and values on which all levels of the sport would develop. Central to this was, 'continual substantial growth in participation … with corresponding growth in coaches, referees and other volunteer roles' (ARU, 2004, p. 19). For this to be achieved, the ARU and the unions needed to provide a solid foundation on which to base the grass roots development of the sport. At the ARU state unions' conference in 2002, volunteer management was regarded as a priority issue. One of the outcomes of this conference was that the ARU commissioned a research project into volunteer management practices of its CRCs (Cuskelly et al., 2006).

An element of the ARU's contemporary strategic management communicates how growth objectives would be met, and inherently, how sustainable growth would be achieved. Like most of the community sport delivery system in Australia, CRCs are largely managed and operated by volunteer management committees or boards. The CRCs utilize volunteers to deliver services to their members in roles such as coaching, managing, refereeing and all operational roles on game day. The volunteer base of the ARU is vital for its operations and a critical dimension in fostering the growth and development of the game. It is therefore important that the ARU and its network of CRCs understand how to best manage and work effectively with its volunteers. In 2005, the ARU had:

- over 800 community rugby clubs;
- 165,000 registered players;
- 18,000 volunteers within it CRC structure.

The post Rugby World Cup strategic plan, *True Vision*, acknowledged the efforts and skills of volunteers and their contribution to providing a safe and fun environment for all who enjoy playing the game. In particular, *True Vision* outlined the need for 'enhanced emphasis on infrastructual support – mainly in the form of support and recognition for our volunteer-based management environment' (ARU, 2004, p. 19). *True Vision* espoused six values across all levels of the organization, no matter whether they are players, administrators, staff or volunteers to foster a rugby culture both on and off the field (ARU, 2005, p. 7). The six values are:

1 *Innovation*: We ensure Australian Rugby has the leading edge through innovation, and sets the standard by which others follow.
2 *Integrity*: Australian Rugby operates in a transparent and ethical manner.
3 *Professionalism*: We promote the excellence in our approach to the corporate realities/imperatives of Rugby.
4 *Teamwork*: We focus on results using the discipline, cooperation, mateship and camaraderie associated with Rugby.
5 *Pride*: We exemplify the spirit of Rugby.
6 *Energy*: We work with enthusiasm and go the extra mile.

While innovation and professionalism may be seen to reflect the new corporatization of elite rugby union, the other four values are inherent to the CRCs, as the organizations continue to reflect the amateur and altruistic notions of the sport of rugby. The values statements were characteristic of a top–down organizational approach that aimed to promote and reward volunteer participation within the organization. Strategies included an $18 million investment in the grass roots operations of the ARU, 'the single biggest grass roots investment ever undertaken by the Australian Rugby Union ... providing unprecedented assistance at the grass roots level' (ARU, 2004, p. 3). Of the $18 million, 'more than $0.75m [was] to be invested in 2004 and 2005 with the aim to identify and recognize "volunteers" individual, invaluable contributions to Australia Rugby' (ARU, 2004, p. 28). Secondary features of this strategy were to develop a Customer Relationship Management database, 'MyRugbyAdmin' (ARU, 2007b) to better manage volunteers' relationship with the Rugby community, and establish a Volunteer Recognition Programme. The 'Volunteer Recognition Program was developed to raise the profile of Community Rugby volunteers and to reward those volunteers who have contributed to the development, promotion and or advancement of rugby union within Australia. The program will continue as more and more volunteers are needed to ensure the growth of the game' (ARU, 2004, p. 8).

The strategies inherent in *True Vision* were designed to instil the six values at all levels of Rugby, as well as facilitate an improved participative experience for volunteer coaches, referees and administrators of the ARU (ARU, 2004, p. 28). The professional reorganization of the game at an elite level occurred over a relatively short period of time whereas the grass roots did not undergone the same level of change and it continued to reflect the largely institutionalized amateur ideals of rugby (Skinner et al., 1999). As John O'Neill suggested, one cannot exist without the other, as the ARU relies significantly on the grass roots volunteers to facilitate participation growth and are the 'fabric' and 'lifeblood' of the game (ARU, 2004, p. 3).

Volunteer Trends and the Role of Volunteer

The significant economic and social contribution of volunteers to the Australian community has been well documented and, community sport, a major Australian social institution, is largely dependent on its volunteers. Without volunteers community sport would cease to exist, sport complexes would close, sport events would decrease and physical activity levels would decline. National sport organizations and the Australian Sports Commission recognize the importance of volunteers in the community sport system and the need to investigate volunteer retention. Ron Graham, Chairman of the ARU commented in his 2005 report that the many people who contribute to the ARU are 'not only employees … but also volunteers … on a range of levels that often go unrecognized' (ARU, 2005, p. 5).

The ARU have set specific objectives to attempt to facilitate sustainable growth in participation of the game. However, the basic infrastructure at the community level is largely dependant on volunteers. This scenario exposes tensions between the professionalism at the elite levels, and amateur notions of volunteerism at the grass roots. As long as the ARU largely relies on volunteers to facilitate growth at the grass roots, trends in sport volunteerism will affect the ARU's operations. Within the time period 1995–2000, on average, sports volunteers annual hours of participation has decreased, and there has also been a decrease in the amount of successive years a volunteer remains involved (Cuskelly et al., 2006). Further, there has been a significant decrease in the proportion of key volunteers within clubs who contribute over 140 hours a year (Cuskelly et al., 2006). These observations have significant implications for the longevity of individuals volunteering and the long-term retention of sport sector volunteers.

Considering the strategic objectives of the ARU, as well as their commitment to support the grass roots game, volunteer social trends are important to consider in conjunction with previously identified environmental pressures. Apart from the rugby-specific pressures brought about by a professionalism, sport volunteers contend with the pressure to improve coaching standards, comply with legislative requirements (e.g. responsible service of alcohol, child protection and privacy laws) and to address public liability. These pressures can be detrimental to the motivation and retention of volunteers within the CRC's, and 'many volunteers are currently just surviving' (Cuskelly et al., 2006, p. 7). The social trends are particularly evident in metropolitan areas of increasing demands on their time and resources, bringing 'into question the sustainability of the community sport system in its current form and its capacity to continue to provide services to club based sport participants' (Cuskelly et al., 2006, p. 2).

Case Analysis

We have argued here that volunteers are the lifeblood of community sport and the volunteers are crucial in the sustainability of rugby union. Without a dependable, committed, passionate and sustainable pool of volunteers, the game could not continue to function at the community level, and certainly would not be able to expand its participant base. While the ARU needed to change and professionalize to survive as part of a globalized professional sport environment, the impact of the changes on the volunteer base was far-reaching and perhaps underestimated. Additionally, as more revenue flows into the sport, there is likely to be further tensions between grass roots volunteers who give their time freely and the perceived 'riches' of the elite players and professional sports administrators. Most recently, the very public negotiations for the high salary for marquee professional player Lote Tuqiri's five-year contract, reportedly worth $5 million, caused a great deal of public derision within grass roots rugby. These changes have been compounded by bureaucracy, statutory and regulatory compliance requirements which have combined to create tensions and increase the workload amongst the community rugby volunteers. This raises some interesting issues to be considered in relation to the juxtaposition of organizational changes with rugby union and societal changes in the nature of volunteering. In particular, how can rugby union respond to these changes to ensure a continuing influx of community volunteers as well as retaining existing volunteers?

Within the Australian sporting landscape, rugby union faces some interesting challenges including the growth of 'soccer' (football) and its renewed image and growing appeal. The extent to which rugby can maintain or indeed increase its market share within certain demographic markets, both as a participant and spectator sport remains to be seen. In recognizing the invaluable service that volunteers provide in keeping the game vibrant and viable at the club level, the ARU is striving to better understand their volunteers to attract and retain a sustainable cohort. The degree to which the ARU will succeed is ultimately tied to approach to managing their volunteers. The implementation of an effective volunteer management approach is a critical human capital issue. Human resource management (HRM) theory and the concept of motivations for sports volunteers (MSV) offer the ARU a framework with which to strategically address volunteer management.

Human Resource Management and Motivation to Volunteer

While there is no universal list of 'high-performance HRM practices' (Pfeffer and Tromley, 1995; Becker and Gerhart, 1996; Guest, 1997) the fundamental issues of how to recruit, develop and motivate key people are central to all HRM. HRM encompasses seven discrete HRM practices, namely: planning, recruitment, screening, orientation, training and support, performance management and recognition. Motivations for sports volunteers (MSV) Wang (2004) can be conceptualized as having five dimensions:

1 *Altruistic values*: Volunteering because of personal values and beliefs, enjoy helping other people and being a person who likes to be involved.
2 *Personal development*: Volunteering to gain experience, for the challenge and being with people with similar interests.
3 *Community concern*: Volunteering to make a contribution to and service the community.
4 *Social adjustment*: Volunteering because it is important to significant others who support their volunteer activities.
5 *Ego enhancement*: Volunteering to feel part of the club, because volunteering is fun and to feel needed or important.

Based on the dual approach of investigating an HRM framework and understanding the conceptualizations of MSV, the nature of volunteering within the ARU can be explored as a multidimensional construct. Several issues are addressed, including use of HRM in CRC volunteer management practices, the retention of volunteers through CRC practices and an understanding of MSV within CRC settings. The relationships that volunteers develop with the CRCs provide significant implications for volunteer management and retention.

Understanding Volunteer Management Practices: A Taxonomy of CRCs

The ARU research study involved an extensive methodology of 16 focus groups of club administrators, a survey of 375 community clubs' volunteer management practices, a survey of 402 volunteers and 48 volunteer interviews. This section provides an analysis of volunteer management practices through a taxonomy of community rugby clubs developed from the study. Based on the work of Taylor (2004) rugby union clubs have been categorized into three volunteer management club types as outlined in Table 28.1 (Cuskelly et al., 2006b).

Table 28.1 Characteristics of community rugby club volunteer management types

Traditional	*Operational*	*Contemporary*
• Minimal use of widely accepted volunteer management practices. • Focus tends to be on immediate problems. • Unplanned approaches in the recruitment, training, support and recognition. • Unlikely to have job descriptions, a volunteer manual, orientation or induction sessions or use have targeted recruitment of new volunteers.	• Some formalized volunteer management practices. • May utilize code of conduct, position descriptions, opportunities for training, and/or volunteer awards/recognition. • Recruitment largely by word of mouth.	• Relatively formalized volunteer management practices across most or all areas. • Tendency to plan strategically for the training, support and recognition of volunteers, but not for recruitment. • Many of these clubs have strategic plans, volunteer manuals, position descriptions, induction programmes, scheduled training and development, mentoring schemes, succession management plans, volunteer recognition awards.

The study found that contemporary club types generally used more formalized volunteer management practices than operational club types, which, in turn, used more formalized practices than traditional club types. Clear patterns were not discernible based on the nature of a club, i.e. whether it is junior, senior, womens' or combined (junior and senior) clubs. A notable pattern was that almost half of all senior-only clubs were categorized as traditional clubs and more than half of the combined senior and womens' clubs were categorized as contemporary, although the total number of combined senior and womens' clubs was relatively small. The degree to which each club type reported using the seven HRM practices outlined earlier are displayed in Figure 28.1 and can be summarized as:

• Traditional club types use HRM to a lesser degree than contemporary club types.
• The largest differences between the three club volunteer management types are in volunteer screening and performance management.
• Planning for volunteer involvement and recruitment practices tends to be informal even in the clubs categorized as more formalized (contemporary club types).

Motivations for Sport Volunteers

The study found that strongest motivators for rugby volunteers were altruistic values, community concern and ego enhancement. Social adjustment and personal development were less important motivators for club rugby

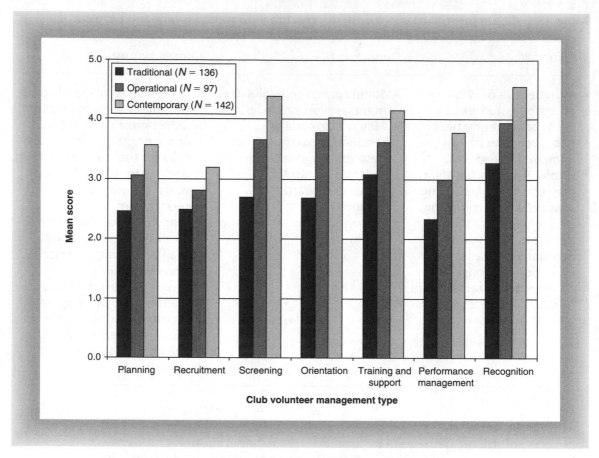

Figure 28.1 Mean scores on volunteer management constructs by club volunteer management type (Cuskelly et al 2006b)

volunteers. Female volunteers reported significantly higher scores than male volunteers on all five MSV constructs. Of the individual motivation statements surveyed, the five most important motives to volunteers included:

1 I enjoy being part of a club.
2 Volunteers make a valuable contribution to the community.
3 Volunteering does something good for the community.
4 I consider myself to be a person who gets involved.
5 I volunteer because I enjoy helping other people.

Volunteer Retention, HRM and MSV: Implications for Management

The ARU needs to create a sustainable base of volunteers to support the participatory environment, which will assist in achieving organizational objectives of participation growth. By analysing the ARU case through both lenses of HRM and MSV, the multidimensionality of the case is revealed

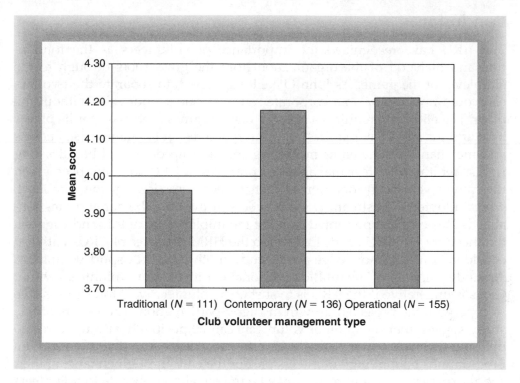

Figure 28.2 Volunteer retention mean score by club volunteer management type

and several lessons become evident for ARU and sport managers. An important question is the extent to which volunteer retention might be positively or negatively influenced by club volunteer management type. As shown by Figure 28.2, there was evidence in the ARU study of significant differences between traditional clubs and the two other club types. This means that volunteers in traditional clubs are less likely than volunteers in operational and contemporary club types to continue to volunteer.

Understanding the club volunteer management type and the relevant HRM practices can be further contextualized through the relative importance that volunteers place on HRM practices. Volunteers identified the importance of factors that positively affected their intention to continue volunteering. First, volunteers were more likely to stay with their club if they believed the club cares about their performance. Second, several volunteers identified the importance of informal and formal recognition of their efforts. Third, volunteers' likelihood to continue volunteering were significantly influenced by opportunities to have fun when volunteering, and to be part of the wider club activities. Fourth, volunteers who were coerced into their volunteer position and fifth, volunteers who felt that the club was doing little to find a replacement for them were both less likely to continue volunteering. These five factors provide a basis for HRM strategies to retain volunteers in CRCs.

Conclusion

The ARU have recognized the importance of volunteers as the foundation and lifeblood of the organization from the grass roots through to the elite level of the game. As John O'Neill suggested, to separate the two levels would not be wise in a corporate sense, as one cannot exist without the other. The elite level requires a strong, coherent grass roots base for its player base and the elite level requires community interest in the game to sell tickets and merchandise, as well as marketing sponsorship deals and broadcasting rights. Yet, the volunteer management practices of CRCs had not been given the same level of consideration as management practices for the elite level, which adopted mainstream HRM practices at the time the game professionalized. This case has presented some of the implications of this and suggests that need for the ARU needs to develop the HRM practices of CRCs with full consideration and knowledge about study motivations for sport volunteers. An understanding of the multidimensional nature of sport volunteers within CRCs is imperative if the ARU is to sustain a volunteer workforce this is able to cope with the projected growth in rugby participation. The results of this study suggest that retention of volunteers can be positively affected through defining their roles, monitoring their performance, conducting a recognition programme and making volunteers part of the club through enhancing their social experiences. These results may be universally applicable to volunteers of other community sport organizations.

Case Questions

1 Do a SWOT analysis for keeping volunteers involved in rugby. Remember that strengths and weaknesses relate to internal factors (i.e. in relation to the ARU) and opportunities and threats are external factors (i.e. changing community demographics/work patterns, popularity of other sports).

2 The case analysis discusses the role of human resource management practices. What do you see as the strengths of using this approach in managing volunteers? What are some of the constraints or barriers?

3 Discuss the taxonomy of community rugby clubs and offer some strategies for retention of volunteers for clubs in each category of the taxonomy.

4 How might you take into account the heritage and tradition of rugby union in developing volunteer management strategies?

5 This case offers the opportunity for other sports to apply the lessons learnt to their organizations. Given that nearly all sporting organizations use volunteers in a variety of roles, choose an organization that you are familiar with and determine the relative roles and responsibilities of its volunteer workforce.

Case Resources

Abrams, J., Long, J., Talbot, M. and Welch, M. (1996). Organisational change in national governing bodies of sport. Working papers from the *School of Leisure and Sport Studies*. Leeds Metropolitan University, Leeds.

Amis, J., Slack, T. and Hinings, C.R. (2004). Strategic change and the role of interests, power and organizational capacity. *Journal of Sport Management*, Vol. 18, No. 2, pp. 158–198.

Anheier, H.K. (2005). *Nonprofit Organizations:Theory, Management, Policy*. Routledge, Oxford.

Auld, C. (1997a). Professionalisation of Australian sport: The effects on organisational decision making. *European Journal for Sport Management*, Vol. 4, No. 2, pp. 17–39.

Auld, C.J. (1997b). *Professionalisation of Australian Sport Administration: The Effects on Organisational Decision Making*. Paper presented at the Australian Sports Commission, Canberra.

Auld, C. and Cuskelly, G. (2001). Behavioural characteristics of volunteers: Implications for community sport and recreation organisations. *Australian Parks and Leisure*, Vol. 4, No. 2, pp. 29–37.

Auld, C. and Godbey, G. (1998). Influence in Canadian national sport organizations: Perceptions of professionals and volunteers. *Journal of Sport Management*, Vol. 12, pp. 20–38.

Australian Bureau of Statistics (2004a). *6285.0 – Involvement in Organised Sport and Physical Activity*, Australia, April 2004, from http://www.abs.gov.au/AUSSTATS/abs@.nsf/ProductsbyCatalogue/751BF8F6B90522DECA2568A90013936C?OpenDocument

Australian Bureau of Statistics (2004b). *4177.0 – Participation in Sports and Physical Recreation*, Australia, 2005–2006, from http://www.abs.gov.au/Ausstats/abs@.nsf/e8ae5488b598839cca25682000131612/9fd67668ee42a738ca2568a9001393ac!OpenDocument

Australian Bureau of Statistics (2007). *4441.0 – Voluntary Work*, Australia 2007, http://www.abs.gov.au/ausstats/abs@.nsf/mf/4441.0 due for release in April 2007

Australian Rugby Union (2007). *About Us*. http://www.rugby.com.au/home/home/home_page,1025.html

Australian Rugby Union (2007). *Community Rugby*. http://www.rugby.com.au/community_rugby/community_rugby_-_landing_page,21783.html

Australian Sports Commission (2000a). *Active Australia/Association Management Program: Legal Issues and Risk Management*. ASC, Canberra.

Australian Sports Commission (2000b). Canberra. *Volunteer management program – Volunteer management policy*.

Australian Sports Commission (2007). *Club Development Network – Volunteer management modules*. http://www.ausport.gov.au/clubs/volunteer_prog.asp

Australian Sports Commission (2007). *Club Development Network – Volunteer management modules.* http://www.ausport.gov.au/clubs/volunteer_club_mngmt.asp

Chelladurai, P. (1999). *Human Resource Management in Sport and Recreation.* Human Kinetics, Champaign, Ill.

Clary, E.G. and Snyder, M. (1999). The motivations to volunteer: Theoretical and practical considerations. *Current Directions in Psychological Science,* Vol. 8, No. 5, pp. 156–159.

Clary, E.G., Snyder, M. and Ridge, R. (1992). Volunteers' motivations: A functional strategy for the recruitment, placement, and retention of volunteers. *Nonprofit Management and Leadership,* Vol. 2, No. 4, pp. 333–350.

Cnaan, R. and Goldberg-Glen, R.S. (1991). Measuring motivation to volunteer in human services. *Journal of Applied Behavioural Science,* Vol. 27, No. 3, pp. 269–284.

Cuskelly, G. Hoye, R. and Auld, C. (2006a). *Working with Volunteers in Sport: Theory and Practice.* Routledge, New York.

Cuskelly, G., Taylor, T., Hoye, R. and Darcy, S. (2006b). Volunteer management practices and volunteer retention: A human resource management approach. *Sports Management Review,* Vol. 9, No. 2, pp. 141–163.

Davies, J. (1998). The value of volunteers. *Australian Parks and Recreation,* Vol. 34, No. 1, pp. 33–35.

Doherty, A.J. (1998). Managing our human resources: A review of organisational behaviour in sport. *Sport Management Review,* Vol. 1, No. 1, pp. 1–24.

Dorsch, K., Riemer, H., Paskevich, D., Chelladural, P., Sluth, V. and Choptain, N. (2002, May 29–June 1). Differences in volunteer motives based on organization type and level of involvement. Paper presented at the *17th Annual North American Society for Sport Management Conference.* NASSM Abstracts, Canmore, Alberta.

Frisby, W. and Kikulis, L.M. (1996). Human resource management in sport, in Parkhouse, B.L. (Ed.), *The Management of Sport: Its Foundation and Application,* 2nd edition. Mosby, St Louis.

Green, B.C. and Chalip, L. (2004). Paths to volunteer commitment: Lessons from the Sydney Olympic Games, in Stebbins, R. and Graham, M. (Eds.), *Volunteering as Leisure/Leisure as Volunteering: An International Assessment.* CABI International, Cambridge, UK.

Houlihan, B. and White, A. (2002). *The Politics of Sport Development: Development of Sport or Development Through Sport.* Routledge, Cambridge.

International Rugby Board (2007). IRB Organisation, http://www.irb.com/EN/IRB+Organisation/ (accessed 14.4.07).

James, M., Nichols, G. and Taylor, P. (2002). *Volunteering in English sport: An interim discussion in relation to national governing bodies of sport.* Paper presented at the Volunteers in sport, Sheffield University, Eastbourne, pp. 1–17.

Pegg, S., Lewis, J. and Dyer, M. (2001). Evaluating the work satisfaction of volunteers engaged in the recreation sector. *Leisure Futures (Leisure Cultures)*, Praxis Education, 2003, pp. 2145–2153.

SCORS Research Group (2001–2005). *Exercise, Recreation and Sport Survey (ERASS)*. Australian Sports Commission, Canberra. http://www.ausport.gov.au/scorsresearch/research.asp

Taylor, P. (2004). Driving up participation: Sport and volunteering, in Sport England (Ed.), *Driving Up Participation: The Challenge For Sport*. Sport England, London.

Taylor, T., Darcy, S., Cuskelly, G. and Hoye, R. (2006). Using psychological contract theory to explore issues in effective volunteer management. *European Sports Management Quarterly*, Vol. 6, No. 2, pp. 123–147.

References

Australian Broadcasting Corporation (2003). Money makes the World Cup go round, in Australian Broadcasting Commission (Ed.), *Rugby World Cup Australia 2003*. Australian Broadcasting Commission, Sydney.

Australian Rugby Union (2003). *John O'Neill named Sport Executive of the Year*. Australian Rugby Union, Sydney.

Australian Rugby Union (2004). *Annual Report*. Australian Rugby Union, Sydney.

Australian Rugby Union (2005). *2005 Annual Report*. Australian Rugby Union, North Sydney, Australia.

Australian Rugby Union (2007a). *About Rugby*. Australian Rugby Union, Sydney.

Australian Rugby Union (2007b). *History of the ARU*. Australian Rugby Union Ltd., Sydney.

Becker, B. and Gerhart, B. (1996). The impact of human resource management on organizational performance: Progress and prospects. *Academy of Management Journal*, Vol. 39, No. 4, p. 779.

Cubby, B. (2006). in Herald, S.M. (Ed.), Sports Blog: O'Neill quits! *Sydney Morning Herald*.

Cuskelly, G., Hoye, R. and Auld, C. (2006a). *Working with Volunteers in Sport: Theory and Practice*. Routledge, London.

Cuskelly, G., Taylor, T., Hoye, R. and Darcy, S. (2006b). The advantage line: Identifying better practice for volunteer management in community rugby clubs. Australian Rugby Union Ltd, Griffith University, University of Technology Sydney, La Trobbe University.

Dabscheck, B. (1998). Trying times: Collective bargaining in Australian rugby union. *Sporting Traditions*, Vol. 15, No. 1, pp. 25–49.

Dabscheck, B. (2003). Paying for professionalism: Industrial relations in Australian rugby union. *Sport Management Review*, Vol. 6, No. 2, pp. 105–125.

Guest, D.E. (1997). Human resource management and performance: A review and research agenda. *International Journal of Human Resource Management*, Vol. 8, No. 3, pp. 263–276.

Hutchins, B. and Phillips, M. (1999). The global union: Globalization and the Rugby World Cup, in Chandler, T.J.L. and Nauright, J. (Eds.), *Making the Rugby World: Race, Gender, Commerce*. Routledge, London. pp. 149–164.

International Rugby Board (2007). *IRB Organisation*. International Rugby Board, Dulbin.

Masters, R. (2003, Saturday 22 February). Festival of the booty. *Sydney Morning Herald*.

O'Brien, D. and Slack, T. (2003). An analysis of change in an organizational field: The professionalization of English rugby union. *Journal of Sport Management*, Vol. 17, No. 4, pp. 417–448.

O'Neill, J. (2007). in Darcy, S. (Ed.), *Speech to the Tourism and Transport Forum Hoteliers Conference*. Sydney, Australia.

Pfeffer, J. and Tromley, C.L. (1995). Producing sustainable competitive advantage through the effective management of people. *Academy of Management Executive*, Vol. 9, No. 1, p. 55.

Skinner, J., Stewart, B. and Edwards, A. (1999). Amateurism to professionalism: Modelling organisational change in sporting organisations. *Sport Management Review*, Vol. 2, pp. 173–192.

Skinner, J., Stewart, B. and Edwards, A. (2003). The Postmodernisation of Rugby Union in Australia. *Football Studies*, Vol. 6, No. 1, pp. 51–69.

Slack, T. (1997). *Understanding Sport Organizations: The Application of Organization Theory*. Human Kinetics, Champaign, Ill.

Taylor, P. (2004). Driving up participation: Sport and volunteering, in Sport England (Ed.), *Driving Up Participation: The Challenge for Sport*. Sport England, London.

Thomas, D. (1997). The rugby revolution: New horizons or false dawn? *Economic Affairs*, Vol. 17, No. 3, pp. 19–24.

Toohey, B. (2007, 11 February). ARU boss feeling the heat. *Daily Telegraph*.

Wang, P.Z. (2004). Assessing motivations for sports volunteerism. *Advances in Consumer Research*, Vol. 31, pp. 420–425.

29

Boca Juniors, the half plus one of the America's population team: the restructuring of the club

Santiago Ramallo and Nick Wilde

Case Focus

This case focuses on the problems faced by marketing managers of football clubs in developing markets like Argentina.

Keywords
• Stadium development • Stadium utilization • Income generation • Key stakeholders • Brand management

Case Summary

The last 10 years has seen a major transformation of Boca Juniors both at home in Argentina and in the whole of Latin America. Since the election of Club President Mauricio Macri in 1996, the club has embarked on exciting new marketing activities, with a greater emphasis on developing their brand.

Boca Juniors are without doubt the most popular club side in Latin America, with what is reputed to be '50 per cent mas uno' or 50 per cent plus one of the whole population. While not statistically accurate, one only needs to travel around Argentina to see how popular they are. They could easily be compared to Manchester United, but in fact their national support is greater.

The past 10 years has seen continuous growth with the net worth increasing from $USD 10 million to 40 million. The club has also matched this success on the playing field with 15 championships won during the same period. This success makes them one of the most successful clubs sides in World Football. According to the information provided by the International Federation of Football History and Statistics, Boca Juniors are ranked in the top 10 clubs in the world and have been placed as high as 3rd.

Case Elements

Boca have always been considered as one of the top two clubs in Argentina, but unlike several of the leading world football powers, clubs in Argentina are usually only considered 'big' based on the number of championships they have won and by the number of fans they have. However, in order to compete on a more level playing field with giants such as Manchester United, Juventus, and Real Madrid, Boca have placed greater emphasis on positioning itself as a 'global player.' Perhaps the greatest difference between Boca Juniors and a club like Manchester United, is that they are still organized as they were when they were first formed in 1905 as a not-for-profit company, with its Board of Directors not receiving any financial remuneration.

Macri set out clear goals for the club in his attempt to modernize and make it more competitive. Greater emphasis was placed on developing new players through its youth structures, to reestablish itself as the most dominant club in Argentina, to position itself as a leading club in world football and to improve the financial status of the club. Clubs in Argentina, in line with a number around the world, are renowned for their financial mismanagement. Another feature of football clubs in Argentina is that they are also sporting and cultural institutions, sharing their facilities with a range of other sports and cultural activities. This also extends to the facilities of the clubs. The main facility at Boca Juniors is the impressive 'Bombonera' stadium, but it is surrounded by a number of other sporting facilities. While these sports have co-existed for a number of years, it makes the issue of ground development much more complicated.

One of Macri's first tasks was to set up a new marketing division under the name of Boca Crece (Boca Grows) with a separate management structure. Boca Crece was tasked with the job of developing new marketing activities and exploiting their enormous brand potential. Greater emphasis was placed on international activities and Boca Crece began to target important overseas markets with a range of initiatives. These markets included the USA, where Boca has an impressive Latin American following, Japan, with a passion for overseas football and the developing Chinese market, where only a handful of clubs had gained any presence.

The club still had to deal with its internal management and the highly politicized atmosphere which is a key part of Argentinian football clubs. Macri had been elected with a majority vote but club 'socios' (or members with voting rights) and like any political party he is responsible to these voters. Boca were in fact the first club to implement these changes and it was some five years later that Racing Football Club was saved from bankruptcy by the formation of a separate company, Blanquiceleste S.A, a limited company. On both of these occasions there was strong resistance to these changes, another situ-ation which Macri had to overcome.

In Argentina fans demand that their clubs win and pay no attention to the financial situation of the club. Members are highly critical of their clubs when they are not successful and demand frequent changes. Any attempt to set up limited companies is seen as a threat to the future of the club and fans fear that their voting rights will be lost and that these new companies will simply take away money from their clubs. However the future of these clubs lies in their long-term financial success and the employment of professional full-time members of staff. Full-time members are able to deal with the day-to-day problems and help keep a balanced financial position. These duties include dealing with players, negotiating their contracts, setting up TV rights, selling merchandise, and maximizing their brand potential. How then was Macri able to be successful? This is how he did it:

- *A new managerial approach*: Where none of the former employees were dismissed, as each one of them had experience which had made a valuable contribution to the club. However, reorganizing the club, meant incorporating highly trained people and creating new departments, with greater focus on the correct administration of the club, supported by the experience of the older employee's experience.

- *Change in the club's structure*: The aim was to get rid of the indefinite re-election of managers, as before there were 30,000 members but only 3000 voted. This meant that very influential people were able to easily win elections. This was changed so that any new managers had to back up their performance by investing some of their own personal assets. This also placed greater emphasis on managerial responsibility and this was seen as critical in stopping earlier financial losses in the club.

This also meant that managers, who do not work full-time for the club, become independent from the main operations of the club, as they have little time to spend at the club. It stands to reason that somebody who is working part-time at the club should not be involved in major strategic decisions. There had been a tendency to employ partly qualified people, of friends of people within the club, which was holding back the club. While these people clearly loved the club, they were not the right people to help take the club forward and compete in an ever more competitive and complex global market.

- *Development of players from within the club*: It is for that reason, that Boca Juniors' objective was to reorganize the club, but any reference to the club as a sports business was not very popular with some people within the club. They saw this as a threat to the other club activities. They had also in the past relied on the sale of players to other clubs as a way of covering the enormous deficits that they tended to accumulate in the pursuit of success on the field.

Macri realized that in the previous 30 years the majority of players who were part of the Boca Juniors squads had been purchased from other clubs with very few players developed through their own junior teams.

It was common practice for clubs to buy players in the expectation that future success would generate additional income, only to find that this in fact didn't happen. There was also an expectation that future sponsorship deals or TV contracts would also generate additional revenue, and in the worst case scenario they could sell on their purchased players at a profit. Again this is an old-fashioned view of football club management and explains why so many clubs are in deficit. Sound financial management was therefore a priority as was the introduction of a greater emphasis on player development.

The economic situation had also impacted on the finances of Argentinian football clubs. In 2001 the Argentinian peso was devalued from 1 peso to the dollar to 3 pesos to the dollar. This meant that selling players to overseas clubs became more of a priority to Argentinian clubs. Put quite simply, the sale of a player to a European club for $USD 1 million was worth 1 million pesos, but after the devaluation it was worth 3 million pesos. In fact any income generated overseas was an important source of revenue. It was possible to clear club debts by selling only one player every year, however this resulted in the export of virtually all of the most talented players in Argentina.

Boca's greater emphasis on developing players also meant that they had to invest more money in these activities. Boca increased the number of scouts it had both nationally and internationally in the pursuit of the most talented young players. This has proved to be successful with a higher percentage of their own junior players breaking into the full squad. They hired Griffa and Maddoni to oversee this new department. In many cases boys are recruited from other cities and brought to Buenos Aires where the club takes care of their sporting and social development. After 1996 more than 50 players progressed from junior sides to the main squad, and in many cases made up half of the club's first team. They were still able to sell some of these players abroad, but it meant that they spent less on buying players from other clubs.

Case Diagnosis

Macri changed the direction of the club and set it up for future success both at a sporting level as well as financially. Success followed and Boca started to pull away both from other Argentinian clubs as well as from other Latin American teams. From 1998 until 2001, Boca won everything,[1] and immediately after this many doors started opening. Economic growth followed. Their success and more professional approach in their marketing efforts saw an increase in sponsorship revenue, increased sales of merchandising, and on overall increase in brand value. The Boca brand was one of the biggest brands of any business in Argentina. The club embarked on lucrative overseas tournaments and their success in the South American Libertadores Cup also brought in additional revenue.

Boca placed greater emphasis on ticket sales to its matches and to take advantage of the increased interest in the club as a result of its success. They began to sell season tickets and started to sell out every week. They are now unable to accept any more memberships and operate a waiting list. The stadium capacity is 50,000 and they have around 60,000 members. They placed greater emphasis on hospitality and upgraded areas of the ground. New packages were developed for corporate clients and the ever increasing number of overseas visitors who wanted to watch games. They also embarked on a highly successful merchandising strategy with a range of traditional and innovative items. It seemed that the Boca logo brand could be used to licence a whole range of products.

---

[1] Championships: *Apertura* 98, 00,03 & 05; *Clausura* 99 & 06; Libertadores de América 00, 01, 03; Intercontinental: 00, 03; Sudamericana 04, 05. Re-copa Sudamericana 06.

In April 2004, Gavin Hamilton reported on the Boca Juniors versus River Plate game, the biggest derby game in Argentina. He suggested that the Celtic versus Rangers game, which for many football followers is the most intense derby match in the world, was like a 'primary school kick-about compared to the Boca versus River game. It was also reported as one of the 50 sporting events to see before you die.

Nowadays Boca has the most modern and impressive Museum from the world of football who receives more than 300,000 tourists a year.

However there are a number of issues that the club now faces. Its stadium, La bombonera is in need of development and is considered to be unsafe. There are plans to move the stadium but there will be strong opposition as La Boca is considered to be their spiritual home. It seems unlikely that they will be able to rebuild in the same district. However a new stadium would enable the club to generate more revenue from increased parking, improved hospitality, catering, conferencing and banqueting. It might also enable them to address the issues of safety and poor access. One casuality of these changes might well be the atmosphere at the ground. Part of the appeal of the Boca stadium is the show and the passion and noise generated by supporters, supported by the use of firecrackers and flares. A new stadium is likely to take away some of this atmosphere. However, on the other hand, increased safety might attract more families to the games.

The biggest threat to the club is the new Fédération Internationale de Football Association (FIFA) regulations on all-seater stadia, which will reduce the capacity to 30,000. While the club has plans for a new stadium, the location still remains a problem with most plots that are available in other parts of the city.

In terms of merchandising income, Boca shares with River Plate (the two biggest clubs in Argentina) 80 per cent of the market and the remaining 20 per cent is split between the other clubs. The geographical distribution of clubs is also very different to other countries with at least 60 per cent of all clubs based in or around Buenos Aires. Of the 23 provinces in Argentina only five are represented by a team in the first division. Perhaps there are franchising options in other parts of the country, but how well would this be received in Argentina? What is clear is that very few clubs fill their stadia and work with a very flat pricing structure. No club sets prices based on the importance of a match as they do in some other countries.

Boca also still have a problem with certain groups of their fans. They are often compared to hooligan gangs in the UK, Holland, and Italy and are referred to as Barra Brava. While there are several theories about their structure, it is difficult sometimes to separate myth from reality. While they are involved in violent acts against fellow supporters they are also seen as 'mafia' type organizations (Taylor, 1998; Duka and Crolley, 1994) and have some influence within clubs. It is likely that they would have to be consulted about future moves. Others, however, believe that developing a new stadium might break the power of the Barras Bravas. There are no simple solutions to this problem but this issue will need to be confronted.

Case Questions

1 To what extent does success on the sporting field affect the income streams of football clubs like Boca Juniors? Do all football clubs have to be successful on the pitch in order to survive?

2 What are the advantages and disadvantages of being a not-for-profit football club like Boca Juniors as opposed to a limited company? What problems will the club face if it decides to franchise its name to other parts of the country, or even overseas?

3 Taking into consideration the fact that Boca Juniors need to develop a new stadium, what would you suggest is included in the design of this stadium? How would you convince the fans and other stakeholders that it will be necessary to move the stadium away from La Boca and change the name of the stadium from 'La Bombonera' to the name of a new sponsor? Suggest what kind of brand would be the most appropriate for Boca Juniors, and what attributes it would need to bring in order to support this famous football club brand.

4 How should Boca Juniors develop further income streams for the club? For each idea, suggest approximately what percentage of its total income should come from these activities

5 Suggest how you might convince FIFA that some standing areas should be allowed for Argentinian football stadia? Given the nature and spectacle of its football support is the imposition of all-seater stadia going to have a detrimental effect on Argentinian football?

6 Do you think that the current economic situation will make it difficult for Boca Juniors to maintain its position as one of the leading football clubs in the world?

7 Should Boca Juniors consider being part of a new international club competition along with other leading world football clubs? Would being part of a major international club competition be a way of keeping its best players, and making the team more attractive to future audiences?

Case Resources

Reading

Aguiar, F. and Ramallo, S. (2006). Argentina: marketing in Argentine football, a snapshot, in Desbordes, M. (Ed.), *Marketing and Football: An International Perspective*. Elsevier, Oxford.

Duka, V. and Crolley L. (1994). Argy-Bargy at the match: Football Spectator Behaviour in Argentina: A case of Seperate Evolution. *The Sociological Review*. pp. 272-293.

Hamilton, G. (2004). *The Observer*, 4 April 2004.

International Federation of Football Statistics (2006). Accessed on 15 May 2007 www.iffhs.de

Taylor, C. (1998). *The Beautiful Game. A Journey Through Latin American Football*. Victor Golanz Publishing, London, England.

TV Program 'Hablemos de Football,' in Espn, May, 2007 special guest: Mauricio Macri.

Websites

Boca Juniors Official website: www.bocajuniors.com.ar
www.lamitadmas1.com.ar
www.estoesboca.com.ar/el_mas_campeon.htm

30

Grand Slam Committee moves to regulate tennis wear logos

Simon Chadwick and Geoff Walters

Case Focus

The case examines the move by tennis' Grand Slam Committee (GSC) to regulate the size of manufacturer's identifiers and logos placed on the apparel of professional tennis players.

Keywords

- Legal action
- Competition law
- Manufacturer's identification
- Sportswear
- Tennis
- Brand

Case Summary

In April 2006, sportswear company Adidas issued a claim in the English High Court against the International Tennis Federation (ITF) and the four Grand Slam tennis tournaments: Wimbledon, the French, the Australian and the United States Opens. The claim alleged infringements of European competition law resulting from a ruling by the Grand Slam Committee (GSC – a representative body consisting of the four grand slams and the ITF) that Adidas' Three-Stripe design was to be considered a manufacturer's identification for the purpose of the GSC's rules and was therefore subject to size restrictions imposed by these rules. This case study therefore sets out to examine some of the issues underpinning the legal case, and traces its development from instigation to resolution.

Case Elements

Over the last two decades, sport has become an increasingly important industrial sector. For sports themselves, faced with rising costs and commercial opportunity, many have adopted new approaches to management. Alongside this, related organizations, ranging from the media corporations through to sportswear manufacturers and sponsors, have also sought to utilize sport as a focus for their commercial and marketing activities. At the centre of these developments are the individuals, teams, leagues and competitions responsible for creating the contests that evoke a plethora of deep emotions amongst sports fans and other consumers alike.

Professional tennis is typical of the commercial changes that have come to characterize 21st century sport. The top male and female players are sporting and cultural icons, attracting major sponsorship and endorsement contracts, appearing in promotional campaigns for major brands across the world, and securing huge financial rewards for their appearances and tournament victories. As such, these players have become hugely wealthy; yet some critics are sceptical about the benefits of the commercial and financial development of the sport. For instance, many will talk of Anna

Kournikova, the darling of marketers, brand managers and sponsorship agents, but someone who nevertheless failed to win a single Grand Slam tennis tournament.

Tennis tournament organizers, keen to attract major stars to their events, have added impetus to the clamour to be associated with the world's leading players, and prize money at the leading tour tournaments has therefore risen dramatically. At the same time, tournament managers have become more commercially savvy, providing better facilities for increasingly demanding fans whilst seeking to maximize capacity utilization in order to promote revenue growth.

In combination, the growth of globally high profile tennis players and tournaments has provided fertile ground for a multitude of related organizations including sportswear manufacturers and sponsors to become involved in the sport. Such is the power of tennis, that some organizations are using the sport as a specific focus for the strategic development of their businesses. This is not so surprising because global media coverage of the sport is growing and leading performers therefore remain in the spotlight for fans and consumers across the world. In many ways, tennis is therefore a perfect global platform upon which corporations can produce and market, amongst other things, shoes, shirts, shorts and racquets. Witnessing Federer at Wimbledon or Mauresmo at the US Open can have a major influence on people's perception of a sportswear brand; indeed there is compelling evidence to indicate that people respond positively to such associations and we have therefore seen sportswear and non-sportswear brands fighting it out with each other to win the right to place logos on the equipment used tennis players.

Over the last few years, the tennis has come to be dominated by a small number of very powerful global sportswear manufacturers. Many of the world's leading tennis players are now associated with them and, such is the market power of these corporations that they have engaged in intensive non-price competition. This has resulted in intense competition to be associated with tennis' leading performers, with product innovation and design, and with a growth in the size of logos appearing on tennis wear. However, the latter has become a particular problem for tennis tournament managers, who are keen to protect against tennis players becoming little more than walking advertisements for the world's leading sportswear brands. These concerns are particularly acute where leading tournament managers, such as Wimbledon, take pride in and value the look and feel of the tournament including the clothing worn by players.

At one level, there is a philosophical issue underpinning these concerns; in tennis there is a certain ethos that the game should be played in a particular way and that rampant, unfettered commercialism should not be allowed to impinge upon the sport. At another level, there is an issue of power and position; tournaments are held to be the property of the event owners, not sportswear companies, and managers therefore see it as a duty and a responsibility to protect their properties. As such, a conflict of interest has arisen between sportswear manufacturers who have paid huge sums to be associated with leading tennis players and are seeking to maximize the return on their investments, and tournament managers who wish to retain control of their events and what happens at them.

This case therefore sets out to examine a major incident in this relationship: the attempts of the GSC to regulate the use of brand logos on tennis wear. In particular, the case focuses on the legal action taken by Adidas against the GSC as the result of attempts to restrict the use of the corporation's 'Three-Stripes'. The basis for Adidas' action is firstly considered, and this is followed by an examination of the market for tennis wear and the leading producers. Thereafter, the development of Adidas and the corporation's involvement in tennis is examined, as is the involvement of rival manufacturers. The case concludes by examining the way in which the legal action was settled as well as identifying some potential implication of this.

Instigation of Legal Action

In April 2006, sportswear company Adidas issued a claim in the English High Court against the ITF and the four Grand Slam tennis tournaments: Wimbledon, the French, the Australian and the United States Opens. The claim alleged infringements of European competition law resulting from a ruling by the GSC (a representative body consisting of the four grand slams and the ITF) that Adidas' Three-Stripe design was to be considered a manufacturer's identification for the purpose of the GSC's rules and was therefore subject to size restrictions imposed by these rules. The basis for the GSC's decision arose from concerns that Adidas were being given preferential treatment as the Three-Stripes were in their opinion clearly more of a marketing tool/logo than simply a design feature and therefore fell within the scope of their rules. According to ITF and GSC regulations, on logos and manufacturer's identifications should be restricted on tennis apparel to 26 sq. cm.

Adidas have incorporated Three-Stripes into their sportswear designs for almost 70 years, but a number of other sportswear manufacturers have recently complained to various governing bodies and federations about them. They have claimed that the Three-Stripes are distinctive and recognizable, and therefore it is unfair that they are not caught by the size restrictions imposed by virtually all governing bodies on manufacturer's identifications such as the Nike swoosh, the Lacoste crocodile and the Puma cat.

A number of US sports already interpret Adidas' Three-Stripes as a form of manufacturer identification and have subjected them to size restrictions. Moreover, in early 2005, the International Olympic Committee announced that at the Turin Winter Olympics in 2006, the Three-Stripes would be deemed a manufacturer's identification and subject to the size rules. Despite these actions, Nike, amongst others, has staged protests against what they have perceived to be Adidas' favoured position. During the Berlin and Rome Masters tennis series events, the company sent Rafael

Nadal and other players out with over sized Nike 'swooshes' on their shirts. The 'swooshes' were clearly and blatantly in breach of each competition's rules governing the size of manufacturer's logos.

In May 2005, the GSC decided that the Adidas Three-Stripes was a manufacturer's identification or logo for the purposes of their rules and they informed Adidas of their decision. The GSC acknowledged that it could take Adidas time to redesign retail stock and they deferred implementation of the rule with respect to the Three-Stripes until the Australian Open in January 2006. The next few months saw frenzied negotiations, threats of litigation and resulted, in October 2005, with an extension of Adidas' grace period until June 2006. This extension in turn resulted in threats of legal action from Nike and the other manufacturers. In March 2006, Adidas pushed for a further extension but, when the GSC refused, they instigated legal proceedings in April 2006.

Adidas claimed that the GSC's implementation of their rule was an infringement of European competition law. In particular, Adidas expressed concerns that the lead times for designing products did not give them sufficient time to redesign their retail products and therefore their sponsored players would have different shirts to Adidas' retail products. This would put them at a competitive disadvantage in relation to their competitors. Adidas also claimed that the GSC's implementation of the rule was discriminatory as it picked on their Three-Stripe design but not the distinctive designs of their competitors, such as Nike's sunray or Diadora's Two-Stripe design. In another move by Adidas, the company made an application for an injunction to prevent the GSC applying their rule before a trial, in effect suspending the rule for Wimbledon and the US Open tournaments.

In response to Adidas' actions, the Grand Slam tournaments and the ITF all applied for summary judgement, that is a declaration from the court that Adidas did not have a reasonable chance of succeeding at trial and therefore the case did not justify a full trial. Although this was difficult for them to prove, the Grand Slams felt it was worth trying as the consensus was that Adidas had a weak case. At an interim hearing in the London High Court in May 2006, Adidas made some amendments to their claim: firstly, the company withdrew it's injunction application against Roland-Garros and Australia (principally as it was felt there would be time for a full trial before these events next took place, in 2007); secondly, in the light of GSC concerns about how other sportswear manufacturers would react if a Adidas was awarded an injunction, Adidas gave the court an undertaking stating that if an injunction was granted, but they lost the case at a full High Court trial, they would indemnify all losses suffered by other manufacturers who sponsored grand slam tennis players as a result of the competitive advantage Adidas enjoyed in that period.

The following judgement on the interim hearing was made in June 2006: (1) the judge struck out the part of Adidas' claim where the company alleged they were at a competitive disadvantage as they were not given enough time to comply with the rule that was being imposed on them; (2) the judge did not strike out the remainder of their claim and accepted that there was a chance that Adidas would succeed in their claim that, in implementing the Dress Rule governing logo size and the nature of manufacturer identifications appearing on tennis wear, the GSC and ITF had discriminated against Adidas; (3) on the basis of an Adidas undertaking, the judge granted the company an injunction against Wimbledon and the US Tennis Association preventing them from implementing the Dress Rule before full trial could take place; (4) the judge ordered an expedited trial to take place in October 2006.

In August 2006, the case became a rather more complex one when Nike and Puma instigated their own legal action against the GSC claiming that they had been prejudiced as the GSC hadn't applied their Dress Rules. The move was widely seen as being a ploy to ensure Nike and Puma were given a voice in the negotiations to settle the case.

Resolution of the Case

Following months of negotiations and the threat of further legal action by Adidas' rivals, the parties involved in the case agreed to an out of court settlement in September 2006. It was accepted by all parties that the Adidas Three-Stripes is a manufacturer's identification, but the ITF Dress Rule was amended to increase the space for manufacturer's identifications so that a 52 sq. cm. patch may be placed on the sleeves of a tennis shirt by a sportswear manufacturer. In cases where a manufacturer includes their name in this patch, the manufacturer's identification can only be 25 sq. cm. in size. It was also agreed that Adidas has a grace period until the Australian Open in 2007 to produce ITF Dress Rule compliant shirts. Thereafter, tennis shirts produced by all manufacturers will be regulated by the new code.

Conclusions

At the end of the legal case, it would appear that honours were even. The GSC asserted some control over tennis, restricting the growth (both in size and number) of sportswear manufacturer logos, thus addressing concerns about commercialism impacting upon the sport. Whether or not this will be a long-term solution to controlling the 'walking adverts' the GSC was so concerned about remains to be seen, especially as various tennis tournaments continue to work in partnership with sportswear manufacturers. For instance, despite the some times bitter nature of the GSC's dispute with Adidas, the company remains a major partner of the French Open staged at Roland Garros. Given the proliferating costs of staging Grand Slam tennis events allied to the exposure that being associated with them delivers to commercial partners, there is no doubting the mutual dependence that exists between the GSC and Adidas, and indeed other sportswear manufacturers. How such relationships are managed, especially in the light of concerns about the sanctity of sport, would therefore appear to be a major issue for parties involved in the aforementioned legal case. Given the cost and consequent revenue pressures nevertheless facing sporting events, the decision to more stringently regulate sponsorship and advertising is an interesting one, raising a number of issues. Amongst these, is the extent to which sportswear manufacturers (and other commercial partners) will accept or tolerate their regulation before seeking other promotional opportunities or, as happened in this case, they instigate legal proceedings to protect their positions.

For the other suppliers of tennis and sportswear, most notably Nike and Puma who joined the proceedings in August, their immediate concerns have been allayed. Adidas' use of the Three-Stripes has at last been brought under control, thereby limiting, if not eliminating, any commercial or competitive advantage the company has secured. In one sense, this is a little naïve; despite the ubiquity and power of, say, Nike's swoosh, Adidas enjoys a historical accumulation of brand equity that will be difficult to undermine or challenge, even in the light of the Dress Rule change. Many consumers, both of tennis wear and sportswear generally, are highly aware of the Adidas brand and are able to readily associate the Three-Stripes with the brand. While reducing the size of a manufacturer's identifier or of a logo might diminish visibility of the Three-Stripes, the positive cognitive and behavioural impact of them will remain. Therefore, just as Adidas is being forced to re-design its tennis wear to comply with the new regulation, their competitors equally face a challenge: to re-design their tennis wear in order to compete with Adidas' Three-Stripe design. In the short term at least, there is likely to be a period of uncertainty as the leading manufacturers interpret the new ruling, and make their competitive and commercial responses to it. Now there is clarity in the Dress Rule, one can begin to think ahead and speculate how long it will be before we see tennis shirts with, for example, larger swooshes or longer leaping cats running down their sleeves.

Following years of largely unregulated use of the Three-Stripes, Adidas will be allowed to continue using arguably their most valuable asset. Whether or not company officials feel aggrieved is a moot point. Because the Three-Stripes remain, it means the company will retain one element of competitive advantage that it has over its rivals. It also means the company will not have to radically change one of sportswear history's most recognizable images. However, given the company's contention that the Three-Stripes are a historic design rather than being a direct form of commercial promotion or a logo, will no doubt concern them. Not least amongst these concerns will be the opportunities it presents to their rivals. Although it has not been the policy of, for example, Nike to place extended or enlarged 'identifiers' or logos on the sleeves of their tennis wear, the potential for this to happen has now been established. The competitive response of Adidas' rivals may be the real downside to what Adidas is otherwise likely to perceive as a legal victory.

The tennis and sportswear markets are incredibly competitive, locally and globally, and Adidas will be loathed to concede ground to its major competitors, especially its closest rival Nike and newer, increasingly aggressive rivals such as Diadora. Adidas' recent acquisition of Reebok will help in this fight, but the way is now clear for other tennis wear manufacturers to instigate design changes that may ultimately be more innovative, visible and/or appealing to consumers, consequently putting Adidas in the shade. With exciting games between the top tennis players always assured, what clothes they wear and what they look like are going to make for an equally interesting contest in the future.

Case Diagnosis

Brand recognition and brand association have been key elements to Adidas' strategy for over 50 years, ever since the 1952 Olympics at Helsinki when Adi Dassler realized the value in increasing public awareness and perception of the Adidas brand through the Three-Stripes and athlete endorsement. This was the reason he persuaded the Karhu executives from Finland to part with the Three-Stripes. Later, Horst Dassler was described as 'one of the first entrepreneurs to recognize the transformation of the games from an amateurish affair to a grand televisual spectacle and the benefits that sponsors could derive from increased exposure and renewed public interest' (Magdalinski and Nauright, 2004, p. 193).

There is relatively little research on brand recognition/awareness/perception of Adidas although, according to Marinovich (2006), the distinctive three-striped logo of Adidas has brand recognition worldwide of more then 90 per cent, while Hem and Iversen (2004, p. 87) argued that the Adidas Three-Stripes is an example of an abstract form of logo that is unrelated to the word mark, and therefore the Three-Stripes in their opinion is a logo that is synonymous with the Adidas brand. Results from the 2006 Keynote Survey on the Clothing and Footwear Industry show that in terms of brand perception, 36 per cent believed that Adidas and Nike offered better quality than most other clothing and footwear. This was most apparent with the 25–34 years age group, with 58 per cent believing that Adidas or Nike offer better quality.

There have been various academic studies undertaken in which the Adidas brand has been used in a study of either sportswear or sports sponsorship. These are that studies are profiled below:

Yoo and Donthu (2001): A Joint US/South Korean study based on a sample of 460 people examining brand equity across a number of brands including cameras, televisions and sportswear. Results showed that 94 per cent of the sample had purchased athletic shoes at some point with Adidas being the second most popular purchase choice, behind Nike, in the sportswear category. Sample members exhibited strong awareness of the Adidas brand and made strong associations with it. Awareness and association were measured using the following:

- 'I can recognize Adidas among other competing brands';
- 'I am aware of Adidas';

- 'Some characteristics of Adidas quickly come to mind';
- 'I can quickly recall the logo of Adidas'.

South Korean respondents were identified as having the strongest awareness of and association with the Adidas brand (ahead of all other sportswear brands). Amongst US and US/South Korean respondents, the Adidas brand returned the second strongest awareness and association figures, after Nike.

Nicholls et al. *(1999)*: Investigated brand recall and brand preferences, relating to event sponsors, amongst spectators at Ryder Cup and Lipton tennis tournaments sponsors. Based on samples of 562 at the Ryder Cup and 200 at the Lipton tennis tournament, the following results were obtained.

Unprompted Brand Recall

- *At Ryder Cup*: 10.2 per cent of respondents were able to recall that Adidas was a sponsor of the tournament.
- *At Lipton tennis*: 20.0 per cent of respondents were able to recall that Adidas was a sponsor of the tournament.
- The difference between these two figures was statistically significant indicating that tennis audiences have a stronger recall of the Adidas brand than do golf audiences.

Brand Preference

- *At Ryder Cup*: 5.4 per cent of respondents expressed a preference for the Adidas brand;
- *At Lipton tennis*: 16.0 per cent of respondents expressed a preference for the Adidas brand;
- The difference between these two figures was statistically significant indicating that tennis audiences have a stronger brand preference for the Adidas brand than do golf audiences.

Walsh (2005): PhD study examining the responses of people to one aspect of logo redesign: the shape of the logo. Major sportswear brands were selected for the study because they were identified as brands and logos with which consumers have especially strong associations. The Adidas brand was represented in the study by the diagonal Three-Stripe logo. The central focus of the study was to test the commitment of consumers to a brand as logo design was changed. Commitment was held to be the degree of psychological attachment, the emotional bond or the behavioural loyalty of consumers to a brand. Adidas was identified as having the largest number of strongly committed consumers and the second lowest number of weakly committed consumers (after Nike). Strongly committed consumers (e.g. Adidas purchasers) responded in a disproportionately negative way to logo change: the greater the logo change, the greater the resulting negative evaluation. The opposite was true for weakly committed consumers. This confirms the importance of the Three-Stripes logo for the Adidas brand because changes to it resulted in changes in consumer behaviour that would in reality be adverse to the continued success of the brand.

Elliott (1994): Explored the symbolic meaning of a number of sports brands amongst 53 school children and 82 university students. Amongst the brands included in the study were leading sportswear brands, including Adidas, the meanings of which were assessed according to the following criteria: fashionable, unfashionable, sports, expensive, high quality, low quality, value for money, comfortable, uncomfortable, product features, advertising and country of origin. One notable observation to make is that the associations the sample population made with product features included grip, technology and chunkiness but not product design. Adidas' Three-Stripes were not therefore identified as a feature of the product or as a design element. What was identified as being significant in helping people associate with, were the visual elements of marketing, for example a logo or name. The 'sign' value of a brand was highlighted as being particularly important; for instance, the Adidas Three-Stripes can be thought to signify credibility, fashionability and socially acceptability. The study concludes that 'artifactual symbolism, (i.e. images and symbols such as the Three-Stripes for example) are important influences on the meanings consumers attribute to them but are nevertheless difficult to control. This means that what a brand is intended to communicate to a marketplace and to consumers is often not received in the way intended. Hence, although Adidas might insist that the Three-Stripes are a design feature rather than, for instance, a logo, consumers may not process such a communication in the intended way, actually perceiving the Three-Stripes to be a brand mark or logo.

Belen del Rio et al., *(2001)*: A preliminary study of 400 individuals in Spain to identify six sports shoe brands showed that 64 per cent had used and had sufficient knowledge of the different features of Adidas sports shoes compared with 57 per cent for Nike and 65 per cent for Reebok. These three were by far the best known brands in the study.

Ross and Harradine (2004): UK-based study showed that there is high brand recognition among children for sports brands including Adidas. They focused their work on a group of children of primary school age in a school in the North-East of England. They found that in their initial focus group meetings at least 75 per cent of children in different age groups (4–6, 5–7, 7–9, 9–11) recognized Nike, Adidas, Reebok and Umbro. Even in the age group 4–6, the pupils were aware of the concept of branded sportswear, suggesting that children become aware of brands at an early age. In the class of 9–11-year olds, 87.5 per cent were aware of the four brands and had a more sophisticated understanding with all claiming they could tell the difference between counterfeit brands and the real thing. Moreover, 82.75 per cent of the older group of children were able to recognize six out of six brand logos without the identification of the brand name. Adidas was the top or equal top choice across all age groups when the children were asked to name their preferred choice of brand.

Hogg et al. *(1998)*: A study by Hogg et al. on a group of children aged between 7 and 10 years revealed that they clearly recognized brand names and logos, such as the Three-Stripes and the Nike Swoosh. These studies suggest that the decision by Adidas in 1993 to concentrate on the 'lucrative, but fickle teenage market' (Lane Keller, 1999, p. 110) was successful in terms of raising brand recognition.

Although the number of freely available market studies and academic papers examining the sportswear market is fairly limited, there is some evidence to indicate the power of the Adidas brand. It is notable that Adidas and, more specifically, the Three-Stripe logo is highly effective in evoking a positive response amongst consumers, in tennis, in a range of other sports, across products and across age ranges. The extent to which people can identify and then associate the Three-Stripes with the Adidas brand is especially telling. This clearly establishes strong awareness, recognition and recall as being significant effects of the Three-Stripes. Such effects are highly likely to be linked to positive purchase behaviour. This means that consumers are more likely to buy an Adidas product ahead of an alternative or rival product on the basis of the psychological impact that the Three-Stripes is thought to have. In addition, there is clearly some evidence to indicate that Adidas' involvement in tennis has a notable effect on tennis audiences. It is therefore my view that the transportability, ubiquity, prominence and effect of the Three-Stripe logo is such that its appearance in, for instance, a tennis tournament, is also likely to have a significant and positive impact on sportswear market segments that are either indirectly or unrelated to tennis.

Case Questions

1 What do you think are likely to have been the main reasons for the GSC seeking to regulate the size of logos and manufacturer identifiers appearing on the shirts, shorts and socks of tennis players?
2 Why do you think leading sportswear brands, in this case Adidas, objected (and in other sports continue to object) to the form of regulation covered in this legal case?
3 To what extent do you think that a logo or a symbol appearing on a tennis shirt is likely to evoke a positive reaction amongst shoppers and buyers of sportswear?
4 On what basis did Adidas take legal action against GSC and why, ultimately, do you think the resolution noted in the case study was reached?
5 What lessons do you think the legal case brought by Adidas against the GSC provides for other sports and for other sportswear manufacturers?
6 As a marketing manager for a leading sportswear manufacturer, how would you attempt to creatively address the regulation of logo size on tennis shirts?

Case Resources

Reading

Badenhausen, K. (2004). King of the court. *Forbes*, Vol. 174, No. 1, pp. 93–94.

Belen del Rio, A., Vazquez, R. and Iglesias, V. (2001). The effects of brand associations on consumer response. *Journal of Consumer Marketing*, Vol. 18, No. 5, pp. 410–425.

Brunner, C. (2006). *All Day I Dream About Sport: The Story of the Adidas Brand*. Cyan Books, London.

Davis, J. (2005). Secrets of success: It's the cost of a pair of shoes. *The Independent*, 10 April, p. 15.

Elliott, R. (1994). Exploring the symbolic meaning of brands. *British Journal of Management*, Vol. 5, pp. 13–19.

Garratt, S. (2002). When is a trainer not a trainer? *The Times*, 19 October, p. 28.

Heard, N. (2005). *Trainers: Over 300 Designs from Rare Vintage to the Latest Designs*. Carlton Books, London.

Hem, L. and Iversen, N. (2004). How to develop a destination brand logo: A qualitative and quantitative approach. *Scandinavian Journal of Hospitality and Tourism*, Vol. 4, No. 2, pp. 83–106.

Hogg, M., Bruce, M. and Hill, A. (1998). Fashion brand preferences among young consumers, *International Journal of Retail and Distribution Management*, Vol. 26, No. 8, pp. 293–300.

Keynote (2005). *Sports Clothing and Footwear Report*. Keynote Reports Limited, Hampton.

Keynote (2006). *Clothing and Footwear Industry Report*. Keynote Reports Limited, Hampton.

Lane Keller, K. (1999). Managing brands for the long-run: Brand reinforcement and revitalization strategies. *California Management Review*, Vol. 41, No. 3, pp. 102–124.

Magdalinski, T. and Nauright, J. (2004). Commercialisation of the modern Olympics, Chapter 9, in Slack, T. (Ed.), *The Commercialisation of Sport*. Routledge, London, pp. 185–204.

Marinovich, S. (2006), Much ado about Adidas stripes. *Business Week Online*. Accessed 28 April from http://www.businessweek.com/innovate/content/apr2006/id20060428_729369.htm

Nicholls, J.A.F., Roslow, S. and Dublish, S. (1999). Brand recall and brand preference at sponsored golf and tennis tournaments. *European Journal of Marketing*, Vol. 33, No. 3/4, pp. 365–386.

Olins, J. (1992). Going for gold, *The Sunday Times*, 12 July, p. 14.

Roberts, L. (2001). The brand new heavies: How Adidas muscled their way back into the game with Nike. *The Sunday Mail*, 17 June, p. 46.

Ross, J. and Haradine, R. (2004). I'm not wearing that! Branding and young children. *Journal of Fashion Marketing and Management*, Vol. 8, No. 1, pp. 11–26.

Smit, B. (2005). *Pitch Invasion: Adidas and the Making of Modern Sport*. Allen Lane, London.

Tait, N. (2006). Adidas moves to get logo dress code ruled out of court. *Financial Times*, 24 May, p. 5.

Wallace, C. (1997). Adidas goes for gold. *Time Australia*, 27 January, available from http://www.time.com/time/magazine/1997/int/970120/business.adidas_goes.html

Walsh, M.F. (2005). Consumer response to logo shape redesign: the influence of brand commitment. Unpublished PhD Thesis, University of Pittsburgh.

White, J. (1997). The big match. *The Guardian*, 1 July, p. 54.

Yoo, B. and Donthu, N. (2001). Developing and validating a multidimensional consumer-based brand equity scale. *Journal of Business Research*, Vol. 52, pp. 1–14.

Websites

Adidas – www.adidas.com
Diadora – www.diadora.com
Fila – www.fila.com
Hi-Tec – www.hi-tec.com
International Tennis Federation Grand Slams – http://www.itftennis.com/abouttheitf/worldwide/grandslams/
New Balance – www.newbalance.com
Nike – www.nike.com
Prince – www.princetennis.com
Puma – www.puma.com
Sergio Tacchini – www.sergiotacchini.com
Wilson – www.wilson.com

Further Information

Users of the case may want to take a look at the Wikipedia entries for the following:

Australian Open – http://en.wikipedia.org/wiki/Australian_Open
French Open – http://en.wikipedia.org/wiki/French_Open_%28tennis%29
Grand Slam Tennis – http://en.wikipedia.org/wiki/Tennis_Grand_Slam
International Tennis Federation – http://www.itftennis.com/
Tennis – http://en.wikipedia.org/wiki/Tennis
US Open – http://en.wikipedia.org/wiki/U.S._Open_%28tennis%29
Wimbledon – http://en.wikipedia.org/wiki/The_Championships%2C_Wimbledon

Index